D0229811

ATHENS: A HISTORY

Robin Waterfield

ATHENS: A HISTORY

From Ancient Ideal to Modern City

MACMILLAN

First published 2004 by Macmillan
an imprint of Pan Macmillan Ltd
Pan Macmillan, 20 New Wharf Road, London N1 9RR
Basingstoke and Oxford
Associated companies throughout the world
www.panmacmillan.com

ISBN 0 333 98991 0

1 3 5 7 9 8 6 4 2

A CIP catalogue record for this book is available from
the British Library.

Typeset by SetSystems Ltd, Saffron Walden, Essex
Printed and bound in Great Britain by
Mackays of Chatham plc, Chatham, Kent

For Ingrid, with love

'There is no end to it in this city: wherever we walk, we set our feet upon some history.'

Lucius Cicero to his cousin Marcus, 79 BCE

Where'er we tread, 'tis haunted, holy ground;
No earth of thine is lost in vulgar mould,
But one vast realm of Wonder spreads around,
And all the Muse's tales seem truly told,
Till the sense aches with gazing to behold
The scenes our earliest dreams have dwelt upon.

Lord Byron, *Childe Harold's Pilgrimage*

A Greek landscape does not give us – if we know how to listen and how to love – an innocent tremor of beauty. The landscape has a name, it is bound up with a memory – here we were shamed, here glorified; blood on sacred statues rises up from the soil, and all at once the landscape is transformed into rich, all-encompassing history, and the Greek pilgrim's whole spirit is thrown into confusion.

Nikos Kazantzakis, *Travels in Greece*

Contents

THE CITY AT LEISURE

THE CITY AT WORK

THE DOWNFALL OF ATHENS: A GREEK TRAGEDY

THE HELLENISTIC AND ROMAN CITY

ATHENS REDUCED AND REINVENTED

EPILOGUE

Acknowledgements

I would like to thank the Royal Literary Fund for supporting my work with teaching fellowships for the academic years 2001–2 and 2002–3. Bill Hamilton, my agent, combined enthusiasm with pragmatism in the right measures, and my son, Julian Waterfield, also offered early encouragement. George Morley, an old friend, turned out to be the perfect editor in London, and Chip Rossetti in New York was patient at a critical stage and made a number of improvements. Among those Greek friends who have eased the passage of the book I should mention especially Irini Livanou and Dimitri Peretzis. Two other friends kindly agreed (in one case, at short notice) to be my readers: many thanks to Professor Paul Cartledge of Cambridge University and to Andrew Lane. Josine Meijer and Maximiliane Pike helped bring the pictures to light. I would also like to thank the several groups on my Page & Moy tours of the sites of ancient Greece who unwittingly served as guinea pigs for some of the material in this book.

Introduction

In 1912, in his essay 'The Future of Constantinople', Joseph Conrad wrote that Athens was 'matchless in the wonders of its life and vicissitudes of its history'. It was and still is a wonderful place, and its history has indeed been extraordinary. However many times I visit it, there is always something new to surprise me; however long I study its history, there are always new angles and quirks and possibilities to explore. The purpose of this book is to trace the life of the city of Athens, from its earliest beginnings up to relatively recent times, with the intention not of expounding a grand thesis but of telling a story – or rather of telling several stories, because no city is so monolithic that it offers only one throughout its history.

As a glance at the Contents of the book reveals, I have spent a disproportionate amount of time on the ancient city. There are good reasons for this: there is far more evidence for the ancient city, up to the end of the fourth century BCE (I use BCE and CE, not BC and AD) than there is for the next 2,100 years; and in 1834 CE Athens became the capital city of the new nation-state of Greece, so that the history of the city merged with the history of the country, which is another book altogether. I have therefore dealt with the era since 1834 in some haste, although up until then I have been reasonably thorough.

Just as important as lack of evidence in dictating this strategy is the fact that the ancient city is what most people think of when they hear the word 'Athens'. Yes, recent visitors will have other memories and associations: the old airport with its uncomfortable seating and lack of air conditioning, the traffic, the smog, the friendly locals and cheap restaurants, the taste of ouzo with the sunlight filtering through a shady vine. But the chances are that they went there to visit the antiquities – the sites and the outstanding museums – and for thousands of others too, who have never had the chance to travel there, Athens represents one of the high points of ancient culture. Within the two centuries of its greatest and most glorious period, Athens sowed the seeds of Western culture in art, architecture, painting, sculpture and drama, both serious and humorous. What is more, it did so under the most unlikely circumstances: it was too small, one would think, to have produced so many geniuses in such a short space of time, and it was beset by the radical instabilities of the ancient Greek world, where warfare, disease, drought and malnutrition were all too familiar.

Above all, the Classical city practised a form of direct democracy which has been held up over the centuries as a model of perfection or a recipe for disaster. Political theorists have always looked to ancient Athens to help them make up their minds about where exactly on the political spectrum they want to stand. Recent debates about American democracy have also often found it useful to take ancient Athenian democracy as a starting point, and to ask, 'How near or far do we want to be to *that* system?'

This book contains, then, a selective history of Athens – enough to give the reader a good idea of the main events, while avoiding the controversies and academic debates which are thrown up by the frequently ambiguous or even downright contradictory evidence. One of the main reasons the history of Athens is so enjoyable is that it has been driven from start to finish by a number of powerful and fascinating individuals: Solon, the poet-statesman who was held to have founded Athenian democracy; Peisistratos, the tyrant of Athens who developed the city's potential as a centre of culture; the cunning Themistokles, who championed the Athenian navy and so played a key role in repulsing the Persians; Perikles, the leader of the city at the height of its power and splendour. Then in post-Classical times, we find a string of influential foreigners, from Romans up to the English poet Lord George Byron, who died during Greece's war of liberation against Turkey, and Lord Thomas Elgin, who plundered the Parthenon. The stories of these men and of others (men and women) feature here alongside the hard historical facts and events they initiated. Throughout the book we will see, implicitly and explicitly, that the engine of history is often the whims and personalities of powerful men and women, as much as economic or other impersonal forces.

This emphasis on personalities has often been criticized: in the case of ancient Athens, historians have been reluctant to rely too much on the personality-focused histories of the Greeks themselves, who were little concerned with broader historical factors, such as economics. But in fact the emphasis is true for much Athenian history. Athens was, by our standards, a small town, where everyone knew everyone else and personal reactions and relations were important. Moreover, there were no political parties in ancient Athens. Laws were proposed by individuals in pursuit of their own vision. Of course, it was often the case that one man's vision was similar to that of a predecessor or colleague, but this still falls short of party politics.

Then there was the unique institution of ostracism. Once a year the people had the option (which they did not necessarily take up) of sending a prominent person into exile for a maximum period of ten years. Whenever the option was taken up, threatened individuals became rivals, each trying to ensure that someone else was ostracized. Nothing could more clearly show the individualistic nature of politics in ancient Athens. Nowadays, if a prominent politician departs, another steps up to continue the party's programme; in Classical Athens, each politician had his own programme, which he saw through in the first instance with the help of a few friends.

Of course, this is not to say that Athenian politics was led entirely by a few individuals. Ancient Athens was, for the 200 years of its prominence, a participatory democracy, and individual politicians could not see their visions through without the support of the mass of the population, who were politicized to a remarkably high level. During this critical period of Athenian history, progress was made by means of debate and dialectic between the masses and the members of an elite. The city had, in a sense, a mixed constitution where both the people and the elite had to take account of each other's desires and objectives.

The history of Athens is, as I said, informed by a number of stories. The architecture of this book is constructed largely out of two, though the two are closely related. The first six sections of the book tell an epic and moral tale, of how from humble beginnings the city rose to greatness and fell due to arrogance. Athens epitomizes the condition of all assertive and successful states that overreach themselves in the belief of their own essential superiority. She was the only city in ancient Greece which could have fostered cooperative values, but she deliberately turned her back on them. I portray the city's rise and fall as a tragedy, and as the gradual betrayal of the kind of values represented in the ancient Greek world by the Olympic ideal. The final sections of the book tell how the city learnt to cope with the tensions created by the painfully clear contrast between an awesome past and a diminished present.

The rise and fall of Athens infuse the city's story with a timeless truth, first articulated by the historian Herodotos of Halikarnassos, who was writing in Athens at the time of its greatness. Close to the beginning of his *History* (1.5), he issued the following implicit warning: 'I will cover both major and minor communities equally, because most of those which were important in the past have diminished in significance by now, and those which were great in my own time were small in times past. I will mention both equally because I know that human happiness never remains long in the same place.'

The idea that individuals and states, when prosperous, run the risk of growing too far, too fast, and bringing about their own downfall is a commonplace in ancient Greek literature, and seems to me to be true. The Greeks loved to generalize and abstract, and their philosophers elevated the principle to a universal law. Anaximandros of Miletos gave the law its earliest formulation around 550 BCE when he described excessive growth as 'injustice': it is a necessary law, he wrote, that things 'give justice and reparation to one another for their injustice in accordance with the ordinance of Time' (Fragment 1). In due course of time, the mighty will fall, and they sow the seeds of their own fall just by being mighty. This is a lesson which certain modern states should heed.

Moralizing about history does of course carry the risks of anachronism and hindsightedness. Nevertheless, this is what I unashamedly do in this book. One of the important reasons for the popular (non-academic) study of history is and always has been to learn from past mistakes and try to avoid them in the future. Although it has proved almost impossible for people in power to do this, the effort is still worth making. And Athens does have a lot to teach us in this respect. But the first purpose of the book is to give an entertaining history of Athens, incorporating the most up-to-date insights of the best scholars.

At the heart of Athens' history, then, is a tragic drama. Just like the protagonist of an ancient tragedy, the city looked after its own self-interest with single-minded ruthlessness, but sealed its doom by misjudging where its self-interest really lay. Classical Athens' rise and fall were even more abrupt than Herodotos could have anticipated: it all took a little less than 150 years, roughly from 480 to 340 BCE. The candle-brief glory of Athens is what makes its tragedy so poignant and resonant: it was played out on a human, comprehensible scale. There is something about Athens which haunts us, more than the longer-lasting grandeurs of Rome or Egypt do. It is somehow both remote and familiar, its story simultaneously archetypal and personal. The typical ancient Athenian free male citizen spent a lot of his life outdoors, in the public spaces of the city rather than at home, and there is something public about Athenian history: its good points and bad points are exposed and available for contemplation and analysis.

Even after Athens' glory days were over, the story continued, not just because the city then suffered the consequences of its downfall, in terms of decline and obscurity, but more importantly because the very abruptness of its rise and fall made the Classical city paradigmatic and dictated not just how Athens was perceived, but also its future history. If ever a city's present was bound up, at every subsequent period, with the myth of its past, that city is Athens. It is not just that the city is still crucially dependent on the tourist trade; throughout her history, if the past was remembered, the city survived and endeavoured to hold her head up high; if it was forgotten, the city floundered and shrank.

The past remained the source of life for the city. Roman leaders and eastern potentates showed their respect by renewing the city's buildings; in more recent times the arrival of notable artefacts in European museums inspired the neoclassical fad, which prompted European intervention in Greece's war of liberation, which in turn enabled Athens to rise again as the capital city of a new Greece. However, I deeply hope that the 2004 Olympics will open a whole new era for Greece. It is time for Athens to take her place as a modern European city, part of the network of cities around the world, not just part of Greece. To my mind, Athens will be able to do this once she has reason to be proud of recent achievements, not just the long-distant past. The Olympics may prove to be exactly the catalyst for this reaction.

THE OLYMPIC IDEAL

1

The Festival at Ancient Olympia

Nothing beats water, and gold, bright as firelight, gleams
More than all other lordly wealth. But, dear soul of mine,
If you want a real contest to celebrate, just as you need search
The barren skies for no bright star more warming than the sun,
So the supreme games of which to sing are those of Olympia.

(Pindar, Olympian Odes 1.1–12)

Once every four years, from the traditional, though probably not authentic, starting date of 776 BCE, men from all over the Greek world, from Spain to the North African coast to the Black Sea, converged on Olympia. They came to this well-watered town in the western Peloponnese, surrounded by low, wooded hills, to compete against one another in the games. They competed as individuals, not as representatives of their native or adopted cities. There were plenty of other games in Classical Greece – especially in Nemea, Delphi and Corinth, where the other 'crown' games (those with only a wreath as a prize) were held – but at best they stood as the World Athletic Championships today do in relation to the modern Olympics. There was honour to be won in any of the games, but nothing compared with the prestige of the Olympics. The ancient Olympic Games continued to be held for over 1,000 years until Theodosios the Great, Emperor of Rome, banned them in 393 CE. Theodosios was a Christian, and the Olympic Games were a religious festival in honour of Zeus.

A student of the ancient Greeks, as of any alien culture, is constantly having the rug pulled out from under his feet. He spends half his time seeing, with a sigh of relief or a jolt of self-recognition, similarities between them and us, in respect of their cultures and even their characteristics. But he spends the rest of his time aware

of profound differences – and the fact that the Olympic Games
were a religious festival is one of these differences. Nowadays,
athletic competitions are strictly secular, unless they are in thrall
to the great god of commercialism. But a visitor to or participant in
the ancient Olympic Games would have witnessed not just athletic
competitions, but also feasts, processions, prayers and sacrifices, on
every day of the festival. The association of athletics and religion at
Olympia was probably fostered mainly by the belief that Zeus would
enjoy the display, though we cannot entirely rule out the idea that
the competitors were offering a sacrifice – their energy – to the god.

The combination of religious festival and competition was by
no means restricted to the Olympic and other games: dramatic
contests, for instance, were part of festivals to the god Dionysos.
Or again, even a spontaneous celebration might include a rapidly
organized athletic contest, if there were enough men present to
make it worthwhile. The ancient Greeks invented sport. They were
naturally competitive, and would not have understood the sentiment
that taking part is as good as winning. For the Greeks, winning was
everything, and losers felt ashamed at their failure:

> They cower in back alleys,
> Keeping away from their enemies,
> Full of remorse at their failure.

(Pindar, *Pythian Odes* 8.86–7)

Athletics, then, was peculiarly Greek, and when the successors
of Alexander of Macedon hellenized the East, they took the craze
for athletics with them. The Jewish author of the apocryphal Maccabees, writing in the second century BCE, complained that young
priests in Jerusalem were practising the discus rather than their
duties (2 Maccabees 4:14–15), an Indian king of the first century CE
had a Greek-style training-ground built so that he could throw
the discus and javelin, and numerous Eastern cities instituted
Greek-style athletic festivals of their own. By the end of the first
century CE, there were over 300 athletic contests around the Greco-
Roman world.

In order to allow athletes and visitors to travel in safety from
their homes to Olympia, there was a sacred truce. Well in advance,

heralds travelled the length and breadth of the Greek world announcing the precise date of the games and the extent of the surrounding truce. The date was roughly known already, since the games were held every four years, and always in the late summer, with the central day of the festival falling on the second full moon after the summer solstice. This is a very hot time of year in Greece for athletics, but little agricultural activity took place at this season, and so more people were free to attend. The athletes themselves were of course amateurs, although for the glory of their family and native city they shunned other work (if they were not already non-working aristocrats) for some weeks or months while they trained for the event and became used to exerting themselves in the summer heat. There were trainers, especially for wrestlers, and manuals on exercise and diet. There was also a considerable amount of medical knowledge about sports injuries.

The Greeks had a habit of making up myths and legends to explain the origins of their customs, and there was one about the truce as well. It was said that King Iphitos of Elis, the town north of Olympia which was responsible for the running of the games, asked the Delphic oracle what he should do to stop the Greeks fighting one another. The oracle replied that he should declare a sacred truce for the duration of the games. For several months surrounding the games, then, warfare throughout the Greek world subsided. In the ancient Greek world, this ceasefire is quite remarkable. Their history shows that the Greek states were belligerent, constantly fighting someone or other, and involved in complex networks of shifting alliances, dictated usually by self-interest. There is no little irony in the fact that one of the things we most admire in the ancient Greeks is their love of freedom – and yet one of the chief manifestations of that love was their constant striving to control in some way the futures of their neighbours.

Geography is not quite destiny – after all, Greece never again split up into numerous independent states – but certainly the landscape of Greece encouraged these rivalries. In the first place, it was quite likely that a community was cut off even from its nearest neighbours by rugged landscape – Greece is dominated by mountains – or, in the case of the islands, tracts of open sea. In the second place, fertile agricultural land and timber forests were scarce and worth fighting over. Over the centuries, one such citizen-state (the cumbersome but fairly accurate translation of the ancient Greek word *polis*) usually gained control over a number of outlying smaller villages, as Athens gained control of the surrounding district of Attica, or Megara did of the Megarid, and so on. Mountains and coastline formed natural barriers to this expansion. The upshot was that on mainland Greece there were twenty-five or so regions – Attica, Thessaly, Boiotia, Lakonia, Epeiros, Phokis, etc. – each invariably with at least one major town, and now with borders and inevitable border disputes with its neighbours. Since much Greek history is incomprehensible otherwise, it is vitally important to realize that there was no independent and unified nation of Greece until the nineteenth century CE, though the mainland and the Aegean islands were regarded more or less as a whole under the Roman, Byzantine and Ottoman Empires.

The centre of the Olympic complex was the Altis, a grove sacred to Zeus. Over the centuries, as well as a colossal temple of Zeus, many other buildings sprung up and were developed and redeveloped, until the modern visitor is faced with a perplexing mass of stone-strewn sites, intersected with paths. This is at least some kind of reflection of the crowded scene of ancient times, as thousands of spectators, peddlers, prostitutes, entertainers, athletes and officials wound their way between the sacred buildings and hundreds of statues. Dominant over all was the great temple of Zeus, which by the end of the fifth century housed one of the seven wonders of the ancient world, the 13-metre-high, gold-and-ivory statue of Zeus seated on his throne, the creation of Pheidias of Athens. The temple too was built on a magnificent scale, to accommodate such a priceless statue, and visitors could climb to an upper floor to get a closer look at the top half of the statue. In addition to this enormous temple, there were important temples to Hera and Rhea (the mother of the gods), a shrine to the local hero Pelops (after whom the whole Peloponnese – the 'island of Pelops' – is named), an oracular shrine of Zeus, council-houses and colonnades, treasuries filled with offerings from successful athletes or their native states, a huge gymnasium (big enough to house an indoor running track) for the athletes to train in, and a number of other grand buildings.

Zeus's altar, on open ground in the Altis, attracted attention for its famously huge mound of solidified ash, the result of centuries of burnt animal offerings; it marked the spot where Zeus is said to have hurled his thunderbolt when laying claim to the sacred enclosure. Spectators jostled one another for a view of the statues of past heroes – and, right by the entrance to the stadium, they could see the name-and-shame bronze statues of Zeus, inscribed on the pedestal with the names of those who had attempted to cheat or bribe an official in past games. There were very few of these, considering the long history of the games, and they were paid for by the cheat or his native city. Towering over all other statues was Paionios of Mende's symbolic figure of Victory, dedicated at the end of the 420s BCE by the people of Messenia. Perched on top of a column 9 metres tall, it depicted Victory swooping down to Olympia. Enough remains of the statue, now splendidly housed in the new museum at Olympia, for us to regret that it is no longer complete, for its grace and the impression of speed given by the way Victory's flimsy clothes cling to the front of her thighs and swirl out behind. In Roman times the complex was extended, with baths and a hotel, for instance. Before the construction of the hotel, we should imagine visitors slinging a piece of material over bushes or the branches of trees as a crude tent. And then there were the facilities for the games: the stadium for the foot-races, the hippodrome for the horse events, the sandpit for the wrestlers and boxers.

The noise and bustle would be familiar to modern visitors, were they transported in time back to the ancient Olympics. But apart from this, many aspects of the festival would seem strange. Most importantly, there were far fewer events in the ancient Olympics – no synchronized swimming or beach volleyball, for instance, nor even a marathon race, despite its supposed ancient Greek origins. When the festival first started, it was limited to a foot-race or two, and everything was on a far simpler scale, but by Classical and later times more events had been added and the festival had expanded into an elaborate five-day extravaganza. We should imagine the games spreading from a local village affair, designed originally to initiate young men into adulthood, until they encompassed the entire Greek world.

The Olympic Events

Two days before the official start, all the contestants and officials were required to walk the 60 kilometres from Elis, where they had congregated a month earlier to train under the supervision of the committee. On the way to Olympia, the formal procession stopped from time to time to perform a sacrifice or carry out some other rite. Then on the first day there were sacrifices, and the competitors and purple-robed judges swore oaths of fair play; well-known orators might give speeches in a semi-competitive fashion, and in later years there were competitions for trumpeters and town-criers. The second day saw the chariot- and horse-races, and the pentathlon, followed by feasting and relaxation in the evening. The third day was especially distinguished: in the morning all the officials, athletes and representatives of Greek cities accompanied the priests of Zeus and 100 oxen in a procession to the altar, where the animals were ritually sacrificed; and in the afternoon the foot-races were held. The evening of this central day was the occasion for a public banquet. On the fourth day it was the turn of the wrestlers and boxers, and there was the gruelling race run in armour. Finally, on the fifth day, as well as the inevitable sacrifices and feasting, all the victors of the games displayed themselves to the crowds in a procession to the temple of Zeus, where they were crowned with wreaths of wild olive, their only prizes, as a sign that they were dedicated to the god. This is a simplified calendar: various events came, and sometimes went, at various times in the games' history.

Victors were heroes, and in some cases literally gained that semi-divine status, when their native city honoured them with worship and sacrifices after their deaths. There were few dissenting voices. The travelling bard Xenophanes of Kolophon (c. 570–c. 480) sourly complained that success in the Olympic Games did nothing to enhance the good government of a city (Fragment 2.15–22), and there were others too who preferred a less superficial way of judging success as a citizen. But success enormously enhanced the prestige of the winner in his native city; in seventh-century Athens, a victor called Kylon even tried to translate his popularity into control of the state. A rich winner might enhance his fame by paying a poet to compose a victory ode in his honour: Simonides, Pindar, Bakkhylides and Ibykos are the best-known poets of such odes, and the show-off Alkibiades had the internationally acclaimed playwright Euripides compose one for him. However, the craze for paying for this form of immortality lasted only a little over 100 years, before giving way to commissioning a sculptor to carve a statue.

The lack of cash value of the prizes reflected not only the Greek ideal that fame was more valuable than material wealth, but also the fact that the games were originally intended for the wealthy elite, who did not need the money, despised working for money, and enjoyed the resonance the games had with the heroic past of Homer's poems; as Homer has a couple of his heroes say at different points of the *Iliad* (6.208, 11.783), it is the hero's job to strive 'always to be the best, superior to others'. In fact, the participants in the Olympic Games for much of their history (certainly down to about 450 BCE, and longer for the equestrian events) did predominantly come from the elite, and the games were viewed as a place for equals from different cities to meet and attempt to establish superiority. It was noble to compete with equals, but the conditioned attitude towards inferiors was contempt. When Alexander the Great was asked if he would enter the sprint race, he replied that he would if his rivals were fellow kings. However, during their lifetimes, Olympic victors could expect to be heaped with honours at home; despite the fact that there was no cash prize at the games, some states, including Athens, gave generous amounts of money to Olympic victors, and we also hear of alternative forms of reward, such as rent-free accommodation, or exemption from certain taxes, or being fed at public expense once or twice a week for the rest of one's life.

The only events were boxing, wrestling, pankration, four footraces, the pentathlon (long jump, discus, javelin, sprinting and wrestling), chariot-racing and horse-racing. The Greeks had other sports – ball-games and swimming, for instance – but they never aroused as much enthusiasm and competitiveness as the Olympic events. It is easy to see that the Olympic events are those which developed skills useful in warfare; one plausible theory of sport claims that it is little more than ritualized warfare – 'war minus the shooting', as George Orwell said of professional football. For the

Greeks, though, the pretext may have been military training, but in reality the games were an outlet for their incredible competitiveness.

Of all the events, the stade run was the most prestigious, as the 100 metres is today: from a fairly early date the winner had the whole four-year period of that Olympiad named after him. As the name implies, the stade was simply one length of the stadium, a little less than 200 metres; in legend, this was the length the mighty Herakles could run without drawing breath. The other running races were the *diaulos* ('double pipe', two lengths of the stadium), the long *dolikhos* (probably 20 stades at Olympia), and a 2-stade race run in armour, or at least helmet, greaves and shield. There might be as many as twenty starters in each race, and the first three were occasionally won by the same man, who was hailed as a triple winner. The fact that all three races were held on the same day makes this rare achievement all the more remarkable. There is no better monument to the popularity of the games than the capacity of the new stadium, built in the middle of the fourth century BCE: over 40,000 spectators could be seated on its banked slopes.

The rules governing the ancient pentathlon are obscure, and there is no scholarly consensus. Possibly, the first competitor to win three events was declared the overall winner. The first three events were those peculiar to the pentathlon – the discus and javelin, and the long jump (which might actually have been a triple jump). If there was no clear winner after these three events, the contestants ran a stade race, and then, if necessary, wrestling decided the competition among those who were closest to winning.

The 'heavy' events, as they were known (from the sheer weight of the participants), were the combat sports: boxing, wrestling and pankration. In boxing, any form of blow was allowed, possibly even kicking, but no grappling. There were no timed rounds: the boxers, who wore light, criss-crossed leather thongs on their hands for protection, or heavier thongs to maximize damage, just went on and on at each other, sometimes for hours, until one was compelled to admit defeat. Clinching was not allowed, and the boxers fought in a ring, to ensure that they remained within striking distance of each other. The description of a boxing-match which begins the second book of the *Argonautica* of Apollonios of Rhodes, a poet of the third century BCE, shows that the attraction (if that is the right word) of the sport was the same then as now – a combination of admiring strength and skill, and waiting for the blood to flow.

Wrestling was again somewhat different from the modern event. The wrestlers grappled upright, with no part of the body except the feet allowed on the ground: a win was gained, then, by three throws – by some part of the loser's back, shoulders, chest or stomach touching the ground three times. All kinds of tactics were allowed, including strangleholds and breaking one's opponent's fingers. Pankration was similar to wrestling (and both in legend were said to have been invented by Theseus of Athens), except that the winner had to compel defeat rather than throwing his opponent, because in this event the contestants were allowed on the ground – and in fact were allowed to do almost anything. In theory, biting and gouging were forbidden, but in practice fighters often got away with them. Vase-paintings depict contestants with bloody hand-prints on their bodies, and show that one could even knee or kick one's opponent in the genitals. The enormous popularity of the heavy events is shown not just by the presence in every Greek town of any size of at least one wrestling-ground, either as a separate facility or as part of a gymnasium, but also by the frequency with which they occur as metaphors in all kinds of ancient literature.

We know far less about the equestrian events, simply because no Greek hippodromes survive. As a result of earthquakes, flooding, and changes in the courses of its rivers, the whole site of Olympia, for all its size and fame, was completely buried from some time in the Middle Ages until the eighteenth century. Proper excavations began in 1875, and by this time the hippodrome had long been washed away. It was about 600 metres long and was wide enough to allow up to forty chariots to race at once.

There were two chariot-races: a 4-kilometre race for colts in a pair, and a 13-kilometre race for older horses, usually mares, in teams of four. Accidents were common, especially when rounding the turn, and there was no suspension in the chariots as they jolted over the broken ground. Naturally enough, then, the wealthy owners tended not to race their own chariots, but entrusted this to trained slaves, whose lives were expendable. This is how Alkibiades could boast that in the games of 416 he entered seven chariots in the four-horse event, and came first, second, fourth and seventh.

We do not hear what happened to his other teams: presumably they crashed. And this was also how a woman could claim victory in an Olympic event, as (most famously because she was the first) Kyniska of Sparta did twice, early in the fourth century BCE. Xenophon, the friend and eulogistic biographer of her brother King Agesilaos, says that it was the king's doing: 'Agesilaos persuaded his sister Kyniska to breed a team of horses for chariot-racing and so, when she won a victory at the games, he proved that to keep such a team is not a mark of manly virtue but merely of wealth' (*Agesilaus* 9.6). And he did mean wealth: good, level land is so rare in southern Greece that to give some over to horses or their high-grade fodder rather than to staples was sheer ostentation, unless they were warhorses. Even though the games as a whole were the province of an elite, the equestrian events were the province of an elite within the elite.

Although the stade foot-race was the most prestigious, the four-horse chariot-race was a close second, and was certainly the most exciting to watch, for many of the same reasons that Formula One racing is popular today – that is, in expectation of thrills and spills. The most famous written account of sports events in the ancient world must be the funeral games in honour of Patroklos in Homer's *Iliad* 23, but a vivid impression of a chariot-race is given by the Athenian dramatist Sophokles in his play *Electra*, written around 415 BCE. At this point in the play an old retainer of Orestes is trying to convince Klytaimnestra, the devious, husband-slaying mother of both Elektra and Orestes, that his master died during the Pythian Games at Delphi. So he gives him a death which is both heroic and plausible:

> But when one of the gods is against you, not even the strong can escape. When the day of the swift chariot-race dawned, he entered the contest along with many other charioteers. [He lists ten in all, from various Greek cities.] Their starting positions depended on how the lots fell out, and the appointed judges put them in their places, until at the sound of the bronze trumpet off they raced, calling out to their horses and shaking the reins in their hands. The whole course was filled with the rattle of chariots; dust rose into the air; they were all tightly bunched together and used their goads unsparingly as each

tried to overtake the others' wheels and panting horses, with either their backs or their spinning wheels spattered with foam flying at them from the nostrils of their rivals' horses.

So far all the chariots had remained upright, but as they came out of the turn from the sixth to the seventh lap, the Ainian's hard-mouthed horses lunged violently forward and crashed straight into the Barkaean chariot. After that, as a result of this single accident, one collided and smashed into another, until the whole Krisaean plain was filled with wrecked chariots. When he realized what was going on, the Athenian charioteer cleverly pulled his team aside and reined them in, so as to pass the seething chaos of the surging mass of horses in the middle of the track. Orestes was in the rear, holding his horses back and trusting that the final stretch would bring him victory. When he saw that there was only one other left, he hurled a shrill command into the ears of his swift horses and set off after him. The two teams were neck and neck, with first one and then the other a head in front of his rival.

Orestes kept the hub of his left wheel close to the post at every turn, and gave the right-hand trace-horse its head. He succeeded in keeping the nearest wheel away from the post on every turn, and the poor man remained safely standing, with his chariot upright, for all the remaining laps, until on the last lap he slackened the left rein before the horse had made the turn and grazed the edge of the post. The hub of the wheel split and he was hurled over the chariot's rail. He became tangled in the well-trimmed reins, and as he fell to the ground his horses were scattered all over the track.

At the sight of his fall from the chariot, the crowd cried out in grief that the young man should meet with such misfortune after having achieved so much. At one time he was dashed to the ground, at another his feet were tossed skyward, until the other charioteers were finally able to check his horses' rush and free his blood-streaked body. Not even any of his friends would have recognized the wretched corpse.

(Sophokles, *Electra* 696–756)

Compared with this, the other horse events were tame. Again, though, the jockeys were likely to be slaves, because, with no saddles or stirrups, and riding over ground already chewed up by the chariot races, the events were tougher than they might have been. There was one race of 6 stades, another for colts, and a third for mares, in which for the last stretch of the race the rider dismounted and ran alongside the horse; this last race, like one in which mules drew carts, did not prove popular and both lasted for only about twelve Olympiads in the fifth century BCE.

For all the track and field events, the athletes were naked. Originally, they had worn loin-cloths, but these fell into disuse by the sixth century. To increase comfort (or at least to decrease discomfort) the penis was infibulated – the foreskin tied back against the body with a leather thong. There were no issues of modesty: part of the point was to display a fine, well-muscled body, gleaming with olive oil. The noblemen of Greece were, in the phrase coined in fifth-century Athens, 'the beautiful and the good', and the assumption that a fine exterior was a reflection of virtuous character was rarely questioned. The Olympic Games were a summation of the aristocratic ideals of physical skill, beauty and strength, of competition, and of honour freely or grudgingly given by one's peers.

Nudity and the application of oil, which serve no practical purpose (except in wrestling), may be seen as ritual aspects of the games, bearing in mind that they were part of a religious festival, but they also afford us a glimpse of the homoeroticism of aristocratic Greek life. Eros, the god of love or, more literally, sexual passion, was (along with Hermes for communication and Herakles for strength) the guardian deity of Greek sports: the gymnasia were always places where those with the time to do so would meet, make conversation and admire the young men at their training, and the Olympic Games were in this respect gymnasia expanded on to a panhellenic stage. In Britain nowadays teenagers use the word 'fit' as a synonym for 'good-looking' or 'sexy': the Greeks would have understood this perfectly, since a fit young body had a certain 'bloom', they said, which made it desirable. They themselves were inclined to attribute the origin of homoeroticism to the practice of exercising naked in the gymnasia.

Married women, apart from the local priestess of Demeter, were not allowed to attend the games, but unmarried women were. Since women tended to be married off around the age of thirteen or fourteen, this was a severe restriction. It may seem to make little sense to stop married rather than unmarried women from seeing naked men, but this is just another occasion when Greek practices confound the modern mind. In any case, the prohibition of women says more about Greek attitudes to women than it does about any sense of modesty or the opposite. Besides, many of the athletes would be in their mid-twenties, close to the age of marriage, and the girls' fathers – as well as the girls themselves – took the opportunity to pick out prospective husbands. The eroticism of the games was not only homoeroticism.

We do hear of women's games at Olympia (and elsewhere), but we know little about them, other than that a shorter stade race was the only event, and they were open only to girls (in three different age groups) who were, as the Greeks put it, still untamed by marriage and so wild enough to run. The games started about 580 BCE and were, appropriately, sacred to Hera, Zeus's wife. In this case, the female athletes were not naked, but wore a loose, light dress which exposed the right breast and rose higher than the knees. They were probably held just before the male games – which helps to explain the presence of unmarried women as spectators at the main games.

Following the Roman conquest of Greece in 146 BCE, Romans gained the right to participate in the games. The Romans admired Greek athletic contests, and set up their own to rival them, but they acknowledged the supremacy of the Olympics and supported the games both financially and otherwise. Wealthy Romans repaired the temple of Zeus after earthquake damage, built new buildings or renovated old ones, and in general smartened up the site. There were innovations (a temple and a Zeus-like statue of Augustus, for instance) and aberrations (as when the mad emperor Caligula tried to replace the head of Zeus on Pheidias' statue with his own, or when Nero insisted on winning events), but on the whole the Romans preserved the ancient lineage of the games, while developing its panhellenism in the direction of further internationalism.

Panhellenism: The Olympic Ideal

In one respect, the Greeks were certainly no different from all other peoples at any period of human history: they approved of cooperation, but were more often driven by competitiveness. In fact, competitiveness was so natural to the ancient Athenian outlook that we come across many examples of it in unusual circumstances – such as the dramatic competition which has given us so many masterpieces of literature. But competitiveness underlay Athenian values at a much deeper level, and explains a great deal about the city's history. It was natural for Athenians to assume that those who made a contribution to the city's welfare should have a right to a voice in its politics: this created the us-and-them division between citizens and non-citizens. A natural extension of this principle was the idea that the city that made the greatest contribution towards the defence of Greeks against non-Greeks (another competitive division) had a right to greater wealth and prestige and power over other cities: this was the implicit justification for an imperialism that was more or less free of guilt. And it was natural for each Athenian individual to envy those of his fellow citizens who were well off. This did not – or not just – lead him to want to bring others low, but rather to aspire to the same level of comfort himself. It was precisely the fact that almost all Athenians shared these views that allowed them to cooperate with one another and form a stable and cohesive state; paradoxically, competition led to cooperation.

The Olympic ideal reflected both sides of the coin, both competition and cooperation. The Olympics were an occasion for prowess and manly excellence, but at the same time the games were chiefly responsible for fostering a feeling of fellowship among Greeks. They spoke more or less the same language, worshipped more or less the same gods, retold more or less the same myths, shared Delos, Dodona and Delphi as common shrines, had recognizably similar ways of life both in private and in public, looked through Homer's poems to a glorious shared past – and when threat came from abroad more or less united against it. They even called themselves by a common name, 'the Hellenes' (our 'Greece' and 'Greeks' come via the Latin from a much rarer Greek word). But Greece was never united politically: it was a set of shared ideas and practices, rather than an entity defined by territory or nationhood, and it was easier for Greeks to say what they were *not* (foreigners, slaves, gods) than what they were.

It was chiefly during the Olympic Games that the common ground, rather than the differences, was allowed to come to the fore. It is no coincidence that Zeus was the patron deity of the Olympics: as the head of a sprawling family of squabbling deities, he was the perfect patron for the major panhellenic festival. We should not overrate the inclusiveness of the games, however: they were strictly a Greek affair, with non-Greeks ('barbarians') utterly excluded, unless they were slaves involved in the equestrian events. It was one of the Elean officials' main tasks in the weeks preceding the games to ensure that all entrants were true Greeks.

A *de facto* panhellenism distinguished the games and was taken for granted by their aristocratic participants, but it took the Athenians to convert panhellenism into a political ideology, because Athens was the only truly cosmopolitan city of ancient Greece, before the Hellenistic period. Its unique emphasis on culture attracted artists, intellectuals, tourists and businessmen from all over the Greek world, it was less xenophobic than most Greek states, and it had extensive trading links with just about everywhere else. Even the Athenian Empire was founded on treaties with tributary states that stressed a form of panhellenism. Moreover, culturally, Athens was the location for three important panhellenic events. The City Dionysia, the festival at which many of the great tragedies and comedies were put on, was open to all Greeks, as was initiation into the Eleusinian Mysteries, one of the most important cults of the ancient world; and the athletic competitions of the quadrennial Great Panathenaia were as open to all Greeks as any of the longer-established games (though in fact they were dominated by Athenians).

Athens was also the natural home for panhellenism because it was the place where the Greek democratic experiment was taken furthest. At Olympia, men met as equals; panhellenism regards all Greeks as equals; Athens was the place where male citizens were (in theory, at least) equal before the law. Therefore, panhellenism had a greater chance in Athens because it was a logical extension of democracy.

But we should not get too excited about panhellenism. It was very strictly the idea of concord or unity among *Greeks*, and always included, explicitly or implicitly, the notion that non-Greeks were 'other', and were therefore legitimate targets of Greek aggression. Easterners especially were considered effete and, according to several writers, were 'natural slaves', whereas a Greek felt a certain repugnance about enslaving a fellow Greek. The palatable idea of the unity of all Greeks was just one side of the coin, with the other being contempt for barbarians. Panhellenism was at best xenophobic, and in its bastardized form overtly racist – but it was a step in the right direction. As this book progresses, we will see how and why Athens ultimately failed to take the step.

Antiphon of Athens was a voice crying in the wilderness. Writing towards the end of the fifth century BCE, he stated his case clearly:

> By nature there is nothing at all in our constitutions to differentiate Greeks from barbarians. We can consider those natural qualities which are essential to all human beings and with which we are all equally endowed, and we find that in the case of all these qualities there is nothing to tell any of us apart as Greek or foreign. For we all breathe the air through our mouths and nostrils, laugh when our minds feel pleasure or cry when we are distressed; we hear sounds with our ears; we see with our eyes thanks to daylight; we work with our hands, and walk with our feet . . .

At this point the fragment (44B), preserved on papyrus, breaks off, to our frustration. But Antiphon, and the occasional character in a Euripidean play, were forerunners: it would be about 100 years before the radical idea of the kinship of all humankind was taken seriously, by Theophrastos of Eresos, who succeeded Aristotle as head of the Lykeion school, and among the early Stoics.

Long before Stoicism, Athens had a chance to use her influence to foster unity among the Greeks. Later generations looked back at the Persian Wars and saw a time when panhellenism could have blossomed. Herodotos of Halikarnassos (modern Bodrum in

Turkey), the historian of the Persian Wars, had an Athenian respond as follows to Spartan fears that Athens would come to terms with the Persians and desert the Greek alliance:

> You should have known that there isn't enough gold on earth, or any land of such outstanding beauty and fertility, that we would accept it in return for collaborating with the enemy and enslaving Greece. Even if we were inclined to do so, there are plenty of important obstacles in the way. First and foremost, there is the burning and destruction of the statues and homes of our gods; rather than entering into a treaty with the perpetrator of these deeds, we are duty-bound to do our utmost to avenge them. Then again, there is the fact that we are all Greeks – one race speaking one language, with temples to the gods and religious rites in common, and with a common way of life. It would not be good for Athens to betray all this shared heritage. (*Histories* 8.144)

Herodotos was writing at the beginning of the Peloponnesian War, when Athens had already betrayed the 'shared heritage', and had flipped the coin so that instead of Greek unity, panhellenism tended to mean a pact of aggression against non-Greeks, especially the Persians. He may be expressing nostalgia for a missed opportunity, but the idea was current at the time, brought to the surface by the wave of emotion following the almost miraculous defeat of the Persian invaders.

Conservative Athenian aristocrats were especially likely to espouse panhellenism: after all, they found more affinity with their peers in other cities than they did with the poor of their own cities. So Kimon, one of the leaders of Athens after the Persian Wars, persuaded his fellow citizens to help Sparta during the time of their greatest crisis, the long slave revolt which followed a devastating earthquake around 460. Kimon argued that Athens should 'not allow Greece to become lame, or Athens to lose its yoke-fellow' (Plutarch, *Cimon* 16). However, the reality of the time was that tension was increasing between Sparta and Athens. It would take work for panhellenism to become any kind of reality.

The panhellenic banner continued to be waved from time to time in Athens. Some time in the early 440s the great Athenian statesman Perikles invited every Greek city, regardless of location or size, to send representatives to a huge conference. The agenda included rebuilding the Greek temples and shrines which had been destroyed by the Persians, keeping the seas clear of Persian warships, and organizing panhellenic sacrifices to thank the gods for the Greek victory over the barbarians. It is true that Athens herself would have been the chief beneficiary of such moves, since many of the destroyed shrines and temples were in Attica, and much of the shipping facing danger on the seas was travelling to and from Athens' port, Peiraieus, to the city's economic benefit; but it would be overly cynical to think that Perikles did not also have more idealistic motives, such as healing the rift between those Greek states which had fought against the Persians and those which had not. The combination of selfish and altruistic motives is familiar in politics. After the Second World War, for instance, the US Marshall Plan offered aid to Europe, including the USSR. Had it gone ahead in this form, the Americans would have gained power in Europe at the expense of the Russians – but they undoubtedly also wanted to alleviate European suffering. Perikles was promoting Athens as the leader of a unified Greece: naturally, the Spartans refused to attend, just as the Cold War Russians rejected the Marshall Plan, and the conference came to nothing.

Some years later, in 443, Perikles tried again to place Athens on a panhellenic pedestal. Following the lead of a rival politician, he fostered the foundation of a panhellenic colony in southern Italy. Traditionally, the original inhabitants of new colonies all came from a single city, and owed ties of allegiance to the mother city. Thourioi, in southern Italy, was to be something different – a city inhabited by families from all Greece. Once again he sent messengers around Greece to recruit colonists. It is hard to find a cynical interpretation of Perikles' actions over Thourioi (except that it was excellent propaganda), because he could not have guaranteed Athenian control there: the majority of the inhabitants were to come from the Spartan stronghold of the Peloponnese. Ten years after the new city's foundation, Athens had an opportunity to assert its right to be called the mother city, but declined.

Thourioi was a genuine panhellenic settlement, and it is not surprising to find that two of the original colonists were the historian

Herodotos and the boy who would later return to Athens and become the famous orator Lysias. We have already seen Herodotos expressing panhellenic ideas, and in 384 Lysias gave a powerful speech at Olympia, the epicentre of panhellenism, in which he pleaded for the Greeks to put aside their differences and unite. This plea echoed that of a speech of the Sicilian orator Gorgias, delivered at Olympia in 392, and was in turn echoed a few years later by Isokrates of Athens, in his great *Festival Speech*. The Olympics were the natural setting for the expression of such ideas.

Before long, the pure panhellenism of Herodotos and Perikles had become compromised. The historian, mercenary soldier and educated polymath Xenophon (*c.* 425–*c.*354) veers between respect for some Persian customs and contempt for others, and he portrays his hero, Agesilaos of Sparta, as motivated by a panhellenic hatred of Persians. The most self-serving form of panhellenism is found in the speeches of Isokrates (436–338). Time and again he urges the Athenians to lead their fellow Greeks in the conquest of the East, not just in revenge for the Persian invasion (which was already over a century old at the time of most of these speeches), but as a means of relocating disaffected Greeks of the poorer classes who might threaten the stability of the status quo, in which wealthy landowners such as himself effectively ruled the roost. By the time he was old – and he lived to be very old – it was clear that the only hope for Greek unity was by external conquest: Isokrates nailed his panhellenic colours to the mast of Philip II of Macedon and urged him to unite the warring Greek states in a crusade against the Persians. Before long, but after Isokrates' death, lame Philip's son Alexander the Great and his successors had indeed conquered and hellenized the East – but they had also proved themselves the conquerors, not the saviours, of the rest of Greece as well.

There was a far higher degree of cultural unity in the Greek states under Macedon, but strictly this form of unification represents a failure of panhellenism, since the Macedonians were not full Greeks, however much Alexander might disguise the fact by usurping panhellenist propaganda for his own ends. Even if they did not become a nation as we understand the term, by the era of Roman domination Greeks felt themselves to be a community, wherever they lived, with its own identity and historical continuity. In the

2

Nineteenth-century Athens and the
1896 Olympics

The 2004 Athenian Olympics will cost Greece roughly a billion dollars. Billions more will be exchanged before, during and after the proceedings. Tens of thousands of athletes, trainers, psychologists, members of the press, and so on will converge on Athens, to be joined by hundreds of thousands of spectators. Approximately half the population of the planet will follow the events on television and in the newspapers. A modern Olympic festival is a vast juggernaut, virtually out of control – yet more than any other institution of the modern world, it was set in motion by one man, a philhellene with a vision.

Baron Pierre de Coubertin (1863–1937), a dapper Frenchman with a splendid moustache, was an admirer of the kind of English education we associate with Thomas Arnold and *Tom Brown's Schooldays*, with its combination of sport and intellectual pursuits – a combination which in turn was based on Greek values. The idealistic baron believed that the ancient Greek world had seen a perfect amalgam of mind and muscle, from which all the virtues flowed effortlessly. Inspired especially by the German excavations of Olympia, he set about reviving the games as a kind of modernization of the ancient Olympic ideals of panhellenism and peace.

There had been other games here and there which styled themselves the 'Olympics' – in the Cotswolds in England, for instance, in the seventeenth to nineteenth centuries, and others in Shropshire – but this was little more than the self-aggrandizement of local games. De Coubertin's vision was of a truly international festival of sport, a genuine successor to the panhellenism of the ancient Olympics. He did not innocently believe that such a festival would automatically lead to world peace, but he did believe that it would foster respect, as an important first step, and this was the ideal for which he strove all his life and on which he exhausted his family fortune. After his death, his body was buried in Lausanne, but his heart was cut out and taken to Olympia, where it is buried under a monument in the grounds of the local Olympic headquarters.

There had been earlier attempts to revive the Olympic Games in Athens. William Brookes, the driving force behind the Shropshire games, approached the Greek ambassador in London with the idea in 1880, but was politely rebuffed: there was no way that Greece could afford to host such an event. More importantly, Greeks themselves had tried to get something off the ground. The most persistent such attempts came from the Athenian plutocrat Evangelos Zappas, who was motivated by a desire to see his native country achieve international recognition.

At his own expense he put on games in Athens in 1859. There was no stadium, and the events were run in the squares and streets of the city. The ensuing chaos may be imagined, and there was insufficient enthusiasm for the games to be repeated at four-yearly intervals, as Zappas had hoped. When he died in 1865 he left a substantial amount of money for further games, which were held in 1870, 1875 and 1889, at various locations in and around the city, including the (then partially excavated) ancient Athenian stadium and a specially constructed exhibition hall, still standing, called the Zappeion. De Coubertin has been criticized for claiming that he revived the games, when in fact Zappas had done so before him, but Zappas's games were for Greeks only, like the ancient Olympics, and so represented no real advance, no recognition that modern games must be truly international. The same can be said of most of the other nineteenth-century attempts to revive the Olympics in America and various European countries.

By the early 1890s, de Coubertin had travelled widely to witness at first hand the state and status of sports in other countries. America opened his eyes to the immense popularity of sporting events, and the 1889 Paris Universal Exposition showed him how attractive and powerful international public spectacles could be, and how important their ceremonial and processional aspects were for harnessing, raising and releasing the emotional aspects of such events. The Exposition even included some sporting contests, and displayed a model of ancient Olympia, based on the new archaeological discoveries. De Coubertin had published books and articles on educational reform, and become an influential member of French sporting and educational circles. He was ready to take the plunge, to see whether his vision could become reality.

The omens were not promising. Whenever de Coubertin spoke in public about reviving the Olympic Games, his audience applauded politely and assumed that he was talking symbolically. Only very few people understood that he was in complete earnest, and so he resorted to guile. He hijacked the 1894 meeting of the main French umbrella organization for sports, and invited sportsmen and educationalists from seventy-nine countries around the world. When replies were slow, he made personal visits abroad to chivvy attendance.

On the agenda were a discussion of amateurism and professionalism in sport, and the question of the establishment of international Olympic festivals. De Coubertin was a skilful negotiator: he knew the art of camouflaging the important question with other issues, and in the advance agenda he buried the question of the revival of the Olympics under a welter of issues concerned with the definition of amateurism in sport. But when the 2,000 delegates arrived, they found to their surprise that there were two new, unheralded items on the agenda, to do with establishing the rules for future Olympic Games and a committee to oversee them. Swayed by torchlit sporting competitions, which were punctuated by musical fanfares, the delegates passed all the proposals: the games were to be held at four-yearly intervals, and were to continue the spirit of the ancient games rather than being exact imitations. Other proposals laid the foundations for the kinds of rules which are still in force. Dimitrios Vikelas of Athens was appointed the head of the first International Olympic Committee, a post he held for two years only, when de Coubertin himself took over until his retirement in 1925. Much of the world's press thought the idea a non-starter.

Vikelas's appointment was a clever move. De Coubertin wanted the first new games, now scheduled for 1896, to be held in Athens, for sound symbolic and philhellenic reasons, but he knew Greece's history of poverty and expected official opposition. He needed a local representative whom he could trust. King George I of Greece had given his blessing, but the government was another matter. Despite pressure from Athenian shopkeepers and cab-drivers, who could foresee healthy profits, Prime Minister Harilaos Trikoupis, who had entered upon his third term of office with promises of fiscal conservatism, continued to argue that the country could not afford to host the games. De Coubertin showed his cunning again: on a visit to Athens in November 1894 he first won both the press and more members of the royal family round to his point of view, and then, pointing especially to existing sports facilities in Athens (the ancient stadium, the Zappeion, the cavalry grounds, the bays for the water events), he concocted a ludicrously low budget for the whole event.

When the opposition party declared itself in favour, Trikoupis bowed to popular pressure (there was a general election in the offing), and de Coubertin later talked of his 'conquest of Greece'. Gifts of money poured in from wealthy Greek expatriates and the Zappeion Commission, and special postage stamps were issued to raise further funds. One particularly well-off Alexandrian Greek, Giorgios Averoff, personally guaranteed all the money needed to refurbish the ancient stadium, first laid out by Lykourgos in 330 BCE, and then rebuilt in magnificent style by the quintessential private benefactor of Athens, Herodes Atticus, in the second century CE. It was severely damaged in the Herulian sack of the city in 267, and then left to disintegrate.

Herodes Atticus had built the stadium out of marble from the nearby quarries of Mount Pentelikon; for Athenian pride in the revived Olympics nothing less would do, and the ancient quarries were re-opened for the new stadium (though it was finally completed only in 1906). De Coubertin himself was hugely energetic. He drew up the invitation list of individuals and clubs, tried to patch up hostilities between countries, designed a velodrome for the cycling contests (though this was not the velodrome that was eventually built), and worked out the programme. Once everything was in place, as the first leg of his journey back to France, the baron made a long-delayed pilgrimage to Olympia. He later said, 'I became aware in this sacred place of the enormity of the task which I had undertaken in proclaiming five months earlier the restoration of the

Olympic Games after a gap of 1,500 years, and I glimpsed all the hazards which would dog me on the way.' But none of the hazards proved insurmountable, and the games went ahead as planned.

Nineteenth-century Athens

Zappas was right and the Greek government was wrong – or at least, this particular government was wrong: others had pursued policies throughout the nineteenth century that were perfectly in keeping with Zappas's desire to make a point to the civilized European nations. After the final liberation of Greece from Ottoman rule in 1833, and the declaration of Athens as the capital city in the following year, Athens pursued an active policy of modernization and assimilation to Western Europe. There were those who argued that the temporary capital, Nauplion in the Peloponnese, should continue as the capital, but the goddess Athena had been the symbol of resistance during the War of Independence, and Athens' ancient reputation as the centre of Greek culture tipped the scales.

It was not altogether a popular choice: the city had been deteriorating for centuries and had suffered terrible damage during the War of Independence. Athens had no schools or hospitals, and a population of fewer than 2,000 (although this rapidly increased); most of the streets were clogged with rubble, and only about 150 houses were habitable. The food supply was erratic; the surrounding countryside was infested with bandits; the largest house, just outside the city, had only eight rooms – it was bought by the new government as the king's residence, until larger accommodation, and eventually a draughty palace, could be built. But Athens was chosen over her rivals because of its historical resonance, and extremely rapid progress was made in rebuilding Athens and Peiraieus.

The city was completely redesigned (in several phases), with wide avenues and imposing neoclassical buildings. It reinvented itself from lowly status as an overgrown shanty town until by 1900 it had become an elegant European city of about 125,000, and the way it did so was by looking simultaneously to the ancient past and to the possible future as a European city. Likewise, the 1896 Olympics revived the history of ancient Greece and located it in a modern setting. The winners even received, in addition to medals, crowns of olive cut from a tree in the Altis at Olympia.

By glorifying and modernizing the city with grand neoclassical structures, the Athenian royalty and governments were walking a number of tightropes simultaneously. After the submission of Greece to the Turkish Empire, there had been a huge diaspora of Greek-speaking people around the Mediterranean, following the trade routes, with the result that by the time of independence only about 800,000 of them lived within the boundaries of what at the time constituted Greece, while the rest were still scattered throughout the Turkish Empire (Greeks referred to the Asia Minor coast simply as 'our East') or the trade routes in Europe. Even after independence, many Greeks preferred to live in Turkish territory, where taxes were lower and prospects seemed better. After all, the three great centres of Greek commerce – Thessaloniki, Constantinople and Smyrna – were still in Ottoman territory.

At a political level, then, the Athenian authorities were reminding these expatriate Greeks (many of whom had amassed considerable fortunes) of their homeland, and encouraging them to return, or at least invest in the prospective glorious future of Greece; they were using Athens as the focus of the awesome task of fulfilling what was known as the 'Great Idea', the creation of a nation and a concept of nationality out of elements which, historically and geographically, had little to unite them apart from language and the supposition of a shared ancestry.

They – the politicians and thinkers who were focused on Athens – were also implicitly undermining the aspirations of those Greeks whose version of the Great Idea anticipated a revived Greek or Byzantine Empire, centred upon Constantinople. This dream would not finally be extinguished until the 1920s, but the grander Athens became, the clearer it was that it, not Constantinople, was to be the centre. In particular, the building of the first university (1837), the royal palace (1842) and the cathedral (1862) secured the right of Athens to be the capital city of all Greeks everywhere. In 1833 the Church of Greece had become autocephalous, instead of being answerable to the patriarch in Constantinople (though the patriarch did not recognize this state of affairs until 1850), so the building of the cathedral in Athens was especially significant. What is more, the authorities ploughed ahead with this building programme against the odds: the country as a whole was heavily in debt, local people grumbled about the demolition of their homes to make way for grand new avenues, and about inadequate compensation, newspapers carped about slow progress.

At a symbolic level, the nineteenth-century building programme is even more revealing. Largely as a result of a craze for ancient Athens – a craze which was stimulated by a combination of idealistic academics, political philhellenes such as Lord Byron, and glamorized tourists – neoclassicism was the dominant architectural idiom of the time, from the Brandenburg Gate in Berlin down to humbler town halls and banks all over Europe and the United States. The chief catalyst was the four-volume work by the painter James 'Athenian' Stuart and the architect Nicholas Revett. They spent two years in Athens, mapping and painting, and produced the beautiful *The Antiquities of Athens* between 1762 and 1814. It immediately became one of the main textbooks for aspiring European architects. Lord Byron made an excellent joke at the expense of the neoclassical fad: on first seeing the Parthenon he said, 'Very like the Mansion House.'

By adorning itself with grand neoclassical buildings, Athens was declaring itself a member of the family of Europe, no longer of Turkey. At the same time, of course, neoclassical forms recalled Athens' ancient heritage, and so reconnected Athenians with their neglected cultural heritage as they came out of what was in effect a Dark Age. By the same token, serious archaeological work also began immediately after liberation, an archaic form of the language was given the seal of approval, and drachmas replaced Turkish piastres. By looking to the past they were building a future. The myth of ancient Athens, filtered through European scholarship and imagination, allowed the city to reinvent itself. Athens still lacked its own cultural identity: it was emulating Paris. If you did not know that this was a description of 1850s' Athens (by one of the maids of honour of Queen Amalia, King Otto's wife), you would never guess:

> On Sundays a very good band plays in a large square. Six cafés have been opened there; at six in the evening it was crowded with little tables and surrounded by people in carriages, while

the King and Queen usually stopped in their drive or ride to
listen to the music ... The latest Paris fashions and foreign
naval uniforms completed the picture.

There was, however, another side to nineteenth-century Athens.
The rapid growth of the city meant that many districts had poor
housing and sanitation, and all the usual urban problems: a high
level of street crime (around 1890 Athens experienced 107 murders
per 100,000 people, compared with two for Western European cities
such as London, Paris and Berlin), burglary, beggary and prostitution. Nevertheless, visitors who kept to the centre were surprised at
how clean and elegant the city was, and to see street signs in French
as well as Greek. The town was, in the words of the ironic, elusive
poet Constantine Cavafy, on his first visit from Alexandria in June
1901, 'very, very pretty – quite European, in the French and Italian
line'.

It would indeed have been the best time to live in Athens: the
city was small and unpolluted; the buildings were low, the streets
wide, the squares open and the gardens shady; the Akropolis was
still visible from all directions, and other ruins poked proudly above
the ground. The cafés of Athens were famous until they were swept
away after the Second World War – Iannakis's, Zavoritis's, Zakhar-
atos's. There were plenty of theatres, but they were not considered
first-rate by those who had seen the real thing. By now, however,
as any visitor knows, the forces of Greek nature have obliterated
many of the Parisian features of the city and made it wholly Greek
– which is to say, not entirely European, but a blend of Europe and
Anatolia.

But some magnificent nineteenth-century buildings survive: the
university buildings, the National Library, the National Archaeological Museum, a number of churches, Heinrich Schliemann's
mansion, and several other former private residences, some of which
are now museums. The Byzantine Museum, for instance, is housed
in the Florentine-style former residence of the splendid Duchesse
de Plaisance (1785–1854). Sophie de Marbois, daughter of the French
consul to the United States, married one of Napoleon's generals
and was a lady-in-waiting to the Empress Josephine. In 1829 she left
her husband and went off to live in Athens and then Beirut with

her young daughter. The death of her daughter in Beirut prompted her return to Athens, and she could be seen walking the streets, dressed in a parody of ancient Greek clothing, and talking to the casket she carried in her arms, which contained her daughter's ashes. She treated the royal family and anyone who was not of her class with equal disdain, and attracted to Athens the cream of French intellectual life. She insisted that after her death a daily bottle of good burgundy and a bouquet of flowers were to be placed by her tomb, but though her grave is still visible in the city's First Cemetery, the practice appears to have lapsed.

The 1896 Olympics

At several levels, then, the choice of Athens as host of the 1896 Olympics was perfect. The games were opened on 6 April, the day after the Greek Easter, which only added to the festive atmosphere throughout the city. Most modern Greek sources, who obviously have not checked original newspapers, say that the games began on 25 March, but this is a wishful projection of the start back on to the seventy-fifth anniversary of the uprising that led to independence. There were an estimated 100,000 spectators – one of the largest gatherings of people for peaceful purposes the world had at that time ever seen. An American visitor, Burton Holmes, wrote: 'The sight is one which thrills us, one the like of which has never before been witnessed in our modern age. The first glimpse of the crowded Stadium is to be numbered among the great sensations of a lifetime.'

Flags and statues adorned the stadium. The Greek royal family received a tumultuous ovation on entering. When the king pronounced the games open, a flock of pigeons was released and cannons boomed. Every night there were street parties, despite the unseasonable cold. The theatres were packed, and bands played the national anthems of the countries of origin of the contestants. Hundreds of Athenian schoolboys put on a gymnastic display in the stadium. The Olympic Anthem, written by Kostis Palamas and set to music by Spyros Samaras, was heard both at the beginning and at the end of the games – and has been repeated at many Olympics since. It is now the official Olympic hymn.

Other features, familiar to us from recent Olympics, were absent. There was no procession with the Olympic flame at the host stadium to mark the start of the games: the lighting of the flame and the symbolic run with the torch were inventions of the tableau-conscious organizers of the 1936 Berlin games. The famous five-ring symbol of the Olympic flag was also nowhere to be seen. The German film-maker Leni Riefenstahl perpetuated the idea that it was an ancient symbol by having it carved on to a rock at Delphi for her documentary on the 1936 games; in fact, it was invented in 1913 by de Coubertin, to represent the five main regions of the world.

The 1896 Olympics were an all-male affair. The music and spectacles, although a pale reflection of current razzamatazz, were more impressive than many of the events, since only the Americans and some of the English believed in pre-contest training; more-over, the cinder track was too soft, and the ancient stadium too tight at the turns, to encourage fast times. Only nine sports were represented: track and field, cycling, fencing, gymnastics, shooting, swimming, weight-lifting and wrestling. Rowing and sailing were cancelled due to bad weather. There were 311 participants, 230 of whom were Greek. This imbalance reflected the doubts most countries felt about the long-term viability of the project, and their lack of local Olympic committees to handle everything from publicity to transport. In Britain, fliers were printed only a few weeks before the games started, with the result that only six or eight athletes attended. Although, with fourteen athletes, the Americans were not the largest team (there were more French and Germans), they were the only ones to field a reasonable number of men who were both well equipped and well trained, and so they won a disproportionate number of the events.

The climax came on the fifth day with the marathon race, run over a roughly 25-mile course from the village of Marathon to the stadium in the city. This was heralded as the first-ever 'revival' of the run of the ancient messenger who carried the news of the Greek victory from the battle of Marathon to Athens in 490 BCE. Unfortunately, there is little evidence for this ancient run. Herodotos, the historian of the Persian Wars, tells a story (*Histories* 6.105) about a runner called Philippides or Pheidippides who was sent from Athens to Sparta (about 140 miles or 225 kilometres) to ask the Spartans for help against the imminent Persian landing at Marathon. In other words, Herodotos, our closest source, does not mention anyone running a distance of 25 miles or so, let alone a run to or from the village or battle of Marathon. This story surfaces only 500 years later in an essay by Plutarch of Khaironeia, a great storyteller. He says that an Athenian soldier called Eukles ran in armour from the battlefield to Athens, 'burst through the doors of the leaders' meeting-room, and had time only to say, "Greetings! Victory is ours!", before expiring' (*On the Fame of Athens* 347c). Plutarch attributes the story to earlier writers, but we cannot be sure of its authenticity. A somewhat later writer, the witty belletrist Lucian of Samosata, tells the same story as Plutarch, but with the name taken from Herodotos (*On a Slip of the Tongue in Greeting* 64.3). This amalgamated version, perpetuated by, for instance, Robert Browning in his 1879 poem 'Pheidippides', is the one which has become familiar to us. There is little historical foundation for it, but it is a very satisfactory legend.

In any case, in 1896 the event was eagerly anticipated, for its historical resonance with Athens' heroic past, and for its novelty. As a contest, it was hardly known in the modern world (even the annual Boston Marathon did not start until 1897), and no one quite knew what to expect: would athletes even be capable of completing the course? A little tampering with the rules allowed in a few more entrants, including a shepherd called Spyros Louis from the village of Maroussi, north of Athens, who had been excluded from the Greek team by his relatively poor performance in the qualifying trials, and by the fact that, as a peasant and not a gentleman, he was not a member of any athletic club. Fifty thousand people packed the stadium and thousands more lined the route.

The marathon started at two in the afternoon, and as time went by tension mounted in the stadium. The spectators could hardly keep their attention on the events going on there. Rumours began to circulate that Edwin Flack, an Australian competing for imperial Britain, was well in front. But then definite news arrived that a Greek was in the lead. Shortly afterwards, sunburnt and covered in dust, Louis entered the stadium, showing hardly any signs of tiredness. He had run an intelligent race, keeping well back, and apparently even stopping for a glass of wine at one point. The athletes who went out hard in the afternoon sun dropped like flies on the uphill sections. Louis came in seven minutes ahead of the second runner, who was in his turn half a minute ahead of the next. All three were Greeks. One of them, however, the third-placed Spyros Belokas, was later disqualified: he had accepted a lift on a cart for some of the course.

The crowd erupted in a frenzy of flag- and hat-waving, shouting and shedding tears of joy. The band was forced to play the Greek national anthem over and over again. Prince Constantine and his younger brother George flanked Louis as he ran the last 200 metres in the stadium, with flowers and bouquets raining down on him. Even the king was on his feet and waving his hat in the air. Then the princes raised the victor on to their shoulders. Caught up in the deep emotions of the moment, none of the foreigners present regretted for a moment that one of their own countrymen had not won the race. De Coubertin, sensitive as usual to symbolic moments, always remembered the scene in the stadium as one of the most extraordinary spectacles he had ever seen.

Only one Greek paper, a few days later, complained about the bending of the rules, which had allowed a peasant to compete, rather than the social equals of the representatives from other countries. In ancient times, as we have seen, a successful athlete might expect to be heaped with honours and privileges on his return home. Pretty much the same happened to Louis. In an ecstasy of patriotism women tried to press gold chains and watches on him, men substantial amounts of cash; others offered free meals for a year, free hair-cuts, coffee twice a day for life, whatever he wanted. Louis refused all these gifts. (One young lady, at least, was certainly grateful for this. Before the race she had promised to marry the winner, if he was Greek. But she had assumed that all the contestants were from her own upper stratum of society, and was taken aback to find that she had pledged herself to a villager.) These refusals were typical of the self-effacing young man, who never traded on his great fame in future years, and hardly turned up for the victory banquets and celebrations, preferring to share his pride with his family and fellow villagers. Forty years later, however, he agreed to lead the Greek team in the opening procession of the Berlin Olympics. In the meantime, his name had become proverbial: 'to do a Louis' means to exert oneself, or sometimes to take off fast. And now the new Olympic stadium is named after him.

The snobbery and elitism which were part of the 1896 games were inevitable. When all is said and done, Pierre de Coubertin was a nineteenth-century baron. His conception of the games was that they should be strictly for amateurs, but that restricted them, in effect, to the moneyed elite who had the spare time to train. Remember the marvellous scene from the 1981 film *Chariots of Fire*, about the 1924 Olympics, in which Lord Andrew Lindsay, played by Nigel Havers, practises the high hurdles on his estate with glasses of champagne balanced on the hurdles against any contact: this is scarcely an exaggeration of the reality, in the days before sponsorship and appearance money.

The games were declared a great success – something that would not happen again until 1908 or 1912. But nothing is untarnished: having made the games their personal project, the Greek royals were busy downplaying the part of de Coubertin and the rest of the Olympic committee, and even snubbing them by omitting to thank them in their speeches. The king also hinted, and the Greek press insisted, that the games should find a permanent home in Athens. But de Coubertin and others had not been impressed by some aspects of the infrastructure. Travel facilities were particularly restricted, and visitors from abroad were few. In any case, de Coubertin's vision was of a truly international event, and so the 1900 games were accordingly scheduled for Paris. De Coubertin's compromise solution was to suggest to the king that Greece should host panhellenic games at four-yearly intervals between the international Olympic Games. The issue remained unresolved for some time. An alternative proposal, by Vikelas, was that the Olympics should be biennial, with Athens hosting every other games. But de Coubertin, wielding the authority of President of the IOC, was unyielding and eventually won the day, though in the event the intermediate panhellenic games took place only in 1906.

In de Coubertin's view, the Athenian Olympics had proved his thesis that the games could foster fellowship and ultimately peace between nations; he had seen displays of patriotism without nationalism, of honest rivalry and mutual respect, and of shared enthusiasm for physical prowess. In ancient times Athens had been the home of panhellenism; in modern times Athens hosted the first of a great series of truly international events. The circle was complete.

THE EARLY CITY
AND THE FOUNDATION
OF DEMOCRACY

3

Athens in Prehistory

Nearly everyone has heard of Theseus. For generations, children have been brought up on tales of his and Herakles' exploits, and may find it hard to distinguish the two heroes. Which of them killed the Krommyonian sow? Was it Theseus who overcame the bull of Marathon and Herakles the Cretan bull, or was it the other way round? Strangely, both the fame of Theseus and his similarity to Herakles are enduring results of Athenian propaganda of 2,500 years ago. Theseus was not always a hero to compare with Herakles. Towards the end of the sixth century, however, Peisistratos, the tyrant of Athens, was attempting to consolidate his rule by uniting all of Attica under a common banner. On the boundary of Athenian history and prehistory was the incorporation of all the towns and villages which made up the region of Attica, with Athens at their head, and this incorporation was supposed to be the work of Theseus. The echoes were useful to Peisistratos: suddenly the cult of Theseus rose to greater prominence and more heroic deeds were attributed to him; suddenly these deeds were more commonly depicted on Athenian vases and sculptures, often the bearers of propaganda.

Then in 490, long after the death of Peisistratos and during the formative years of the Athenian democracy, the rumour circulated that the ghost of Theseus had appeared during the battle of Marathon, when Athenian troops under Miltiades routed the first Persian invasion of Greece. Never one to miss an opportunity, Miltiades' son Kimon, the architect of the Athenian Empire, set sail around 475 for the island of Skyros, the legendary location of Theseus' death and burial, and recovered his bones – which is probably to say that he found and raided a prehistoric burial chamber. The Greeks knew of Mycenaean tombs, of course – the dome-shaped tholos tombs were too big to pass out of memory –

and they not infrequently became the sites of hero cults. Or perhaps he dug up the fossilized skeleton of a dinosaur. At any rate, the skeleton Kimon found was welcomed back in Athens with enormous pomp and ceremony. A new shrine was built for Theseus, a splendid new festival was instituted (and was paid for by a tax on those who claimed to be descendants of the boys and girls he had rescued from the Minotaur), and even more stories gathered around the legendary hero.

Some of the stories were traditional, and could not be too blatantly distorted for propaganda purposes; others merely reflected the interests of fifth-century Athens – including, in these Cold War years of increasing tension with Sparta and her Peloponnesian League, the desire to have a hero to rival Peloponnesian Herakles. Often, little attempt was made to disguise the anachronisms. Around 420 BCE, for instance, Euripides staged his play *Suppliant Women*. The mothers of the Argive heroes who fell in their ill-fated campaign against the city of Thebes have come to Eleusis, the sanctuary of Demeter and Persephone near Athens, to beg Theseus to compel the Theban authorities, by force of arms if necessary, to give up the bodies of their sons for proper burial. It takes a little while, but he is eventually won over.

Why should Athens, unprovoked, interfere in the affairs of another city? Theseus' answer, in Euripides' play, is that Athens has a proud tradition of supporting the weak against the strong. But he refuses to set out against Thebes until the Athenian people have given their assent. Paradoxically and anachronistically, although he is the king, Athens is portrayed as a democracy and, in a debate with a Theban herald, Theseus is loud in his affirmation of the virtues of democracy over the evils of monarchy, which is equated with despotism.

This was one aspect of the Theseus of fifth-century Athenian legend and cult – the personification of Athenian democracy and philanthropy. Suppliants could turn to Athens in their hour of need; if their cause was just and their oppressor a tyrant, they would receive a favourable hearing. The largest group of stories, in direct rivalry with Herakles, had Theseus civilizing the wild elements of the world. So he killed brigands, overcame the Krommyonian sow and the Marathonian bull, defeated unruly centaurs and tamed (and slept with) husbandless Amazons. For fifth-century Athens saw herself, with considerable justification, as the representative – the perfection, some said – of culture and civilization.

A third group of stories had Theseus protecting and maintaining the routes of Athenian shipping and trade. He was even said to be the inventor of coinage, and Athenian silver, acceptable all over the Mediterranean world, was one of the mainstays of Athens' supremacy as a trading power in the Classical era. One of the earliest stories about Theseus, and certainly the best known, tells of his voyage to Crete and slaying of the Minotaur. This story too was made to fit a commercial context, since it is explicit in some fifth-century versions that Theseus ended the control King Minos of Knossos exercised over the seas. It was even commonly said that Theseus scuttled Minos' fleet as he left Crete.

Many of the legends about Theseus, then, are scarcely historical. The Theseus legends began the long tendency of Athens to look to the past to create its present: they are projections back into the past of contemporary concerns, and above all of the three pillars of Athenian greatness in the fifth century: commerce, culture and democracy. Athenian supremacy and pride in all three explain a great deal about the city's history, and we shall see how the Athenians built on these apparently innocent foundations to create a monster, a hybrid of good intentions and bad policies, which exposed the flaws in the system and, with hindsight, made the tragedy of the city inevitable. Pride does indeed precede a fall.

Mycenaean Athens

In reality, Theseus was no democrat, but one of a line of kings who ruled Athens with absolute power, from a palace perched on the top of the Akropolis, for about three centuries from the fifteenth century BCE. Later legend supplies only an incomplete list of these Bronze Age kings, and the order is uncertain. The most famous were Kekrops, Erikhthonios, Erekhtheus, Pandion, Aigeus, Theseus and Kodros, all of whom became the stuff of tall tales in antiquity and street names in modern Athens. The earliest of them were portrayed as only semi-human, with their lower halves being serpentine. They

were said to personify the proud Athenian boast that their people
were autochthonous – sprung from the soil following premature
ejaculation by the god Hephaistos during a bungled rape of Athena,
and never ousted by invaders. And it is certainly true that when
the so-called Dorians began to enter Greece from the north around
1200 BCE, they bypassed Athens altogether, leaving it free to develop
internally.

Many ancient Greek citizen-states had an akropolis. The word
literally means 'the high point of the city' or 'the high city', and it
was typically a natural rock, offering a place of defence and refuge
in emergencies. The earliest Greek cities were all close to the sea,
but not right on the coast. Pirates and diseases ravaged the low-
lying coast, so it made sense to build a few kilometres inland, and
to centre the state on a defensible high point. Originally, then, the
Athenian Akropolis housed the king's palace and the most important
religious shrines, and also other noble houses, while the king's
subjects, numbering no more than a few hundred, went about their
daily business below. The Akropolis is 156 metres high, and its
geological structure – limestone on a layer of schist – means that
rainwater can be trapped between the limestone and the schist to
form underground pools and springs that can be tapped by wells
and supplemented by rainwater cisterns. With the fertile plain
below, it therefore offered everything that early settlers might
want, and the Akropolis was inhabited from Neolithic times (about
5000 BCE) onwards.

There were other springs on the southern and northern sides,
but the well best known as the Klepsydra ('hidden water' or 'water-
stealer') on the north-west corner was the most abundant, and stone
steps and Roman work can still be seen there. The existence of
sweet water deep within the Akropolis was said to be the gift of the
god Poseidon to the city. In the time of Kekrops, Athena and
Poseidon were in dispute as to which of them should be the patron
deity of the new city. Athena gave the gift of the olive tree, while
Poseidon struck the rock with his trident and out gushed fresh water
(or, in another version, salt water – but what would be the point of
that?). The people, recognizing the commercial value of the olive
and its suitability for the dry Attic climate, chose Athena, but over
the centuries many besieged soldiers could attest to the importance

of fresh water on the Akropolis. This myth too may reveal long-forgotten historical events. The ancient Greek name for Athens is a plural word, because once there were several villages, which came together under the auspices of the goddess Athena – 'the communities of Athena', as it were. If the chief deity of one of these original villages was Poseidon, the myth reflects his losing out to Athena.

Nowadays there are few visible remains of Mycenaean Athens apart from a number of massive blocks of the thirteenth-century defensive wall on the Akropolis, but we know enough about the culture to be able to reconstruct the broad picture. The name 'Mycenaean' comes from the most famous site, Mycenae in the Argolis area of the Peloponnese, but it is misleading if it is taken to imply that Mycenae was the overlord of other places. Over 400 Mycenaean sites have been discovered all over mainland Greece, and it looks as though they were independently ruled, though with various ties to their neighbours. It is true that in the Homeric poems Agamemnon, the king of Mycenae, is the commander-in-chief of all the Greek forces, but it is impossible to tell to what extent this reflects historical reality. So far from forming any kind of unified 'Mycenaean' nation, the towns self-destructed in the century from 1250 onwards as a result, probably, of warfare with their neighbours, not of external invasion. The Dorians did not so much invade as infiltrate Greece, taking advantage of the increasing weakness of Mycenaean towns.

Mycenaean civilization was glorious and rich, testimony to the continuing and continuous Greek love of fine artwork. The king's palace was decorated with lovely, colourful wall-paintings, heavily influenced by the representational style developed much earlier in Crete. The sheer size of the stonework, and the quantity and quality of the gold and silver treasures discovered at Mycenae and elsewhere, are evidence of a highly developed and hierarchical society, in which the kings and nobles were given to ostentatious displays of their wealth. The huge beehive-shaped tholos tombs and the massive walls are the most obvious survivors of such display for the modern visitor. Allowing for the distortions of poetic licence and the passage of time, Homer gives us a word-picture of a fantastic Mycenaean palace when Odysseus approaches the palace of Alkinoos, in the seventh book of the *Odyssey*. Surrounded by rich orchards and fields, it has golden doors with silver posts, a bronze threshold with a silver lintel, and a doorknob of gold. Gold and silver statuettes of dogs symbolically guard the doorway. Inside, golden statues of young men hold torches to light the noble banqueters at their plentiful feasts, while men and women of the lower classes prepare various goods for internal use and for export.

The king of a Mycenaean community was simultaneously the political and religious leader of his people, and the CEO of a commercial enterprise. The palace complex, though nowhere near the scale of the Minoan palaces on Crete, contained rooms for the storage and inventorying of goods, as well as rooms for bathing and dining and audiences with the king. There was a degree of specialized literacy, with scribes recording on clay tablets in the early Greek script called Linear B (a syllabary consisting of about ninety signs) the king's possessions and various other commercial or religious transactions. Mycenaean economy was redistributive, like that of New Kingdom Egypt: all produce belonged to the king and was gathered into the palace before being redistributed to his subjects according to their status and needs.

This, in outline, is the lifestyle we should project in our imaginations on to Theseus and the kings who preceded him in Athens. But then, around 1100 BCE, as a result of warfare with neighbouring communities and the cutting of the lucrative trade routes in the Near East, Mycenaean Athens collapsed. All over Greece, people left the towns to live and work in hamlets; in Attica they went above all to the eastern coast. In Greece, the days of luxury goods, magnificent burials and international trade were over, and the population fell. Literacy vanished – highly specialized pursuits are always precarious. The palaces, if they were not altogether abandoned, were broken up into smaller housing units. Knowledge of the splendour of Mycenaean civilization was so thoroughly lost that later Greeks, in awe at the size of the stonework, attributed it to the Kyklopes, a race of giants; and where names were remembered, such as that of Theseus, they were supposed to belong to the protagonists of a bygone era in which heroes sacked Troy, tamed the wild, and made hazardous voyages to the East to collect a golden fleece.

The End of the Dark Age

After the time of the kings, in Athens as elsewhere, culture went into such a rapid decline that the next 300 years, up to about 800 BCE, are known as the Dark Age of Greece. But Dark Ages are dark only to historians, because they have no internal or external written records of what was happening. People lived and worked during these centuries, and progress was made in a number of fields. Linear B was replaced by a more user-friendly alphabetic script (basically the Phoenician alphabet with the critical addition of vowels); bronze gave way to iron for edged tools and weapons; clothes with buttons were replaced by clothes fastened by pins. Homer wrote his poems around 750 BCE, and he represents the end of a long line of oral bards who travelled the Dark Age communities, entertaining their hosts with songs of the feats of the heroes.

A new way of decorating pottery, called 'proto-geometric', arose during the Dark Age and soon became the geometric style familiar from countless pots in museums all over the world, in which almost the whole surface area of the pot is covered in a tapestry of inanimate geometric designs such as the meander pattern or swastikas, painted in layers which draw our attention to the overall shape of the pot. By the 800s, as a result of contact with the Near East, artists were beginning to rediscover vestiges of naturalism and representation, forgotten since Mycenaean times. They painted stylized, stiffly angular pictures on the pots: a funeral scene, perhaps, for a funerary urn, or a Homeric scene of heroic warriors fighting. This was the emergence of the narrative art for which Greece, and Athens in particular, became famous: decoration began to tell stories.

This was the period of Athens' first prominence in the pottery business: there was a high demand for decorated pots for domestic and funerary usage, and for more ordinary ware for transport and storage, and by about 900 Athens had become a commercial centre. Athenian geometric pottery styles and decorations were widely copied. Culture revived in Attica first after the collapse of the Mycenaean civilization because the Dorian newcomers bypassed the region and so it suffered less disturbance. Athens retained this position as the most prosperous city in Greece for about 150 years, until others caught up and Athens had to make another leap of creativity – the refinements her artists and potters introduced to black-figure decoration – before she could overtake them again.

One of the most important phenomena of the Greek Dark Age was migration, which was at least in part a response to the arrival of the Dorians. Around 1000 BCE, mainland Greeks travelled to the west coast of Asia Minor and established themselves there, initially in small communities numbering no more than five or six hundred inhabitants. The land is more fertile there than barren Greece, and that was no doubt the attraction. By 800 these communities fell into three bands from north to south, each speaking a different dialect of Greek. Athens was involved in this movement, not only because native Athenians were among the emigrants, but also because the city served as a staging-post for emigrants from all over mainland Greece. In later years Athenians invented a hero called Ion to be the founding father of all the Ionic-speaking communities in Asia Minor, and claimed kinship and natural alliance with these communities. At the beginning of the fifth century, Athens acted on this claim when she went to help the Ionian cities in their rebellion against the mighty Persian Empire – and the whole of Greece nearly paid the ultimate penalty.

4

Archaic Athens

The Dark Age came to an end around 800 BCE, and the next 300 years are conventionally known as the Archaic period of Greece. Here at last we are in the realm of protohistory rather than prehistory, because we have not only the archaeological record, but also just enough writing to be able in some cases to tell, or at least guess, not only what people did, but why they did it. The two chief phenomena that characterize this period are colonization and the development of the unique political structure of Greece, the *polis* or citizen-state. Although Athens had been essentially involved in the earlier period of migration, she sent out few colonies during the Archaic period: population growth and movement there were largely confined within the borders of Attica.

Athenian control of Attica made it the second largest state in mainland Greece, with a territory of about 2,400 square kilometres (about the size of Suffolk, or a little larger than Rhode Island); there was room for internal expansion, rather than having to seek foreign fields, and in the eighth century there was an enormous growth in the population. In territorial terms, only Sparta was larger, with somewhat over three times the area, after it had conquered its neighbours. In Attica, however, the long-standing close relationship between Athens and the outlying villages meant that, however far within Attica they lived from Athens, all men were equally Athenian citizens, rather than conquered slaves.

Apart from Athens and Sparta, few states in Greece exceeded 500 square kilometres, and many were considerably smaller, with populations even at their peak rarely exceeding a few thousand citizens (free adult males). Little of the land was fertile, and the tendency to divide it evenly among sons was reducing many families to poverty. The poet Hesiod, writing in Boiotia around 700 BCE, grimly suggests that his audience 'pray for just one son to maintain his father's house, for then domestic wealth will increase' (*Works and Days* 376–7); and the broader picture is given by a famous saying recorded by Herodotos: 'Greece and poverty are foster sisters' (*Histories* 7.102). And so people went in search of richer lands – or at least richer lands for themselves, if they came from the stratum of their native city which was not already wealthy in land. Others went as a form of political exile, and took a founding band with them; others went for adventure, and to secure a strategic location along a trade route for the good of their native city and their own pockets. Metals and timber were in especially high demand, but grain came a close third, since both the climate and the soil of Greece are better suited to poor barley than to wheat, which is less resistant to drought.

By the end of the Archaic period, as a result of migration, the Greek world extended all over the Mediterranean and the Black Sea, and there were over 1,000 Greek communities. In Plato's memorable image (*Phaedo* 109b) the Greeks were scattered around the coastlines 'like frogs (or ants) around a marsh'. The new colonies remained linked to their mother city by ties which varied from strong to virtually non-existent. Typically, only 100 or so men went out on these colonizing expeditions, and they took local women as their wives to perpetuate the new community.

Athens itself is surrounded on three sides by hills and on the fourth by the sea – a natural combination of defence, access to the sea for trade, and a small but fertile plain (now lost under urban sprawl), punctuated by hills – especially, of course, by the Akropolis and the Lykabettos hill. The plain is bounded to the east by Mount Hymettos (1,027 m), to the north-east by marble-rich Pendeli (1,109 m; its ancient name was Brilessos or Pentelikon), to the north by the ranges of Parnes (1,412 m) and Kithairon (1,409 m), and to the west by Mount Aigaleos (468 m), which lies just north of Peiraieus. To the east and south, beyond the immediate hills, there was more agricultural land.

The topographical isolation of each city led over the years to a common civic culture. Each community was economically and politically independent of its neighbours, unless it had been conquered or chose to form an alliance or needed to trade. There was an urban centre, surrounded by agricultural villages as in a house the hearth is surrounded by rooms. In the urban centre there was an agora, a central square where most of the administrative and commercial functions of the state took place. The akropolis became reserved chiefly for religious buildings, but could be used as a place of refuge in emergencies.

The ideal of self-sufficiency meant that a *polis* had to be small to work – small both in extent and in overall population, including the inhabitants of the outlying villages. Even at its height, in the middle of the fifth century BCE, the total population of Attica never exceeded 350,000, and over a quarter of these were slaves. In the seventh book of his *Politics* Aristotle suggested that the free population of a citizen state should not exceed about 10,000, a number that could be surveyed all at once; that all the citizens should be capable of recognizing one another; and that the physical size of a city should not exceed an area within which a single town-crier could be heard summoning the citizens to a meeting. He clearly thought that Athens had grown too large.

Within this structure, however, a number of different constitutions could and did develop, depending essentially on how much power lay with how many of the male citizens, and the championing of alternative political systems was to become one of the major excuses for warfare between Greek states. But throughout their history it remained essential to citizen-states of whatever political persuasion that their political life was entirely in the hands of the free male citizen population, who were more or less accountable to their fellow citizens, and ultimately to the laws, for their political and public actions. An ancient Greek *polis* was its citizens: the name 'Athens' referred only to the physical city with its buildings and open spaces; as a political unit, the name was 'the Athenians'. The Spartans, then, did not make war on 'Athens', but on 'the Athenians'.

In the kind of symbolic gesture that resonates through the ages, the overthrow of the last king in Athens was soon followed by the transference of the seat of government from the palace on the Akropolis to the agora in the lower town. The Akropolis became the centre of the public religious life of the city, but was not again for many centuries the administrative hub. Gradually, the old king's main functions became separated out, until by the eighth century there were three dominant officers in Athens: the polemarch ('war-leader'), the 'king', who was responsible for religious matters, and the arkhon ('leader'), who was responsible for all civic affairs and who gave his name to the year ('in the year of Solon's arkhonship'). Somewhat later, in 683, a board came into existence of six officials, the *thesmothetai*, who were responsible for law and order, and these nine between them were collectively called the 'arkhons', even when some of their functions had devolved on to lesser officials.

By historical times, the arkhonship had become annual. After-wards, arkhons automatically became life members of the Council of the Areiopagos, named after the Hill of Ares, just west of the Akropolis and south of the agora, where they met. This Council, the descendant of the council of elders which had once advised the kings, was responsible for most of the important political and judicial functions of the city. Since election to arkhonship was open only to wealthy landowners, who called themselves the Eupatrids, the 'well born', the Areiopagos Council effectively ruled Athens as an aristocracy, although election to the arkhonship had to be ratified by the Assembly of all the people.

There was still little formal structure to Athenian society at the beginning of the Archaic period. The dominant way of life was rural, and Attica was a mass of small villages. But individual households or householders acknowledged themselves members of several larger units. All those households which traced their lineage back to a common ancestor formed a clan. At the same time, by virtue of certain shared cults and rites, they were members of phratries (literally, 'brotherhoods'). And at the top of the pinnacle all Athenians were divided among four tribes, again with common rites and functions. It is unlikely that these groupings formed the kind of tidy pyramid beloved of scholars from Aristotle onwards, from household to clan to phratry to tribe. For a start, less than half the population belonged to a clan: clans came together to exert pressure or to exact privilege, and especially to perpetuate Eupatrid dominance. The householder's obligations, as resident in a particular area and as related to particular families, simply meant that he was a member (not necessarily in a formally defined sense) of a number of greater or smaller groupings, largely based on kinship and location. This kind of set-up automatically allows particular families to develop a power base – which is to say that it is the type of set-up that develops within and sustains an aristocracy.

Hoplites and Tyranny

For much of the eighth and seventh centuries, Athens was inward-looking and agrarian, concerned to protect her borders rather than expand abroad. But border wars proved unsettling. Warfare had previously tended to be heroic in scale and nature: individual aristocratic champions fought it out in one-to-one combat, while the masses lobbed stones and insults at one another. Now, however, as a result of trade, iron was readily available. Better weaponry and more effective armour could be developed, and at no great cost. States increasingly had to try to outnumber their enemies by deploying larger numbers of troops. The Greek response was to develop the hoplite phalanx.

Hoplites were armed, typically, with a bronze helmet (the designs of which found various ways to compromise either protection or visibility), a bronze breastplate, greaves for the shins, and above all a large, round, two-handled shield, about 90 centimetres in diameter, made of bronze-covered wood, and weighing about 7 kilograms. They carried a long, iron-tipped spear and a short, iron sword. They fought in a phalanx – a tightly packed formation in lines. While advancing, the shield on a hoplite's left arm protected the left half of his body and the right half of the body of his neighbour; even in combat, when the necessity of standing sideways-on in order to wield his spear meant that a hoplite's shield offered less protection to his neighbour, it was vital for the line of battle to remain solid. As long as no cracks appeared, the line was virtually impregnable, and the hoplite phalanx became one of the most successful military formations in history. For over 500 years, from the end of the eighth century, it dictated military strategy throughout the Greek world, until the superior Roman legionary formation defeated the Macedonian phalanxes in 197 BCE.

Hoplites had to fight on level ground or risk breaking ranks. Skirmishing, light-armed troops were used for foraging and the destruction of enemy farmland, but not until the fourth century

were they organized and used regularly for battle. Until then, battle
tactics involved a head-on collision between two hoplite phalanxes.
Each tried to outflank the other, while compromising between
avoiding being outflanked and being stretched too thin, and the
soldiers in the front line literally pushed with their shields against
the opposing rank, while stabbing with spear or short sword above
or below the shield – either of which blows, if successful, would
inflict horrible wounds in the groin or the neck, often leading to
mutilation or slow death. When one of the lines caved in and the
phalanx turned to flee, the victorious phalanx, if disciplined, would
not pursue the losers, for fear of scattering and becoming easy prey
for re-formed opponents. There were no reserves (until the late fifth
century, when armies began to get more professional), and conse-
quently the battle was effectively over when one phalanx gave way,
so that battles were often rapid and casualties were rarely heavy.
The victors were content with occupying the field, burying their
dead, taking prisoners for later ransom or sale, and stripping the
living and the dead of their armour, some of which was piled up in
honour of Zeus as a trophy at the point of the field where the
enemy had turned and fled.

In most states, about a third of the population could afford
hoplite arms and armour, so that each state could call on a relatively
large fighting force (there was of course no standing army) – up to
8,000 men for a large city. In a hoplite phalanx, then, the wealthier
smallholders and artisans stood shoulder to shoulder with aristocrats.
The political consequences were inevitable. Just as in Britain the
introduction of the longbow shifted political power down the social
scale, so the Greek middle classes (to use this term for anyone who
was not so badly off that he could not afford the gear) became
aware that they were just as important for the defence of their city
as the aristocrats, and so there was no reason why they should not
be equal participants in the political processes. The aristocratic code
of success and individual heroism began to give way to the view
that to stand out in any sphere was to invite the jealousy of the
gods, who would humble the proud.

The days of aristocracy were doomed, but social changes like
this are rarely seamless. In Greece, the typical pattern was that a
single champion came forward either to represent the middle class

with their new or budding political and commercial conscious-
ness and to wrest power from the old aristocracy, or to attempt to
re-establish the authority of the aristocracy in the context of the
new dispensation. This champion then ruled as an autocrat, and
even attempted to pass the reins of power down to his sons. In
actual fact, in Greece none of these dynasties lasted beyond the third
generation, once people realized they had simply exchanged one
form of powerlessness for another. With hindsight, the short term
of these dynasties is not surprising, since autocracy is the antithesis
of politics, and all Greek citizens, from now on, assumed a natural
right to participate to some extent in the public affairs of their
citizen-state. It was a common Greek boast that they were the
subjects and slaves of no one and nothing except the laws – which,
of course, they made themselves.

They called these rulers 'tyrants', and although the word came
to carry the same despotic meaning that it does in English today,
it originally meant no more than an unconstitutional, but not
necessarily oppressive, sole ruler. One of the most famous of such
tyrannies was the rule of Kypselos and his descendants in Corinth.
Corinth was an extremely wealthy trading city, the first major city
of Greece and probably the first to adopt hoplite tactics, and so the
Kypselid dynasty seized and retained power there earlier than in
other Greek states. Kypselos came to power around 655; about
twenty years later an Athenian tried to follow suit:

> There was an Athenian called Kylon, an Olympic victor, of
> high birth and power. He had married the daughter of a
> Megarian called Theagenes, who at that time was the tyrant
> of Megara. Kylon consulted the oracle at Delphi and was told
> by the god that he should occupy the Akropolis of Athens during
> the greatest festival of Zeus. Once he had been given troops by
> Theagenes, and had persuaded some of his associates to join
> him, he occupied the Akropolis, with a view to establishing
> himself as tyrant, during the Olympic Games in the Pelopon-
> nese, because he thought that this was the greatest festival of
> Zeus and was peculiarly relevant to him as an Olympic victor
> ... When the Athenians realized what was going on, they
> came from the countryside *en masse* to resist him and his men,
> and besieged them on the Akropolis. After a while, they grew

bored with the siege and most of them withdrew, leaving the blockade up to the nine arkhons and giving them full powers to do what they thought best. . . . The siege was going badly for Kylon and his men, who were short of both food and water, and so Kylon and his brother ran away. The rest were in dire straits, and some of them were even dying of hunger, so they took refuge as suppliants at the altar on the Akropolis. When the Athenians who were responsible for the blockade saw that the Kylonians were dying in the sanctuary, they told them to come out, with the promise that they would come to no harm, but once they had brought them away from the sanctuary, they killed them. On the way out some of Kylon's men took refuge at the altar of the Holy Goddesses, but even so the Athenians did away with them.

(Thucydides, *The Peloponnesian War* 1.126)

The famous story which Thucydides here passes over – and it was undoubtedly a later invention by the Alkmaionids, who were chiefly responsible for the murder of Kylon and his supporters – was that the suppliants attached themselves to Athena's altar with string, and then came down from the Akropolis. On the way down, the string broke, and the Alkmaionids, taking this as a sign that the Kylonians had lost the goddess's favour, fell on their defenceless enemies.

Kylon had badly misjudged the passion of the resistance he would meet: his aristocratic opponents were prepared even to commit sacrilege to prevent his becoming tyrant, and the Alkmaionid family was formally cursed for its part in the affair. Kylon had also misjudged the amount of popular support he would receive. Athens was still relatively poor in the middle of the seventh century, so there was not enough political awareness among the middle classes to seriously disturb the status quo for the time being. The city did not even adopt hoplite tactics for another twenty or so years.

Nevertheless, Athens was not isolated from other cities. The changes taking place across Greece threatened the traditional rule of the aristocrats. As a short-term measure, in 621 they appointed a man to draw up a legal code for the city. Drakon was not a reformer, but for the first time the unwritten laws of Athens were written down and set in stone. This was a necessary measure to prevent arbitrary application of the laws and uncertainty about one's own behaviour: there were now standards to which one could refer. The implication is that significant numbers of people were capable of reading, and this is borne out by some wonderful graffiti found in Egypt: early in the sixth century nine Greek mercenaries scratched messages and their names on to the left leg of a colossal statue of Rameses II at Abu Simbel. Potters and vase-painters were beginning to inscribe their pots, and some tombs gained inscriptions too. Literacy hugely increased as the sixth century progressed.

Although it did take the vital step of distinguishing between homicide and manslaughter, Drakon's code was in many respects primitive, with fines expressed in number of oxen, with the institutionalization of traditional notions such as the religious pollution caused by murder, and with death as the penalty for a wide range of crimes. There was a famous *bon mot* of a later Athenian orator called Demades, who said that Drakon had written his laws not in ink, but in blood; we still use the word 'draconian' for a harsh legal code. This is probably an exaggeration, but little is known about Drakon's code because, except for its provisions about murder, within thirty years it had been superseded by further reforms; it did, however, mark a clear stage in Athens' progress towards the centralization of legal justice. Previously, it had been up to the injured party or his relatives to exact compensation for crimes against an individual; now the state saw it as its duty to interfere in such cases. It goes hand in hand with this that Drakon for the first time distinguished Athenians from non-Athenians: murdering a non-Athenian, for instance, incurred a lesser penalty. Attica was beginning to cohere around Athens and around a notion of citizenship.

5

Solon, Poet and Statesman

With or without an intermediate period of tyranny, the typical pattern of constitutional change in Greek states in the seventh century was that aristocracy gave way to a form of government in which the middle class was prominent. Athens was unique (as far as we know) in staving off the arrival of a tyrant and in paving the way this early for a broader, more democratic constitution. Both the staving and the paving are due to the character of one man, Solon, who refused the tyranny when it could easily have been his, and whose vision was clearly of a more equitable future for his native city.

Later Athenians looked back to Solon as the founder of their democratic constitution, and despite the fact that the constitution he gave the city was a graduated timocracy, he did begin the process of moving political power further down the social scale than it had previously been, and he set his people on the path of an overriding concern with social justice by framing laws which supported weaker members of society against the stronger. He is also the first person in Athenian history whose political motives we can assess, because he wrote poetry (the only medium available at the time for didactic work), and most of the extant fragments of his poems are concerned either with his reforms or with justifying them to his critics.

In 594 he was elected arkhon with plenipotentiary powers to deal with a crisis. Precise details of the emergency are lost to us, and are the subject of fierce scholarly debate, because although Solon talks about them in his poems, the language he uses is imprecise, and we lack the background picture which would bring what he says into sharper relief. It is, however, clear that the basic problem lay with what he calls the 'injustice' and the 'greed' of the rich. A sign of the ostentatious wealth of some Athenians at the time is that they were commissioning the first of the famous *kouros* marble statues, usually about life-size or larger, of young men, as dedications or to adorn a tomb. Heavily influenced by Egyptian ways of portraying hair and facial features, with one leg placed in front of the other and with washboard torsos, they are among the best and most famous of early Greek works of art. They are not very realistic, but they are striking for their pose and grand assurance. There were also female *korē* statues, whose main difference was that they were clothed, while the young men were portrayed naked. Nude female statues were a much later invention.

The aristocratic system of clans and phratries allowed the rich to exploit the poor in a number of ways, and even, Solon says, to enslave them – which perhaps fell short of literal enslavement, but involved demanding either labour or a crippling share of the smallholders' produce, or both. Some Athenians even fled abroad, seeking their fortunes elsewhere in preference to the grinding poverty they found at home. Moreover, the aristocratic system had run its course: the middle class was demanding a say in politics, the poor were demanding the removal of an unjust system, and aristocratic feuds were getting out of hand. The Eupatrids had traditionally offered military protection in return for hired labour, but in a hoplite age this was redundant. Athens was close to civil war. And so Solon achieved, or had thrust upon him, the vision of Athens as a collective whole. The greed of the nobles was bad not just for the oppressed, but for everyone. From now on Athens was to be a community in which all the elements worked together as much as possible.

Solon was himself a Eupatrid, but he had enough patriotism or idealism to avoid merely perpetuating the interests of his own class. He had a Hebrew prophet's sense of injustice, but a greater grasp of practical realities. And enough of his aristocratic peers must have been frightened by the prospect of revolution or tyranny to choose the lesser of two evils and allow the reforms to go ahead, despite the fact that Solon blamed the rich for the unrest:

> This great city's own, their minds set on wealth,
> Are foolishly bent on her destruction. Unjust
> Are the decisions of the leaders of the people,
> And the consequences of their arrogance will be dire,

For they know not how to check their excess . . .
They rob and plunder right and left,
Sparing neither sacred nor public property,
And they fail to guard the solemn foundations of Justice.
Though silent, she knows what is happening
And what has gone before, and in due course of time
She comes to exact full compensation.
The entire city is bound to suffer from this wound,
And before long she falls into grim slavery,
Which wakens from their sleep civil strife and warfare,
The destroyer of the lovely youth of many men . . .
These are the evils abroad among the people,
But many of the poor go to foreign lands,
Sold and bound with foul fetters . . .
Thus the public ruin comes to each household,
And the courtyard doors can no more keep it out:
It leaps over the high walls and seeks a man out
Even if he hides in the corner of an inner room.
This is what my heart bids me tell the Athenians,
How ill rule brings countless evils for the city,
While good rule orders and smooths all things.

(Fragment 3, selections)

If these were the problems, what was the solution? Another fragment outlines the measures he took:

Did I stop before I had achieved any of the purposes
For which I summoned the people to assembly?
In the court of Time my deeds will gain the best of witnesses –
The black earth, mighty mother of the Olympian gods.
For I removed the markers which were everywhere fixed in her,
And now she is free, who once was enslaved.
I brought back to Athens – to their fatherland,
Founded by the gods – many who had been sold abroad . . .
And those at home who were suffering the shame of slavery,
Trembling at their masters' moods, I made free.

(Fragment 24.1–9, 13–15)

More and more land, whether privately owned by smallholders or held publicly by phratries, was falling into the hands of the few big landowners. In a series of reforms which he proudly called 'the disburdening', Solon not only permanently banned loans taken out with the borrower's own person as security and issued a general amnesty for all those who had been enslaved in this way, or had fled abroad, but he also limited the amount of land anyone could own. In the future, even the estates of the super-rich never exceeded a few hundred scattered acres. This spelled the end of the quasi-feudal system whereby a man was obliged to perform services for a master. Athenian democracy depended on the existence of free land-owning citizens: it was Solon who made this future possible for the city. Many peasants still paid some form of rent to landowners, but they were no longer juridically dependent on them. From now on, they were more free and more politically involved than any peasant class anywhere has ever been. Ironically, however, in guaranteeing for the Athenian peasant relative freedom from exploitation, Solon created the gap which was later filled by foreign slave labour, as those in search of cheap labour began to import more slaves.

A New Dispensation for Athens

Agrarian reforms alone, however, would not guarantee the future. Fundamental constitutional changes were also required, to ensure that the peasants remained free. At the same time, because Athens was fast becoming the central seat of the government of Attica, it needed a workable system of government which would reflect the notional equality of all inhabitants of Attica as free citizens. Solon made wealth rather than birth the criterion for political office.

He divided all Athenians into four property classes. Only the wealthiest were eligible for the highest political offices, while the next two orders, the horsemen and hoplites, could join the new Council Solon created, and the thetes (casual labourers and poor peasant farmers) were for the first time allowed to participate in the popular Assembly, which was now open to all citizens regardless of rank. By dividing Athenians into property classes, Solon was beginning to define Athenian citizenship. A citizen was basically someone who owned property in Attica, of whatever amount, and the more property he had the more fully he was allowed to play a part in the political process. Thereafter, however, citizenship was passed down by descent: if your father or, later, both parents were Athenian citizens, you were too. Non-citizens were not allowed to own property in Attica.

The new Council of 400 (100 from each tribe) served as a kind of intermediary between the nobles and the people. Before the Assembly convened and voted on any issue, the Council discussed the matter and prepared the agenda. To ensure that no individual could use membership of the Council as a platform for personal power or corruption, election was by random lot, and nearly all Athenian officials served on committees, rather than having personal authority. Since the use of the lottery particularly characterized the Athenian democracy from its inception, it is worth pausing to consider how radical its implications were. There could be no more direct way of asserting that all Athenian citizens (or at least, all those eligible for any particular post) were equally equipped to serve their city.

The arkhons were chosen, though not at this stage by lot, from a shortlist prepared by the four tribes and approved by the Assembly. There had been a popular Assembly before Solon, but it had met at the whim of the aristocrats. After Solon, however, the Assembly met at regular intervals, and therefore began to gain its own independent existence and purposes, though at this stage it could only vote on proposals, not debate them. However, Solon gave the common people greater power, and guaranteed their juridical independence from the landowners, by establishing the Heliaia, a court of appeal manned by their peers. Although the main judicial functions remained in the hands of the Areiopagos and the various individual officials, anyone could now appeal against their verdicts to a popular court.

By means of these constitutional reforms, Solon more or less invented the notion that an individual, just by virtue of being a member of a community, has certain basic rights which cannot be bought or sold, undermined or abolished. But he did not stop there: he drew up a new law code, confirming and codifying Athenian traditions in everything from public morality to criminal law, and structured the religious life of the city around a calendar of regularly repeated rituals. He also laid the foundations of the boom in Athenian trade and pottery by offering foreign craftsmen Athenian citizenship if they would settle there with their families (that is, if they could guarantee the continuity of their craft), by encouraging those who had fled in poverty to the city from the countryside to take up urban trades too, and by banning the export of any natural product except olive oil. He clearly saw that specialization would ensure the prosperity of both individuals and the city as a whole, and in order to ensure Athens' place in the international market-place, he legislated for the adoption of the Euboian standard of weights, the only one at the time which was widely recognized around the Mediterranean.

Solon's reforms were not excessively radical. He himself saw that he had steered a middle course:

> For to the common people I gave sufficient rights, neither too many
> Nor too few. And I ensured that those with power,
> Admired for their wealth, should suffer nothing shameful.
> I stood with my strong shield protecting both sides,
> And stopped either gaining unjust victory over the other.

> (Fragment 5)

Although some in Athens wanted to see more radical reforms, Solon tried to achieve a balanced constitution, in which both the rich and the poor shared power. Plutarch was probably paraphrasing Solon's own words when he said: 'His thinking was that if the state was moored, so to speak, with two anchors – the two Councils – it would be better equipped to ride out any swell' (*Solon* 19). After overseeing the passage of his reforms, Solon left Athens for ten years of self-enforced exile. We cannot rule out the simple desire to travel and to trade, but he also undoubtedly wanted to avoid the temptations tyranny is bound to offer a would-be benevolent dictator, and to prevent people looking to him to interpret the laws: the laws were to stand on their own. Athens was not the only democratic state in the Greek world, but the experiment went further there than anywhere else. It was Solon who set Athens on the path of radical democracy, by converting the Athenian majority from subjects to citizens.

6

The Peisistratid Renaissance and the
Athenian Revolution

Solon's reforms did not settle Athenian affairs. A Eupatrid called
Damasias tried to establish a tyranny in the 580s, and aristocratic
feuding continued:

> There were three factions. One was made up of the men of
> the coast; they were led by Megakles the son of Alkmaion, and
> they wanted above all to see a balanced constitution. Another
> was made up of the men of the plain; their goal was oligarchy
> and their leader was Lykourgos. The third was made up of the
> men from beyond the hills; their leader was Peisistratos, who
> was regarded as being the most inclined towards democracy.
>
> (Aristotle, *The Athenian Constitution* 13)

Each of these factional leaders had a regional power base, roughly
located by the names of their followers. Each of them also represented different points on the post-Solonic political spectrum:
Lykourgos wanted to abolish Solon's reforms altogether, Megakles
wanted to keep them, and Peisistratos wanted more radical reforms
to help the poor. After a dozen or so years, it was Peisistratos who,
having risen to prominence in Athens' campaigns to secure the vital
trade route through the Hellespont to the Black Sea, was to come
out on top, at least partly because he was a masterful manipulator
of people's perceptions.

First attempts to seize power resulted in flight abroad, but he
used the time wisely. He made a fortune from mining concessions
in Thrace and developed some powerful friendships among tyrants
elsewhere in the Aegean. His money and his new friendships enabled
him to raise a mercenary force, with which he returned to Athens
and seized control. For the next nineteen years, from 547 until his

death in 528, he ruled Athens as tyrant. After his death, his eldest son Hippias ruled until 510, and collectively this period is known as the Peisistratid period – the '-id' ending in Greek signifying 'the family of . . .'. By cunning, force of arms and plenty of internal sympathy, Peisistratos succeeded where Kylon and Damasias had failed, but he maintained his rule by strength of personality rather than force of arms.

Later Greek historians looked back on Peisistratos' reign as a golden age, and he was indeed a mild and enlightened monarch. There was even a story which endowed him, somewhat implausibly, with the common touch and a concern for the lot of the poor. During one of his tours of Attica, to see how his people were coming along:

> Peisistratos saw a man who was digging and working land which was nothing but rocks, and in surprise he told his slave to ask the man what he got from the land. 'Plenty of troubles and pains,' said the man, 'and of these troubles and pains Peisistratos has to take his ten per cent.' The man gave this reply because he didn't recognize Peisistratos, but Peisistratos was delighted with his candour and industriousness and freed him from all taxes.   (Aristotle, *The Athenian Constitution* 16)

Athens first became a major cultural centre under the Peisistratids. The most famous poets of the Greek world took up residence in Athens, and other arts flourished too. In vase-painting, the century of Athenian black-figure work gave way to red-figure painting by about 530. Red-figure work involved painting rather than black-figure incision, and so artists working in red-figure could achieve great realism. As opposed to the static universality of Archaic art, or the sultry severity of the brief intermediate period, in Classical art bodies were shown live and in motion, fleeting through time. Athenian artists were unsurpassed in later years or in other cities. Red-figure work continued in Athens up until about 320, when relief ware became more popular all over the Greek world, but the best work was done in the first fifty or sixty years following its abrupt introduction around 530.

Peisistratos considered himself the special ward of Athena, and he repaid her well. He rebuilt and refurbished her temple on the

Akropolis on a magnificent scale, and he further developed her
annual festival, the Panathenaia, which had already become the
centrepiece of the Athenian religious calendar. Once every four
years, as the Great Panathenaia, the festival was carried out in an
especially splendid fashion, with, among other things, panhellenic
athletic and equestrian competitions (the winners of which were
rewarded with valuable prizes of olive oil in special amphoras) and
recitations of Homer. The incorporation of athletics into a civic
festival was clever, since earlier Athenian athletics had been a more
spontaneous affair, restricted to and reflecting the rivalry between
aristocratic clans: Peisistratos defused the potentially disruptive
nature of these competitions. And in emphasizing Homer, the
Peisistratids chose precisely those poems which are scarcely biased
towards any particular part of Greece. Those later Athenians who
had panhellenic pretensions were doing no more than building on
Peisistratid foundations. The tyrants not only put in motion a
general programme to downgrade local cults in favour of pan-Attic
cults centred on Athens (symbolized by the fact that the sanctuary
of the Twelve Gods in the agora became the point from which all
distances to and from Athens were measured), but they also began
to position Athens in the centre of the Greek universe.

There had long been the competitive singing of choral odes in
honour of Dionysos, especially in the countryside, but the Peisistratids made the spring festival of Dionysos in Athens particularly
glorious. There was a procession with the cult statue from the
outskirts of Athens to a new temple built at the southern foot
of the Akropolis, a procession with sacrificial bulls, phalluses and
new wine, and plenty of feasting and revelry. The recitation of odes
began to develop towards something more recognizable as drama,
as the chorus-leader came to separate himself from the main chorus
and entered into a kind of dialogue with them. All the chorus-leader
had to do was take on the role of a particular character, and drama
was born. The Athenian playwright Thespis was the first to do this,
in 534, and that is why actors are still called 'thespians'.

The Peisistratid building programme was not restricted to the
temple of Athena on the Akropolis and a new temple of Dionysos.
This was Athens' first great period of monumental stone temples.
A temple of Olympian Zeus was planned just to the east of the city

on such a grand scale that it was several centuries before anyone could afford to complete it. The temple of Artemis at Brauron (Peisistratos' native town) was built in stone; a new initiation hall was built at Eleusis, the site of the most important mystery cult of Demeter and Persephone, and the Peisistratids encouraged non-Athenians to participate in the cult as well, making this too a panhellenic centre.

Among their secular works, perhaps the most important were concerned with water – always a serious business in a country as dry as Greece, and Attica is the driest region of mainland Greece. They built the first aqueduct, an underground channel bringing water into the agora from springs on Lykabettos and ending in a splendid fountain-house. Another fountain-house – the Enneakrounos, or Nine Spouts – was built on the southern side of the Akropolis. They continued the development of the agora, begun under Solon, as the administrative centre of Athens and hence of Attica as a whole, and laid out the earliest substantial gymnasia in the suburbs outside the city walls. In terms of the amenities that make a city not just survive but flourish, Peisistratid Athens became the city to imitate.

Athenian trade had been doing well throughout most of the sixth century, but Peisistratid foreign policy put it on an even firmer footing. It is not an exaggeration to say that the Peisistratids were, perhaps unwittingly, laying the foundations of the Athenian Empire of the next century. The silver mines at Laureion, close to the south-eastern tip of Attica, were developed and Athenian coinage was standardized. The famous 'owls', named after the symbol of the goddess Athena that adorned the silver coins, became the only currency which was accepted all over the Mediterranean: traders could be certain of the weight of the coins (the picture of the owl hindered shaving) and of the purity of the silver. Peisistratos secured trade routes, by force of arms if necessary, and in another propaganda coup resuscitated the pan-Ionian sentiments of Athenians – the basis of the Empire – by ritually purifying the central Ionian sacred site, the island of Delos, and reworking the temple of Apollo there, and by welcoming Ionian refugees from the expansion of the Persian Empire.

However, the Peisistratids were also in some respects tyrants in the modern sense of the word. They lived in an ostentatiously large house on the south side of the agora, took steps to neutralize opposition, and used Scythian mercenaries to police the city. Above all, of course, there is little scope for political ambition under tyrants, and this in the end proves to be their downfall. In the long run, the Peisistratids broke the power of the aristocrats more effectively than Solon had, because they accustomed them to a subordinate position – subordinate at first to a tyrant, but before long to the sovereign people. In the short run, however, the overthrow of the Athenian tyrants was very much an aristocratic affair. At first, the tyrants had ruled with the complicity of Athens' great noble families, such as the Alkmaionids, the Gephyraioi and the Philaids, but at some point they fell out. Many of the Alkmaion-ids and the Philaids went into exile, and it was two of the Gephyraioi who became credited with the downfall of the tyranny.

What happened was that Hipparkhos, one of Peisistratos' younger sons, fell in love with a young man called Harmodios, and made advances to him. Having been rejected, he wanted to humiliate him in some way, so he insulted his sister. On top of his unwelcome advances, this was too much for Harmodios and his lover Aristogeiton. Using the joyous confusion of the Great Panathenaia of 514 as cover, they assassinated Hipparkhos, in the expectation that other noble Athenians would escalate the affair into an uprising against the tyrant, Hippias. In the event, however, they acted alone: Harmodios was killed immediately, and Aristogeiton was executed a short while later.

After this, Hippias began to behave like a true tyrant, with a campaign of terror in the city. The focus of Athenian resistance was the Alkmaionid family, in exile. They first attempted to oust Hippias on their own, but after their defeat they called on Sparta for help. Sparta had a reputation as a liberator of states from tyrants, and was only too glad to comply: it suited its policy, led by the power-ful and far-sighted king Kleomenes, to make Athens a member of the Spartan alliance of Peloponnesian and central Greek states. Besides, the Alkmaionids had the support of Delphi, since they had lavishly rebuilt Apollo's temple there after a devastating fire, and so every time the Spartans consulted the oracle on any matter, the reply included the message: 'First free Athens.' The first Spartan expedition, sent by sea, was defeated by Hippias and his supporters, but Kleomenes returned in greater force by land and succeeded in blockading Hippias on the Akropolis. An attempt by Hippias to smuggle his children out of Athens ended with their falling into Kleomenes' hands, and the tyrant surrendered and fled to Persia.

Athens owed her freedom from tyranny to a foreign power. It is not surprising that before long the official Athenian version of the events ignored the fact that Harmodios and Aristogeiton had been acting on personal motives, conveniently forgot that Hippias had ruled for four oppressive years after Hipparkhos' murder, and brushed Sparta's involvement aside. Harmodios and Aristogeiton became 'the tyrannicides', and bronze statues of the pair by Antenor – the earliest political monument in Europe – were set up in the agora. When this pair of statues was removed by the Persians in 480, a new set was immediately commissioned. The legend was that important to the Athenian democratic self-image: it was an exemplar of how model citizens combined personal loyalty to each other with public benefaction, and of how one could die nobly for one's city. By word of mouth and in popular songs the action of the tyrannicides became a victory – even a kind of charter myth – for democracy:

> Harmodios and Aristogeiton, here in this land
> Your deeds will live for ever in song,
> Because you slew the tyrant
> And gave the Athenians democracy.
>
> (Athenaios, *Professors at the Dinner-table* 695b)

In 510, however, all this talk of democracy would have been premature. The aristocrats still seemed securely in control of the city. It would take a revolution to dislodge them.

The Athenian Revolution

Following the expulsion of Hippias by Kleomenes, Athens was effectively a client state of Sparta, and with Spartan encouragement in 508 an Athenian aristocrat called Isagoras attempted to set up an oligarchic government. Isagoras' main opponent was an Alkmaionid called Kleisthenes. At least partly as a means of defeating his opponent, Kleisthenes addressed the Assembly and proposed a number of radical constitutional reforms. Isagoras began to lose out, and he called on Kleomenes for help. Kleomenes responded by ordering the Athenian people to expel Kleisthenes (and others associated with the Alkmaionids), using the old Kylonian curse as a pretext. Kleisthenes and many others left the city, but there was still unrest, and Kleomenes sent a garrison to police the city and to oversee the establishment of an oligarchy of 300 of Isagoras and his associates. The people resisted, besieged Kleomenes and his troops on the Akropolis, and after three days let them leave the city peacefully. The Athenians were free, and Kleisthenes and the other exiles were recalled. The critical moment here was the spontaneous Athenian uprising against the Spartan garrison and the attempted oligarchy. The people rioted – but this was still Kleisthenes' doing: he had inspired them with promises of representational government.

It is hard to tell after all this time whether Kleisthenes was a democratic idealist or was simply trying to get the better of his aristocratic rival. At any rate, once he was in effective control of the city, he passed the series of reforms that turned Athens into a primitive democracy. Family rivalries caused his eclipse soon after the reforms had become law, but his legacy was a lasting one.

The whole of Attica was divided by Kleisthenes into three geographical areas with approximately equal populations: the various coastal regions, the inland, and the city (including the plain and coastline near the city). Each region contained a number of demes (wards or parishes; there were 139 in total) which were distributed unequally, within each region, between ten *trittyes* (literally 'thirds'), so that there were thirty *trittyes* throughout Attica. Kleisthenes then took one *trittys* from each region and combined them into a tribe, so that there were ten tribes, with the members of these tribes drawn from all three regions and a more or less random selection of demes. Fellow tribesmen from different *trittyes* might well live miles apart from one another, and have no familial ties.

All political appointments and the provision of hoplite regiments for the army were based on the new tribal system. The old tribal system of kinship had put power in the hands of the land-based aristocrats, and this had led to the loyalties, rivalries and factions which had bedevilled Athenian life for over a century. In the long run, Athens would never become a world-class state if it was held back by internal feuding. Kleisthenes' reforms broke the power of the aristocrats once and for all, and ensured that the Council and the Assembly had enough muscle to counterbalance the aristocrats in the future. At a stroke, Kleisthenes replaced a vertical, tribal ethnicity with a horizontal sense of identity based on Athenian citizenship. He also enrolled many non-Athenians and even slaves into the new demes, which ensured a loyal substrate of confirmed democrats.

Membership of the new Council was raised to 500, with each tribe supplying fifty councillors, and every deme supplying a quota according to its size. Councillors were chosen by lot, as were their understudies, who were available in case of inability to attend a meeting. Thetes became eligible for the Council as well as the Assembly, but for the time being this made little difference, since there was no pay for public service and thetes could not afford to take time off: since the Council met about 260 times a year, working as a councillor made a heavy demand on one's time, and few meetings were attended by the full 500. Throughout democratic Athens' history, the Council tended to be dominated by the better-off.

The Kleisthenic Council was the effective ruler of Athens. It controlled state finances, especially through various subcommittees, and managed all non-routine business; no proposal could come before the Assembly which had not been debated and ratified by the Council, and the Council also attached its recommendations to every item on the Assembly's agenda; it posted the business for all ordinary meetings of the Assembly and had the right to call extraordinary meetings if necessary; it supervised the work of all the various bureaucratic committees which ran the daily functions of the state; although the formal declaration of war was up to the Assembly, it was the Council which negotiated with foreign states and received their representatives; the Council also received certain judicial functions which had previously belonged to the oligarchic Areiopagos Council.

Since it was impractical to have 500 councillors in permanent

session, each year was divided into ten sessions, with the councillors
of each tribe acting as a sitting committee, the *prytaneis* ('presidents'),
for one of these ten periods, and then reporting to the full Council
when it met. No one could be a member of the Council more than
twice in a lifetime, and even then not in consecutive years. And
no one could be chairman of the *prytaneis* more than once: every
day a different chairman was chosen from among the fifty members
to be, in effect, the head of the Athenian state, symbolized by his
custody of the city's seal and the keys to the temples where the
state's treasures and archives were stored. It was hard, then, for
an individual to gain prominence, and as many people as possible
would gain political experience. This in turn guaranteed a politicized
Assembly, since the people who served as councillors were the same
people who attended the Assembly.

People were also politicized at the deme level, since deme
assemblies decided all local issues, including the election of a
demarch (mayor) and the choice of candidates for the Council.
Kleisthenes regulated local governmental procedures and made them
uniform throughout Attica; in many ways the procedures made the
demes microcosms of the city itself. Over the years, it emerged that
one of the important functions of deme politics was to connect
members of even the most remote villages to those members of
their deme who were wealthy enough to take part in central politics
in the city. From the time of Kleisthenes, membership of a deme
was the essential prerequisite for Athenian citizenship and was
passed down from generation to generation, wherever you actually
lived, so that if you wanted to refer officially to a citizen you called
him, for instance, Sokrates the son of Sophroniskos of the deme
Alopeke. The deme provided a network of loyalties which replaced
the old kinship system.

The aristocrats and tyrants had referred business to the Assembly
only as a last resort. Kleisthenes ensured that all state business would
be legal only if ratified by the Assembly. The new power of the
Council meant more power for the Assembly, and before long this
was confirmed with the establishment of a permanent meeting-place
for the Assembly on the hill of the Pnyx, just west of the Akropolis
and the Areiopagos hill. There were ten statutory meetings of the
Assembly each year, and membership was open to any adult male

citizen. In addition to passing all laws, decrees, treaties and so on, it had the right to propose further motions for debate in subsequent meetings, and to introduce emendations to proposals.

Decisions in the Assembly were taken by a show of hands (and so in his play *Women in Assembly*, produced in 393, the comic poet Aristophanes crudely imagines women, were they to come to the Assembly, being confused, since they were more used to raising their legs), with a simple majority carrying the day. The only exception to this was the process of ostracism, another measure put in place by Kleisthenes to curb the power of individual aristocrats who might be aiming for tyranny. Each year the Assembly could decide to cast a secret ballot which would result in a ten-year exile for one man, whoever gained the majority of the votes, provided that a minimum of 6,000 votes were cast. Each attending citizen wrote on a broken piece of pottery (a sherd, or *ostrakon* in Greek) the name of the person he wanted to see removed, or if he was illiterate arranged for the sherd to be inscribed with the name or got hold of a pre-inscribed sherd. Although Kleisthenes made ostracism available to the people as a political weapon, it was not used until the 480s, and then gradually fell into disuse over the next sixty years.

One of the most significant aspects of Kleisthenes' reforms is that he effectively redefined Athenian citizenship, in contrast to the looser arrangement that had served up till then. Formally, a citizen had to be enrolled in a tribe and a deme, but the unwritten understanding was even more important. An Athenian citizen was expected to be useful to the city. This meant that, after the age of eighteen, he would participate in the civic religious rites which kept the gods smiling on the city, and after the age of twenty could attend and participate in the meetings of the popular Assembly. At thirty he could serve as a juror in the law courts or on the Council, and could vote and stand for any of the public offices of Athens. He could own land in Attica, and if there were any handouts he could receive them, after having been means-tested. He was expected to serve unpaid in the army or navy, and, if rich, to perform certain services that stood in Athens in lieu of taxation.

In return he enjoyed the protection of the laws of Athens, and could benefit from its culture and good order. In most or all of these respects a citizen was clearly distinguished from, on the one hand, Athenian women and children, and on the other hand from slaves, foreigners and resident aliens ('metics', from the Greek *metoikoi*), all of whom had fewer or no rights, and above all could not own land (though privileged metics might in exceptional cases be granted this right). Athenians rapidly became extremely proud of their constitution and their citizenship:

> So Athens flourished. Now, the advantages of everyone having a voice in political procedure are not restricted just to single instances, but are plain to see wherever one looks. For instance, while the Athenians were ruled by tyrants, they were no better at warfare than any of their neighbours, but once they had got rid of the tyrants they became vastly superior. This goes to show that while they were under an oppressive regime they fought below their best because they were working for a master, whereas as free men each individual wanted to achieve something for himself.　　　　　(Herodotos, *Histories* 5.78)

The pride that followed from widespread involvement in public life gave Athenians the energy to develop their city both internally and in relation to their neighbours.

7

The Persian Wars

In 549 the Persians under Kyros the Great conquered Media and three years later took Lydia, ruled by Kroisos (as in our 'as rich as Croesus'), along with the Greek cities on the Asia Minor coastline, which were dependencies of Kroisos' empire. In 539 Kyros conquered Babylon (and freed the Jews from their fifty-year captivity), and in 525 his mad son, Kambyses, gained Egypt. In 512 Dareios, who had come to the throne nine years earlier, invaded Europe and occupied most of Thrace. By 510 Macedon too – that is, much of what nowadays we think of as northern Greece – had submitted in the Persian fashion, by offering the king or his envoys earth and water. The mainland and island Greeks suddenly found themselves on the borders of the largest and most aggressive empire in the world, over a million and a half square kilometres in size, and capable of drawing on troops from the Hellespont to Pakistan, and from Georgia to Egypt.

There is one aspect of the birth pangs of Athenian democracy at the end of the sixth century which I have not yet mentioned: Persia came close to being its midwife. In 506, following or during Kleisthenes' reforms, Isagoras attempted to return and install himself as tyrant, again with Spartan backing. Faced with the threat of absorption into the Spartan alliance and the stifling of their fledgling constitution, the Athenians came up with a desperate ploy. They sent envoys east, to Sardis in Lydia, to ask the Persian satrap, Artaphrenes, for an alliance with his master Dareios; the satraps of the Persian Empire were partly dependent governors and partly independent princelings and generalissimos. It is hard to guess what was going through Kleisthenes' mind, if the embassy was his doing. He must have known that the Persians would offer military assistance only if Athens agreed to become a vassal state. And this was indeed what Artaphrenes demanded, prompted no doubt by Hippias, the exiled Athenian tyrant, who was resident in his court. Miles from home, the Athenian delegates had to make a quick decision: they agreed to Artaphrenes' terms.

Meanwhile, back in Greece the Spartans and their allies formed themselves into a three-pronged invading force, with the Spartans and Corinthians to the west, the Boiotians to the north, and the Euboians to the east. But at the last minute the Corinthians and one of the two Spartan kings withdrew, leaving the western attack to retreat in disarray. The Athenians defeated the Boiotians and on the same day crossed over to Euboia and defeated its army as well. By the time the envoys got home, then, the Spartan threat had evaporated, and in their new confidence the Athenians punished the envoys and refused to acknowledge that they were now officially vassals of Dareios.

The issue came to a head in 499. Aristagoras, the puppet ruler of the important Ionian city of Miletos in Asia Minor, renounced his tyranny and declared himself the leader of the anti-Persian faction of the city. Miletos rose in revolt, and many other Ionian cities and communities followed. Aristagoras tried to enlist the help of the Spartans, the supreme military force on the Greek mainland, but the Spartans were justifiably daunted by the huge size of the task, so he next turned to Athens. Swayed by Aristagoras' appeal to pan-Ionian sentiment, and irked by Hippias' threats from Sardis, the Athenians agreed to support Aristagoras with twenty ships, fully half of their fleet at the time, and they were joined in this doomed venture by five ships from the small town of Eretria on the neighbouring island of Euboia. In 498 Aristagoras launched an ill-judged assault on Sardis, in which he and his Athenian allies succeeded only in setting fire to residential areas of the city before being turned back. The Athenians sailed home, but it was, in the words of Herodotos, 'the beginning of misfortune for both Greeks and barbarians' (*Histories* 5.97). This action of theirs meant that they came to the attention of the Great King himself, not just Artaphrenes:

> Meanwhile, news reached King Dareios of the Athenian and Ionian capture and burning of Sardis, and he was told that the man who had gathered the troops together, and was therefore the instigator of the whole affair, had been Aristagoras of

Miletos. It is said, however, that his first reaction to the news was to discount the Ionians, because he was confident of punishing them for their rebellion, and to ask who the Athenians were. On hearing the answer, he is said to have asked for his bow; he took hold of it, notched an arrow, and shot it up towards the sky. And as he fired into the air, he said, 'Lord Zeus, make it possible for me to punish the Athenians.' Then he ordered one of his attendants to repeat to him three times, every time a meal was being served, 'Master, remember the Athenians.'

(Histories 5.105)

One of the nice aspects of this story is Herodotos' suggestion that even in the 490s the Persian king would not have known who the Athenians were. This is probably not true, since Greek craftsmen were in demand in the Persian Empire, and the flow of information and skills ran both ways. But Herodotos' implicit message is this: however insignificant Athens was at the time, within thirty or forty years she controlled a sizeable Mediterranean empire. The transition from backwater state to international power was astonishingly swift. And the other irony implicit in Herodotos is that having defeated Persia's imperialist ambitions in the Aegean, Athens became an imperialist power herself.

Aristagoras died soon after the attack on Sardis, but the Ionian rebellion continued until 494, as one by one the cities, which never fully united, were besieged and captured. Miletos was the last to fall, and the city was razed to the ground. Many inhabitants were slaughtered, the rest enslaved or deported. The news stunned the Greek world, and especially the Athenians – so much so that in 493 the dramatist Phrynikhos is said to have been fined for putting on a play entitled *The Fall of Miletus* and reminding the Athenians of the disaster and their impending doom. Perhaps the only good fall-out from the affair was that Miltiades found it sensible to leave his mini-kingdom in Thrace and return to his native Athens.

Miltiades and Marathon

Miltiades was an unlikely hero. More a self-interested pirate than a loyal citizen of Athens, he had left his native city around 516 and set himself up as master of the western tip of the Khersonese, the narrow peninsula (now called Gallipoli) on the northern, European side of the Hellespont, and ultimately of the nearby islands of Imbros and Lemnos as well. He had gone with the blessing of the Peisistratids to secure the vital grain route through the Hellespont from the Black Sea, but by the late 490s the encroachment of the Persians made it wise for him to return to Athens, and within a year (once the Athenians had made sure that he did not aspire to be tyrant) he had been elected one of the generals.

Meanwhile, Dareios had indeed not forgotten the Athenians. An abortive naval expedition in 492, under Mardonios, a son-in-law of Dareios, was wrecked off the coast of the Athos peninsula (famous today for its monasteries). By the summer of 490, the Great King's military commanders had assembled a vast fleet of warships at the Aegean island of Samos. As numerous nations have learnt over the centuries, the Mediterranean can never be conquered or controlled without a strong navy. The Persian mission was to devastate Eretria, capture Athens, re-install Hippias as tyrant, and thereby have Attica as, in effect, a bridgehead in mainland Greece. The first part of the mission went well: the armada sailed across the Aegean, stopping at island after island to punish or recruit the inhabitants, and Eretria was betrayed to the invaders by the pro-Persian faction within the town. Just across the narrow strait separating Euboia from mainland Greece lay the village of Marathon, on Attic soil. The shoreline there was perfect for beaching the fleet, and the level plain beyond the shore suited the deployment of the highly trained cavalry with which the Persians expected to overcome any armed resistance. They were only 40 kilometres from Athens.

Terror and a determination to resist gripped the Athenians in equal measure. Political differences were put on hold, and the city presented a united front. They dispatched a runner to summon Spartan help, but the Spartans procrastinated: the phase of the moon was wrong, and there was danger of a slave rebellion. Only a handful of troops from the tiny Boiotian town of Plataia, an ally of Athens, came to reinforce the vastly outnumbered Athenian hoplites. In a display of boldness which must have seemed outright stupidity to fainter hearts, Miltiades and his fellow generals chose to march out against the overwhelming Persian army. They encamped on rising ground to dissuade a Persian attack, and the two sides watched each other for several days.

Miltiades was in favour of attacking the Persian army, if an opportunity presented itself, and he eventually won over his fellow generals. The sacrifices were favourable, and the Athenians and Plataians moved down the slope and took up positions opposite the invaders, 10,000 facing 20,000 or more. Choosing a moment when the dreaded Persian cavalry was deployed elsewhere, the Athenians advanced, and for the final 100 metres or so broke with hoplite tradition and charged across the ground separating the two armies, to foil the famous Persian bowmen. The two Greek wings – Athenians on the right and Plataians on the left – had been strengthened, and in the centre the Athenians only just managed to hold their ground before beginning to disintegrate and fall back. But the two wings were victorious. They routed the enemy, but with admirable discipline turned to assist the centre, rather than pursuing their fleeing opponents. Before long the entire Persian army was withdrawing in disarray to their ships. After some bloody hand-to-hand fighting right by the ships, the Persians managed to take to the safety of the sea. They were poised to sail around Attica to Phaleron and attack Athens more directly, but a signal from pro-Persian and Peisistratid elements among the Athenians warned them against it. The Athenians raced home to defend their city, and the Persians sailed away.

The Athenians lost 192 men, while the lighter-armed Persians lost over six thousand; the ghosts of the dead men and horses were said in later years to haunt the battleground every night. The miraculous victory elevated Athens to the front rank of Greek states, so that from now on she was a direct rival of Sparta. Within twenty-five years the Athenian artist Mikon had painted the battle scene on the walls of a new stoa or colonnade – henceforth known as the Painted Stoa – right in the heart of Athens.

Marathon really is one of those great 'what-if' battles whose

outcome decides the course of history for a substantial region of the
world. If the Greeks had lost there (or, since they won, if they had
lost any of the cardinal battles of the subsequent Persian invasion),
European culture as we know it would have been strangled at birth
and autocracy would have swamped the fierce independence of the
Greek citizen-states. Miltiades was hailed as the hero of the battle,
but politically his day was done and he died a couple of years later.
In a marvellous gesture he dedicated the helmet he had worn at
the battle in the precinct of Zeus at Olympia; it survived, and can
be seen in the museum there. Olympia was the panhellenic centre
of excellence, and so a suitable destination for the symbol of Greek
military prowess and of superiority over the barbarian.

Themistokles and the Second Persian Invasion

Dareios deeply resented the ignominy of defeat by a flea-sized city
just across his borders, and when he died in 486 he bequeathed the
task of vengeance to his son, Xerxes. But Xerxes was delayed by
more pressing engagements: in rapid succession he had to quell
rebellions in Egypt and Babylon. Finally, he began to focus on
preparing a successful invasion of Greece. He bridged the Hellespont
and Thracian rivers, built roads and fortresses along the route, dug
a canal through the Athos peninsula, and mustered a vast army and
navy.

At the same time, however, a man was becoming prominent in
Athens who would become a byword for the peculiarly Greek virtue
of cunning intelligence. Themistokles was a new man, not from one
of the main aristocratic families of Athens. From the time of his first
appearance on the Athenian stage, he was concerned to strengthen
and maintain the Athenian navy. His first major coup, in 493, was
to move the centre of Athens' seafaring activities a few kilometres
north, from the old harbour of Phaleron to the Peiraieus peninsula,
which with three natural harbours was better suited to future
requirements, and was easier to fortify. Miltiades briefly eclipsed his
younger rival, but Themistokles grew in power and stature through
the 480s. Through the process of ostracism, introduced by Kleisthe-

nes but never previously used (or not with any result that has left a trace in the historical record), he got rid of powerful rivals and particularly those who were thought to be pro-Persian or Peisistratids. The Athenian people were trying out their new powers; from now on, in order to be successful, any Athenian politician would have to keep on the right side of the masses.

Themistokles was instrumental in a far-reaching constitutional measure which came into force in 487 and decreed that even the nine arkhons were not to be elected, but chosen by lot. From then on, personal authority or the judicious distribution of wealth could not guarantee a man the arkhonship, and this office was sidelined as a route to or measure of power. For the next seventy years, ambitious Athenian politicians sought one of the ten generalships, instituted around 500, since this was now the only important position still open to voluntary election and to which one could be repeatedly re-elected, even year by year. Because the reform of 487 weakened the power of the Areiopagos, which was manned by ex-arkhons, it is commonly represented as a democratic move, and so it undoubtedly was meant to be. But in fact it gave Athens a mixed constitution. Politics could now become a profession: ambitious men could try to gain election to a generalship. But only the wealthy could afford to make politics their profession, and so Athens became a democracy in which executive power was in the hands of all the people, while advisory power was in the hands of a plutocracy. At a broad level, this remained the nature of Athenian politics for much of the fifth century.

By 483 or 482, Themistokles was the most prominent public figure in Athens, and he used his position to push through a proposal that must have required all his cunning and rhetorical powers. A rich new vein of silver was opened up in the mines at Laureion, and Themistokles persuaded the Athenians not to share the surplus out among themselves, but to use it to develop a war fleet. The immediate excuse was an ongoing war with the city's trade rival, the island of Aigina, but the Athenian navy would soon turn out to be critical in the defeat of the second Persian invasion: by the time of the pivotal battle of Salamis, Athens was able to launch over 200 ships with experienced crews.

In 481, faced with the imminent invasion of a Persian army consisting of, at a conservative estimate, 200,000 land troops and a navy of 800 warships, the Greeks convened an emergency conference in Corinth. It was poorly attended, because many Greek states, not unnaturally, preferred to capitulate to or side with the Persians, or to maintain an uneasy neutrality. The amount of pro-Persian feeling in Greece should not surprise us. It was not quite treason or treachery, because there was no Greek nation to betray and panhellenism was not deeply rooted; in any case, the Persian Empire tolerated cultural diversity. Anyway, the delegates from thirty-one states – fewer than 5 per cent of the mainland Greek states – agreed to put aside their mutual and often long-standing differences, and chose the Spartans, with their military expertise and leadership of a powerful coalition of Peloponnesian states, as the overall commanders of the Greek forces. They realized that they had little hope of defeating the Persians on land, and devised their strategy accordingly. They formed two lines of defence: one in the north, directly in the line of the Persian approach, at Thermopylai and Artemision, and one to fall back on in the south, around the isthmus to the Peloponnese.

Following the betrayal and glorious defeat of the Spartan king Leonidas and his vastly outnumbered troops at the narrow pass of Thermopylai, which gave Xerxes his first taste of the passion with which love of freedom inspired the Greeks, it was the turn of the largely Athenian navy at Artemision. Perhaps they could check the inexorable advance of the Persian forces south through Greece. The Athenian leader was Themistokles. Even though quite a few Persian ships had been destroyed in a storm, the Greeks were still hugely outnumbered, but they held their own in the indecisive battle, before falling back south to the island of Salamis, in the Saronic Gulf near Athens.

Nothing could now stop the Persian advance, and the Athenian fleet was used, on Themistokles' orders, to evacuate the city and ferry its inhabitants to safety. It must have seemed to be the end of the world: the Athenians did not know whether they would see their native city again or whether, if they ever did return, it would be as insignificant members of an increased Persian Empire, slaves to the Great King. The warm summer breezes blew through the columns of deserted temples and empty streets, and rustled the leaves of unattended olive trees. Only a few priests and diehards remained on the Akropolis.

The Persian fleet was stationed in the bay of Phaleron, right by Athens itself, while the army marched on, through Boiotia and into Attica. The Akropolis was besieged and soon taken. The few defenders were massacred and the temples were plundered and burnt to the ground. Many of the Greeks at Salamis regarded this as effectively the end of the war on the mainland and were now concerned only to retreat to the Peloponnese and make a last stand there. In fact the Peloponnesians were already in the process of building a defensive wall across the isthmus near Corinth. But this strategy was doomed to failure: even if the wall succeeded in holding up some of the Persian troops, others could be landed beyond the wall, since the Greek fleet could not patrol the whole coastline of the Peloponnese.

Themistokles tried to persuade his fellow commanders to stay at Salamis and risk a sea battle there. He was not entirely successful, and at this point Herodotos tells an extraordinary story (*Histories* 8.75):

> Themistokles quietly slipped away from the meeting, briefed one of his men (a house-slave of his – his children's attendant, to be precise – whose name was Sikinnos), and sent him over to the Persian camp in a boat … Sikinnos sailed over and said to the Persian commanders, 'I am on a secret mission for the Athenian commander, who is in fact sympathetic to Xerxes' cause and would prefer you to gain the upper hand in the war rather than the Greeks. None of the other Greeks know that I am here. The message from my master is that the Greeks are in a state of panic and are planning to retreat. Unless you just stand by and let them escape, you have an opportunity here to achieve a glorious victory. They are disunited, in no position to offer you resistance; in fact, you'll see them pitting their ships against one another, those who are on your side fighting those who are not.'

Themistokles attracted a great many stories to illustrate his cunning and venality, and there may be little or no truth to this episode, but at any rate the Persian fleet did make sure that the Greeks could not leave. They divided their fleet by night into two parts, with each part blocking one of the channels on either side of Salamis. The Greek fleet was confined to the water on the landward side of the island, and the Persians rowed into the attack at dawn. They expected to find the Greeks in disarray, but were faced with a small, but disciplined and determined force. The Greeks pulled back, to draw the Persians further into the narrow straits where their superior numbers would be a disadvantage, and then attacked. The battle was desperate and fierce, but in the end the Greeks won and did so decisively.

Herodotos' description of the battle is long and thrilling, with its focus typically on a few of the individuals involved. Chance has also bequeathed us the only extant Greek drama (apart from comedies) with a historical rather than a legendary setting. The Athenian playwright Aiskhylos (Aeschylus), who was no ivory-tower literato, but fought with distinction at Marathon as well as Salamis, wrote *The Persians* in 472. It tells the story of the invasion from a Persian perspective, and includes this vivid, if poetic, description of the battle by a Persian messenger delivering the news to Atossa, the king's mother (*The Persians* 399–428):

> First their right wing advanced in an orderly and disciplined
>   manner,
> And then their entire force came out against us, and at the same
>   time
> We could hear a mighty shout: 'Onward, sons of Greece!
> Free the land of your birth! Free your children and wives!
> Free the seats of your ancestral gods and the tombs of your
>   forebears!
> For all is at stake in the struggle at hand!' Then from our side
>   arose
> An answering roar in the Persian tongue, and the hour was upon
>   us.
> Straightway one ship drove its brazen weapon against another –
>   A Greek ship it was that began the assault, and sheared off the
>   entire stern
> Of a Phoenician vessel. Then ship after ship steered straight at
>   another.
> At first the surging Persian fleet held firm, but when the ships
> Were massed together in the straits, unable to assist one another,

And were being struck by the bronze-tipped beaks of their own
    side,
They began to smash the whole of each other's array of oars,
And the Greek ships, alert to their chance, encircled ours
And began to ram them. Our ships capsized, and the sea so filled
With wrecks and dead men that the water could not be seen.
The beaches and rocks were strewn with corpses, and every ship
Of the eastern armada rowed away in disorderly flight.
But as if our men were fish caught from the deep, tunnies
    perhaps,
The Greeks began to strike them, to chop them up, with broken
    oars
And fragments from the wrecks, and screams and cries of pain
Filled the open sea until the dark of night veiled the scene.

Xerxes, who had watched the battle and the massacre of his floundering troops from a high point in Attica, was utterly dejected. After the battle, he took what was left of his fleet back to Asia, to forestall opportunistic rebellions back home, to secure his line of retreat and to guarantee provisions for the bulk of the land army, which stayed behind, under Mardonios, to continue the campaign the following year. Mardonios attempted to detach the Athenians from the Greek alliance, but was firmly rebuffed. He invaded Attica for a second time, before withdrawing to Boiotia, but on the same day in 479 the Greek army annihilated the Persians on the Greek mainland at Plataia and on the coast of Asia Minor at Mykale. The Persians withdrew, to lick their wounds and prepare for the future; the Athenians returned, to rebuild their shattered city. Within a few days, the sacred olive tree on the Akropolis, in legend the original gift of Athena to the city, put forth a new shoot from its burnt and scarred trunk, signifying the invincibility of Athens. Not even Persian fire and sword could lay the Athenians low.

This was Athens' finest hour. Themistokles was the acknowledged saviour of Greece, and the city expressly waved the banner of panhellenism, both by expressing what was common to all Greeks (see p. 19), and by continuing the ongoing fight against the Persians. From obscure origins, a small and impoverished city had risen to power and prominence. A new era was possible: although few of the Greek states had been actively involved in the repulse of the Persians, others would now line up behind them. Under the dual leadership of Sparta and Athens, all Greeks everywhere could unite and cooperate. But those who entertained this dream were to be sorely disappointed.

THE CLASSICAL CITY:
DEMOCRACY AND EMPIRE

8

Cold War, Empire and Democracy

Greece has little to offer in the way of material comforts, but it occupies a strategic position in the Mediterranean and so it has commonly been invaded. What we think of as the apex of ancient Greek culture occurred between two of these invasions – by the Persians at the beginning of the fifth century and by the Macedonians towards the end of the fourth. Thanks in no small part to Athenian military prowess, the Greeks turned back the Persians, but the Athenians were also responsible for the defeat by the Macedonians, in the sense that in the intervening period they (and others) had, by both commission and omission, promoted inter-Greek rivalry and weakened the citizen-states until they were vulnerable to Macedonian conquest. The Olympic spirit of panhellenism informs the history of the times: panhellenic ideals and rhetoric began in the face of the Persians, but were so thoroughly trampled on and distorted by the Athenians that in the end Athenian orators welcomed the non-Greek Macedonians as the bearers of these ideals and conquerors of the Persians.

Athens and Sparta emerged from the Persian wars as the two leading states in Greece. In Athens everyone was agreed that their city should take the lead in finalizing the defeat of the invaders, but there were two main options for what to do after that. Themistokles championed the view that Athens should establish herself as the supreme power in Greece and prepare, therefore, for conflict with Sparta. In keeping with this view, he ensured that, despite Spartan opposition, the city's defensive wall was hastily rebuilt and that Peiraieus was further fortified. The new wall determined the size of the city of Athens for centuries to come: it followed the contours of the land, and the city was therefore irregular in shape, but kept the Akropolis more or less in the centre; the total area enclosed was about 4 square kilometres. Classical Athens was no larger than that.

On the other hand, Kimon, an aristocrat (the son of Miltiades of Marathon) who spent enormous sums on public projects in order to win political support, saw the future of Greece lying in a more panhellenic direction, with Sparta and Athens sharing the leadership of Greece. In the long run, Themistokles' view won the day, but in the short term these political rivalries brought about his downfall: by the end of the 470s he had fallen victim to the democratic process of ostracism, which in the previous decade he himself had wielded to good effect against his own rivals.

Ostracism involved exile, but no loss of rights back in Athens, so that an ostracized man could, for instance, still hold property in Attica. In many cases, he might even expect to be recalled to Athens before his term of exile was up. But while Themistokles was in exile in Argos, he was accused by the Spartans of having collaborated with the Persians – perhaps at Salamis, or perhaps afterwards, during the 470s. He was hounded from place to place in Greece and by 463 fetched up – no doubt to his enemies' delight – at the court of the Persian king in Sousa. The new king, Artaxerxes I, received him kindly, and gave him the income from three towns of Asia Minor as a stipend. In return, he demanded Themistokles' help in the continuing warfare against Kimon. Finding himself unable to betray his native city, Themistokles committed suicide in 459.

As events turned out, however, Kimon's policy antagonized the Spartans no less than Themistokles' would have done. For in securing Athenian dominion over an enormous area of the Mediterranean and Black Sea coastlines, he forced the Spartans into an aggressively anti-Athenian position, out of the desire to preserve Sparta's prominence and prestige. Following the Persian defeat, the Ionian cities and the Aegean islands remained free, or in a state of rebellion against Persia, but in need of protection. For the first few months, the Spartans and Athenians shared this task and made vital gains: by conquering most of Cyprus and retaking Byzantion they secured the southern and northern approaches to their part of the Mediterranean from the east. But the allies were not convinced that the Spartans were wholehearted in their dislike of Persia, and before long, to the intense annoyance of Spartan hawks, the leadership devolved on to Athens alone. This was not surprising, given the importance of naval strength to the security of the Aegean.

Athens used the continuing threat of Persia to remain on a war footing and, in 477, to form a league of Aegean islanders and coastal towns in Ionia, Karia, the Hellespont, Thrace and the Black Sea. The purpose of the league was to free those Greeks who remained under Persian sway, to exact reparations and to ensure permanent Greek freedom from Persia. Tribute was imposed in order to fund Athenian naval incursions against Persia and against the piracy which, until recently, always flourished in the eastern Mediterranean whenever there was no naval power to curb it. With its treasury based on the island of Delos, the member states of the Delian League, numbering about 140 at first, were to provide either money or ships for the war effort. The original tribute was fixed by an Athenian statesman called Aristeides, who had been prominent at Salamis; his assessment was so fair that he gained the nickname 'the Just'. Delos was the perfect symbolic centre because it was sacred to Apollo, the father of Ion, the eponymous founder of the Ionians, whose mother-city Athens felt herself to be, and was the site of an important annual panhellenic festival.

Most of the allies chose to provide money rather than ships (which required considerable expense and expertise to build and man), and in the long term this choice was a mistake: it awarded the Athenians a virtual monopoly on naval experience in the Aegean. Perhaps because they realized the opportunity this gave them, the Athenians began to behave with more arrogance, using military muscle to compel some Aegean states, especially those with strategic importance to Athens herself, to join the alliance, and punishing others for wanting to withdraw from it. The most vigorous exponent of this budding imperialism was Kimon. A brilliant and bold strategist, he crowned his efforts against the Persians with the utter destruction of their fleet at the battle of Eurymedon (the modern river Köprü Irmagi in southern Turkey) in 469 or thereabouts. Money raised from spoils from the battle was put towards the building of a new wall on the southern ramparts of the Akropolis.

'Rebellion', or attempting to leave the League, usually meant defaulting on the required payment of money, rather than armed insurrection, but the first to rebel was the ship-contributing island of Naxos in about 470. Thucydides commented (*The Peloponnesian War* 1.98): 'When the Naxians rose up in revolt the Athenians mounted a campaign against them and besieged them until they surrendered. This was the first allied state to be enslaved, contrary to accustomed practice, but later the same thing happened to others too.' The suppression of the Naxian revolt took place less than ten years after the League's formation, supposedly as an alliance of equals. When the wealthy island of Thasos rebelled in 465, in the face of aggressive and unreasonable demands from Athens for a share in its commercial profits, Athenian commitment to the cause of imperialism was such that they besieged the island for three years until forcing capitulation. This had little to do with the Persians, and everything to do with the ships, timber and precious metals which Thasos controlled and Athens needed. Nor did it have anything to do with the League: there is no evidence that other members were consulted over the action at any stage.

This is not to say that the Athenians did nothing against the Persians. Far from it: Kimon was always harrying them in the 470s and 460s, many Greek cities were liberated from Persian control, and in the early 450s a League fleet of 200 ships went to help a rebellion in Egypt (and, incidentally, to secure Athenian access to Egyptian grain). Nor is it to say that the Athenians did not on the whole act with decency. At its height the Athenian Empire consisted of about 300 states, and while secession was depressingly regular, it was never concerted. And when, for instance, the small town of Methone on the Thermaic Gulf failed to pay its tribute, Athens appreciated its special difficulties and tolerated late payment of arrears. There was widespread trouble after the loss of the fleet in Egypt in 454: for a while Athens had to focus on settling its own imperial affairs before returning to Cyprus and Egypt in 451 to continue the war against Persia, this time with more success. However, even if, in general, the Athenians were moderate masters, and left their subject states a considerable degree of autonomy, this does not alter the fact that the whole idea of mastery, of empire, ran counter to the ingrained Greek ideals of autonomy and self-sufficiency. Imperialism is also the opposite of the Olympic spirit: both are international in outlook, but only one treats others as equals.

The Spartans looked on the Delian League with increasing and increasingly justified suspicion: after all, they argued, after Eurymedon the Persian fleet was no longer as much of a threat to the Aegean as the Athenians continued to make out. But power struggles within the Peloponnese, stirred up by the exiled Themistokles, prevented the Spartans doing more than worrying, until in 465 they were poised to help the Thasians by invading Attica. The hawks must have been in the ascendant in Sparta at the time, as this would undoubtedly have precipitated a war between them and the Athenians, but internal problems drew their teeth: a terrible earthquake devastated Sparta and their thousands of slaves seized the opportunity to revolt. This slave rebellion occupied all of Sparta's military muscle for several years, and they were so desperate that they called on their neighbours, even the Athenians, to help them.

Thucydides, one of the world's great historians (and not least because he saw, with absolute clarity, that states invariably prefer self-interest to morality), marks the occasion with chilling words: 'For the first time, as a result of this expedition, there was open hostility between the Spartans and the Athenians' (*The Peloponnesian War* 1.102.3). For the Spartans dismissed the Athenian force, with Kimon at its head, and sent them back home, unsure whether they might not even side with the rebel slaves. The Athenian response to this insult was to ostracize Kimon for his pro-Spartan tendencies, form alliances with Sparta's enemies, such as Argos, and settle refugee Spartan slaves.

This spelled the end of the anti-Persian alliance with Sparta. There was appalling tension between the two rivals, and this state of affairs deteriorated over the next twenty or so years of Cold War, punctuated by occasional and sometimes serious clashes, and by treaties and truces which did little to disguise the fact that each side was actually positioning itself for war. The worst phase came in the 460s and 450s, a period of hostility which is sometimes known as the First Peloponnesian War, though Athens clashed more with Sparta's allies than Sparta itself. Sparta, however, was involved in the battle of Tanagra in 457, which, along with another battle on Boiotian soil, at Koroneia in 447, put an end to Athens' hopes of a mainland empire. Even though compelled by necessity and defeat, the decision to focus on a maritime empire was rewarding and momentous.

Athenian authoritarianism grew, and resentment and fear rapidly built up among those of the allies who were more in love with freedom. By the time the Peloponnesian War was imminent, the Empire was widely unpopular, since many Greek states either wanted to rid themselves of Athenian rule, or were frightened of being absorbed. Perikles, the leading statesman of the time, candidly described the Empire as similar to despotism, and added the pragmatic comment: 'It may have been wrong to take it, but now it is too risky to let it go' (Thucydides, *The Peloponnesian War* 2.63.2). But the prevailing feeling in Athens, as among all imperialists at any period of human history, was that Athenians had a right and a duty to maintain their Empire: not only were they culturally superior, but the strong naturally rule the weak, and in any case the Greeks were in debt to Athens for her defeat of the Persians – a pretext which must have seemed increasingly tired as the years rolled by. The Athenians knew that while claiming to be the benefactors and even the liberators of their allies, they were actually their masters.

By the late 450s, it was becoming clear that the threat of Persia was receding, and the attempt to convene a panhellenic conference was, as much as anything, a way of seeking a new sanction from the Greeks for Athenian dominance. But it came to nothing (see p. 20), and from then on Athens made little attempt to disguise her imperialism. There were two key moments in the transition from league of equals to Athenian Empire. First, in 454 Athens transferred the treasury and the capital of about 8,000 talents, a vast fortune, from the island of Delos to Athens itself, ostensibly in reaction to the loss of the fleet in Egypt. Second, in 449 the Athenians negotiated a peace with Persia (it would be renewed in 423). There was now little military justification for the network of alliances. All imperialist states and nations are driven by the irrational desire to expand merely for expansion's sake; as her population increased, Athens was also motivated by the necessity of securing a reliable source of grain to avoid shortage or even starvation. And so the Delian League became the Athenian Empire.

The League meetings stopped around 435, by which time they had become more or less nonsensical. Even the treaties drafted by Athens for new 'allies' no longer made any pretence at equality, but treated them as subjects, or as 'colonists' with Athens as the fictitious mother city, to carry out decisions made in Athens by Athenians.

The Athenians increased their allies' tribute payments and spent the money on their own interests rather than on defence against Persia, and followed the dictates of expediency rather than equity; they imposed garrisons of Athenian soldier-settlers on troublesome islands and states, or those with the greatest strategic importance, simply by taking the land they needed to do so (albeit in return for a reduction in tribute); they eliminated the navies of potential rivals among the allies; they expected allies to contribute men towards campaigns which had nothing to do with the aims of the League, such as the Athenian invasion of Sicily in 415; they punished rebellion in the most high-handed and brutal fashion; they encouraged the worship of their own goddess, Athena, throughout the Aegean and reserved a sixtieth of the tribute for the goddess; they required the allies to supply sacrificial victims and other religious paraphernalia for the three most important Athenian cults, of Athena at the Great Panathenaia, of Dionysos at the City Dionysia, and of Demeter and Kore at Eleusis; they interfered in the internal affairs of allied states in order to ensure that the most influential men were sympathetic towards Athenian interests and democracy, and installed quasi-oligarchies of Athenian officials to keep an eye on things; certain classes of legal issues affecting the allies were heard in Athenian courts; Athenian weights, measures and silver coinage were imposed on all member states. This imposition of Athenian standards created a kind of uniform culture, but it was not true panhellenism: the panhellenic ideal included respect for diversity, while Athens was well on the way to imposing a homogeneous oneness.

Above all, the Athenians exercised such control of the sea that potential rebels were discouraged by the prospect of an Athenian flotilla off their coastline and of trade embargoes. During the Peloponnesian War, Athenian warships were used to collect tribute from the allied states: the implied threat was obvious. 'Of the mainland cities which are members of the Athenian Empire, the large ones are controlled by fear and the small ones by need. For there is no city which does not need to export or import, and none will be able to do these things unless it accepts the authority of the power that rules the sea' (the 'Old Oligarch' (pseudo-Xenophon), *Constitution of Athens* 2.3). It is true that Athenian suppression of piracy and Persian shipping meant that the allies could trade more easily than before; and, of course, the majority of the people were politically better off under the democracies imposed and maintained by Athens than under oligarchies: as the contemporary polymath Demokritos of Abdera (a member of the alliance) said: 'Poverty in a democracy is as preferable to what is called prosperity under autocracy as freedom is to slavery' (Fragment 251). But the cost in loss of freedom was enormous, and there was a huge backlog of resentment and fear. When in the 440s Athens showed signs of turning her attention west, to Sicily, Corinth (which had strong links with its colony, Syracuse, the major power on the island) joined with Sparta in wanting to check Athenian imperialism and it became only a matter of time before a major war broke out.

Ephialtes and the Law Courts

Following the ostracism of Kimon in 461, his enemies took advantage of the weakness of their opponents and a backlash of anti-conservative feeling to push through further democratic reforms. The time was ripe, because a perhaps unintended result of Themistokles' shift of the Athenian power-base to the sea was that instead of being a hoplite culture, as at Sparta, political power devolved on to the thetes, the lowest class in Athenian society, because they were the ones who rowed the ships.

The mathematics is simple: each Athenian warship had a contingent of about 200, of whom 170 were rowers and the rest marines and crewmen. A fleet of 200 ships therefore occupied 40,000 men. Assuming that a quarter were Athenian citizens, rather than resident aliens (who were liable to military service) or hired mercenaries, and given that the total adult male citizen population of Athens early in the fifth century was probably less than 40,000, it is easy to see that a great many male citizens were involved in the navy. Most of these were thetes, because wealthier men had other military duties, as hoplites or cavalrymen. The thetes had two areas of self-interest: they profited from Athens' possession of an empire, and they wanted a greater say in domestic politics. Ephialtes, with Perikles as his right-hand man, set to work.

Ephialtes' target was the Areiopagos Council, the last remaining bastion of the old aristocracy. Even though its standing had been dented by the reforms of 487, it retained wide-ranging judicial powers, and its prestige remained high as a result of the successful conduct of the Persian Wars by aristocrats. The fact that it heard homicide cases was neither here nor there, but it also had the politically important function of ensuring that the constitution was upheld. This rather vague mandate applied both to public officials and to private citizens. Where the thousand or so public officials were concerned, it meant three things. Before a man took up office, the Areiopagos assessed his worthiness to hold office; during his term of office the Areiopagos kept a watch over his conduct, and afterwards called him to account for his actions and could punish him if they saw fit. Ephialtes deprived the Areiopagos of all these functions and gave them to the popular Council or to one of its subcommittees.

Where private citizens were concerned, the Areiopagos had the right to punish anyone for crimes against the state. Ephialtes made it possible for any citizen to take any other citizen to court for such crimes. The popular Council would hear the preliminary charge, and then the Heliaia would be responsible for the final trial and the verdict. This is not to say that *all* cases involving a public offence were brought to court by private individuals: there were publicly appointed prosecutors for a very few cases. But most were, and this put a great deal of power squarely in the hands of the ordinary citizens of Athens.

It also made ancient Athens extraordinarily litigious and competitive, especially where a man felt that his honour was at stake – a civic equivalent of the typically Greek competitiveness which manifested in the Olympic and other games. The ancient Greeks used the same word, *agōn*, for a law suit and an athletic competition. A trial was, of course, meant to try to establish the objective facts of the case; but it was also a contest between two people, before large numbers of their fellow citizens, at which issues of general interest to the community were raised. A successful prosecution or defence could enhance a man's political career; an unsuccessful one might be politically disastrous.

Solon had established the Heliaia as a court of appeal against verdicts reached by the various administrative officials or the Areiopagos. Each of the main officials tried cases within certain areas: the polemarch heard cases involving resident aliens, for instance, while the king arkhon heard cases of impiety. But since it cost nothing but time to appeal against a verdict, so that the case would be heard in the Heliaia anyway, over the years the officials stopped bothering to deliver verdicts at all, and simply presided over the preliminary hearing of cases within their province. Although until Ephialtes' time the Heliaia remained in theory no more than a court of appeal, in practice it had already become the supreme court of Athens. Ephialtes was only acknowledging the status quo and putting the purely judicial side of things on a more formal foundation.

For the Heliaia, the people sitting as a court, these extra judicial powers came with a satisfactory degree of political clout as well. They heard cases where a public official was accused of crimes against the state; they were the court of appeal for the assessment of the conduct of public officials before, during and after their term of office. And by 415 they were hearing cases where the defendant was accused of having introduced an unconstitutional proposal in the Assembly; this acted as a check on the ability of politically active orators to introduce revolutionary measures. If it was the opinion of the court that the proposal was constitutional, it was deemed to have passed into law: the Heliaia was the people of Athens as a political entity.

In 458 Aiskhylos portrayed the Areiopagos in his *Eumenides* as a court for the trial of cases of homicide, and indeed that was about all that was left to it, and even then only when the accused was an Athenian citizen. The number of times a year the Areiopagos met was reduced, and before long the number of ordinary meetings of the Assembly was increased to forty a year, so that the Assembly could govern Athens, with its mass of domestic and imperial business, in every detail. Ephialtes himself was murdered by a hired killer not long after pushing through these reforms, but the Areiopagos did not try whichever individual or group was behind the assassination, because none was ever found.

The final nail in the coffin of Areiopagite supremacy came in 457, when the arkhonship was opened up to the third of the four property classes established by Solon, the hoplites. The Areiopagos was no longer a club for the very rich alone. The thetes, however, never became legally eligible for official positions beyond member-ship of the Council, in case, being poor, they would be tempted to take bribes.

In order to allow the Heliaia and its various sub-courts to function, 6,000 Athenian citizens – 600 from each tribe, about 12 per cent of the male citizens – were empanelled each year, and from this body the jurors were drawn for any given trial. And before long Perikles introduced an important rider: any juror who sat for a trial would be paid a small daily allowance – a democratic move which, along with other state payments introduced later in the century, was facilitated by the allied tribute and prevented wealthy aristocrats from buying the favour of the masses by their largesse. It was now possible for even middle-class citizens to leave their work to slaves, if they could and wanted to, and serve in the Heliaia. In actual fact, relatively few of the young and able-bodied chose to sit as jurors, but it was a popular occupation for older Athenians, as if the daily allowance were a kind of state pension. But the important point about these reforms is this: the fundamental democratic right of trial by a jury of one's peers was invented in fifth-century Athens.

Any Athenian citizen could call anyone else to account for crimes against the state, and the state paid the plaintiff if his prosecution was successful. This was highly democratic, but it was liable to a peculiar weakness. Ever since Solon's day, it had been illegal to export any foodstuffs except olive oil. Occasionally, how-ever, people tried to smuggle figs across the border. If one of your fellow citizens denounced you as a fig-smuggler, he was a 'sycophant', a 'tale-teller about figs'. Although periodically steps were taken to curb it, sycophancy became virtually a profession in Athens, since even the unjustified threat of being taken to court for some crime against the state (usually involving something more serious than figs) often prompted an out-of-court payment to the sycophant. It is easy to see how the modern meaning of the word emerged, since Athenian sycophants were, ostensibly, currying favour with the authorities. Of course, things could backfire: Sokrates once advised his old friend Kriton, who was being harried by a sycophant, to find someone to protect him from such attacks. The man he found threatened the sycophant himself with court action, until he dropped the charge (Xenophon, *Memoirs of Socrates* 2.9.1).

The Athenian legal system was liable to other weaknesses as well, largely due to its lack of professionalism. Apart from homicide, Athenian laws tended not to define the offence, but to say something like 'If a man commits impiety, he shall be liable to such-and-such a penalty', without defining what impiety was. It was up to what has been called 'the inherited conglomerate' to define impiety and so on in the minds of the jurors, but there was plenty of room for ambiguity – and therefore for the jurors to be swayed by persuasive argumentation rather than mere evidence. Nor were there professional advocates (although there came to be a few professional speech-writers for those who could afford their services) or judges present to define for the layman what such disputable terms might mean. At the most they had precedents from earlier lawsuits.

There was, of course, nothing resembling what we today would count as forensic evidence. Nor was there anything like a regular police force, although the streets were patrolled after dark by Scythian public slaves and there was a ten-man committee of 'city regulators' whose jobs included making sure that the streets were clear of sewage and refuse, and that the city's street-walkers did not overcharge their customers. It was up to the litigants themselves to gather evidence and witnesses before the case was tried, and witnesses could not be cross-examined by the opposing litigant (though they could be accused of false witness in a subsequent action).

Jurors could number in the hundreds in several important classes of case (partly as a hedge against bribery or intimidation), so that the rhetorical manipulation of crowd psychology became as critical in the law courts as it was in the Assembly. And besides, in a town as small as Athens many of the jurors knew the defendant and had made up their minds before even hearing the evidence and arguments. That this was not considered corrupt is proved above all by the fact that there was a cult in Athens of Rumour or Hearsay; and indeed the origin of the jury system in Britain is that the 'twelve good men and true' were supposed to be local and to know in advance the facts of the case or at least the character of the defendant.

Speeches tended to consist of indirect defence: 'Look at all the services I have done the state! How could you think that such an upright person could have committed the heinous crimes with which I am charged? Besides, do you want to deprive my children of their father? Now look at the corrupt characters of my accusers . . .' Slander and innuendo were as effective as evidence, and the jurors might boo and cheer to express their approval or disapproval. What worked was appealing to the conditioned prejudices of the audience, however vague and undefined they may have been, and especially casting aspersions on your opponent's value to the city: the courts were political arenas, where the jurors considered themselves representatives of the people. The law was less objective in Classical Athens than it is, or is supposed to be, in our day: it was the community which judged you, as much as some impersonal body of law.

Trials were limited to a single day. Cases involving private interests allowed each litigant two speeches, so that each had the opportunity to reply to the other. In cases involving public interests, however, the prosecutor and the defendant each gave their main speech, and then there was the assessment of the penalty: the prosecutor made a suggestion, and the defendant made a counter-suggestion. There was no impartial judge to summarize cases and advise the jury on relevant points of law; there was no formal discussion among jurors – just immediate voting on guilt or innocence, and a fixing of the penalty. In no kind of case was unanimity required, just a simple majority.

The potential within the Athenian legal system for abuses should not blind us to the fact that it was a good attempt, under relatively primitive conditions, to make public servants accountable, to ensure justice for all, and to put judicial power in the hands of the majority. Control of the law courts by the few has been a common problem in unequal societies, but one which Classical Athens securely avoided. In Euripides' *Suppliant Women*, in the course of an anachronistic democratic manifesto, King Theseus says (429–37):

There is nothing more pernicious for a city than a sole ruler,
Above all because in such a situation there are no public laws,
And one man has usurped the law and taken rulership for
    himself.

That spells the end of equality. A written code of law guarantees
Both weak and wealthy an equal share of justice,
So that it is possible for a weaker member of society,
When accused by someone well off, to respond in the same terms,
And for an insignificant man to defeat an important man.

It is hard for us today, surrounded by states which are or which
claim to be democratic, to understand how extraordinary an institution democracy is, especially the open and hands-on version found
in Classical Athens (as opposed to our voting for decision-makers to
represent us in a remote parliament). But take a step back and think
about it: why would any state give all power directly to the common
people, rather than to a few professionals? Even other Greek states
that adopted democracy limited the number of male citizens with
the right to vote. Direct democracy is a bizarre practice – but this
is exactly what the ancient Athenians chose to do, and with the
reforms of Ephialtes and Perikles the experiment was more or less
finalized. The three essential features of democracy were in place –
the features picked out by Herodotos in perhaps the earliest statement of political theory in the Western world (*Histories* 3.80):
selection by lot, accountability of officers and decision-making by
the assembled people. To use modern buzzwords, Athenian democracy was open and transparent. The next fifty years would tell
whether it would work.

9

Periklean Athens

Perikles, whose Alkmaionid mother was a niece of Kleisthenes, came to the fore in the 460s and 450s, especially during the so-called First Peloponnesian War, as an able military commander, a committed patriot and a passionate advocate of democracy and empire. While Ephialtes was alive, he was somewhat in the older man's shadow, but after his murder he came into his own, and by 450 was the undisputed first man of the city. From 443, when the last of his serious rivals was ostracized, until his death in 429 from the plague that decimated Athenian manpower in the early years of the Peloponnesian War, he held repeated generalships every year. Thucydides wryly commented that 'Athens, in theory a democracy, was tending to be ruled by the most prominent man' (*The Peloponnesian War* 2.65). Or, as a contemporary comic dramatist remarked, the Athenians passed into his hands:

> The revenue from cities, and actual cities, to enslave or free as
>   he chooses,
> Their walls of stone, to build up or tear back down again,
> Their treaties, forces, government, peace, wealth and prosperity.

(Plutarch, Pericles 16)

When the comic poets nicknamed Perikles 'Olympian', this was satire with an edge to it, because he could certainly be high-handed at times, as well as being somewhat reserved and aloof in public. A small but telling example will illustrate the extent of his sway over the Athenian masses. By the 450s, the benefits of Athenian citizenship were considerable, and there were also thousands of resident aliens in the city, attracted by the commercial opportunities there, so in 451 Perikles tightened up the requirements for citizenship. Whereas previously one was a citizen if one's father was a citizen, now both parents had to have been citizens. The move was designed not just to restrict the numbers of new citizens, but to hurt aristocrats, who would marry someone of their own class from outside Athens rather than someone from a class lower than theirs – and, ironically, the new law would have excluded Kleisthenes, Themistokles and Kimon, among many others. Now, it so happened that both Perikles' legitimate sons died from the plague in 430, but he also had a son by his partner, the cultured and beautiful Aspasia, originally from Miletos. Perikles went before the Assembly and begged them to waive the citizenship requirements in the case of this son. They agreed to do so.

Despite all this, Thucydides and the comedians are exaggerating. It is true that democracy is fragile: the boundaries between it and a more hierarchical form of control blur as soon as any individual gains power and authority. But Perikles did nothing unconstitutional, and his career was marked by his support and increase of democratic institutions, not by any impatience with them. In 429, shortly before Perikles' death, the Athenian people impeached him for embezzlement, and deposed him; but he was soon reinstated. At any point in his career they could have accused him of desiring sole rule, but they never did. At every point in his career he had political opponents and he had to argue for each and every one of his proposals: they rarely went through simply on his authority.

There is no doubt that he owed his prominence to his personal qualities, especially his gifts as an orator (he had the ability to translate the complex business of empire into terms the layman could understand), and his determination and acknowledged expertise as a statesman. In many ways the flavour of Athens in the 440s and 430s, at the height of its cultural greatness and splendour, seems to be attributable to Perikles' influence. Perikles epitomized cultural values by surrounding himself with intellectuals and, more importantly, by pursuing the building and rebuilding programme which has secured Athens' fame for all time. Many of the buildings whose sad, splendid remains we still see in Athens were started during his rule and owe their existence to his decision to make his city the fairest in the world.

The development of Athens as the cultural centre of Greece is inseparable from her development as an imperial power. For forty or so years after the flurry of intellectual and artistic activity under the Peisistratids, there was little to attract poets, sculptors and the like to Athens, but once she had at her command the resources and wealth of an empire, she could afford to pay more than any other city for precisely those intangible 'extras' that constitute the heart and soul of a culture. And so they came to the 'violet-crowned city', as Pindar described Athens in a lost poem – Ion of Khios to write dramas; Polygnotos of Thasos, the master painter, who showed all future generations how to paint realistic figures in great dramatic scenes; Hippodamos of Miletos, polymath, political theorist and idealistic town-planner, who designed the layout of Peiraieus when it took over from Phaleron as Athens' port; Herodotos of Halikarnassos, the first real historian and ethnographer, and a superb storyteller; Anaxagoras of Klazomenai, who introduced Athenians to proto-scientific speculation on the origin and constitution of the universe; a host of Sophists including the greatest of them, Protagoras of Abdera, Gorgias of Leontinoi, Prodikos of Keos and Hippias of Elis. And then there were native intellectuals as well – the playwrights Aristophanes, Aiskhylos, Sophokles and Euripides; Antiphon the Sophist; Sokrates, the Western world's first and most important philosopher; Thucydides the historian.

But having said that Perikles epitomized Athenian culture, one has to be careful to strip off layers of nineteenth-century eulogy, in which he became the consummate statesman and man of culture, and Athens in the 440s and 430s the perfection of all that makes life worth living. In nineteenth-century Europe, it was easier to be complacent about imperialism than it is now. And there is no doubt that Perikles was a hard-line imperialist. His aggressive stand over defaulters and his determination to see Athens rise at all costs were directly responsible for the Peloponnesian War, and therefore for the downfall and loss of much that he deemed good and great about Athens.

The rise and fall of Athens as an international power was the swiftest in history, and for that reason alone the city epitomizes and reveals the factors which invariably cause such rises and falls. The adventurousness and swiftness of resolution which allowed Athens to become great are the direct result of universal commitment to the greatness of one's native state. As long as countries believe in their divine right to power, they will continue to be great, if greatness is measured in terms of military might, aggressiveness and control. But at the same time they will be sowing the seeds of arrogance and excess which are likely to result in their eventual downfall.

Educated minds at the time could see the Athenians' actions as manifestations of the delusion that inevitably leads to a tragic downfall. Close to the beginning of his *Histories*, Herodotos expounded the tragedy of Kroisos of Lydia, as a moral tale for the edification of Athenian leaders, but his words fell on deaf ears. By not being content with what he had, by succumbing to the largely irrational impulse for further conquests, Kroisos had attacked the Persians in 547 and lost his Empire.

The island of Samos had always occupied a special place among the Athenian allied states. It was one of only three islands that continued to supply ships rather than tribute, and it had been staunchly loyal to Athens through thick and thin – which explains the otherwise surprising fact that Athens had never tried to replace its oligarchic constitution with a democracy. In 440, however, Samos was in dispute with Miletos. Athens offered arbitration, Samos refused, and Athens took the side of democratic Miletos. Perikles took command of the fleet and launched a surprise attack. The island fell into his hands, and he installed a democracy and an Athenian garrison. But the oligarchs, supported by the local Persian satrap and led by the philosopher Melissos, counter-attacked and retook the island.

The Athenian garrison and a small fleet were soundly defeated. Perikles returned in 439, his fleet reinforced by contingents from Khios and Lesbos (the other two allied states retained a navy), and forced Samos to rejoin the Athenian alliance. Samian prisoners-of-war were branded like runaway slaves or cattle, though the later rumour that Perikles crucified some prisoners was probably untrue. The suppression of Samos was hazardous, and threatened Athenian domination of the sea. It exposed the dangers of imperialism, but Perikles rode out the storm on a raft of flowery rhetoric (at the memorial service for the dead, he said, 'When a city has lost its young men, it is as if spring has gone from the year') reinforced by steel: for the duration of the war the comic poets were not allowed to mention Samos.

In 446 Athens had negotiated a thirty-year peace with Sparta, which sanctioned the status quo: Athens (with a fleet now of 300 warships) could keep and expand her Aegean Empire, while Sparta consolidated her network of alliances centred on the Peloponnese, Boiotia and Sicily. The treaty provided no real peace at all, since it did little to defuse the tension between the two superpowers: at the most it was a kind of truce, a temporary suspension of hostilities between the 'First' and 'Second' Peloponnesian Wars.

As the immediate threat of all-out war seemed more remote, the Athenians, at Perikles' instigation, secured the passage of timber, precious metals and grain, with the foundation of colonies in Thrace and the Black Sea. Especially important was the foundation and fortification of Amphipolis in 437 on the Strymon river between the Athos peninsula to the west and Thasos to the east (on the site of an earlier failed colony of the 460s). From the middle of the century, Athens had been more and more reliant on imported grain, with a population now in excess of what the land could support. Of the accessible sources, Egypt was in Persian hands, North Africa was controlled by the Carthaginians, and Sicily had more ties with the Peloponnese than with Athens. The islands of Euboia and Lemnos could supply only so much, and so the Black Sea coastal towns were increasingly vital to Athens' survival and welfare, and the route through the Hellespont and along the Thracian coast loomed large in Athenian minds when they were considering foreign policy. Rather than expansion, security and maintenance were Perikles' objectives at this time.

Sparta looked on Athenian enterprise with dismay. She was only just restrained, by Corinth, from offering military assistance to Samos in 440. The shine rapidly wore off the peace of 446.

Perikles' Building Programme

Perikles' decision to spend allied tribute on the glorification of Athens was not universally welcomed by his fellow citizens, but he came up with a specious argument to justify it:

Of all Perikles' policies, this was the one which his enemies particularly maligned and criticized time and again in the assemblies. 'The fame and reputation of the Athenian people are suffering,' they howled, 'because of the transference of the common Greek funds from Delos to our own keeping. Moreover, Perikles has undermined the most plausible excuse we had to offer our critics, namely that the removal of the treasury from there was prompted by fear of the Persians, in the sense that we wanted to have it in a safe place where we could guard it. The Greeks regard it as outrageously arrogant treatment, as blatant tyranny, when they can see that we are using the funds they were forced to contribute for the military defence of Greece to gild and embellish our city, as if she were a vain woman adorning herself with costly marble, statues and temples at 1,000 talents a time.'

In response Perikles used to tell the Athenian people that, since they were defending the allies and keeping the Persians at bay, they were not accountable to them for the money; the tribute the allies paid consisted only of money, not of horses, ships or soldiers, and money, he claimed, belongs to its recipients, not its donors, as long as the recipients provide the services for which they are being paid.   (Plutarch, *Pericles* 12)

Apparently, Perikles' arguments won the day, because the building programme continued for about twenty years of his leadership, with himself as official supervisor of some projects, and unofficial supervisor of them all. One of the popular benefits of the work was, of course, that huge numbers of Athenian and foreign craftsmen were kept in state-paid employment for so long. But the main benefit was intangible: the new buildings taught Athenians to regard their city as the world leader. As the al-Qaeda terrorists were well aware on 11 September 2001, buildings are potent symbols.

The Periklean building programme included temples and other buildings elsewhere in Attica (the famous temple of Poseidon on Cape Sounion, for example). The scale of the programme as a whole, and of individual buildings, was extraordinary. The Athenian democracy left monuments of a stature normally associated with self-aggrandizing tyrants or absolute rulers.

Perhaps somewhat oddly to us moderns, who are used to

depressingly functional factory buildings and so on, the ship-sheds and the mercantile centre Perikles built in Peiraieus around 446 were considered alongside the Parthenon and the Propylaia as the finest architectural achievements of the era, though nothing remains of them now to enable us to assess this ancient opinion. In the course of the fifth century, the city had come to depend more and more on the sea. Themistokles may have wanted to move the administration and ultimately all the major functions of the city down to the coast, 7 kilometres distant, but although Peiraieus quickly became the city's business centre, that was too ambitious a project. Instead, in the early 450s the Athenians constructed two enormous walls, on foundations begun by Kimon, connecting the city to the coast and enclosing Phaleron to the south and Peiraieus to the north. These walls joined on to the Themistoklean wall of 479. These new walls made Athens a kind of inland island, capable of housing more or less the entire population of Attica in an emergency, and with a permanent lifeline to the coast. By the time of Perikles' supremacy, however, Phaleron had become totally eclipsed by Peiraieus as the city's port, and in 445, at the instigation of Perikles, Phaleron was eliminated, and a narrow corridor of two walls, the old northern wall and a new middle wall, connected Athens to Peiraieus.

Another building undertaken a few years later in the 440s was the Odeion or concert hall, underneath the south-eastern corner of the Akropolis. The Odeion had a unique pyramidal roof, supposedly modelled on the design of the Xerxes' war tent, but the roof (which was made of masts and yard-arms from captured Persian ships) had to be supported by a veritable forest of internal pillars, which made the building rather impractical as a concert hall: it was intended for external display as much as internal use, and with its ironic Persian features served an important propaganda purpose.

The most famous and enduring Periklean constructions, however, were religious in function and located on the Akropolis – and of these the best-known is the Parthenon, the temple of the virgin goddess Athena. Work began in 447 and the bulk of the monumental temple, including the cult statue, was completed by 438; the sculptures that adorned the temple took a further two or three years from 434. The chief overseer of the project was Perikles' close friend, the sculptor Pheidias, who was also commissioned to make the new cult statue. The architects were Iktinos and Kallikrates.

Pheidias was a fully paid-up Periklean. He had made his name a decade or so earlier, especially in Athens with his sculpture of Athena Promakhos (the Defender), a large bronze statue which greeted visitors to the Akropolis as they entered through the western gateway. This statue was so tall that sailors used it as a landmark, when the sun glinted off the tip of the spear and the crest of the helmet. If the message conveyed by Athena Promakhos was straightforwardly pious, Pheidias' other famous statue was somewhat more sinister. He had also sculpted another significant Athena situated on the Akropolis – the Athena Lemnia, erected in celebration of Athens' imperialist settlement of an Athenian garrison on the island of Lemnos in 450. Lemnos was important to Athens not just as a source of grain itself, but as a stepping-stone on the grain route from the Black Sea.

The Parthenon replaced a temple of Athena which was begun in the 480s, destroyed by the Persians, and never later completed. There was already an old temple to Athena, to the north of the Parthenon (its foundations can still be seen between the Parthenon and the Erekhtheion), and it remained in use, but the new one was a proclamation of the glory of Athens and a visual confirmation of the success of Perikles' policies. Aesthetically, it is an extraordinary piece of work. Its massive appearance is achieved by its unusual size: the sides are roughly 70 metres long, and the ends over 30 metres. It has seventeen columns along each side, and eight along each end. Since perfectly straight lines, if they go on for some distance, appear to the human eye slightly curved, the architects introduced slight curves and bulges and inclines to compensate, so that the building does appear rectilinear, and the bulk of the Doric columns is lightened. In fact, there is hardly a straight line to the Parthenon: the floors on all four sides are slightly arched, as are the entablatures above the columns; the spaces between the columns are irregular; the inner walls lean a little, and no columns are perfectly perpendicular, but they tilt a little inward (continued upward, they would meet about 1,500 metres in the air); the rows of columns are slightly convex; the columns do not taper evenly, but in a slight arc; the corner columns are thicker than the rest. The temple was made from 13,400 blocks of Pentelic marble.

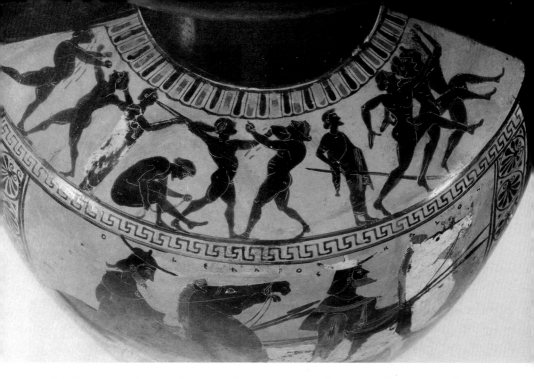

1. This vase, made around 520 BCE, shows runners on the right, and two pairs of boxers, with one of each pair bleeding heavily from the nose. They are being urged on by a pipe-player. The seated man appears to be preparing for some event.

2. The referee is using his wand to signal a foul, by touching the errant contestant. It looks as though the pankratiast on the right is biting his opponent.

Clockwise, from top left. 3. Themistokles 4. Perikles 5. Demosthenes
6. Sokrates 7. Aristotle 8. Herodes Atticus

9 & 10. A geometric grave amphora made in Athens in the first quarter of the eighth century BCE. By this time artists were beginning to supplement purely geometric designs with some representation, here of a funeral.

Above. 11. Horsemen from the Parthenon frieze. Note the liveliness typical of the best sculpture of the period. Pheidias and his team of sculptors could achieve remarkable results even with shallow stone-work.

Left. 12. The 'Athena of Varvakeion', a small Roman copy of Pheidias' cult statue in the Parthenon.

Opposite. 13 & 14. Metopes from the Parthenon with scenes from the battle of Centaurs and Lapiths. This was a popular subject for temple sculptures, representing the overcoming of disorder by civilized human beings.

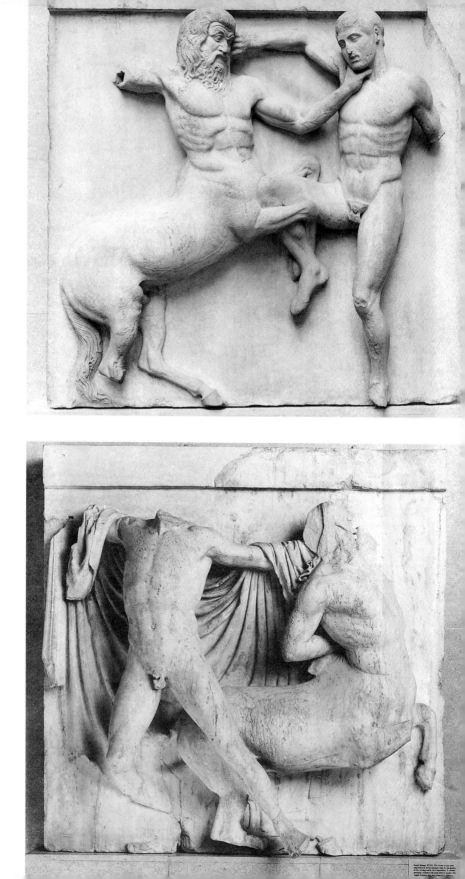

15. A well-preserved *kouros* statue from Attica, made towards the end of the sixth century to mark the tomb of a certain Kroisos. A verse was inscribed on the base: 'Stop and mourn at the grave of dead Kroisos, killed by savage Ares in the front rank of battle.'

16. The female equivalent of the *kouros* statue was the *kore* (girl) statue. Here is one from about 520 BCE, from the Akropolis of Athens. Glimpses of the original paintwork remind us that temples and statues were colourfully decorated.

Right. 17. One of the most famous pictures by the Athenian vase-painter Exekias is this one of the legendary hero Ajax planting his sword before committing suicide. It was painted around 540 BCE.

Below, left. 18. This red-figure krater from early in the fifth century BCE shows a scene, possibly from a play by Aiskhylos, in which half of a chorus of young men dance towards a figure seated as a suppliant on an altar.

Below, right. 19. On this panel of a black-figure vase an older man (the one with the beard) is importuning a younger man. The other two men are potential rivals for the boy's favours, and the one on the right has brought a deer as a courting gift.

20. Scenes from a symposium, on a cup by the Foundry Painter. The man on the far right is playing *kottabos* (p. 157); his companion is lusting after the pipe-girl prostitute; the next man is already drunk, and his couch-fellow is well on the way to joining him.

21. Scenes from the schoolroom. In this red-figure cup by Douris (c. 480 BCE), one boy is reciting to his teacher, while another is practising the lyre; the man seated on the right is a *paidagōgos*.

The sculptures of the eastern pediment (the triangular crown over the entrance) displayed the birth of Athena from the head of her father Zeus; the western pediment showed the triumph of Athena over Poseidon (see p. 42). Ninety-two sculptured slabs or panels (whose technical name is 'metopes') ran all around the building, depicting on the eastern front the defeat of the unruly Giants by the gods; to the south the victory of the human Lapiths over the marauding Centaurs, and the birth of Erikhthonios, the legendary snake-king of Athens; on the west the battle of Greeks and Amazons; and on the northern side the legendary Trojan War. All the sculptures, most of which have by now been destroyed, were in the new realistic style, with recognizably everyday gestures and postures; most were carved with consummate skill, though one or two of the surviving panels, if the truth be told, reveal poor workmanship.

The propaganda value of the sculptural themes is obvious: they celebrate Athena, the patron deity of Athens, and they depict Greeks, and especially Athenians, overcoming the forces of disorder and irrationality. Erikhthonios stood for Athenian autochthony – the belief that Athenians had inhabited Attica since time immemorial. Democrats fostered the idea of autochthony because it was a good leveller: every Athenian was as good as every other. So the sculptures were utterly commensurate with Perikles' vision of his city and in keeping with the Athenian democracy's tendency to use art to present the city's aesthetic ideals (especially on pots) and socio-political role models (especially on public statues).

Many grandiose temples had an inner peristyle of columns in addition to the outer peristyle. On the Parthenon, a ground-breaking frieze ran around the temple above the inner peristyle, which took the narrative style of Greek art a step further by telling a continuous story. The story started on the western frieze, the first to be seen as you approached the temple from the Propylaia, and then carried on clockwise around the temple. Walking around it gave an ancient Greek the experience of a moving picture. The story it told was one of the main Athenian foundation myths, the legend of Erekhtheus' sacrifice of his daughters. Faced with a barbarian invasion, the gods told King Erekhtheus that he would have to sacrifice one of his three daughters, and in order to save him from the painful choice all three chose to die. In the ensuing battle, Erekhtheus lost his life, but the city was saved. The frieze was an astonishing piece of work: never more than 6 centimetres deep, it nevertheless managed to give a reasonably lifelike portrait of teams of horses four deep. There was also another frieze, around the inside of the eastern porch, which was so badly damaged by fire in the third century CE (marble crumbles under heat) that only the fastidious restoration work currently being undertaken has revealed traces of it.

The inner chamber of a Classical temple, where the cult statue was housed, is called the 'cella'. Within the cella of the Parthenon stood Pheidias' famous statue of Athena. The statue was 11.5 metres high, and therefore almost touched the ceiling of the temple. A wooden image was covered in gold and ivory – ivory for the face, arms and other visible parts of her body, and for the traditional Gorgon's head on her breastplate; gold, 40 talents (1,150 kilograms) in weight, for her robes and the snake fringes of her shield. The gold plates were removed early in the third century BCE and replaced with gold leaf, and the statue vanished altogether in the early Byzantine period; but it was still standing a few centuries earlier, so that the travel-writer Pausanias saw it in the second century CE. He has left us a brief and rather flat description (1.24.5–7):

> The cult statue is made of ivory and gold. In the middle of its helmet is a sphinx ... and on either side of the helmet are carved griffins ... The statue of Athena stands upright in an ankle-length robe, and on its breast is an ivory representation of the Gorgon Medousa. Athena holds in one of her hands a Victory, about four cubits tall, and in the other a spear. At her feet lies a shield and, by the spear, a snake (which might be Erikhthonios).

From other sources we know that the shield and the goddess's sandals picked up themes from the metopes: on the outside of the shield was the battle of Greeks and Amazons, on the inside was the battle of gods and Giants, and on her sandals were Lapiths and Centaurs (which Pheidias had also sculpted on the shield of Athena Promakhos). If Athens saw herself as the patron of civilization, her patron goddess was to epitomize that aspiration.

As with all ancient temples, we will go sadly astray if we imagine the Parthenon gleaming, as it does today, in skeletonic white marble. The pillars and ornamental sculptures were painted, and the temple itself was filled with treasures and dedications – gold and silver implements, thrones and couches and weapons and armour. It blazed with colour and wealth – and thieves were held at bay not just by superstition, but by security fences between the outside pillars and barriers at the eastern and western ends.

The Propylaia, the magnificent gateway on to the Akropolis, was the next to be built. Designed by the architect Mnesikles, it and the Parthenon cost, in modern terms, many millions of dollars. The Propylaia, a five-gated, double-banked entrance with wings on either side containing colonnades and ceremonial halls, occupied more or less the whole of the western brow of the hill. At least one of its halls was decorated with paintings by Polygnotos. The Propylaia was never entirely completed: the war intervened and drained both manpower and money. The various gateways in the Propylaia allowed access for both humans and the numerous animals led for ritual slaughter at one of the altars on the Akropolis.

Two final projects on the Akropolis were started after Perikles' death, but are very much part of the programme he initiated. The delightful small temple of Athena Nike (Athena as Victory), which stands like a bastion on the south-western corner of the hill, was designed by Kallikrates, one of the architects of the Parthenon, and had a frieze of Greeks and Persians fighting. The so-called Erekhtheion (actually another temple of Athena, to house her most ancient cult statue) was built on the northern side of the Akropolis, in an area long used for religious purposes. Its construction too was interrupted by the war, although we know that the famous Porch of the Karyatids, with its pillars of statuesque young women, was more or less complete by 413.

There was an ancient story that Perikles delayed his entry into public life because he somewhat resembled the tyrant Peisistratos and did not want to attract unwelcome comparisons or early ostracism. But Peisistratos was an unconstitutional ruler, whereas Perikles adhered strictly to democratic rules and regulations. The only respect in which he and his circle deserved the title 'the new Peisistratids' (Plutarch, *Pericles* 16) was that they continued the cultural programme the tyrants had initiated. Although there had been plenty of building, both religious and secular, between 510 and 450, both the Peisistratid and the Periklean periods display a concerted effort to glorify the city and her goddess.

Perikles ensured that the city he loved became synonymous with architectural majesty and beauty. Although time and historical events have been as merciless as usual, although many of the sculptures from the pediments and friezes have been destroyed or are scattered in museums around the world, although it is hard for the modern tourist to ignore the crowds with their cameras and vociferous local guides, and although for many years the Parthenon and other monuments have been inaccessible and shrouded in scaffolding or even demolished, a visit to the Akropolis is essential for anyone with even an hour to spare in the city. Perikles' buildings were designed with a message for their time, but also to be timeless, and people still stand in awe at the city he created.

Perikles' Athens: The Peak of Perfection?

It is all too easy to disparage the naivety of eighteenth- and nineteenth-century scholars who saw Classical Athens as perfect and paradigmatic, for both its artistic and political achievements. In actual fact, the myth of Athenian perfection was consciously developed by Perikles himself. The myth was made concrete in the buildings whose construction he oversaw, but it was also expressed in his speeches. The most important of these, and one of the outstanding rhetorical showpieces of all time, is the Funeral Speech put into Perikles' mouth by the historian Thucydides, and based on his own and others' recollections.

In the winter of the first year of the Peloponnesian War, Perikles spoke in the burial grounds of the Kerameikos district of Athens at the memorial service of those who had fallen in battle. He took the opportunity to celebrate the city, to show that these young men had not died in vain. The speech is long, and these are only excerpts:

> In our political life we do not emulate the customs of our neighbours; no, rather than imitating anyone else, it is more

the case that we are an example for others to follow. Our constitution is called a democracy because government is in the hands not of a few but of the majority; where private disputes are concerned everyone is equal under the law, and men are preferred for public office not because of their rank but because of their excellent qualities, according to their merits and their distinction in some field. On the other hand, no one is prevented by poverty or public obscurity from benefiting the city in any way he can. Where our public lives are concerned, we live in the state like free men, and the same goes for the lack of suspicion with which we deal with one another in our daily pursuits. We do not react with anger if one of our neighbours indulges himself, nor do we put on the kind of ill-humoured expression which is bound to cause offence, even if it is actually harmless. Although we deal comfortably with one another in our private lives, in our public lives a deep respect stops us doing wrong, because we obey the authorities and the laws – especially those which have been established for the benefit of victims of wrongdoing and those which, though unwritten, bring acknowledged disgrace on their transgressor.

Moreover, we have provided very many ways for the mind to relax from its toils: we have instituted contests and sacrifices throughout the year, and our private households are elegant, so that day by day pleasure banishes distress. The city is so great that everything is imported into it from all over the world, with the result that we enjoy goods from abroad as though they were as familiar as local products.

We are also superior to our enemies in our training for war. We do not close our borders, and we never use the deportation of foreigners to prevent someone either learning or seeing something which, once discovered, might help the enemy. This is because we rely less on schemes and deceit than on our own innate courage in action. And whereas their educational system has men from a very early age set out in pursuit of courage by means of laborious exercises, we live our lives without constraints and yet are just as ready to face any danger we might be pitted against . . .

Our love of beauty does not make us extravagant, and our love of intellectual pursuits does not make us soft. We use our wealth as an opportunity for action rather than as an excuse for boasting, but we also refuse to accept that poverty is shameful; what is more disgraceful is not attempting to escape it. A man's concern with his domestic affairs does not stop him being equally interested in political affairs, and our various business interests do not make us any the less informed about public matters. We are the only people who regard a man who is uninvolved in public matters not as carefree, but as useless. We ourselves either assess issues or think deeply about them in an appropriate manner, because we do not think that words injure actions: no, it is worse to rush into action without having first learnt what we should be doing . . .

We have also always differed from others with respect to our ability to do good, because we acquire friends by being the givers, not the recipients, of favours. The friendship of a benefactor, who is concerned to use his good will to preserve the gratitude due to him from the recipient, is more secure, while the friendship of a debtor is less enthusiastic, because he knows that when he comes to repay the good deed, he will do so not as a favour, but as a debt. So we alone do good to others freely, without thought of expediency, but basing ourselves only on our generosity.

In short, I declare that the city as a whole is an education for Greece, and that, in my opinion, every individual can gain from us the ability to face, as a free and independent agent, the widest variety of circumstances with consummate grace and versatility. That this is no idle boast, designed for the present situation, but actual fact, is proved by the very power of the city, which is a consequence of precisely these qualities. Athens is the only city existing today to approach the hour of trial in a condition which surpasses what men say about her. In the case of Athens alone no enemy invader feels annoyed at receiving rough treatment at her hands; in the case of Athens alone no subject complains that he is ruled by unworthy people. We provide unmistakable evidence of our power; there are plenty of witnesses, and future generations will wonder at us, just as the present generation does. We need no praise-singing Homer nor any other poet whose words may give temporary pleasure, but whose conception of the facts falls short of reality. No, we have compelled every sea and every continent to open up to our daring, and everywhere we have planted everlasting monuments of our successes and our failures.

(Thucydides, *The Peloponnesian War* 2.37–41)

The speech overflows with civic pride – it is a poignant snapshot of the last moment of Classical Athens' splendour – but also with boasts that need some qualification. Some of them are wildly unrealistic, such as the claim that all Athenians were law-abiding citizens. In every society there are good people and bad people, and in Athens the veneer of respectability could rapidly wear thin. At the height of the plague in 430, for instance, people began to think that life was so short and uncertain that they might as well indulge themselves and do anything they could get away with, and they ignored both human laws and the gods, since the rich and the poor, the good and the bad, were all dying equally.

Other claims are simply untrue. One of the most famous sentences in the speech is the one translated 'Our love of beauty does not make us extravagant' – this from a man who had spent the equivalent of millions of dollars embellishing the city. And he ignores the unwelcome nature of Athenian imperialism (although it is true that the worst was yet to come) in claiming that Athens acquires friends by doing them favours. Other lies or half-truths will become clear in later chapters. Athens was not, for instance, as tolerant and liberal a society as Perikles liked to paint it: anyone who stood out was liable to be the butt of gossip or even official interference. The only boast that rings entirely true concerns the cultural superiority of Athens to other Greek cities. But for the moment I want to focus on his claims about Athenian democracy. The speech is such a famous manifesto for democracy that during the First World War posters with extracts from it were carried by London buses.

Athenian democracy was not without its contemporary and native critics, notably Isokrates, Plato and the 'Old Oligarch', the name given to the author of the *Constitution of Athens*, a short, immature and clumsily composed essay or pamphlet preserved among the works of Xenophon. These ancient critics focused on a narrow range of problems: that democracy was over-reliant on an unsatisfactory legal system, that it left politics in the hands of the ignorant (or at least non-expert) masses, who were easily swayed by demagogues or political coteries and so failed to deliver a coherent foreign policy, that it failed to recognize talent and made unequals equal, and that it promoted class divisions and civil strife. This last claim is certainly untrue, since for the roughly 200 years of its history democratic Athens was remarkably stable, and finally succumbed only to external invasion. It was not a monolithic stability, however. The inherent tensions between rich and poor, or between professional politicians and the masses, were held in check by the thoroughness of the radical democracy, but erupted into conflict twice in the history of the democracy. Otherwise the power of the people was such that they could channel the family-centred ambitions of the elite into internal competition – into public debate in the Assembly, for instance – where the rules were dictated by the people and the popular constitution.

There is some truth, however, in the other complaints. Above all, the radical nature of Athenian democracy meant that there were no permanent government officials, no Civil Service. Most officials were chosen year by year, and while this meant that control remained in the hands of the people, the cost was a lack of professionalism, or an over-reliance on those few, like Perikles and the demagogues who followed him, who were professional politicians.

In his speech Perikles claimed that everyone in Athens was equal before the law, which is true, and that everyone participated in the city's political processes. Even allowing for the fact that 'everyone' here means only men (not women), and only Athenians (not resident aliens or other non-citizens), and only free men (not slaves), the claim is untrue. Many Athenian citizens lived too far away from the city – on Salamis or Euboia, for instance, or in the further corners of hilly Attica, which had at the most only poor roads or cart tracks – to make a trip to the Assembly feasible, even if their work schedule or finances allowed it. Payment for attendance was not introduced until 403 (though councillors and other officers, whose work was more time-consuming, had been paid since the middle of the fifth century). Then again, the Pnyx, where the Assembly met, could accommodate at the most only 6,000 people out of the roughly 50,000 who by now had the right to vote, and the constitution enshrined this limitation by fixing the quorum for the most important issues at 6,000. In other words, while 'everyone' had the *right* to vote in the Assembly, in practice not all that many exercised that right. Normal attendance at the Assembly numbered about 2,000 until the fourth century, when pay for attendance and an enlarged and more comfortable Pnyx made participation more attractive.

Even fewer exercised the right to speak in the Assembly, to debate any issue. Although by formula, after the presiding committee had raised some item on the agenda, the town-crier would ask the assembled people, 'Who wants to speak?', it is a familiar fact of life that in mass meetings very few people – and usually the same people over and over again – do the speaking. The right to speak one's mind was one of the theoretical mainstays of Athenian democracy, and in the theorists' idealized version of an Assembly meeting, the banner of freedom of speech was constantly waved. In practice, however, the vast majority of Athenians were led by increasingly professional orators, and limited themselves to cheering and heckling.

These orators – few in the fifth century, rather more in the fourth – were the closest Athens got to professional politicians. They were attracted by the hereditary prestige their families could gain, by power, and by the prospect of financial gain from bribes and spoils of war; on the other hand, if they fell foul of the system, they could become liable to ostracism, heavy fines (up to and including confiscation of property), and even the death penalty. But in order to attain political prominence, the aspirant had to stay in the limelight for a number of years, and probably to have studied under a rhetorical teacher: all of this took money, and almost all the main politicians of Athens, particularly in the fifth century, were well off – despite Perikles' claim that poverty was no bar to playing a full part in the city's political processes.

In a play of 424 BCE, the comic poet Aristophanes satirized the power political speakers wielded in a mock address:

> O People of Athens, how fine is your rule,
> When all men fear you as they would a tyrant.
> But you're so easily led: you love

To be flattered and deceived.
You're impressed by every new speaker.
Just now your mind is on vacation.

(*Knights* 1111–20)

But although the oligarchs and the comic poets liked to criticize or poke fun at the Athenian people for their reliance on demagogues, it was hollow criticism: the system worked well precisely because there were those who, for whatever reasons, were prepared to make politics their primary occupation. This is why, for instance, the Assembly generally turned a blind eye to politicians taking bribes (Demosthenes' opposition to Philip II of Macedon, for instance, was funded by the Persian king) or helping their friends: they needed the politicians, and the continuity and professionalism they supplied, and they were realistic enough to recognize that the politicians needed to make a living and to repay debts. Nor were the people as fickle as their enemies liked to make out: there was a strict requirement that any new law, or even proposal, should not contravene an existing law, so that the Assembly could not just pass any old measure into law according to its whim or the whim of a persuasive speaker.

Although it is easy to see that a smaller percentage of the population was actively involved in the political processes and procedures than Perikles would like us to believe, to modern eyes the extent of participation by men of all ranks is startling. In a city of maybe 50,000 citizens with full rights, 6,000 jurors were empanelled each year. Then there were 500 councillors and a further 700 minor officers and bureaucrats. Several thousand spent half a day or longer up to forty times a year in the Assembly (which for obvious reasons met on days when the courts were not sitting). If we count religious festivals as political – as the Greeks would, since it was part of one's civic duty to maintain a good relationship between the gods and the city – then we can count the thousands more who filled the streets or the theatre during the great festivals, of which Athens had more than any other Greek city.

For all its flaws, Athenian democracy worked. It is hard for the unbiased historian to rank any constitutional system over another in terms of efficiency. All of them are flawed, and many seem unwieldy, but business still gets done, and cynically one might say that the purpose of most constitutions is just to slow things down, to provide a check on proposals being passed into law faster than is wise. In this respect the Athenian system worked as well as most, and it had the important benefit that every participating citizen felt essentially involved in his city's future and destiny. This sense of involvement went a long way towards papering over the cracks in the system, especially the discontinuities caused by annual elections, because politics was the main topic of conversation among the majority of male Athenian citizens, so that whether or not they were currently in office, they knew what was going on.

The outstanding features of Periklean Athens are imperialism, participation, wealth and high culture. They are interconnected. Participation fed and was fed by patriotic pride in the city. This pride led to the conviction that Athens was greater than any other city and therefore had a right to rule over others and to be belligerent in the face of opposition from Sparta or elsewhere. Imperialism created the wealth to attract artists and sponsor them, and the leisure for such pursuits. Pride created the desire to embellish the city with magnificent buildings and to foster her reputation as the supreme city of culture. The Athenian people usurped the role of aristocrats and collectively sponsored art.

One consequence of this pride, however, was the swamping of panhellenic sentiments. This is not only because such pride is necessarily parochial. Panhellenism was a feature of aristocratic Greek life, but by the last quarter of the fifth century the aristocrats and their ways were becoming sidelined, even a source of suspicion. If they felt a natural affinity with their peers in other cities, that might now be seen as a betrayal of Athens. In democratic Athens, as the opponents of democracy complained, the thetes dictated the terms of life – and they were the ones who were fanatically loyal to the city. There was no longer much room for panhellenism: other Greek states threatened the Empire of Athens and therefore the sovereignty of the common people. Perikles' attempts to combine panhellenism with his fervent democracy failed, and they were doomed to failure.

The single most important reason for Perikles' enduring popularity was that he was the first to articulate a vision of the future towards which events of the past fifty years seemed inevitably to be driving Athens – a vision of material and cultural glory for the city, and of leadership of all Greeks everywhere. Moreover, he stayed in power long enough to fix this vision in the hearts and minds of the Athenian people, rich and poor. Almost the whole citizen body of Athens was united behind Perikles in pursuit of this vision: the business of Empire provided the issues most commonly debated in the Assembly, everyone benefited from the material wealth the Empire provided, and the rich in addition could gain enormous prestige from being seen to champion Athenian interests. But it was a natural consequence of this vision that those who did not agree with Athens' divine right to leadership would have to be swept aside, if they put up any resistance. War became inevitable.

THE CITY AT LEISURE

10

Religion

As a result of the city's wealth and of Perikles' programme of embellishment, Athens became the cultural centre of the Greek world and a magnet for artists and thinkers. This was the first peak of the city's internationalism. Not unnaturally she felt herself to be the centre of the Greek world, and the ideal of panhellenism took root in her outlook – but evidently not in her policies, which remained as self-interested as ever. This clash between ideal and real lies at the heart of the tragedy of the city: the potential was there for a broader perspective, but it never became real, and since Athens now had the power to pursue its self-interest very aggressively, it was in the process of sealing its doom. Under the high notes of cultural splendour and brilliance lay a heavy bass beat of warfare and impending destruction.

When considering what we might broadly call the Athenians' 'leisure' pursuits, we must start with religion, because the Greeks started and ended with religion. Religion was embedded in every aspect of life, from morning to night. Religion was not a separate sphere, as it is for most of us today in the West: awesome events were not just symbolic of divinity, but were themselves gods.

The political and religious histories of Athens intertwine, especially because an individual's involvement with the public life of the state included his performance of actions which we would now categorize as religious. It was one of the duties of a citizen to keep the gods smiling on the city, and he did this chiefly by participating in the public rites of the city. But his private, family rituals were part of the same process, and it was therefore possible for the state to interfere in them, and even condemn a man as impious for his private actions. The most notorious case of such interference was the trial of Sokrates.

Athens and Attica, like other regions of Greece, had their own

specific forms of worship, their local heroes, and so on. The
persistence of traditional forms over the centuries is remarkable
and speaks volumes for the hold religion had over the minds of the
Athenians, although there were changes and developments. For
instance, some of the gods became more popular under titles
different from those of the fifth century, as, for instance, the cult of
Zeus the Saviour spread throughout Attica in the fourth century.
Gradually, too, because of Athens' willingness to allow foreigners
to reside in or near the city and because of the flexibility of Greek
religion, foreign deities were introduced into the cultic pantheon;
this happened especially in Hellenistic times, when Athens was
part of or was influenced by large international empires. Another
phenomenon of the Hellenistic period, from the last quarter of
the fourth century BCE to the beginning of the first, is that more
exclusive forms of worship, by private individuals or small groups,
became more acceptable. But in what follows I shall wield a broad
brush and ignore all these developments.

In Homer's and Hesiod's epic poems, the earliest works of
European literature (written between 750 and 700 BCE), the authors
present the end result of a lengthy process of simplification due to
prominence and conquest: the gods govern the most important
aspects of a peasant community's life, and are those of the dominant panhellenic culture of the Greek world. Anthropomorphism is
the outstanding characteristic of Homeric religion, but we must be
careful here. When the Greeks portrayed their gods as young and
attractive, this might not mean that they thought they looked like
young, attractive human beings, but that they thought that youth
and beauty were qualities that evoked or represented the divine.
Moreover, outside of literature, sculpture and vase-painting, the
gods were defined largely by their functions, not by any appearance.

On the whole, though, the mental picture the Greeks had of
their gods involved a full-blooded anthropomorphism. Not only did
the gods have family trees, they also had family squabbles. Being
pictured as super-humans, they could not be omnipresent, though
they were sometimes regarded as omniscient. But we hear of the
gods even washing, walking, eating, drinking, being wounded and
making love. They were spitefully pleased at an enemy's downfall
and could be swayed by appeals to logic and reason. The gods were

just many times more powerful than petty humans; the only utterly irreconcilable gulf between the two species, which makes Homer's *Iliad* a tragic poem, is that the gods are carefree and immortal.

For Homer and most Greeks the world was not governed by immutable divine laws, but by the gods' preferences. This meant that the Greeks lived in a profoundly insecure universe, where anything was possible. The Greeks created the gods in their own image: the climate was fickle and crops could easily fail; they were frequently exposed to the hazards of warfare; disease, disfigurement and early death were common. The gods were the forces that ruled this dangerous universe.

The main god in the Olympian pantheon was Zeus, the sky and weather god. He and his brothers, Poseidon and Hades, divided the three parts of the world between them. Zeus got the sky, Hades the underworld and Poseidon the surface of the earth, so that he was the god of the sea and seafarers, but also of earthquakes. The sky is broad and encompassing, and so Zeus was the father and ruler of gods and men. His wife was Hera, goddess of marriage and child-birth; she shared the latter domain with Artemis, who was also the goddess of hunting and wilderness. Athena was the goddess of craft. Ares was the god of warlike frenzy, and so in myth his lover was Aphrodite, the goddess of beauty and sexual passion. Aphrodite was actually the wife of Hephaistos, the crippled dwarf-god of metallurgy and volcanoes. Apollo was the god of music, prophecy and disease, the link being that he sent things from afar. Hermes was the messenger of the gods, in charge of travellers, communication, writing and magic. Demeter was the goddess of cereal crops. The lists of the canonical Twelve Gods generally also included Hestia, the goddess of hearth and home. Chief among those gods who fell outside the original Olympian pantheon was Dionysos, god of ecstasy and wine. There were only these dozen or so major gods, but they were infinitely extensible through gaining particular cult names: Zeus the Saviour, Zeus of the Hearth, Zeus of the Hilltops, Zeus the Kindly, Zeus the Protector of Stores, and so on and so forth.

In addition to the main gods, there were dozens more, such as Kore or Persephone (the daughter of Demeter), Pan, Asklepios the healer and the witch Hekate. And as well as gods there were *daimones*, good and bad spirits who took a particular interest in human beings and intervened in their affairs. Because the gods were seen as the givers of blessings, they were not commonly held responsible for death or psychological disturbance, both of which were the province of *daimones*. Finally, there were heroes, dead human beings who had achieved local or, in the case of a few like Herakles, international cultic status or even deification. Taken all in all, the natures, functions, names and characteristics of the Greek gods and demigods constitute a serious attempt to explain the nature of the universe, seen as a place of power, and all that it contains.

As with many aspects of Greek culture, it is hard to understand Greek religion without shedding some modern conceptions. The Greek gods were created, for instance, and they were within, not outside, the world. In particular, for most of us moderns, religion is bound up with the ideas of orthodoxy and heterodoxy, heresy, atheism and agnosticism. The Greeks would not have understood much of this. There was no Bible or sacred text to which one had to adhere, no body of doctrine in which one had to believe, no professional priestly hierarchy, no synods to declare what was right and what was wrong, no confessional books in which a writer revealed his or her personal beliefs.

Greek religion was ritualistic. One had to perform certain actions, and they presumably involved emotional commitment, but there was little or no dogma. Moreover, a great deal of religion was not personal, but was part of one's obligations as a member of some community or other – the civic community, the community of peasants, one's family and household, as a craftsman, a demesman or a soldier. A personal relationship with the divine, and moral guidance, was the province of philosophy rather than religion – which in turn shows the gulf between ancient and modern conceptions of philosophy. Today philosophy means conceptual analysis, but in those days it was a way of life, a means of self-improvement.

There were some moral features embedded within normal Greek religion, however. Certain acts were regarded as offending or angering the gods. Murder polluted not just the murderer, but everyone who came into contact with him: punishing the murderer was a religious requirement as much as a legal one. The gods were concerned with justice and would see that the unjust and oath-breakers were punished. The Greeks also held that the gods wanted one to be hospitable to strangers, kind to one's friends, dutiful to one's community and one's parents, fierce with one's enemies; and they believed that – in the long run, at least – arrogance and excess would be humbled. The mechanism for this was often that a god or a *daimōn* took possession of the guilty person, and put into his mind the kinds of thoughts and impulses which drove him to destruction. The uncanny was always a sign of divinity.

The chief means of communicating with the gods were offerings and prayer. Most of these rites were based on reciprocity: either you were giving to the gods in expectation of a return from them in the future, or you were repaying them for some perceived token of good will. Animal sacrifices ranged from a bull ox down to a pigeon or a goose: blood was shed and fire burnt the offering and sent it as smoke up to the gods. Daily domestic sacrifices involved tossing, say, a bun or a handful of grain on to the hearth. A big animal sacrifice was a festive occasion for the community, with a procession before the sacrifice, the ritual offering of the bones and innards (and perhaps one or two choice cuts) to the god, and a feast afterwards to consume the rest of the meat – a practice that aroused St Paul's indignation (I Corinthians 8). If a private individual was performing a sacrifice in his home, in thanksgiving perhaps, he would invite friends to participate in the ritual and have dinner with him afterwards. The communal eating of the meat, binding people to one another, was an essential part of blood sacrifice in Greek religion, and meat was rarely eaten except after a sacrifice.

You might imagine something like the following scene for a small sacrificial ritual. The family and the guests stand around the altar. The sacrificial victim – a piglet, perhaps – stands ready by the altar, kept in place by a slave. The host fetches a burning torch, extinguishes it ritually in a bowl of water, and sprinkles the water for purification on all the assembled people, who stand in solemn silence. He sprinkles water also on the head of the victim, which instinctively nods its head, in assent to being sacrificed to the gods. Then the host takes the knife out of the basket and slits the throat of the victim, while the women give voice to the ritual scream. The blood is caught in a bowl and a libation is offered to the god. The dead creature is carried off to be cooked, and the party begins.

Other offerings included first-fruit offerings – offering a portion of your harvest, or of your catch of fish, or whatever it might be, on the understanding that since the gods had given they deserved at least a portion back. Such an offering was left in a sacred place, sunk in a lake, or burnt as a sacrifice. Votive offerings were made in consequence of a vow: 'If I get out of this storm alive, I'll sacrifice a pig to Poseidon.' 'If Asklepios makes my foot better, I'll dedicate a model of a foot and some money in his shrine.' A portion of booty taken in war was expected to be given to the gods. Girls gave their playthings before they got married, and artisans the tools of their trade when they retired, in acknowledgement of the transition and in gratitude for good times past. Teenagers cut off locks of their hair and gave them to the gods, giving a piece of themselves in return for protection in adult life. States and wealthy individuals made such generous offerings that in major panhellenic sites, such as Olympia and Delphi, state treasuries were built to store them, and all major temples were treasure-houses as well.

A third kind of offering was a libation, the pouring of a little liquid, usually watered wine, on to the ground for the dead (as I confess I did on a visit to the mound of the Marathon dead), or on to the flames of a sacrificial fire for the god, or to anoint a tombstone. Again, usually only a portion of the liquid was poured out, while the rest was passed around the assembled company, binding them to one another.

Libations and sacrifices were usually accompanied by prayers; music might be played and incense burnt, on the understanding that what was pleasing to human beings might well be pleasing to the gods. Prayers could also be offered up at any time. It is not misleading to think of prayer in ancient Greece much as we do today, except that if the Greeks accompanied prayer with a ritual gesture they would stand or kneel with arms outstretched. The god was addressed humbly, and in the prayer you were expected to rehearse a number of his titles, out of politeness and your natural concern to make sure that you got his attention. You would also mention his obligation to you: you have been a loyal devotee and have performed copious sacrifices, and therefore you reasonably expect him to answer your prayer in return. The gods were not always reasonable – they both were and were not similar to human beings – but in all your dealings with them you acted as if they might be.

Purification kept one a part of the community: you accepted its standards of right and wrong, pure and impure, and not to accept those standards was to be an outsider, to be unclean. So rituals of purification accompanied or preceded most Greek sacral acts. Water was the main means of purification, with ritualized sprinkling more likely than full washing. Fumigation was occasionally used to purify rooms. Blood, bizarrely, was used sometimes as a purificatory agent; for instance, before the opening of the Assembly in Athens, officials would carry piglets around, cut their throats and spray their blood over the seats and the members of the presiding committee (no doubt to the delight of the slave-women at home whose job it was to wash the clothes afterwards).

Sacred acts were invariably carried out in sacred places. At the lower end of the scale a sanctuary was no more than a dedicated place with an altar, protected perhaps by a low wall and certainly by being kept untainted by moral pollution; at the other end, it could contain a full-fledged temple with a cult image of the god inside, and priests or priestesses (whose gender usually depended on the gender of the deity). Modern preconceptions about priests must be shed: Greek priests were not intermediaries between the congregation and the divine. Although they did perform sacrifices, any individual could do so, and could pray, pour libations, and so on. As much as anything, the priests of a temple were the Civil Service: they saw that things were done properly, consecrated sacrificial victims, administered the temple, and looked after the cult statue and the temple's finances and dedicated treasures. It was a prestigious, part-time position, not a vocation. Priesthood was often hereditary within a family, though sometimes priests were elected by lot or vote (either from a particular clan or from the whole male or female citizen body). In other words, priests were servants of the community.

We must also shed preconceptions about temples. They were houses for gods, not places of congregation and worship, and they were storehouses for valuable dedications. Very little happened inside a temple and most of them were closed for most of the year, until it was the turn of that particular deity for worship. Congregation took place around the altar (often a mound of turf or a slab of natural rock), which was generally placed in front of – which is to say, usually, to the east of – the temple.

Piety was measurable: the more of the city's cults in which you participated, and the more generous your offerings, the more pious you were reckoned to be. Rich Athenians rarely complained if they were required to pay for a dramatic production, or some other element of a religious festival: it enhanced their piety and their family's standing in the community. Display was important not just for individuals: the Panathenaia, Athens' most important festival, involved a glorious procession and the slaughter of hundreds of victims. The importance of the occasion was measured by the number of people and victims involved.

These were the ways in which mortals communicated with the gods. But the gods also communicated with humans – through dreams, but especially through divination. Divination played a considerable role in ancient Greece: if you needed to know the future, a sneeze or a chance meeting or a stray remark or the pattern of a bird of prey's flight could all be significant. But the Greeks were not obsessive about divination, otherwise there would be no point to the portrait of the superstitious man given by Theophrastos of Eresos in about 320 BCE (*Characters* 16):

> If a weasel runs across the road, he refuses to continue on his way until either someone has passed by or he has thrown three stones across the road. If he sees a snake in his house, he calls on Sabazios if it is yellow or immediately builds a hero-shrine on the spot if it is a sacred snake ... He finds it disturbing if owls hoot at him as he is walking along and carries on only after saying, 'Athena is greater.' ... When he has a dream, he goes to the dream-interpreters, the diviners, the soothsayers, to ask which god or goddess he should pray to.

Divination was usually reserved for crises, such as warfare. To see whether the outcome would be favourable, professional diviners examined the liver of sacrificial victims before battle, and watched to see how the creature's tail curled in the fire, how quickly the flames spread, and so on, and went on sacrificing until they obtained a favourable omen. Since in all probability the other side was doing the same, there must have been some cynics who wondered whether it was all worthwhile. In Athens there were state-sponsored collectors of oracular responses, who could be consulted in an emergency to see if there was an utterance or two relevant to the situation at hand.

The most public form of divination was consulting an oracle. When the state was considering a critical mission, such as founding a colony, or declaring war, or turning some sacred ground over to secular use, or building a temple, they might turn to one of the panhellenic oracles, and especially to the oracle of Apollo at Delphi. The Delphic oracle was famously ambiguous, and the utterances of the Pythia, the priestess there, might well require interpretation, but these are only the best-known responses the oracle gave. More usually one went with a question requiring a simple yes-or-no answer and Apollo or one of his delegates would make a choice. In the middle of the fourth century, for instance, the Athenians were to consult Delphi over whether some sacred land should be left untilled or should be rented out for agricultural use. They prepared two jugs, and sealed statements of the two possibilities, one inside each jug. A delegation took these two sealed jugs to Delphi, where the priests opened one of them and drew out the solution.

The Panathenaia

Athens was famous for the frequency of its religious festivals. In the fifth and fourth centuries, there was a festival on at least a third of the days of the year, in Athens or somewhere in Attica. Some were exclusive (just for women, say, or for the members of a particular clan), and certainly one did not have to attend any or all of them, but there must quite frequently have been a party atmosphere in the streets and houses of Athens. The festivals that are still held in some of the towns and villages of Greece and Sicily give one an accurate impression. The ancient Greeks did not have non-working

weekends, or twenty days a year of paid holiday, or national
holidays: these festival days, whatever other functions they performed, allowed people to rest from work.

The festivals took place on fixed dates of the calendar. The
Athenian calendar consisted of twelve lunar months, alternately of
thirty and twenty-nine days. When things got out of kilter, an extra
month was inserted by repeating one of the months. The new year
began around midsummer, on the new moon before the summer
solstice, with the month of Hekatombaion; then there were
Metageitnion, Boedromion, Pyanepsion, Maimakterion, Poseideon,
Gamelion, Anthesterion, Elaphebolion, Mounikhion, Thargelion and
Skirophorion. Several of these months are named after the chief
festivals which occurred during them. The Anthesteria, for instance,
was a boozy festival, sacred to Dionysos as god of growth, at
which three-year-old children were crowned with flowers. At the
Thargelia, which was sacred to Artemis and Apollo, there was a
concert of dithyrambic verses, and two ugly, poor people were
chosen as scapegoats. The one standing for the men of Athens
wore a string of black figs around his neck, the one standing for
the women wore green figs. These two unfortunates were taken
in procession around the city and then beaten with branches and
driven beyond the city bounds.

The single most important Athenian festival was the Panathenaia. It was the most splendid, the most resonant with civic pride,
and by all accounts one of the most enjoyable festivals of the year.
It was held towards the end of Hekatombaion, and the month was
named after the huge sacrifice, the hecatomb, which was central
to the ceremony. Every fourth year it was held on an even larger
scale and lasted for nine days; the centrepiece was the presentation
of a new robe to Athena, and in addition to the regular activities
there were athletic games, horse-races, boat-races, a contest in manly
strength, a dance in armour, the typically Athenian torch-relay race,
and various musical and poetic events (which by the end of the fifth
century were held in Perikles' Odeion). Victors in all these competitions won prizes of cash or valuable olive oil.

All this added to the holiday atmosphere. But the core religious
function of the festival was the presentation of Athena's new robe.
Nine months before the festival, a picked team of young, unmarried

women began work on the brightly coloured robe, when the loom was ceremonially set up by Athena's priestesses and a band of young girls who were dedicated each year to the goddess. The robe was made out of wool, and was embroidered with a scene portraying Athena's victory over the giant Enkelados. The statue that was dressed in the robe was not Pheidias' enormous and already gaudy masterpiece, but a small and plain wooden statue (perhaps just a stump of olive wood) which by the end of the fifth century was housed in the Erekhtheion on the Akropolis. The robe was transported, like a sail, on a wheel-mounted model ship (to commemorate Athenian reliance on the sea) to the Areiopagos, and then carried up the final slope to the Akropolis.

From dusk of the evening before the procession young men and women had held an all-night vigil, with dancing and the singing of hymns. The following morning crowds began to assemble all along the Panathenaic Way, one of the main roads of ancient Athens, from the Dipylon Gate in the Kerameikos, through the agora to the western entrance to the Akropolis, adorned by Perikles with the magnificent Propylaia. The procession was led by young girls escorting the model ship with the new robe for Athena, and by the priestesses of Athena. Then came a long train of women bearing gifts for the goddess. The dozens of sacrificial victims came next, led or carried by their handlers, and after them came metics, carrying trays of offerings. All were singing hymns, and behind the metics came the musicians playing their pipes and lyres. Older men followed, and representatives of the armed forces, especially the year's ten generals, and young men of hoplite status. They were followed by chariots and horsemen and the winners of the various events in the games which had occupied the previous days. The rear was brought up by representatives of every deme in Attica. During the later years of the Empire, representatives of the allied states were present too, since they were required to supply a cow and a suit of armour for the ceremony.

When the front of the huge procession reached the Propylaia, they stopped and everyone gathered around the foot of the Areiopagos Hill while sacrifices were offered to Athena as guarantor of good health, Athena as guarantor of victory, and Athena the protectress of the city. After this stage only citizens entered the

Akropolis through the Propylaia. The robe was offered to the priestesses, who joyfully carried it into the Erekhtheion and dressed the goddess. All the remaining animals were now sacrificed on the fire that had been lit earlier by a torch carried in a race to the Akropolis from the altar of Eros in the Academy outside the Dipylon Gate. The race began at dawn, and the winner was the first to arrive at the altar with his torch still alight. After the sacrifices, select citizens from each deme were invited to a huge feast in the agora.

The Mysteries of Eleusis

Athenian festivals covered a broad spectrum in terms both of events and emotions. In the month of Boedromion the Great Mysteries of Eleusis were celebrated in a nine-day festival which was far removed from the public pageantry of the Panathenaia: it was the closest Athenian religion came to a cult that offered personal salvation, communion with the divine and a better afterlife.

Today, Eleusis is an ugly industrial town, but for a thousand years it was the site of the most popular mystery cult in the ancient world. The awe in which the place was held survived for many centuries after the demise of Greek religion and the end of the rites performed there. In the early nineteenth century the traveller Edward Clarke came across the ruins and gained official permission to buy a statue and take it back home. His account is fascinating:

> We found it on the side of the road, immediately before entering the village, and in the midst of a dung heap, buried as high as the neck ... The inhabitants of the small village ... still regarded this statue with a very high degree of superstitious veneration. They attributed to its presence the fertility of their land; and it was for this reason that they heaped around it the manure intended for their fields ... They predicted the wreck of the ship that should convey it; and it is a curious circumstance that their augury was completely fulfilled, in the loss of the *Princessa* merchantman, off Beachy Head, having the statue on board.

The statue was recovered and is now in the Fitzwilliam Museum in Cambridge. Clarke goes on to explain how he had to bribe the local Turkish official with a telescope to let him take the statue, and how the locals were reluctant to help move it, out of superstitious fear. In fact, they worshipped it after all this time as St Dimitrios, a corruption of the name of Demeter of Eleusis.

There were a number of mystery cults in ancient Greece. They were often agrarian in origin, celebrating life over death by means of sexual symbolism or even activities. One had to be initiated into them, indicating a fresh start, a new life. Whatever happened in the ceremonies was accompanied by or re-enacted a myth, which often told a tale of the overcoming of terror, itself a kind of rebirth. The initiate was invariably promised a special place in the afterlife as a result of his initiation – one of the few occasions in Athenian religion when people showed an interest in an afterlife, rather than in getting on in this life.

Speaking of the mysteries was forbidden; the root of the word 'mystery' means 'secret'. When Alkibiades was suspected of, among other things, imitating the mysteries with some friends at a drunken party he fled into exile; he was condemned *in absentia*, his property was confiscated, and he was cursed by the priests and priestesses of the state. When Pausanias, the travel-writer of the second century CE, was poised to describe just the buildings, a dream warned him not to. In Alkibiades' case, the state had to intervene, but often the goddess herself punished transgressors: a man once wandered into the sacred area which only the hierophant – the high priest, a hereditary post in an aristocratic Athenian family – was allowed to enter, and shortly afterwards he died of a strange disease. Someone else who climbed a rock to try to see inside fell off and was killed.

Some cults were exclusive, but at Eleusis initiation was open not just to any Athenian citizen, but even to slaves (at least, those who worked in the sanctuary), women and foreigners, provided they could understand the Greek in which all the announcements and rituals were conducted, and provided they were not tainted by any religious pollution. The site was in continuous use for many hundreds of years, and in that time tens of thousands were initiated, but the secret largely remained intact. But by mining hostile Christian writers, the legend of Demeter and Persephone and certain other references, we can reconstruct at least some of what went on.

Initiatory purification took place in the spring in Athens, in a rite known as the Lesser Mysteries. Several months later the Greater Mysteries took place. On 13 Boedromion young men went to Eleusis and the following day they escorted the priestesses back to the city. The priestesses carried the crucial sacred objects hidden inside a special box or basket, and they paused from their journey just outside Athens, at a place called the Sacred Fig Tree. Here they were met by representatives of the state and escorted inside the city walls to the Eleusinion in the agora, where the sacred objects were deposited. After five days of preliminary activities – registration, sacrifices, purificatory rituals, feasting and fasting – on the 19th the initiates processed to Eleusis.

The processional route followed the Sacred Way. A wooden statue of Iakkhos, a boy god usually identified with Dionysos, led the procession; the carrier of this sacred image was followed by the priests and priestesses of Demeter, who looked after the holy baskets with their mysterious contents, then the city officials and representatives of other cities, then the initiates themselves. As they processed, they danced and sang hymns, and swung bundles of branches in time with the rhythm of their chanting. Aristophanes has preserved something like one of the hymns in his play *Frogs* (340–52):

> Wake, for you come wielding the blazing torch,
> Iakkhos, O Iakkhos, daystar of our nightlong rite,
> And the meadow is lit up by fire.
> Moved by the act of worship, the legs
> Of the aged quiver in dance; they shake off
> Their cares and the long years of old age.
> Blessed one, lead with the light of your torch
> The dancing youths to the flowery meadow lands.

The procession passed the temple of Apollo, on the site of what is now the monastery of Daphni, and carried on past the shrine of Aphrodite. Close to here they had a chance to rest, while yellow ribbons were tied on their right hands and left legs by the local inhabitants. When they came to the bridges on the border of

Eleusis, masked or veiled figures made obscene fun of the passing initiates, to humble them so that they would not attract the jealous attention of the gods. After reaching Eleusis, when darkness fell they broke their fast, and turned to singing and dancing around the Kallikhoros Well – the Well of Fair Dancing.

Much of the following day was spent resting and fasting (in honour of Demeter's fast, when she was mourning the abduction of her daughter by Hades) and sacrificing. The main ceremony started that night. The fast was broken by drinking the *kykeōn*, the special potion of the mysteries, made from barley-meal and mint mixed in water. Following the main sacrifice to the goddesses, the initiates made their way through the temple of Hades to an enormous hall with a capacity of about 2,000, and witnessed the priest's revelation of the sacred objects, and a pageant representing Demeter's trials. This year's spring crop of initiates could see only certain objects, but the Watchers – those for whom this was a repeat visit – were shown others as well, while the newcomers veiled their heads. Whatever it was that was shown was supposed to inspire dread, and to simulate death and the underworld, until the assurance of blessing was introduced when the doors were flung open by the Torch-bearer, a priest second only to the hierophant, and firelight flooded in. Kore had returned from the underworld; new life began again. The hierophant announced: 'The Mistress has given birth to a holy boy, Brimo the Brimos.' And in total silence he displayed an ear of corn.

Dancing and the sacrifice of bulls followed. Then two large vessels were filled with water and each person poured a libation, one towards the east and one towards the west, while looking up at the sky and shouting 'Rain!', and down at the earth with the cry of 'Conceive!' Further sacrifices were performed the following day, along with libations and rites for the dead, and then people straggled home on their own, rather than in a formal procession.

11

Drama

The most important of the Athenian religious festivals included two in honour of Dionysos which involved dramatic and choral performances. We are so familiar with acting and actors, on the stage, on TV and in the cinema, that it is easy to forget how extraordinary it must have seemed to an ancient Greek, who was not daily bombarded with moving images. Here, right before his very eyes, the gods and heroes of ancient times were brought magically to life. Drama was an Athenian invention with profound cultural consequences for the Western world, but its original context in Athens was utterly different from that of similar modern forms of entertainment.

There were two main dramatic festivals in Athens, the City Dionysia (late in February in our calendar) and the Lenaia ('Winepress') in the autumn, at the time of the grape harvest. Quite a bit went on apart from the plays – sacrifices, public feasts, religious processions, dithyrambic choruses (choruses singing short, florid, narrative poems), and so on – but the plays formed the heart of the festivals. At its fullest, the City Dionysia went on for five days, with three tragedies (sometimes forming a more or less tight trilogy) and a satyr-play on each of three days, and five comedies the following day. Counting the choral performances, over 1,200 Athenian citizens were involved per year in the two festivals: an astonishingly high number of people were trained to a standard capable of enduring public scrutiny, and overall the festivals represent an amazing level of artistic output and commitment to cultural values.

The stories of satyr-plays were based on Greek myths, with the author free to take as many liberties as he wanted with the story, in order above all to accommodate a chorus of satyrs – in myth, lusty followers of Dionysos, the god of revels. The only genuine satyr-play to survive in full is Euripides' *Cyclops* (408 BCE), the starting point of which is the violent, Homeric story of Odysseus' contact with the monstrous Polyphemos on his way back home from the Trojan War. The original story had nothing to do with satyrs, so Euripides added another, that Silenos, a traditional follower of Dionysos, had been captured and enslaved, along with his band of satyrs, by Polyphemos. The whole story of Odysseus' encounter with and escape from Polyphemos, even the blinding, is treated very light-heartedly and crudely. Odysseus is a braggart, Silenos an alcoholic, Polyphemos a confused bully; typical comic scenes include one where Odysseus is trying to get volunteers from the satyrs to help him blind the giant, and all the satyrs suddenly find excuses: one has sprained an ankle, another has dust in his eyes, and so on.

Comedy of the fifth and early fourth centuries (we have complete plays only from the great Aristophanes, of whose forty plays eleven remain) added wild fantasy and irreverent satire to the knockabout, crude humour of satyr-plays. The most striking aspect of these early comedies is their freedom. The comic playwrights did not have to take their plots from history or legend: they made up their own stories and set them in contemporary times. There was also freedom of expression, unhampered by libel laws or censorship. The characters of the comedies were often well-known figures, either thinly disguised or not at all, and they were held up for all kinds of ridicule and slander. The humour was often obscene or lavatorial. As in satyr-plays, the actors wore costumes with outsize leather phalluses attached, which could be waved about or manipulated at appropriate points in the plays.

The best dramatists of the Greek world were native Athenians, and Athens was widely regarded as the home of drama. The three great Athenian tragedians a little of whose work survives are Aiskhylos, Sophokles and Euripides, all of whom worked in the fifth century. These three Athenians were not the only ones: there were others from Athens (such as Agathon, whose first victory is the occasion for Plato's *Symposium*), and there were those born elsewhere who came to Athens to work. But we have at best only fragments of the work of these playwrights.

The word 'tragedy' preserves the religious context in which these plays were put on. The Greek word originally meant 'goat-song', and referred to the sacrifice of a goat at the start of the festival. We do not think of going to the cinema as a religious experience, but the ancient Greeks went to the theatre to celebrate Dionysos. Dionysos was not just the god of wine, but of release of emotion in general, whether dancing or 'the lightning-bolt of wine' (as the poet Arkhilokhos of Paros put it in Fragment 120) or plays were the means of release. Seeing a comedy or a satyr-play is obviously an opportunity for laughter and letting go, but tragedy was expected to perform a similar function. In his *Poetics* Aristotle spoke of tragedy purifying or purging the spectator. In various ways, all three forms of drama held a mirror up to Athenian society, or more broadly to Greek society, without dictating the results of that inspection.

The theatre was not the province of just the elite: the Theatre of Dionysos in Athens held up to 15,000 spectators. People from all strata of society came, and foreign visitors too, if they happened to be in the city at the time. No women or slaves were allowed, except perhaps a few selected priestesses. People came to enjoy themselves. We can imagine the boos and hisses and claps and laughter accompanying a comedy, but they were not less involved in the tragedies. Once a play by the often radical Euripides was interrupted by the audience, who wanted the playwright to explain why he had put a particularly amoral sentiment in the mouth of one of his characters. The story continues that Euripides told the spectators to wait and see what happened to that particular character.

As if it were not already strange enough that Athenian drama was the core of a religious festival, a Greek playwright put on his play not just to please and instruct, but also to try to win a competition. Each tragic author was competing against the other two, and likewise for the comic playwrights. The first prize in the dramatic contest was simply considerable prestige, for the producer as well as for the playwright. But the really strange thing about the play's being part of a competition is this: when a modern playwright gets a production staged, he hopes it will last as long as Agatha Christie's *Mousetrap*, but when an ancient playwright wrote a play, as far as he knew it was going to be put on once and once only. It so happened that repeat performances of the canonical three tragedians were licensed from 385, twenty years after the deaths of Sophokles and Euripides (and from 341 this became the regular practice), but they did not know that at the time. All the work of composition and preparation led to the giving of a gift to the god.

In essence, the theatre consisted of a large circular area, the *orkhēstra* or 'place for dancing', in the open air at the bottom of a natural slope, where the audience sat. In the fifth century, only the prestigious bottom few rows of the Theatre of Dionysos in Athens were made into stone or wooden seats, while the rest was banked turf and rocks. At the back of the *orkhēstra* was the *skēnē* (literally a 'tent' for the actors to prepare in), which came to be decorated and formed a kind of backdrop: hence our word 'scene'. Scene-painting was rarely elaborate: it usually depicted the façade of a grand building, which could serve as either a temple or a palace. There would be an altar on the ground in front of the façade, and maybe one or two other props, as required. There was a low stage between the *skēnē* and the *orkhēstra*, a central door in the *skēnē* for entrances and exits into the building, and an entrance at either side of the acting area. Early in the play, often in the opening speech, the audience (lacking programme notes) would be told what the scene was and where each of the exits led to, and would have the background to the action and the main characters identified. The roof of the *skēnē* could be used for the appearance of gods, or they could be raised or lowered on a kind of crane, known as a *mēkhanē*. Euripides was so fond of resolving his plots by having a deity fly in on the crane that a proverbial saying arose for help from unexpected quarters; its Latin form is still used in English – a *deus ex machina*.

The most striking aspect of a Greek theatre is its sheer size, and this introduces a third alien feature of Greek drama. The *orkhēstra* alone could be 15 metres in diameter, which means that the *nearest* spectators, in the privileged front-row seats, were already a long way from the stage, where all the action, apart from the choral singing and dancing, took place. If you were in one of the back rows, maybe 50 metres from the stage, the actors would have appeared only a few centimetres high, so that much of what we think of as acting was simply irrelevant. There was no point in raising an eyebrow to express astonishment, because no one in the audience would have seen it. In any case, actors wore masks, which were instantly recognizable to the audience as the King, the Beggar,

the Priestess, the Soldier, or whatever; the masks also had mouthpieces shaped to work as small megaphones, though the acoustics
of ancient Greek theatres were generally excellent. If an actor
wanted to express astonishment, he raised his voice in surprise,
shouted out an oath to the gods, made huge arm gestures and ran
across the stage. Actors – who were all male – were trained as
athletes. Very often words alone, or in company with appropriate
gestures, conveyed the message. One character might say to
another, 'Why are you weeping?', as a way of telling the audience
that this person was weeping.

Athenian drama and Athenian painting developed together. It
was not just that they drew on common legends; we can get a good
idea of the gestures and postures actors used to express emotions
and to represent character from the paintings on vases. From a
more formal point of view, the use of perspective in painting is
said to have been used first in scene-decoration for Aiskhylos'
dramas. The spin-off from this for vase-painting (the only kind of
ancient Greek painting that survives in any quantity) was that artists
began to depict figures higher or lower than one another, on rising
ground. The audience at a tragedy would have been quick to
transfer a sense of perspective from the vases they saw to the stage,
so that if an aged attendant took several minutes to make an
entrance and reach the other characters on the stage – no doubt
muttering darkly all the time about the miseries of old age – they
would understand that there was greater distance involved than the
dramatist could readily portray. And if a whole battle was supposed
to have taken place in the few minutes it took the chorus to sing an
ode, that too was an easy leap to make in the imagination.

Apart from the actors, there was the chorus of twelve or fifteen,
who were often visible in the *orkhēstra* throughout the play. The
chorus-leader had a speaking part, and partook minimally in the
action of the play, but the chorus's main role was to fill in the time
between episodes with singing and dancing. The themes of their
songs were, for instance, mythological precedents for what was
happening in the play, perhaps along the lines of 'I've heard of
the suffering of X, Y and Z, but what we are seeing here today
beats them all.' Or they might express sympathy with one of the
characters and call down curses on others, or chant homilies.

By the end of the fifth century, however, choral interludes were becoming standardized, making them much more an opportunity for the audience to get up and stretch their legs, and for the actors to change costumes, than anything intrinsic to the play. Changing costume did not take much time, though, because for much of the fifth century all actors wore long robes, with only the mask and headgear differentiating them. Euripides introduced the innovation of more appropriate costumes. It was all quite stylized – but then it was part of a religious festival, and Athenian religion was largely performative and ritualistic. A degree of characterization was possible, however, and all the playwrights took advantage of this possibility.

In the sixth century, Thespis was the first to introduce an actor to speak narrative lines and interact with the chorus, whereas previously the festival (if there was anything organized enough to deserve the name before about 500) had consisted only of choral dances in honour of Dionysos. Then soon after the beginning of the fifth century, Aiskhylos introduced a second actor. Although this created the possibility of interaction between the two actors, at first they simply took it in turns to interact with the chorus. Sophokles introduced a third actor, and from then on greater freedom was possible, and the role of the chorus became subordinate to the actors, rather than the other way round. Euripides occasionally had as many as thirty people on stage, but even so there were still at the most only three speaking parts at any one time.

A Greek play consisted of episodes interspersed by choral interludes – speech and song in turns. The episodes were often formal: there had to be a messenger speech, telling the audience what happened off stage, sometimes with a comic tinge; there was invariably a debate between two of the main characters, outlining the rights and wrongs that motivated the action. There were whole episodes of one- or two-line rapid interchanges between two actors. What makes a Greek tragedy, though, is not just the structure, but also its effect. The effect was supposed to be one of emotional release. This is easiest to achieve through the portrayal of suffering, but not all Greek tragedies have *Hamlet*-type endings in which everybody suffers and dies. There are quite a few happy endings, as in Euripides' light-hearted *Helen*. Emotional release was commonly achieved by a reversal of fortune, and by the main character's recognition of where he had gone wrong, or realization that he was subject to divine bad luck. There should be a conflict – of some god against a human being, or between two or more humans. The main character must take a stand on some issue, so that his downfall does not come out of the blue. His or others' actions must be seen to have consequences, furthering the plot but also hastening their doom. The characters invariably display for us human frailty, and that is their only flaw. And since we are all human, that is how their downfall affects us.

The Theatre and Athenian Democracy

Clearly, fifth-century comic playwrights were politically engaged. They were exploiting the very nature of Athenian democracy, the freedom it gave any of its citizens to speak out on political issues. Some of their political jokes were cheap shots, but they also sometimes had a serious point to communicate. When a comic playwright had a character directly address the audience, he invariably used the politicized term 'the people of Athens', and he showed the assembled people their leaders and their policies on the egalitarian grounds that they were as competent to judge them as anyone else.

The theatre was the ideal place for a comic poet to communicate his points, but also for tragedians to air issues of concern to the Athenian democracy. The Theatre of Dionysos, with room for 15,000 people, held the largest mass audience available, since the Pnyx, where the Assembly convened, accommodated only 6,000 at the most, until its capacity was increased early in the fourth century. The audience was, for the period of the festival, the assembled people. In the theatre, citizens were seated in blocks according to their tribe. From the start of the fourth century poor people were given an allowance by the state so that they could attend, and throughout the history of the festival rich people were required to finance the production of plays. If you were a member of a chorus of a play, you were exempt from military service. Only Athenian citizens could be actors, on the grounds that it was one of their civic duties. The right of sitting in the front rows was bestowed by the democracy on those it especially favoured.

The arkhons and generals, the leading figures of the democracy, performed public rites to open the festival. There was a public proclamation of the names of those citizens who, in the course of the preceding year, had in some way benefited the city. Then, for most of the fifth century, there was a display of the tribute given to Athens by her 'allies', and a parade of young men whose fathers had died fighting for Athens. The city was centre stage right from the start. It was presumably awareness of this which perpetuated the custom that women were not allowed to be members of the theatre audience: they were not full citizens, and so they were not there.

The Athenian people assembled in the theatre felt themselves to be more than a passive audience: they were the hosts of the plays, but also the judges, since the official judges were chosen by lot from all the citizen tribes and were influenced by the audience's cheers and jeers. If the Assembly was where overtly political issues were discussed, and the law courts were where Athenian justice was delivered, the theatre was where social customs were subjected to scrutiny. In his play *Frogs* (405 BCE) Aristophanes several times asserted his right – in fact, the right of all poets – to act as the city's adviser.

So political and moral themes relevant to Athenian society were openly explored on stage. It was not the playwright's task to reach any kind of solution, but only to hold a mirror up to society. For instance, in 415, Athens used its might as an imperial power to crush the island of Melos; in the same year Euripides put on his *Trojan Women*, which depicts the suffering of women whose menfolk have been killed by Greeks and whose future holds only the misery of slavery, as was the case for the Melian women. More subtly, although none of the plays raised only one question, they brought to the audience's attention large social issues such as justice, duty and self-restraint. War was an all-too-frequent fact of life and death to a fifth-century Athenian, and war or some other extreme threat loomed large in most tragedies; litigation was one of the mainstays of the democracy, and so the scenes in which moral and political issues were openly debated were of relevance and intense interest.

If the tragedies were shown within a politicized context, this does not mean that we can necessarily find references to particular events, or read characters as particular Athenian politicians. But it does mean that the playwrights were reflecting contemporary concerns, and not infrequently challenging the Athenian people to consider the consequences of their actions. Characters in plays often represented types familiar in Athens (the unscrupulous politician, the democratic leader) and the events shown too often have a contemporary resonance (Athens as welcoming to strangers in trouble, the horrors of war, the difficulties of decision-making, imperialist ideology).

In this context, if all the tragedians included seemingly sycophantic references to democratic Athens, this served only to drive home the point that, for all their legendary settings, the plays had contemporary relevance. It is one of the peculiarities of Athenian democracy that no tracts were written in its defence: it was up to the orators and playwrights to educate their audience in the ideology of democracy. Attendance at the dramatic festivals was part of one's education as a citizen. It served much the same function as attendance at a law court or the Assembly, where speeches articulated just what it was to be a good or bad Athenian citizen.

12

Education: The Sophists and Sokrates

Formal education was woefully inadequate in Classical Athens, but there were many ways, including attending the dramatic festivals, for a child to become expert in the inherited conglomerate – the customs and practices passed down and found acceptable by generation after generation of Athenians.

Up until the age of six or seven, all children were raised at home by their mother and slaves – especially, if the household had one, by a slave called a *paidagōgos* (literally, a 'child-leader'), whose job it was to mind the young master's manners and moral education at home, and to look after him when he was out of the home. The attendant was often a trusted member of the household, but slaves were generally expected to do work that was more demanding physically, and so Perikles once said, on seeing a slave fall out of a tree and break his leg, 'Ah, now he's a *paidagōgos.*'

During this period the child's education consisted largely of stories – exactly the same Greek myths and legends with which we are still familiar today. Many children remained at home for longer, either because their parents could not afford to send them to school or because they were girls, who scarcely needed educating. 'Suppose,' imagines Sokrates in Xenophon's *Memoirs of Socrates* (1.5.2), 'we have reached the end of life and want to entrust someone with the education of our sons or the guardianship of our unmarried daughters?' Sons were to be educated, daughters protected until they were passed into someone else's care. Nevertheless, some girls were taught to read and write, and those boys who were destined for their father's trade learnt the rudiments of arithmetic at home.

By the end of the fifth century, literacy in Athens had spread down to the artisan level, though it was a very different story outside the city, in the small farms of Attica. But by and large Classical Athenian society functioned perfectly well without mass literacy. The uses to which writing was put to secure a greater degree of permanence than the spoken word – from letter-writing to legal documents such as wills and records of commercial transactions, from the writing of literature to civic and political lists, from recording maritime loans to emphasizing magical curses – were usually things with which the masses were largely uninvolved. New laws and other civic information were posted in the agora, but there would always have been someone around who could read them out to those who were illiterate, or educated slaves who could write a letter for them. Even at the higher levels of society and its work, ancient Athens was largely an oral culture: the literate tended to dictate letters rather than write them themselves, and to listen to a slave reading rather than read themselves.

Schooling began in Athens around the beginning of the fifth century, but schoolteachers remained few, underpaid and underrated in the Classical period. Even in the fourth century Demosthenes taunted his rival Aiskhines with being the son of a mere schoolmaster. Only in Hellenistic times did their status improve, as private individuals left bequests to maintain schools; even girls began to go to school. In the Classical period, boys who were lucky enough to gain an education attended three kinds of school, each of which took in a dozen or so pupils. A *grammatistēs* taught them to read and write and do their sums, and made them study and even learn substantial amounts of the Homeric poems. A *kitharistēs* taught them to play either the lyre or the pipes, and with him they studied and learnt the lyric poets. A *paidotribēs* supervised their physical education in a gymnasium or a palaistra (wrestling-ground). And that was it – with a marked lack of concern for critical, experimental or creative thinking.

A typical day involved attendance at the palaistra early in the morning; home for the late-morning meal; and then attendance at one of the other schools in the early afternoon. The strong emphasis on physical training reflected not just the fact that there was no standing army in ancient Athens, so that every citizen was potentially a soldier, but also the Greek love of competition in general. Schooling continued until the early teens, when the sons of poorer families went to work, while those from richer families continued to enjoy considerable leisure until they reached military age.

Students wrote on wax tablets with a *stylos*, which was sharpened at one end for making marks in the wax, and blunt at the other for smoothing the wax over mistakes. Athenian schoolteachers and parents did not believe in sparing the rod (or rather the sandal, which seems to have been the preferred instrument): beatings were the standard punishment for any infringements. The state did not intervene if you chose not to send your son to school. The lax attitude towards education reflects two principles: that children were not highly regarded in their own right, but were seen as adults in waiting, and that the Athenians had supreme confidence in the ability of the inherited conglomerate to condition their children into traditional Athenian mores.

The Sophists

By and large, an Athenian boy's education equipped him to take his place in traditional Athenian society, but it did not expand his horizons, and it was all over by the time he was thirteen or fourteen. However, Athenian society changed rapidly in the first half of the fifth century, and this kind of parochial education was no longer sufficient for everyone. Individual careers and the destiny of the city could hinge upon a carefully crafted speech; greater sophistication was needed to take charge of an empire, with all its financial, logistical and military responsibilities. At the same time, the lottery system of selection for administrative posts precluded the establishment of a professional Civil Service. Athens was a city of amateurs in a sphere where developed intellects and professionalism were sorely needed. This is where the Sophists came in. They were itinerant teachers, from all over the Greek world, who were attracted to Athens because of its wealth.

The Sophists offered to teach a vast range of subjects, from music and martial arts to government, with the emphasis on skills useful for government and manipulating the democratic system. Often, then, they were teachers of rhetoric and argument. Whatever subject they were teaching, they were perpetuating a competitive lifestyle, because they taught 'excellence', in its literal sense of surpassing others. This rudimentary higher education was designed only for the rich, since the Sophists tended to charge exorbitant fees, but it was a step in the right direction, and they also gave displays of their learning or speechifying to wider audiences. Plato and Aristotle made 'Sophist' a term of reproach, on the grounds that their arguments were often invalid (Aristotle) and that they were concerned only with winning arguments rather than improving people (Plato). But originally the word had more or less the same implications as our 'expert': Sophists were clever men who were prepared, for a fee, to impart their skills to others.

The Sophists were a new phenomenon, but they stood on older foundations. There was a tradition of speculative, proto-scientific thought about the origin and constitution of the universe and all that it contained, stretching back to the end of the seventh century, and based chiefly in the Greek cities of Ionia, Sicily and southern Italy. Even crude scientific work, undertaken long before the days of sophisticated measuring devices and experimentation, relies on the assumption that the human mind not only is capable of understanding the universe, but is in fact the correct tool to achieve such understanding. Although the views and theories of the Sophists were considerably different in orientation from those of their scientific predecessors and contemporaries, they continued the tradition by focusing on human potential. The first and greatest of the Sophists was Protagoras of Abdera (*floruit c.* 440), and his saying that 'Man is the measure of all things' – that experience is comprehensible to anyone, just by virtue of the fact that he is a human being – can be taken as a motto not just of the Sophistic movement, but of fifth-century optimism as a whole.

The mood of optimism in fifth-century Athens stemmed from the Athenians' almost miraculous defeat of the Persians, combined with significant advances in technology. There was a feeling that human beings could tame nature and conquer everything – except death, Sophokles added in a famous ode (*Antigone* 332–75). There was intense interest in argument for argument's sake; all kinds of learning were in the air, and even the common people loved to hear tales of far-flung places and different customs that put their own into perspective. Geography, history, rhetoric (with its attendant psychology), science, philosophy (in several branches) and medicine began to be developed, and Athens was one of the first places to employ a publicly funded doctor as a more scientific alternative to traditional folk medicine. It is hardly an exaggeration to say that almost all the great, perennial questions were raised by thinkers (whether historians, philosophers or playwrights) who were either native Athenians or were at least temporarily resident in Athens during the fifth and fourth centuries BCE.

A good illustration of the rationalistic spirit of the times is the difference between the two great historians of the fifth century, Herodotos and the somewhat later Thucydides. In Herodotos major events are divinely inspired: Kroisos is bound to fall (and so the Greek cities of the Ionian coastline are destined to come under Persian domination) because of a sin committed by a family member some generations earlier; Xerxes' decision to invade Greece is at least abetted by a god-sent dream; and so on. But the gods play hardly any part in Thucydides' account of events; the constant for him is human nature. Because people are greedy, the Athenians built an empire; because power is frightening, the Spartans felt that they had to go to war against the Athenians.

In his play *Clouds*, produced in 423, Aristophanes parodied the new learning and teaching. The protagonist of the play was Sokrates, because he was a native Athenian and a well-known figure, but the Sokrates of the play is simply a mouthpiece for a wild assortment of pseudo-scientific doctrines and Sophistic ideas. The play is extremely funny, but on its first showing it would have stirred the Athenian audience into a somewhat nervous form of laughter. There was considerable fear of the Sophists and what they came to represent: they were *deinoi*, a word which simultaneously meant 'clever' and 'formidable'.

Why were the Sophists so disturbing? Reflection on Protagoras' teaching supplies the answer. He set his pupils exercises designed to help them to argue either side of a case. He explicitly developed this teaching into a kind of relativism, whereby there is no absolute right or wrong, but only what seems to an individual or to a state to be right or wrong. 'Man is the measure' precisely because there are no absolute values. This triggered a debate which flourished throughout the latter half of the fifth century and centred on the terms 'nature' and 'convention': were moral values, for instance, merely conventional, or were they somehow dictated by nature?

Ultimately, Antiphon (the first native Athenian Sophist, towards the end of the fifth century) argued that one should obey the natural law of self-preservation, with pleasure as its marker, and obey man-made laws only when doing so contributed to one's self-preservation in the sense that one avoided punishment. Most man-made laws, he argued, are hostile to nature (which is to say that they do us harm) and stem from a concept of justice which fails in practice.

Sokrates and the Religious Crisis

Sokrates (469–399) committed none of his philosophy to writing, with the result that most of what we know of his thought is refracted, albeit in very different ways, through two of his pupils, Plato (427–347) and Xenophon (c. 430–c. 354). Neither of these two writers, however, wrote down faithful records of Sokratic conversations. This means that the historical Sokrates fades into the background, and instead we get what Sokrates might have said had he been addressing the largely practical interests of Xenophon or the more abstract philosophical concerns of Plato. Nevertheless, even modern philosophers look back to Sokrates (or, more strictly, the character who goes by that name in Plato's dialogues), because he made philosophy reflective, which is still its style. Instead of saying, for instance, that self-restraint is good, he asked what self-restraint was, and what goodness was. He introduced a method of questioning in place of the dogmatism of his predecessors, and he redefined excellence in what he counted as properly moral terms rather than by Homeric standards of heroic prowess.

The one thing everyone knows about Sokrates, perhaps especially because of his parallels with Jesus, is that he was put to death (by drinking hemlock). Both were undeniably good and sincere men, both were put to death by their communities, and both – or at least the mythic versions of them that grew after their deaths – have radically changed the Western world. Sokrates was executed by the Athenians in 399 on the charges of irreligion (specifically, not worshipping the gods of the city, and introducing new gods) and corrupting the young men of the city. Whether or not he was actually guilty of these crimes – and we should not forget that he was found guilty according to the due process of Athenian law – there were certainly a couple of subtexts to the trial, which compounded his chances of being condemned.

First of all, as Plato brings out brilliantly in his version of Sokrates' defence speech (usually called the *Apology*), Sokrates had become tarred with the brush of the new learning. Aristophanes' caricature in *Clouds* was at least partly to blame for this. Even granted that, given the performative nature of Athenian religion, religious heterodoxy was a difficult concept and the crime of impiety was notoriously vague, the taint of irreligion had become associated with both the Sophists and the scientists. In the far background was the bard Xenophanes of Kolophon (*c.* 570–*c.* 480), who was no friend of Greek anthropomorphism (Fragments 5 and 6):

> If cows and horses or lions had hands,
> Or could draw with their hands and make things as men can,
> Horses would have drawn horse-like gods, cows cow-like gods,
> And each species would have made the gods' bodies just like
> 　their own.
>
> Ethiopians say that their gods are flat-nosed and black,
> And Thracians that theirs have blue eyes and red hair.

Then Anaxagoras of Klazomenai, for instance, who was a friend of Perikles, claimed that the sun was a lump of burning rock, about the size of the Peloponnese. But the sun was traditionally a god, Helios, riding across the sky in his blazing chariot. In a sense, the whole enterprise of these first scientists was anti-religious: in place of the radically insecure universe with a plethora of whimsical gods, they presented, in their dogmatic fashion (the equivalent to the monumental inflexibility of much of the Archaic art with which they were contemporary), a universe that was comprehensible, because its nature was explicable by reference to only a few causes. They gave reductionist explanations of precisely those awesome meteorological and celestial phenomena which had underpinned Greek religion.

Among the Sophists, Protagoras took a moderate agnostic stance, claiming only that it was impossible to know whether or not the gods existed, and adding: 'There are many impediments to such knowledge, including the obscurity of the matter and the shortness of human life' (Fragment 4). Others went further. Prodikos of Keos denied the existence of the gods on the grounds that they were just deifications of things like the sun and cereal crops, which are essential for life. Kritias – the principal leader of the savage Thirty Tyrants of Athens in 404–3 – wrote a play in which one of the characters claimed that the gods were invented by some clever fellow in the past as a means of curbing even secret crimes by fostering the idea that even if one escaped punishment by men, one could not escape punishment by the gods. Euripides was so fond of putting radical statements into the mouths of his characters that Aristophanes has a seller of wreaths (which were used on festive, religious occasions) complain that thanks to the playwright her trade has halved (*Women at the Thesmophoria* 450–2). In the face of all this, a certain Diopeithes had a law passed in 435 'that anyone who did not pay due respect to supernatural phenomena or who offered to teach people about celestial phenomena should be impeached' (Plutarch, *Pericles* 32). The traditional moral code was under attack, and Diopeithes' decree represents just one aspect of the conservative backlash.

In the second place, Sokrates had some unfortunate friends. Although he himself was of hoplite status rather than one of the wealthier members of Athenian society, his circle consisted largely of the sons of aristocratic families. And several of them fell foul of the democracy. He was friends with Kritias and Kharmides, both of whom were heavily involved in the oligarchy of 404–3; he was particularly close to Alkibiades, who had a dramatic and turbulent relationship with the democracy; a number of his associates were implicated in the scandalous mutilation of the herms in 415 (see pp. 224–5). In short, he consorted with precisely those elements of Athenian society who were or were suspected of being pro-Spartan oligarchs. 'Everyone was mad about Sparta in those days,' said Aristophanes in 414 (*Birds* 1281–2). 'They grew their hair long, starved themselves, never washed, Sokratized.' And so it is far from insignificant that one of the three men who chose to take Sokrates to court was a prominent democrat.

The broad context of the trial was that Sokrates was an individual and he taught his followers to think for themselves, rather than taking anything for granted. As it happens, Sokrates invariably found that, after examination, his views coincided with those of normal Athenian morality, but some of his followers brought him into disrepute by using his questioning method to challenge Athenian customs and standards. In Athens private interests were always expected to be secondary to public concerns, and in religious matters especially, individualism was suspect, since state religion subordinated the practices of individuals to its own requirements. The item in the accusation which charged Sokrates with introducing new gods was a sly reference to the fact that he claimed to have a direct link with the divine, in the form of a little voice which sometimes warned him against certain actions. Individuals were not supposed to have a hotline to the gods, and if there were new gods to be introduced (as there were at the end of the fifth century) the state had to be involved.

Traditional societies, in which religion permeates civic life, are notoriously paranoid about failure to conform. Whatever else Sokrates may or may not have been, he was not a conformist. The corollary of the traditional belief that a pious society will prosper is that a state with a significant number of impious individuals might not prosper. Athens had just lost a disastrous war; Sokrates was a scapegoat. His trial was a response not just to his specific friendships with Kritias and Alkibiades, but to the traumas of recent Athenian history. Sokrates was felt to personify the moral rot that had undermined the foundations of Athens and her way of life.

13

Indoor Life: Sex, Symposia and Sandals

The Symposium

Sokrates clearly felt perfectly at home in the company of his aristocratic friends and followers, and so, for instance, both Plato and Xenophon have left us portraits of him at a symposium, one of the more arcane aristocratic rituals, a hangover from the glory days of the Athenian aristocracy, when these evening meetings had formed the pulse of the city's social and political life. The word *sumposion* literally means 'drinking together', but it is best left transliterated rather than translated, because 'drinks party' has misleading connotations. Like many aspects of Athenian life, the symposium incorporated elements of ritual and religion.

On the arrival of the guests, slaves washed their feet: streets were rarely paved, except for some that were on a slope and would otherwise be washed away in heavy rain. The guests – normally about a dozen – reclined, in the fashion borrowed by Greeks from the Near East, on couches set up around the walls of the main room of the men's quarters of the house. Their left arms rested on cushions and supported the upper half of their bodies, so that their right hands were free for eating and drinking from the small table that was set in front of them. After a light meal, the tables were removed, and the room was cleared and swept. The diners wiped their hands on pieces of bread and tossed them to the dogs, then ritually washed their hands and dabbed a bit of perfume, perhaps of rose or orris-root, on their bodies.

A symposiarch was appointed, known as the 'king', to regulate the evening and decide on the proportions of wine and water to be mixed in the great mixing-bowl. The Greeks usually drank their wine diluted with water, in the ratio of about five parts of water to two of wine, as they thought that over-indulgence in neat wine induced madness. Drinking-cups were shallow, better for sipping than gulping, to curb drunkenness and encourage conversation between sips. Three mixing-bowls of wine were normal for a moderate symposium: 'One for health, the second for love and pleasure, the third for sleep', as the comic poet Euboulos had Dionysos pronounce in one of his plays (Fragment 93). If it went further: 'The fourth belongs to bad behaviour, the fifth to shouting, the sixth to revel, the seventh to black eyes, the eighth to indict-ments, the ninth to nausea, and the tenth to madness and hurling things around.' Xenophanes' more prosaic rule of thumb was: 'It is not excessive to drink as much as allows a man who is not too old to make his way home without the help of a slave' (Fragment 1.17–18). But drunken symposia were at least as common as the more sober variety, and this too was ritualized: drunken guests might spill out on the street in a *kōmos*, a revel, in which the boisterous party careened through the city, still dressed as sympo-siasts and still singing, in search of another house where they could prolong the evening.

The symposium began with purificatory rituals, the donning of garlands, and libations and hymns to the gods. The guests settled down to make conversation, sing songs (either lyric poetry or popular songs such as the one quoted on p. 67), play games (such as *kottabos*, the flicking of drops of liquid and sediment from the bottom of a cup at a bowl or some other target) and be entertained. The entertainment consisted either of a show put on by hired dancing-girls, acrobats or mimes, or of competitive singing by the guests, to the accompaniment of a girl playing the pipes. A myrtle wreath circulated, and any guest who wore it was obliged to sing something. Apart from these slave-girls, it was a strictly male affair.

Visitors to museums housing ancient Greek pots have often wondered why the Greeks depicted sexual scenes on their vases and jugs. These pots were used at symposia, and so they displayed scenes typical of symposia -- drinking (symbolized by the god Dionysos or by satyrs), sex (both heterosexual and homosexual), or the kind of mythological or historical story which would have formed the theme of some of the songs. Symposia were orches-trated to include nothing from the humdrum world: guests ate and drank from crockery decorated with symposiast scenes – with ever-

domesticated animals, fish rarely featured. For a sweet, if something richer than figs was required, Athens was famous for its pastries, sweetened with Hymettos honey. Country-dwellers supplemented their diet with wild-growing greens and berries. Rich and poor alike ate pretty much the same foods, but the rich had more than the poor, and made greater use of the wide variety of seasonings that were available. Generally speaking, Athenians of Classical times cooked in a way that let the natural flavours come through. Bread and porridge were usually made from barley; imported wheat was a treat, but one that was more available to Athenians of the Classical period, because of the city's wealth and extensive trading contacts, than it was to other southern Greek cities.

Cereals were the dominant feature of the Athenian diet. Perhaps as much as 75 per cent of the total intake of the poorer classes and not much less even for the wealthy consisted of grain products. Cereals are an adequate source of calories and protein, and they have a couple of important vitamins (B and E). But they are deficient in other vitamins, and plant protein is not as good as animal protein. Even if these deficiencies were remedied by other aspects of the diet, over-reliance on grain leads to iron and calcium deficiency, because the phytate acid of cereals, found especially in the husk and the germ, impedes the body's absorption of these minerals. So the less well sieved or ground the grain, the greater the chance of mineral deficiency, which would be especially detrimental for women, who need more iron and, when pregnant, calcium than men.

Throughout her history, Athens was plagued by periodic poor harvests, which compounded the inherent deficiencies in the diet. A certain degree of malnutrition was widespread, and helps to explain the high incidence of child mortality, and the relatively short stature of ancient Athenians (men averaged about 168 centimetres, women about 155). The average life-expectancy for women was about thirty years, for men only a little more; warfare, complications arising from pregnancy, cholera, diphtheria, typhoid – all took their toll. Most of the men who made it to adulthood faced a hard life of agricultural toil, supported by an inadequate diet. The disease-ridden and impoverished peasants of Attica resembled the heroic figures of Peisistratean and Periklean statuary about as much as the proverbial sheep and goats. Our picture of Classical Athens would be incomplete without knowing that most Athenians, the founders of much that we hold to be great and good, lived lives that we would count as harsh, either as a result of poverty, or simply because they lacked the material resources of modern societies.

Clothing

Clothing was basically different forms of long rectangles of cloth wrapped around the body and pinned at the shoulder and/or belted at the waist (the closest equivalent in modern times is the Indian sari). Although there were different varieties for different purposes (for riding, for instance, or for children's wear) the two most common items of clothing were the *khitōn* and the *himation*. The *khitōn* was light, and was worn in warm weather or as an undergarment. Athenians wore no underwear – and so it was considered rude or flirtatious to sit cross-legged, in case things could be seen which were better left unseen. The *khitōn* was an oblong piece of linen or wool, usually worn at knee-length by men and ankle-length by women. The heavier *himation* was a much larger oblong, about 2.4 by 1.8 metres. Spare folds could be wrapped around the head for warmth or modesty. Instead of a *himation* women sometimes wore a *peplos*, two oblong pieces of cloth, one for the front of the body and one for the back, gathered and fastened at the shoulders. Taken off at night, clothes became bedclothes, though there were also blankets for the winter.

As for footwear, Athenians rarely went barefoot (Sokrates was the exception in this as in so many other conventions), but wore sandals, shoes or boots. Everyday footwear was made from felt or soft leather, but soldiers had tougher boots, reinforced by hobnails. Felt was also used for warm hats and cloaks. Workmen wore hats to protect their heads from the sun, while women put up their hair with ribbons and snoods. Women wore cosmetics (including potentially dangerous forms of white and red lead) and jewellery, while men usually restricted themselves to perfume for ritual purposes. Women got rid of body hair by shaving, plucking or singeing, and pitch was occasionally used as a primitive form of wax. Men were bearded and wore their hair short; women wore their hair long and up; slave-girls had short hair.

The Household

Despite the enormous wealth of some families, Athenian houses tended to be simple. Although there were of course marked differences between the houses of the rich and those of the poor (in the countryside, many peasants lived with their animals in huts), the rich did not cluster in grand mansions in a small number of exclusive neighbourhoods in town, and real extravagance was reserved for public buildings. Within the 4 square kilometres of the Themistoklean wall, there were about 6,000 private houses, and Peiraieus held another 10,000 or so; country-dwellers tended to congregate in villages, as peasant societies always have. Streets ran narrow, unsanitary and higgledy-piggledy through the town: Hippodamos may have laid out the redesigned Peiraieus, but it was too late for Athens. Typically, houses of over one or two rooms in size were built around a central courtyard, which held the domestic altar, and a well or a cistern for collecting rainwater, and was a place for cooking, weaving and sitting in the fresh air. Houses were turned inwards, focused on the courtyard, rather than out towards the street, unless there was a room dedicated as a shop or workshop, which needed public access. Most of the rooms came off the courtyard, which in larger houses might also be surrounded by a portico with a balcony on top for a second floor. An inconspicuous doorway led off the street straight into the courtyard; outward-facing windows were high and small. Floors were hard-packed soil, or occasionally mosaics. In a grand house, the ground floor held storerooms and the men's quarters or dining room, a kitchen and perhaps a bathroom, while the women's quarters were upstairs – reinforcing in a concrete fashion the distance between women and life outside the house.

There was little or no plumbing. The streets or an out-of-the-way corner of one's courtyard were the most common places for relieving oneself; the mess was sluiced away later by a slave. Some babies had pots, and there were chamber pots for adult use at night or at other times. Sponges were used for cleaning yourself. Apart from the rainwater collected in the cistern, drinking water was fetched from the public fountains – there were two in the agora and others elsewhere – rather than from the Eridanos, the only river actually to flow through the town, which was polluted. The other river of Athens, the Ilissos, ran outside the city wall to the south-east.

The ancient Athenians did not clutter up their houses with furniture. Couches were used for both eating and sleeping (except that women ate sitting on chairs rather than reclining on couches). There were wooden or terracotta chests for storing clothes, valuables and other items; kitchen utensils and good pottery hung on the wall; food was stored in various sizes of jar. There might be a couple of chairs and more stools, and there were small, low tables that could be brought into the men's quarters at mealtimes and then removed or tucked under the couches. Cooking was often done in the courtyard rather than a dedicated room, and ovens therefore tended to be portable.

Walls were invariably plain, but rich families might employ an artist to paint a mural. Although foundations and socles were stone, walls were made out of mud-brick covered in plaster (the ancient Greek for burglar was 'wall-tunneller'), so that none of these paintings have survived, but the marvellous paintings from the Tomb of the Diver in Paestum (Greek Poseidonia) in southern Italy, painted around 480 BCE, give us some idea. In a fashion said to have been started by Alkibiades, scenes from famous plays or legends were popular. Poorer people just left the plaster on their walls bare, or at the most painted them in layers of different colours. Wealthy men bought the richly decorated pots beloved of museum showcases around the world. We should picture a scene illuminated by smoky oil lamps, whose light reflects off gleaming, colourful surroundings.

Although they had a strong sense of kinship, and respect and care for one's parents were legally enforced obligations, ancient Athenian men had far less family life than we assume normal, because they spent so much of their time outdoors or in the company of other men. On the birth of a child the front door was wreathed, in olive branches for a boy, or garlands of spun wool for a girl. Five or seven days after birth, in a rite called *amphidromia*, the baby was carried around the domestic hearth and named, to indicate acceptance into the family. Children were identified by their own name and their patronymic ('Nikias the son of Nikeratos'); the first son was often named after the paternal grandfather, the second son after the maternal grandfather, and the first daughter after the paternal grandmother. A male child or adopted son was presented to his phratry at a festival called the Apatouria, whereas a girl's membership in the family was declared only before close relatives at the *amphidromia*, not before any extended pseudo-family such as the phratry. As a final stage of entry into citizenship, young men had to strip and undergo – more or less as a formality – a scrutiny at the age of eighteen (or rather, to see whether they were mature enough to be reckoned as eighteen-year-olds). If their legitimacy was accepted, they were then enrolled in their father's deme, and hence became full Athenian citizens.

Families were generally small, with two or three children at the most, though since infant mortality was high and contraception primitive a woman might have given birth many more times than that. A man was under no obligation to bring up a child: infants could even be exposed at birth if they were unwanted, though this was rare, and the high rate of infant mortality was usually left to deal with the problem. It was illegal actually to kill infants, but leaving them to die or to be adopted by another family was an accepted loophole. Adoption was very common, especially if the man of the house had no son or direct male descendant. Boys were of course the privileged gender: Poseidippos, a comic poet of the third century BCE, was only exaggerating when he said (Fragment 11): 'We always raise our sons even if we are poor; we expose our daughters even if we are well off.'

Marriage was the entry of a woman (or girl, by our standards) into her husband's household instead of her father's or guardian's. The marriage ceremony was accompanied by rituals oddly similar to those performed over a corpse or marking the entry of a slave into the household – which reflects the fact that in all these cases one person was passing into the control of another (a husband or Hades, the god of the underworld, or the head of the household). Although it was accompanied by sacrifices and by being pelted with dried figs, small cakes and so on, to herald fertility, the marriage ceremony was not a sacrament, and divorce was easy: since the essence of the relationship was cohabitation, the bride just had to return, or be sent back, to her father's house. Her relationship to her husband's family was more tenuous and less sanctified than that of any children she might bear him. Marriage was simply the consummation of a contract entered into previously, perhaps many years earlier, by the groom and the future bride's father or guardian, with or without the help of a professional match-maker. The contract and the ensuing cohabitation were, however, officially recognized by the state in order to determine the legitimacy of children as citizens.

Although husband and wife might come to feel affection for each other, love was rare enough to be remarked on. Upper-class women were often little more than pawns in the dynastic manoeuv-rings of men. Marriage was more common within the same stratum of society than, say, within one's deme, and so there were quite a lot of married cousins in Athens (and half-siblings, and uncles and nieces). Women married far younger than men. The discrepancy in age not only preserved the dominant status of the husband and the Athenian male's desire that his wife should be a virgin; it was also believed, on false medical grounds, that a man's seed was most potent when he was about thirty and a woman's body best suited for childbirth when she was still a teenager.

Sex

The plot of Aristophanes' brilliant and much-imitated *Lysistrata* (411 BCE, in the middle of the Peloponnesian War) is that the women of Athens want peace. In order to persuade their husbands, who have the power to make Athenian policy, to put an end to the war, they decide to deprive them of sex. This is very significant. Although Athenian men had plenty of opportunities for extra-marital sex, Aristophanes' plot makes no sense if they were not usually finding sexual satisfaction within their marriages. There was sexual freedom for men in fifth-century Athens, but we should not imagine that they were consumed by rampant promiscuity. Ancient Athenians were no more obsessed with sex than we are, but they had fewer anxieties about it, and their sexual lives were hardly circumscribed by legislation. In ancient Athens even the taboo against incest was not enshrined in codified law, but left in the domain of the unwritten laws.

There were basically three ways in which a man could get sex with women other than his wife: he could pay a prostitute to come to his house (for a symposium, perhaps) or he could visit a brothel; he could maintain a hetaira, a somewhat more refined prostitute who could entertain with her mind as well as her body and might be hired as a semi-permanent companion; or he could make one of his slaves his temporary bed-mate or a regular concubine. The usual, specious argument to justify the availability of sex for Athenian men was that it preserved the sanctity of marriage: by satisfying their needs with non-Athenian prostitutes they were less likely to prey on the wives of their fellow citizens.

A man could have a free or freed concubine to whom he was not married living with him even along with a wife in the house. This was rare, however, and a man more typically might keep such a mistress before or after marriage. But a fourth-century speaker bluntly said that hetairai were for pleasure, concubines for the body's daily needs, and wives for the procreation of legitimate children and the maintenance of the household (pseudo-Demosthenes, *Against Neaera* 122). What is most shocking and illuminating about this assertion, for all that it is something of an exaggeration, is that all classes of women, whether they are foreign or slave or free, prostitutes or concubines or wives, are treated simply as commodities for the satisfaction of male needs.

The other way in which an Athenian – typically a young man in his twenties, before he got married – could find sex outside of marriage was with a teenage boy. The Athenians had a healthy attitude towards homoeroticism – so much so that nineteenth-century campaigners for greater tolerance looked back to Classical Athens as a golden age. It was not expected that one would be attracted exclusively towards members of either the same or the opposite sex, and in Athenian society homoeroticism was not regarded as perverted against a standard of heterosexuality as 'normal'. In fact, ancient Athenians did not classify sex acts simply by the gender of the partners, but also by social status and by the actions involved – whether the man or his partner was the penetrator or the penetrated.

It was accepted that at a certain time of his youth a teenager had a kind of beauty, and that older men would be attracted to him; ancient Athenian homosexuality was in fact pederasty, in the literal sense of the word. If an affair took place, it was monogamous (there was little homosexual promiscuity) and generally lasted only a few years, as long as the boy kept his youthful 'bloom', as the Greeks called it. Lifelong homosexual relationships between men were extremely rare, though the pair were supposed to remain friends even after the sexual side of the relationship had died down. Homosexual relationships between women were also temporary, even fleeting.

Athenian homoeroticism was largely an upper-class phenomenon, for two main reasons. First, any society which represses its women as much as ancient Athens did runs the risk of forcing its members to find other outlets for their sexuality. There was little of the normal interplay between men and women which underpins a heterosexual society. Respectable Athenian women were not commonly seen on the street, and even in the home there was little communication: 'Don't you entrust more of your affairs to your wife than to anyone else?' Sokrates ask Kritoboulos in Xenophon's *On Estate-management* 3.12–13. When Kritoboulos agrees, Sokrates' next question is: 'And is there anyone to whom you speak less than you do to your wife?' 'There aren't many, if any,' replies Kritoboulos. Homoeroticism was more a feature of upper-class Athens, then, because these people lived in larger houses, in loveless marriages, with more opportunity to segregate their womenfolk, and because their lives were more fenced around by conventional attitudes towards women.

The second factor concerns the somewhat ritualized expectations of a homoerotic affair. A good-looking boy who was in bloom would be pursued by several older men. These older men were the ones feeling passion, and one of them would be successful if he could induce the boy to admire him. This was manly enough to be acceptable, but boys were not expected to flirt to attract lovers, because that was regarded as too effeminate and, taken to the extreme, a convicted male prostitute lost his status as a citizen.

By the same token, anal penetration was considered effeminate, and so sex was generally limited to masturbation or intercourse between the thighs. The boy would most likely feel little or nothing beyond a degree of excitement. He was expected merely to 'gratify' the lover, as the Athenians tended rather delicately to put it.

What the boy got out of the affair – and this is again why it was an upper-class phenomenon – was a form of patronage and mentorship. In return for granting his sexual favours, he would expect the older man to act as an extra guardian in public life, to introduce him into the best social circles, and later, perhaps many years after the sexual side of the affair was over, to help him gain a foothold in the political life of the city; this would seem especially attractive to boys from poorer households who were eager for advancement. The offer of political friendship later in life might seem too little to gain in exchange for sexual favours, but in Athenian political life influential friends were the single most important possession an aspiring politician could have, more important even than a political platform or a good speaking voice. They could do everything from helping in elections to heckling opponents. And they would expect some return if the young man eventually found himself in a position to dispense favours.

The older man was also expected to cultivate the boy's mind, to be an intellectual companion as well as a lover, and so a homoerotic affair was another aspect of acculturation for a teenager. The older man also helped the younger in his physical training in the gymnasium too – affording opportunities for disguising sexual contact as fair play. In fact, the gymnasia were notoriously places where men would meet not just for conversation and exercise, but to eye up the local talent, since the boys exercised naked. As a couplet attributed to Theognis of Megara, an elegiac poet of the sixth century, says: 'Happy is the lover who exercises in the gymnasium and then goes home to spend the rest of the day in bed with a beautiful boy' (1335–6). We meet again the homoerotic side of Greek sport, which infused the ancient Olympics.

Such homoerotic relationships were widely tolerated, but not universally approved. Apart from specialist philosophical disapproval among the followers of Sokrates, who struggled against lust just as they did against all powerful emotions, there is an interesting passage in Plato's *Symposium* (183c–d) which reflects ordinary views. Plato has his character Pausanias claim that the situation in Athens is quite complex. On the one hand, there is plenty of evidence for homoerotic love being perfectly acceptable; on the other hand:

> When you see that fathers stop lovers talking to their boy-friends by putting *paidagōgoi* in charge of their sons with specific instructions to that effect, and that if a boy's friends catch him being approached by a lover, they call him names, and also that older people don't stop them calling him names and don't tell them off as if what they were saying were wrong – when you see all this going on, you might change your mind and think that such relationships are completely unacceptable here.

But this is not surprising. It reflects disapproval not of the older lover for falling in love and trying to attain his sexual goal, but of the boy for yielding. Yielding automatically brought him close to being a second-class citizen – a woman or a slave – and so both he and his father or guardian had to be sure that the benefits of the relationship would outweigh the disadvantages of yielding and of accepting gifts, which of course comes awfully close to prostitution. This might seem calculating, but that is an aspect of Athenian views on friendship in general: they frankly acknowledged that a friend was not just someone for whom you felt affection, but someone who could help you out.

By and large, then, although there was little stigma involved in the relationship itself, people turned a convenient blind eye to the sexual side of the affair. And homoerotic love could even be put on a high pedestal, as it was by Plato in *Symposium* and *Phaedrus*. If women's bodies were little more than commodities, and heterosexual relationships were rarely love matches, a homoerotic affair might well be a man's best chance to experience the overwhelming and glorious emotions of love.

THE CITY AT WORK

14

Work, Money and Taxes

Almost all our evidence for ancient Athenian life is skewed by the fact that books were written by and for the literate male members of the upper class, vases were painted for them, statues sculpted for them, leaving the ordinary working man, the wives and the slaves mute – or with their voices at best heard enigmatically through archaeological evidence or the equally distorting medium of comedy. Yet even in Classical times over 90 per cent of the Attic population were still peasant farmers, living in the countryside rather than the city, and in a mid-fifth-century population of perhaps 350,000, only 50,000 were adult males with full citizen rights. There were about 100,000 slaves and 30,000 resident aliens. What follows is an attempt to penetrate the world of women, slaves and ordinary working men in Classical Athens.

Work is often an emotional subject, and it was certainly so for ancient Athenians. The nobles had definite ideas about what kind of work was appropriate – essentially, managing the managers of your land, and not soiling yourself with the ignominy of manual or indoor labour – but these ideas were of course confined to the upper class, while everyone else made a virtue out of necessity. No one but a member of the leisured class could have written this:

> The manual crafts, as they are called, have a bad name and are not rated at all highly in our cities. There are good reasons for this: those who work at them and apply themselves to them are forced to be sedentary and to spend their time out of the sunlight, and sometimes even to spend their days by the heat of a fire. As a result, their bodies are ruined, and this physical debilitation is accompanied by considerable weakening of their minds too. These manual crafts give people no time to bother with friends or city, and consequently their practitioners are

thought to be bad at dealing with friends and at defending their
cities.   (Xenophon, *On Estate-management* 4.2–3)

Against this rarefied view we can set the inscription on a pot made
by Euthymides around 500 BCE: 'Euphronios never made anything
as good as this!' Craftsmen were plainly proud of their work.

In ancient Athens the distinction between private and public
life was usually sharply maintained. It was widely taken for granted
that the laws were there in part to protect the private sphere. A
person's sexual preferences, for instance, were largely up to him,
without state interference, or with the state only loosely involved
and dealing with ambiguous terms and situations. Adultery was
prosecuted because it could lead to illegitimate, non-citizen offspring, and because the confrontation between adulterer and cuckold
could threaten civic stability, and so the state had a duty to regulate
the action the aggrieved husband could take; likewise, as in the case
of Sokrates, the state could on occasion legislate about a person's
religious life because that was supposed to affect the welfare of the
state as a whole. Otherwise, an individual expected to be left pretty
much to make his own choices. Critics of democracy, arguing that
societies are threatened more by the collapse of private morality
than by anything else short of hostile invasion, complained about
precisely this separation of the private from the public domain, and
found fault with democracy for allowing a citizen freedom to do
whatever he liked.

Work blurred this distinction between public and private. The
job you do, and how much time you spend on it, should be up to
you as a private individual, but in ancient Athens work belonged
to the public sphere, and was therefore an area into which the state
did intrude by means of legislation. For obvious reasons, the stability
of the state depended on people having a livelihood. Solon passed a
law against idleness: it was your civic duty to support your family,
and you could be fined if you failed to make an attempt to do so, at
least by working a smallholding or by casual labour. Another of
Solon's laws was that a father must teach his son a trade or give
him some means of support, so that, in return, the son could look
after his parents in old age. Otherwise, a son was not obliged to
maintain his parents.

Athenian law and tradition defined work and the outside world as the male sphere, leaving the inner space of the household as the private domain of women. It was considered shameful for a man to do things in private rather than in public, and the punishment for a number of crimes involved or included banishing the male criminal from the public places of the city, thus effectively unmanning him. The Athenian ideal was to work for oneself, not for another (unless the other was the state), because working for someone else was paradigmatically what a slave did, not a free man. One way or another, then, a great deal was at stake for an Athenian man, in terms of personal dignity, in relation to whether he worked and what work he did.

Money and Taxes

It is virtually impossible to give meaning to Athenian incomes, since too many of the variables are unknown. We do not know how much many people were paid (and there does not seem to have been a standard wage, but rather a flourishing market economy), nor do we know how much staple goods cost, or what proportion of their foodstuffs were grown on a family's own smallholding. But for what it is worth, a talent of silver weighed just about 26 kilograms; it was divided into 60 mnas, or 6,000 drachmas, or 36,000 obols. At the end of the fifth century, semi-skilled workers might expect to get 1 drachma a day, skilled workers 1 drachma, 3 obols; at the end of the fourth century these wages had risen by about 75 per cent, and 90 per cent of the population earned between 180 and 480 drachmas a year. When Perikles introduced pay for jurors in the 450s, the rate was fixed at 2 obols a day; twenty-five years or so later Kleon raised it to 3 obols. At a guess, at the end of the fifth century, it cost about a drachma a day to keep an adult.

The poor were not directly taxed, but the rich were liable to a peculiar combination of voluntary and involuntary taxation. The city had considerable outgoings on military and naval necessities, pay for jurors and attendance at the Assembly, the building and maintenance of public buildings and roads, religious and athletic festivals, and the maintenance of public slaves, to name just the main issues. Its principal sources of income were allied tribute (in the imperial years), law-court fines, revenue from the silver mines, import and export taxes, the proceeds of auctioning the collection of various taxes (lacking a Civil Service, the state regularly sold the right to collect taxes in a particular area for a year at a time), and the annual poll tax all the 30,000 resident aliens had to pay in order to live in the city (12 drachmas for a man and 6 for a woman). But this was not enough to leave a comfortable margin, and so, lacking any kind of income tax, the rich were required to contribute further. In times of war a special war tax might be levied, but in any given year, from the middle of the fifth century, there were two kinds of service ('liturgy') for the rich, military and festival.

The fitting out and maintenance of warships were incredibly costly: timber and so on had to be imported, crews found, trained and maintained. The military liturgy was the trierarchy, the upkeep of a warship (trireme) for a year, after the state had paid for the hull. This was very expensive, but not much more than some of the festival liturgies. The rich acted as impresarios and funded, for instance, the production of the tragedies and comedies at the dramatic festivals; they paid for public delegations to sacred sites such as Delos and Olympia, and supplied the processions at religious festivals with all they needed; they maintained and trained athletes for any and all games, but especially the panhellenic ones.

There were about 100 liturgies a year, but no one had to undertake more than one a year. Nevertheless, in a lifetime, a wealthy Athenian might expect to spend about 10 talents on liturgies. In the vast majority of cases, this was not regarded as a burden, but a privilege. The Athenian state worked extremely well in this respect: the main taxpayers were generally happy to pay their taxes! There was a high degree of competitiveness among liturgists, who tried to outdo one another for glory and the family name in future generations. But liturgy-level wealth rarely stayed in one family for longer than a few generations: their estates were not huge, and although they might have alternative sources of income (owning a factory, for instance, or loaning money for maritime trade, or hiring out slaves, or collecting the state's taxes), life was hazardous.

Work

Making use of a naïve but straightforward division of Classical Athenian society into three property classes, in the middle of the fifth century BCE, you could describe the upper class as those with inherited estates and capital to invest. Then there was a middle class of smallholders, shopkeepers, small businessmen and master crafts-men, and a lower class dependent on wages earned from the state or from casual labour or piecework on farms, as fishermen, and so on. On my population estimate of 50,000 working male citizens in the middle of the fifth century, the upper class consisted of about 1,000, the middle class of about 30,000 and the lower class of about 20,000. In 317 BCE, when a rough census was taken, the proportions of the much-reduced population had changed: there were about 12,000 in the lower class, 8,000 in the middle class, and 1,000 in the upper class. These figures alone show how serious a matter it is for the historian that only upper-class interests are represented in the surviving literature.

Working the land was fundamental. In Classical Athens the majority of the population owned small plots even if they were not large landowners. There was arable land in the plains around Eleusis and Marathon, in the Kephissos valley and in the agricultural heartland, the Mesogaia. Hill country was extensively terraced to maximize the production of, mainly, barley. Elsewhere, the land was used largely for olives, grapes and figs, sheep or goats, and a little bit of forestry and charcoal production. Attic land is poor and stony, and even small plots were often surrounded by a wall both to make use of the stones cleared from the ground, and to stop the incursion of goats and streams of rainwater.

Agriculture was a hard option. Apart from the poverty of the soil, and the lack of both technology and anything more than a primitive version of the science of crop rotation, there was the weather: idealistic theories about the moderate Attic climate were written by those who did not have to work out in the heat and cold. Peasants lived in huts with their animals in winter, and out-doors in summer. The Greeks did not enjoy agriculture; no one had yet thought to glorify hard work from a Christian or socialist perspective. When the Greeks envisaged a golden age (which they tended to locate in the distant past), it was one in which people did not have to work. Reflecting the picture made famous by Hesiod in his didactic poem *Works and Days*, Plato (whose hand certainly never touched a plough or a mattock) says that long ago:

> Trees and other plants produced huge crops and grew in abundance, without needing to be farmed: the soil yielded them of its own accord. People spent most of their time roaming around in the open air without clothes or bedding, since the climate was temperate and caused them no distress, and the earth produced more than enough grass for them to lie on in comfort.　　　　　　　　　(Plato, *Statesman* 272a)

When we think of large estates, we should not imagine nineteenth-century plantations in the American South, with thousands of acres and an enormous slave workforce to match. Landowners tended to own more than one estate, here and there around Attica or even abroad, with an average size in total of 50 or so acres, and therefore easily worked by just a few slaves, at least some of whom doubled up as domestic slaves. Many of these estates were run by professional managers rather than the owners themselves, who lived in the city and occupied themselves with politics. Tenant farming was rare, except on land owned by a temple or looked after by the guardian of orphaned children.

Smallholders were really market gardeners, growing a variety of crops and fruits; they might own a couple of pigs, a few chickens, bees perhaps, and a goat; if they were richer, some sheep and a pair of oxen or mules. Most peasants diversified – producing small quantities of various foodstuffs for their own consumption, and perhaps a bit of surplus for sale – but, following Solon's edicts, some specialized and therefore had specific surplus produce to sell. Surplus products were sold in the market or exchanged for flour, pots, tools and shoes. These people were unlikely to have accumulated money, and if they lived near Athens or a town like Brauron, they might have doubled up as artisans. In war they had to abandon their land and huddle miserably in a fortress somewhere, while the enemy damaged their trees and stole their crops. It might take them years to recover. In a society such as that of ancient Athens, where most food was grown on your own smallholding for your household's consumption, a poor year – as a result of warfare or drought – could mean hardship, and two such years could mean hunger. The ideal of self-sufficiency was rarely attainable.

Where imports and exports were concerned, the basic commercial functions were handled either by merchants who hired ships to transport their cargo, or ship-owners who owned both the ships and the cargo; on land there were dealers who traded with either of these two categories of seafarers. From the middle of the fifth century, at the latest, Athens was having to import grain in increasing quantities. In the summer sailing season, about six grainships a day would have docked at Peiraieus (from November to March there was hardly any sailing). Other imports, and ships in transit, would account for the same number again: Peiraieus was busy, and at the height of the Athenian Empire in the fifth century, the tribute-paying states were also required to acquire many of their goods via Peiraieus, so that the city became a major centre for international trade in both essential and luxury items. Whatever you wanted was available in the city.

Tramp trade was the norm, with ships carrying mixed cargoes (grain and hides, perhaps, or timber and perfume) and going wherever a particular commodity might fetch the highest price. This made grain-traders a source of bitter humour in Athens, since even when stocks were low, dealers would still bypass the city if they could make more money elsewhere; however, anyone whose ship was registered in Peiraieus was obliged by law to bring his cargo there. In the fourth century and later, traders and the rulers of grain-producing countries might be honoured by the grant of Athenian citizenship if they helped the city in a time of scarcity.

Trade, whether of grain or anything else, was never run by the government (even the concept of 'the government' is hard to square with the ancient Athenian system). Of course, the city was happy with the tax revenue trade provided, but it was in the hands of private individuals. The main imports were grain, slaves, timber and metals. Grain came especially from the Black Sea, but also from Euboia, North Africa, Sicily and southern Italy, Cyprus and the Levant. Timber came from Macedon, Thrace and southern Italy, slaves mainly from Thrace and inland Asia Minor. These goods were paid for by cash or barter or a combination of both. The main export was silver (about 1,000 talents a year in 360 BCE); the Athenian silver tetradrachm became the international currency everyone wanted to use, and most of the coins minted in Athens were for the export market. Other exports were olive oil, olives and honey, and of course fine pottery for the luxury end of the market – but the visibility of this in our museums should not disguise the fact that it was never a major economic factor.

Manufacture meant chiefly the making of everyday pottery, and the working of metal, wood, stone and leather (tanning and cobbling). Textile production remained largely a domestic affair, apart from fulling and dyeing, and the making of some specialist items of clothing. Other small-scale craftwork was undertaken at home too. Pottery clay came from Cape Kolias to the south-west of the city, or Maroussi to the north; it was mixed with red ochre, shaped, dried in the sun, painted and then fired, but only to about 900 or 950 °C, which is much cooler than modern kilns, and so Athenian pottery was rather brittle. There were no production lines, but small workshops, mostly in the Kerameikos (named after the ceramics), in which, typically, the owner and chief designer was free, while the rest were slaves, who kneaded the clay, prepared the glaze and so on, while the master operated the wheel.

Pottery and sculpture workshops often survived for generations, with fathers passing on their skills to their sons, but this did not lead to fossilization: commissions from the rich stimulated innovations. Gradually, the vigorous emphasis on curves and the grace that characterized pure Classical Greek art gave way, in sculpture as well as vase-painting, to a kind of vivid serenity: mastery of technique meant that a far higher degree of subtlety was possible. Filled with confidence now, sculptors began to aim for virtuoso effects, and used the folds of swaying clothing, for instance, to emphasize physical action. A similar floridity appears also on painted vases in the last quarter of the fifth century. While there are still some masterpieces, the style is closer to the posturing of some early rhetoric: all form and little content. Appropriately, the Corinthian column, with its ornate capital, put in its first appearance around this time, in the temple of Apollo at Bassai in the western Peloponnese.

Metal-working – the manufacture of tools and weapons and, to a lesser extent, tableware and jewellery – also took place in small workshops, using charcoal-fired furnaces and bellows. Metal-workers clustered around the temple of Hephaistos, still splendidly preserved on a low hill by the agora – appropriately, since Hephaistos was their patron deity. Softer metals were melted and recast; iron ore was heat-softened, beaten to remove impurities and then shaped.

Other industries were largely based in Peiraieus, especially ship-building, with a workforce of many thousands at peak periods, manufacturing businesses, limestone quarrying, and fishing. Most industries were small-scale; workshops doubled as retail outlets, and rarely reached a size we would want to call 'factories'. Although we hear of one or two exceptionally large businesses, most employed between one and ten slaves. Lack of machinery ruled out the development of larger factories with their attendant economies of scale.

The division between landowners and artisans is absolutely fundamental. All but a very few Athenians were either landowners or artisans, and there were never large numbers of artisans, compared with smallholders. In the fifth century, for instance, at the height of red-figure ceramic production, there were probably no more than 400 potters and painters in Athens. There were few professional teachers, doctors, engineers and so on; politics and the law were part-time occupations; there was no professional Civil Service apart from public slaves, and no offices as we know them today. A few were wholesalers (that is, maritime traders), and otherwise, in the city, there were all the lesser trades, like cook, inn-keeper, midwife, nurse, baker, wreath-maker, miller, shoe-maker, salt-seller, sausage-maker, washerwoman, jeweller, perfume-maker, town-crier, carpenter, maker of terracotta figurines, and so on and so forth. But most were full-time or part-time smallholders.

For all areas of work, technology was, of course, at a very crude level; essentially it was restricted to animal or human power, though there was a wide range of tools suited to each craft. The most sophisticated devices were the potter's wheel, the lathe, the pulley-and-winch system, the magnifying lens (for making fine jewellery, for instance), bellows for generating heat for smelting and welding and heating a kiln, the olive-press, and a simple swing-plough which was enough for the shallow soil of Attica. Despite the crude technology, the sixth and fifth centuries saw not only products of astonishing skill, but also increasing professionalism, confidence and self-consciousness. Experts wrote (now lost) handbooks on painting, the construction of the Parthenon, rhetoric, and a number of other areas of expertise. Another sign of self-consciousness is that some artists affected eccentric dress, while others declared that with them the peak of excellence in their field had been reached.

Since much trade was in the hands of resident aliens, Peiraieus was also the place where most of them lived. Resident aliens were vital to the Athenian economy, and although they could accumulate great wealth and mingle with the highest Athenian society, and although their contribution was valued, they were in certain respects marked off from full citizens. They could not stand for any political office; they could own only movable property and so rented their houses and workshops; they had to have a citizen as a 'protector' or 'sponsor'; they paid the annual metic tax and were liable for military service; in law they had fewer rights than full citizens (for instance, they were liable to summary arrest, rather than just being summoned to court, for an alleged crime); and they lacked the network of interlocking allegiances which underpinned so much of Athenian society. In short, a metic's situation was somewhat precarious. They were in but not of the city, and so tended not to put down long roots, but to move elsewhere after a generation or two.

Since the business interests of Athenian citizens were largely confined to the sphere of the household and its attendant aim of self-sufficiency, and since Athenians had a marked preference for self-employment over working for another, metics, and even slaves, filled the gaps and worked in commercial businesses. Although much of what we think of as affecting the economy of a society (housing and foodstuffs, for instance) never appeared on the open market outside the family, there were bankers and other businessmen who operated with a variable supply-and-demand system and who were separate from such family-based systems; they catered therefore largely for metics and foreigners, rather than traditional Athenian families with their network of helpful friends.

Bankers were not just money-changers (though this role was important in a world where hundreds of states minted their own coins, but the coinage of only a few states was internationally acceptable); just like modern bankers, they accepted financial deposits and were free to invest or make use of these deposits in any way they chose, such as financing a new business, while remaining absolutely obliged to repay the loan in due course. Unlike modern banks, however, Athenian banks were unincorporated businesses, and operated almost entirely without governmental regulation. A wealthy Athenian's funds (and other assets, such as goods made out of precious metals) could be, and often were, discreetly hidden by a banker for years. A scandal from the first quarter of the fourth century vividly demonstrates the point. The officials responsible for looking after the treasures of the goddess Athena worked out a nice scam: they would lend money to a bank and in due course of time keep the profits for themselves while returning the full sum of the capital to the temple. The traditional discretion required of bankers would ensure that no one would know about the transaction, which came to light only because in this case the bank was unable to return the capital amount and the treasurers attempted to disguise the temple's loss by torching the part of the Parthenon where the treasures had been stored.

15

The Agora, Women and Slaves

The prototype of public, male space in Classical Athens was the agora. Imagine an Athenian man, towards the end of the fifth century, entering the agora from the north along the Panathenaic Way. He pauses by one of the boundary stones, with its announcement that 'I am the boundary of the agora', designed to exclude those who were prohibited and to stop the encroachment of the private houses that cluster all around, and ritually sprinkles some water on himself from one of the basins provided for the purpose. After admiring the herms (busts of Hermes used as boundary markers) set up by Kimon at this, the main entrance to the agora, he looks up to see the magnificent new temples gracing the brow of the Akropolis, which looms in the near distance. To his left is the multi-functional Painted Stoa, and to his right the altar of Heavenly Aphrodite and the Royal Stoa (which houses the offices of the king arkhon) and the Stoa of Zeus, overlooked by the gleaming temple of Hephaistos with its sculptures of the labours of Theseus and Herakles.

North of this temple, at the foot of the Kolonos hill, is the Hipparkheion, the office of the two cavalry commanders and their subordinates, with a good view of the Panathenaic Way, where horsemen display their skills during the Great Panathenaia. Further south, along the western side of the agora, he can see, through the trees and over the heads of the crowds, the Council House, the archives building and the circular Tholos where the prytaneis, the executive committee of the Council, live during their term of office. Just out of sight beyond the Tholos he knows there is the Strategeion, the office of the ten generals. Then on the south side of the agora stand the Heliaia, the people's court, and another stoa, where the bankers set up their stalls and the occasional official dinner is held. Next to the stoa is one of the Peisistratid fountain-houses, now bordered by the Mint.

Shops – crude wicker- or canvas-shaded stalls compared with these magnificent edifices – cluster around the south-western, eastern and northern sides of the agora, but the centre is mainly an open space, large enough to accommodate the assembled people before the Pnyx was developed as the official meeting-place, and still containing the stade-length track used for the athletic competitions of the Great Panathenaia. As well as the stoas (colonnades with a roof and a back wall, occasionally graced by projecting wings at either end), plane trees – another gift to the city from Kimon – offer shade. Though nowhere near as crowded with buildings as it was to become later, the agora is plainly the heart of the city, and as our Athenian looks around he can see half a dozen small shrines and hundreds of inscribed stelae, hear several dialects of Greek, see faces both familiar and foreign (but all male, except for a few slave and metic stall-holders), smell from the stalls the odours of bread, olives, worked metal, leather, spices, fish and other foodstuffs. Braziers emit smoke, pedestrians stir up dust, and everywhere there are the sounds of industry, commerce and companionship. He greets friends and hears the latest gossip, reads the public announcements posted on the Altar of the Eponymous Heroes (the legendary founders of the ten Kleisthenic tribes), does some business, snacks and sips at a cup of wine (bought with small change carried in his mouth or a fold of his clothing), peeks at the councillors in their chambers and the jurors in session, wonders whether to attend the Assembly at its next meeting, gawps at conjurors, avoids the beggars and the earnest philosophers discoursing in the stoas to their admirers.

The word 'agora' means 'place where people gather'. The agora was atmospheric, exciting – the centre of activities for every Athenian man who was the slightest concerned with the city's public affairs. It is hard for us to imagine how much free time was available to some people in a slave-owning society, but in clement weather Athenian men spent over half the day there. A good illustration of the centrality of the agora to Athenian life is that one of the most common ways of telling the time was in relation to 'when the agora is full', in the late morning.

Over time it came to be the administrative hub of the city, but retail commercial activities constantly encroached on it. When Solon laid out the agora, the idea was that shopping should be confined to the old agora (roughly where the so-called Roman agora is now, a little to the east), but stall-holders were naturally attracted to the centre of activity. No house within the city walls was more than ten or fifteen minutes' walk away. The agora evolved more or less at random, and even after the destruction of the city by the Persians it was not rebuilt according to any rational plan; splendid official buildings and stoas rubbed shoulders with older structures, some half ruined, and with building work in progress. The agora was destroyed by the Persians in 480 BCE, the Romans in 86 BCE, the Herulians in 267 CE, the Visigoths in 396 and the Slavs in the 580s. Each time it was rebuilt, but also refashioned, with new buildings placed on top of old ones. What the archaeologists have discovered, then, has been accurately described as a palimpsest of hundreds of years of Athenian history, and has bewildered many a passing tourist.

Women

If the agora, the heart of the city, excluded respectable women, what was expected of women in Classical Athens? In the fourth century there was probably a small all-female agora, run by and for poor women, but until then there were few free women to be seen on the streets. Even then, though, there was a law curtailing the value of any financial contract a woman could enter into: she could go shopping, and she could sell goods in the women's market, but that was about it.

The idea that in Classical times Athenian women were more or less entirely confined to the home is an exaggeration – but only an exaggeration. By and large, a respectable woman would go out, if at all, only on absolutely necessary business (perhaps for a females-only religious festival, or to attend a funeral or the birth of a child), and then with her head covered. Essentially, her job was to practise the womanly virtue of self-effacement, to raise children and to keep house. Iskhomakhos, the conservative and patronizing protagonist of Xenophon's treatise *On Estate-management*, summarized his new wife's role to her as follows, after trying to persuade her that the gods have divinely ordained the world so that while a man is fitted for being outdoors, a woman's place is inside (7.35–42):

> You will have to stay indoors and send out the slaves who have outdoor jobs, and oversee those with indoor jobs. You must receive the produce that is brought in from outside and distribute as much of it as needs dispensing; but as for the proportion of it which needs putting to one side, you must look ahead and make sure that the outgoings assigned for the year are not dispensed in a month. When wool is brought in to you, you must try to make certain that those who need clothes get them. And you must try to ensure that the grain is made into edible provisions. One of your responsibilities, however, will probably seem rather unpleasant: when any slave is ill, you must make sure that he is thoroughly looked after ... Anyway, some of your specific responsibilities will be gratifying, such as getting a slave who is ignorant of spinning, teaching it to her and doubling her value to you; or getting one who is ignorant of housekeeping and service, teaching her to be a reliable servant, and ending up with her being of inestimable value; or having the right to reward those in your household who are disciplined and helpful, and to punish anyone who turns out bad. And the most gratifying thing of all will be if you turn out to be better than me, and make me your servant. This will mean that you need not worry that, as the years pass, you will have less standing in the household; instead you will have grounds for believing that, as you grow older, you will have more standing in the household, in proportion to the increase in your value to me as a partner and to our children as a protector of the home.

When a man came of age, he had a variety of different and overlapping roles: as a participant in the administration of the city, as a soldier, as a worker, as a family member, as a member of groups of other like-minded men. Most women had only marriage, childbirth and family life to look forward to. Marriage was supposed to fulfil a woman's nature in the same way that war and politics fulfilled a man's nature. In both drama and real life, the first tears for a dead girl were shed because she would never marry.

Women had a civic duty – to produce the next generation of Athenian citizens – and that was considered to be their main role. One of the ritual sentences pronounced at the betrothal ceremony by the future bride's father was: 'I give you this girl for the ploughing of legitimate children.' If a woman failed to produce a male heir, she might well face divorce; if she did produce a male heir, she would receive more honour from her husband, and perhaps correspondingly more freedom. Hence baby-smuggling was not unknown in Athens.

Although men valued their wives as household managers and as mothers, the leading male was very much the paterfamilias, as was the case in Europe until early in the twentieth century; his were the final decisions, in everything from household finances to how much make-up he felt it appropriate for his wife to wear. The definition of a happy household was one where the wife was subservient in all things to her husband's will and whims. Towards the end of the Peloponnesian War, however, when many Athenian men had been killed, more women were expected to go out to work – so many more that in the 390s Aristophanes could fantasize in *Women in Assembly* that women might take over the reins of government. The two world wars in the twentieth century hugely accelerated female emancipation, and a similar phenomenon occurred in Athens, at least temporarily. Otherwise, women did unpaid work in the home.

Athenian women had few rights under the law – like slaves and resident aliens they were, in effect, legal minors – but they had a kind of secondary status through the protection and representation of a guardian. The guardian would typically be the father until the girl was married, when her husband took over, as the head of the new household into which she had entered. If the father died before his daughter was married, and he had no male heir, the girl was not allowed to inherit the estate, but a male guardian had to be found to look after her and it, and to arrange a suitable husband for her, usually the nearest eligible relative on her father's side, so that 'proper' care could be taken of her father's property. Women, and especially upper-class women, thus often became little more than channels for the perpetuation of property, so that it would not pass out of the original household.

Women married at fourteen or fifteen, men at about thirty. Men died on average at about forty-five. Hence a lot of women remarried; on their husband's death they would return to their father's house, unless he was dead too, in which case a guardian would have been arranged, or unless there was a son old enough to be a householder in his own right. Occasionally, the husband bequeathed his wife to another man in his will. Once established within a household, a woman had free usage, but no property over a stipulated slight value was hers to dispose of. One way or another, throughout her entire life, an Athenian woman was in someone else's charge, denied self-responsibility and self-representation. And so when Athenian women were mentioned in public, in a forensic speech, for instance, they were commonly referred to not by name, but as 'so-and-so's wife' or 'daughter'.

Women's quarters in houses were sometimes lockable from the outside, nominally to protect slave-girls from having sex with male slaves (at any rate, that is Xenophon's reason or pretext in *On Estate-management* at 9.4), but also to keep women in their place, and to preserve the slave-girls for the master's *droit de seigneur*. There was such a high degree of segregation that in the early fourth century the speech-writer Lysias had one of his speakers say (*Against Simon* 6) that the womenfolk of his household 'had lived such a modest life that they were ashamed to be seen even by their own male relatives'.

A perfect symbol of the position of wives is the fact that under Athenian law the punishment for seducing a married woman was far more severe than the punishment for raping her. In certain cases, killing a man who had seduced your wife even counted as justifiable homicide – as summary execution rather than as murder. This difference between the laws governing rape and those governing seduction seems wrong, counter-intuitive, until we remember that wives were the husband's belongings. To seduce a wife was to take her away from her husband, while raping her presumably left her just as loyal as before. Moreover, even more than rape, seduction raised the possibility of the birth of an illegitimate, not purely Athenian child and, especially after Perikles' citizenship law of 451, the Athenian state was always concerned to preserve the purity of its citizens' bloodlines.

Nevertheless, this picture of the utterly down-trodden Athenian woman, from whom no more than domestic industry and frugality were required, needs some qualification. In the first place, it more closely fits upper-class women than poorer women: in poorer households, with fewer or no slaves, women had to do more, take more responsibility and get out more. In the second place, although the frame fits the kinds of passive wives we generally find in male-written literature (such as the young wife of Iskhomakhos in Xenophon's *On Estate-management*), other evidence shows that women could find their own voice. Sokrates was famously hen-pecked by his wife, and Aristophanes shows women nagging their husbands. In *Trojan Women* at 655–6 Euripides has Andromakhe say, even after an extremely demure speech: 'I knew when I should defeat my husband and when I should let him defeat me' – a timeless sentiment, familiar to couples now as then. One of Themistokles' famous sayings described his son as the most powerful person in Greece, 'since everyone else in Greece took orders from the Athenians, while they took orders from him [Themistokles], he did from the boy's mother, and the boy's mother did from the lad himself' (Plutarch, *Themistocles* 18). Men clearly often allowed women authority within the home, their area of expertise.

Then think of the anger and proto-feminism of Medeia in Euripides' play of that name, written in 431. Although the author was a man, he has given us a portrait of a strong woman, who refuses to accept society's norms:

> Of all the living and sentient creatures on earth
> There is none more wretched than we women.
> First, for an outrageous sum of money, we must buy
> A husband, and accept him as the master of our bodies.
> . . . For us everything hinges on whether the husband we get
> Is good or bad. For divorce dishonours women,
> And it is not our right to refuse a husband.
> When we have come into his house, with its strange ways
> And alien customs, which we have not learnt at home,
> We must somehow guess how best to deal with our spouse.
> If after all our efforts in this respect, our husbands
> Share our homes without complaining,

Our lives are enviable. Otherwise, we're better off dead.
If a man is unhappy with the company at home,
He can always go elsewhere for relief from boredom.
But we have to gaze at one person only. Men say
That we live a risk-free life at home, while they fight wars.
What a stupid idea! I would rather stand three times
In the line of battle than give birth once.

(Euripides, Medea 230–251)

For all the power of this speech, though, no Athenian man was an unambiguous spokesperson for women: in Euripides' play the 'mannish' Medeia goes on to commit acts of appalling violence, including killing her own children, and our outrage is bound to colour our response to the sentiments she expresses. Besides, she was an easterner, a princess and a witch, descended from the gods: she was hardly the Athenian girl next door.

It is likely, anyway, that in the home women in Classical Athens could have a voice and make their feelings heard, but it helped if they had some kind of hold over their husband, especially if they came with a large dowry or from a powerful family. Divorce was easy – the woman could just leave her husband's house and return to her father's – but it made most women suspect to future husbands. A big dowry would always help, since a divorced woman was entitled to the return of her full dowry, or if the husband failed to return it, he could be charged an enormous rate of interest on the debt. Dowries were therefore important. They were the woman's inheritance, given by her father or her family on her marriage as a kind of fund to give her security in her future life with her husband. She did not own her dowry, but it came with her, and that gave her some clout.

Women were considered to be closer to beasts than a fully rational man, with strong appetites for sex, food and alcohol. An Athenian man's honour depended in part on the honour of his womenfolk, and he lived in fear of adultery on the part of his wife, although marriage was widely acknowledged as his best chance of 'taming' a woman. Herodotos plays to these fears when he tells an amusing story about an Egyptian king who was blinded as a result of an act of sacrilege (*Histories* 2.111):

Sometime in the eleventh year, after he had been blind for ten years, an oracle came to him from the city of Bouto that the time of his punishment had come to an end and that he would regain his sight once he had washed his eyes in the urine of a woman who had slept only with her own husband and had never been with another man. He tested out his own wife first, but he still did not regain his sight, so then he tried all kinds of women one after another. When at last he did recover his sight, he had all the women he had tested, except the one whose urine he had washed in to regain his sight, assemble in a single town ... and once they were all gathered there he burnt the town down, with them inside it. As for the woman whose urine he had washed in to regain his sight, he made her his wife.

There was a whole townful of unfaithful women, or women who had not been the virgins they should have been at marriage, but only one faithful one! Athenian men were out of the house a lot, and did not know what their wives got up to, and such ignorance breeds fears, especially when combined with the view of women as cunning creatures. The men were out sleeping with other women and with boys, and they judged women by their own standards. Since they were the ones writing the works of literature, they injected the idealized portrait of the demure woman as a model for their wives – partly out of fear that they might not actually be living such lives. They were also hypocrites: a man's normal sexual appetite was considered excessive in a woman, and the same for eating, drinking and talking. But different standards applied: 'A man would seem a coward if he had a woman's courage, and a woman would seem a chatterer if she was as self-contained as a good man,' as Aristotle put it at *Politics* 1277b.

But if women were as cloistered as the standard picture suggests, why would their husbands be afraid that they would form adulterous relationships? They must have had more freedom; they must have had opportunities to escape from their menfolk. And when we look more closely at the evidence, we see that they could get out of the house. Older women worked as midwives; younger women worked in the fields; they all visited neighbours, fetched and carried water, washed clothes in the public fountains, participated in funeral processions, went to the public baths, attended public gatherings such as Perikles' Funeral Speech (which is addressed to the widows and mothers of the dead as well as to their male relatives) and public religious ceremonies, were brought into court by a husband to arouse pity in the jurors.

In most of these cases, they were interacting only with other women, but there were certainly opportunities for them to see and be seen by other men. If Thucydides has Perikles say in his Funeral Speech that women ideally should not be spoken of at all, whether for praise or blame, the implication is that in his time a significant proportion of women *were* being talked about. However, it remains the case that by and large women wanted to live indoor lives, as a sign of wealth and breeding: having to go out to work was an indication of poverty. Hence they cultivated pale skin to show that they rarely went outdoors.

Women lived separate lives to a great extent – separated by convention and ideology rather than by physical constraints – but that is not the same as saying that they lived secluded lives. Education was not widespread even among male Athenians, and women of course received less – men thought they were less intelligent, for one thing – but we do hear of women who could read. It was considered a useful skill for household management. But women attained their greatest freedom in another cultural sphere, that of religion. They were important in Greek religion generally, since as well as being the priestesses of female deities (while male gods tended to be looked after by priests) they were the oracular mouthpieces for Apollo and Zeus at the two most prominent and public panhellenic shrines at Delphi and Dodona. In Athens, they participated in a number of ceremonies throughout the religious year, some obscure and designed only for women (such as the Thesmophoria with its bizarre rituals, including disembowelled and rotting piglets and the telling of crude jokes), some mainstream (such as when young unmarried women carried sacred objects in the Panathenaia), and most concerned with fertility. Fertility was important to a woman's role in the home, and her religious duties invariably reflected her social roles.

Since they were occasions when women could get out of the home and mingle freely with their female peers in larger numbers than usual, female religious rites were popular and well attended, and it is not surprising that women were prominent in the introduction into Athens of new cults in which they could be involved. And men tolerated their womenfolk's absence during these festivals, partly because it was everyone's civic duty to keep the gods smiling on Athens, and partly because they saw it as a necessary holiday from domestic chores. Some Athenian women even went as far as Mount Parnassos at Delphi every year, for a joint festival with the women of Delphi in honour of Dionysos.

Women were especially important when a family member died. The corpse was washed by the women of the household, dressed in white linen, crowned with a vine wreath, and laid out inside the house, for friends and relatives to visit and pay their last respects. This stage, the laying out, lasted a whole day, with intense mourning from the bereaved womenfolk. The corpse was then prepared for burial: it was given a flask of oil, an obol to pay the ferryman of the dead, and a honey-cake to propitiate the underworld deities. Before sunrise on the day following the laying out, and in any case within three days of death, the corpse was taken to its place of burial or cremation, in a procession with men in front of the cart and women behind. Solon passed laws restricting mourners to family members only, up to and including cousins, and outlawing some of the more outlandish expressions of grief, such as raking cheeks with fingernails, but it remained a sign of status to hire elderly women as professional mourners. Women mourners were an old tradition, dating back to Mycenaean times; women were expected to be more emotional than men, and their open grieving was seen as a fitting send-off for the deceased person. Men had ways of expressing grief (such as cutting their hair and wearing black cloaks), but women did the lamenting. There was an annual commemoration of the death-day, but women could visit the grave more often if they felt like it.

We return, then, to the same theme: to Greek eyes, women were less rational than men. In certain religious contexts, their emotional or slightly subhuman nature was welcomed, but otherwise it was more often an object of suspicion and even fear. In his dialogue *Timaeus*, at 90e–91a, Plato speculated that the first race of humans on the earth were all men, but that those who did not fully live up to their manhood were reborn as women, and that was how the race of women began. Proving that scientists are just as liable to prejudice as anyone else, Aristotle too was convinced that the rational capacity of women was inferior to that of men (*Politics* 1260a). The word 'hysterical' properly applied, according to ancient Greek theorists, only to women, because the symptoms of emotional excess occurred when a woman's womb (*hystera* in Greek) slipped. Women were important in the bed, in the household and in religion, but they were never considered equals. It was still a man's world. Even if Athenian women were allowed out of the house more than the traditional picture suggests, it was men who gave them permission to go.

Slaves

It is undeniable that the Athenian economy depended crucially on the availability of slave labour. In Athens and Attica slaves filled the gap left by the Solonic reforms. They did those jobs which in other cultures have usually been carried out by people from the peasant class (such as domestic work) or which fall outside the peasant sphere (such as factory work). This is one reason why Attic peasant life was remarkably stable: there were few pressures to change career. Huge numbers of slaves were imported into Athens in the fifth century, when the Empire gave both the state and individuals disposable income, until there were about 100,000 slaves throughout Attica, of whom about 15,000 worked in the mines of Laureion at times of peak demand for labour, about 50,000 in Athens and Peiraieus, in domestic employment or in factories or on various public duties, and about 35,000 on the scattered parcels of land owned by the rich or, again, in domestic or jack-of-all-trades employment on a farm. Proportionately, there were so many more slaves in the city than in the countryside that, while it makes sense to describe the city as a slave society, rural Attica was a society with slaves. Attic agriculture was periodic, and the poorer small farmers preferred to draw on the help of their neighbours, or hire slaves when they were needed, rather than keeping more than one or two on a permanent basis.

In one of the last shreds of panhellenism, it was considered inappropriate to have a Greek slave (although in wartime the Athenians did not think twice about selling Greeks into slavery elsewhere). The main sources of slaves were Scythia, Thrace and Illyria, countries such as Karia and Phrygia in Asia Minor, and Syria in the Middle East. In Hellenistic times, African slaves became something of a vogue. If they were not slaves born of slaves in Athens, they came as a result of warfare, piracy or kidnapping, and there was a flourishing trade in Athens in these human commodities. Slave-traders, practitioners of a despised profession, followed armies like jackals. The purchase price in Athens varied enormously, according to age, physique, appearance and especially skill (since an owner could quickly recover his outlay by hiring out a useful slave). A poor slave might cost only 50 or 60 drachmas, but wealthy Nikias was said to have paid a whole talent (6,000 drachmas) for a good overseer; in general, unskilled slaves cost about the same as a mule and considerably less than a warhorse.

In talking about the cost of slaves, we are getting close to the nub of the matter: Athenian slaves were chattels; they belonged to their master. Aristotle even defined a slave as an 'animate tool' (*Politics* 1253b–1254a). Not everyone was this extreme or analytical: Aristotle was the earliest thinker bold enough to attempt a justification of slavery by means of a panhellenist theory that some people (not Greeks) were 'natural slaves'. But even if others treated their slaves with kindness, Aristotle was right: under Athenian law slaves could be bought, sold and bequeathed; their children were routinely taken from them and sold elsewhere. The fact that the killing of a slave (by someone other than his master) was accountable under the law means little: there might as well have been a law against stealing or ruining other tools, and the penalty for killing a slave was far less severe than for killing a citizen. In theory the killing or gross maltreatment of a slave even by his master was punishable under the law, but in practice this rarely happened.

Estimates vary and the evidence is sketchy, but probably over half the citizen population of Athens owned one or more slaves. We even hear of thetes owning slaves. Slaves provided both skilled and unskilled labour in the mines, on farms and smallholdings, in workshops and factories, as assistants to every kind of merchant and entrepreneur, in domestic service of various kinds, and for the state.

The thousand or so public slaves were used for building work (though masons, carpenters and sculptors were free), but also as assistants to the various committees, for repairing public buildings, road-building, street-cleaning (largely sewage disposal), working in the Mint, and as a rudimentary police force. Some had very responsible jobs, as the keeper of the state archives, for instance, or as the manager of coins, weights and measures; these jobs were given to educated slaves rather than citizens to avoid corruption. Domestic slaves might do productive work (such as shopping, cooking or weaving) or, in richer households, non-productive work as *paidagōgoi*, hairdressers, doorkeepers, waiters, maids, and so on.

Domestic slaves were on the whole quite well treated; a familiar character from Athenian drama is the loyal, old retainer. As well as domestic slaves, farm or workshop managers might become indispensable to their owners. But, however well treated they were, they were not free: a slave was uprooted from his country and family, and denied a proper family in Athens. If a female slave had a child (the product of a liaison with her master, or after having been introduced by her master to one of his male slaves for breeding purposes), the child belonged to her master. Even those few slaves who did have some kind of family life were all still at the whim of the master, who might disperse them at a moment's notice. As individuals or as a family they had no legal status; they were non-persons. The closest slaves got to recognizable status was that they were ritually introduced into the new household, given a new, Greek name, and allowed to take part in the family's worship.

Even though some slaves may have become 'almost one of the family', resentment could build up. The relationship between masters and slaves was often uneasy, and slaves were notoriously capable of murdering their owners. This was one of the reasons why a period of military training was felt to be essential for an Athenian citizen: 'The citizens of a state serve for free as one another's bodyguards against slaves and criminals, to make sure that none of their fellow citizens meets a violent death,' as Xenophon put it (*Hiero* 4.3). And friendly relations between master and slave were likely to be tinged with self-serving on both sides – the master to get the best out of his slave, and the slave hoping for freedom in the future. Slaves resorted to the few strategies of resistance that were available to them: laziness, theft, breakage, running away. Running away from Athens or Attica was not easy, since there were few places of refuge, home was far away and the journey dangerous. But slaves who accompanied hoplites abroad as their assistants might well desert and go over to the enemy. In Athens, an individual slave who felt badly treated could take refuge at the shrine of the Furies or that of Theseus, and ask to be bought by someone else: that was the extent of his legal 'protection'.

Although Athenian slave-owners were constantly aware of the possibility that one of their slaves might abscond, and took steps to prevent this happening, there were only three occasions in Athenian history when there were collective insurrections, and they did not escalate into the kind of armed rebellions Sparta or Rome witnessed. During the Peloponnesian War, after the Spartan occupation of Dekeleia, thousands of slaves seized the opportunity to run away. Most of them were mine-workers from Laureion, and this was also the source of the only other two large-scale revolts, in 133 and 103 BCE, both of which were spillovers from revolts in Roman Sicily. But the rarity of outright rebellion does not mean that on the whole Athenian slaves were content with their lot. As much as anything it was a product of two facts: slaves spoke a wide variety of languages (until they learnt Greek), and they usually worked alongside only one or two others. Organization of a rebellion was difficult.

There were four major exceptions to the generally benign treatment of slaves in Athens. First, conditions for those who worked in the cramped shafts and galleries of the silver mines at Laureion were appalling, and life expectancy was low, as a result of lead poisoning and a diet inadequate for such hard work. The most expendable slaves worked underground, often in spaces big enough only to crawl in; others above ground at washing and smelting. Archaeologists have recovered shackles at Laureion, but we cannot tell whether all or only some of the slaves were shackled there. Things cannot have been much better for workers in the marble quarries of Mount Pentelikon or the limestone quarries of Peiraieus. Several plutocrats owned large stables of slaves and hired them out for profit: skilled workers went wherever they were needed, and unskilled labourers went to the mines, quarries, shipyards or building works (that is, places where there was fluctuating demand for labour).

The second way in which slaves were treated with cruelty in Athens is that some slave-owners hired out their young female slaves as prostitutes, and some masters certainly expected their female slaves to have sex with them. Third, it was a feature of Athenian law that a slave's testimony was not recognized in court unless the slave had been tortured. As a foreigner, he was taken to be a natural liar; as a chattel, he was taken to speak only in his master's defence; as subhuman, he was taken to be concerned only for his bodily welfare. For all these reasons, torture was thought to be necessary to elicit truthful testimony. In actual fact, though, there were few occasions (only where important state interests were at stake) when slaves actually were tortured for their testimony, since the law was hedged around by complex conditions.

Fourth, with the casual cruelty to which people are liable when society sanctions injustice, slaves were routinely beaten for work-related offences, or just for seeming too uppity. This was so common that the whip became an emblem of slave punishment. Masters employed the carrot as well as the whip, however, recognizing that a willing slave was better than a surly one. And the ultimate inducement was the promise of freedom. In desperation towards the end of the Peloponnesian War, Athens freed those slaves who had risked their lives in battle for the city, and particular owners might free an elderly slave after a lifetime of trusted service; he would then gain metic status, if he chose to remain in Athens. The slave had to buy his freedom with his savings or a loan. Cynically, one might point out that elderly slaves would be difficult to sell and just as expensive to keep as before, and so the master's generosity was tinged with expediency, but the slave's descendants, should he have them, would also become metics, and this was a step up the social ladder, even if it fell short of full freedom. The rate of such manumission increased from the fourth century onwards.

By contrast to the misery of many slaves' lives, we hear of rural slaves working alongside their master in the fields and sharing his joys and troubles, and craftsmen-slaves might even run a shop on their own, paying their master a kind of rent or a percentage of the profits. Unlike slaves in other societies, Athenian slaves could earn money. They were paid the going rate and worked alongside metic or free colleagues, as prostitutes or labourers or clerks or whatever.

Their owners kept a proportion of their income, in theory to cover board and lodging. Some slaves, usually skilled craftsmen, lived apart from their owners, however, in their own small houses or dormitories, which were again rented from the owner.

One or two slaves even became rich men in their own right, before and after being freed by their owners. Pasion, who died around 370 BCE, had been a slave owned by bankers. He was very good at his job, and was eventually freed by his owners. Now with the status of a metic or resident alien, he set up on his own as a banker, and invested also in a shield-making factory. In due course of time, he gained a virtual monopoly on the accounts of maritime traders and became very wealthy indeed. He was eventually made a citizen for services to the state: he had donated 1,000 shields and five warships.

Divisions between non-citizen and citizen could be blurred in social and business contexts, with metics and even slaves filling the gaps in banking and wholesale trade which Athenians were reluctant to fill, and working alongside citizens at other occupations. It was an oligarchic complaint that Athens was too much of a melting-pot, so that it was impossible to tell at a glance the difference between citizen and foreigner, slave and free man, but in fact status distinctions such as that between man and woman, citizen and foreigner, free man and slave, were enshrined within Athenian law and custom, so that if push came to shove the various elements of Athenian society could quickly be put in their proper places.

THE DOWNFALL OF ATHENS:

A GREEK TRAGEDY

16

Open Warfare

A tragedy is a tragedy not because the protagonist is a flawed person, but because he is all too human, and is simply overtaken by the consequences of a stand he took in the past. In important respects, Athens hastened her own downfall, and this lends a tragic twist to the story of the war which broke out between Athens and Sparta, the two chief Greek states in the fifth century BCE. Athens' ruthless and single-minded concerns for Empire and victory at all costs brought about her doom. The arrogant assumption that one has a right to wield power over others may not bring its own nemesis, but it leads one into actions which provoke reactions from others. In the case of Athens, her wholehearted commitment to Empire, and apparently to increasing her Empire, provoked the strongest reaction from Sparta and its allies.

Sparta

The modern visitor to Greece might well wonder why, if the two cities were such great rivals, guidebooks and tour leaders steer him towards Athens, but less commonly towards Sparta. Thucydides prophetically supplies the answer (*The Peloponnesian War* 1.10):

> I think that in the distant future, if the city of the Spartans were to become abandoned, and their temples and the foundations of their buildings were all that remained, men would find it very difficult to believe that they had once been as powerful as their fame made them out to be, despite the fact that they occupy two-fifths of the Peloponnese, and are the leaders not only of the whole Peloponnese but also of many allies else-

where. But because the city consists of a collection of villages, in the ancient Greek way, which were never incorporated, and because it lacks expensive temples and buildings, it would, I think, appear less powerful than it was. On the other hand, if the same thing happened to Athens, the visible remains of the city would make it appear twice as powerful as it actually was.

Although in the seventh and sixth centuries Sparta, the main city of the fertile and rugged Peloponnesian district of Lakonia, was home to poets, sculptors, ivory-carvers, vase-painters and other artists, both native and immigrant, by the fifth century the city had abandoned any pretensions to artistic culture, and had developed along extraordinary lines. The Spartans had no Thucydides to record their deeds, no playwrights to entertain them or Sokrates to challenge them, few grand public buildings and certainly nothing to compare with the Parthenon or Propylaia. Sparta was, in short, a kind of military camp, requiring uniformity and conformity from its citizens, who were known for that reason as the *homoioi*, literally 'the Similars'.

The main reasons for this lie in the late eighth century BCE. While other Greek states, faced with overpopulation or a shortage of good land at home, were sending colonies abroad, Sparta chose to gain extra land by conquering and enslaving her Messenian and Lakonian neighbours. Full-blooded Spartans ('Spartiates') were then hugely outnumbered by helots (as they called their slaves: the word means 'captives'). From the time of a major helot revolt in the seventh century, the Spartans felt compelled to bring up all their male children as warriors, so that the helots could be kept in their place. They were right, pragmatically, if not morally: there were commonly threats of rebellion, which occasionally erupted into reality, and when Spartan power was finally broken in 371 BCE the Messenians seized the opportunity to make their rebellion permanent.

From about 550 until the third century BCE, Spartan culture remained more or less stable – and it was one of the most bizarre cultures the world has ever seen. Young men were brought up in communal dormitories and, when they were older, military messes, to which they owed unswerving allegiance. In fact, they owed more allegiance to the mess, and hence to the state, than to their parents. Parentage could even be oblique: since eugenics were paramount, elderly husbands could invite younger men to sleep with their wives if they felt that a good soldier would be the result. Babies were tested soon after birth for their potential, and deformed infants and weaklings were exposed to die, or even thrown down a gorge. From the age of six or seven, when they were removed from their mothers, until they were thirty, when they were allowed to take up normal family life, Spartan men lived and ate in barracks, separated into year-groups, while their wives took correspondingly more responsibility for domestic matters. Barracks food was notoriously disgusting to non-Spartans: one visitor from luxurious Sybaris in southern Italy wittily said that after tasting their food he understood the Spartans' readiness to die in battle.

On graduating from military academy at the age of twenty, as part of his initiation into full citizenship (which included ritual flogging at the altar of the goddess Orthia), every Spartan male was given a plot of land in the fertile valley of the Eurotas river. Worked by the state-owned slaves, this provided the food he had to supply for his mess, and also fed his household. Surplus, and so the accumulation of wealth, was permitted; at any rate, plenty of Spartans were rich enough to enter chariots at the Olympic and other games. Loss of this plot of land and expulsion from the mess were the ultimate punishments, equivalent to disenfranchisement; cowardice in battle was the main crime for which this extreme penalty was reserved.

The Spartans, then, were a land-owning oligarchy or aristocracy, a hangover from almost prehistoric times. They grew their hair long, to distinguish themselves from their slaves and from the intermediate *perioikoi*, the inhabitants of towns in Lakonia and Messenia other than Sparta itself, who were the free but non-voting farmers, artisans and tradesmen of Spartan society. Few Spartiates did these jobs: they were bred and trained to be warriors, and on land they were the supreme Greek fighters for many decades.

Marriage was by capture:

Their marriage ceremony involved the forcible abduction of the woman . . . The abducted woman was handed over to the so-called bridesmaid, who would cut her hair very short, dress her in a man's clothes and shoes, and leave her lying alone on a straw mattress without any light to see by. The groom ... first dined in his mess and then slipped into the room, undid the woman's belt, picked her up, and carried her over to the bed. He spent only a short time with her before leaving quietly, and returning to the same sleeping-quarters he had been sharing before with the other young men. This pattern continued in the future: he would spend the day with the men of his age-group, and take his rest with them as well, but he would visit his wife secretly, taking every precaution out of embarrassment and fear of being seen by anyone in the house ... They went on behaving like this for quite a long while; in fact, in some cases there were children born before the men saw their own wives by the light of day.

(Plutarch, *Lycurgus* 15)

If the manner of preparation of the bride smacks of homosexuality, that is not surprising: homosexual affairs between men of the same mess and platoon were encouraged and institutionalized. The older partner was partly responsible for the training of the younger, and the underlying thinking was that a young hoplite was less likely to break rank and expose his neighbour to danger if his neighbour was also his lover. So until his marriage a young Spartan man in all likelihood had experienced heterosexuality only with slaves and only homosexuality with his peers: the strange marriage ceremony eased the transition to heterosexuality with a peer.

The brevity of a Spartan's visits to his wife until he was thirty was another means of decreasing loyalty and affection for anything other than the state. The stealth with which the groom approached his bride was also par for the course. All the young men were trained to forage for their food from the land (especially useful in small-scale guerrilla actions against rebellious helots), and being caught was one of the worst forms of disgrace. Hence apocryphal stories arose, such as the one of the young Spartan who had a live fox hidden under his clothes; on his way back to his mess with this prize, he was engaged in conversation by an older man, and silently endured having his stomach ripped open by the fox.

The training in stealth could take on inhumane forms:

From time to time the young men's commanders would send those who gave them the impression of being the most intelligent out into the countryside – to different districts at different times – with nothing more than a dagger each and a bare minimum of supplies. By day the young men spread out and found remote spots where they could hide and rest, but at night they came down to the roads and murdered any helots they caught. (Plutarch, *Lycurgus* 28)

This was just one of several ways in which helots were treated as less than human. Every year the ephors – who along with the two kings were the effective rulers of Sparta – declared war on the helots, so that for a Spartan to kill a helot was not murder but an act of war. As well as the five annually elected ephors, the main Spartan council was the *gerousia*, a council of twenty-eight elders who were joined by the two kings (who had additional rights and powers as well). There was an assembly of all Spartiates, but it generally did little apart from rubber-stamping the decisions of the ephors and *gerousia*.

The Spartan authorities felt it their chief duty to preserve Spartan culture, with all its austerity. Over the years they banned the use of coined money, preferring to use iron bars as currency, to prevent hoarding and to ensure that wealth was conspicuous; they also banned imports (a stricture hugely helped by the fertility of Lakonia and 'the land that once had been Messenia', as Thucydides calls it from time to time, with heavy irony), discouraged visitors, and passed laws against luxurious living. Soldiers at war have no need of luxuries.

The militarization of Sparta in the seventh and sixth centuries was accelerated by an aggressive policy towards other Peloponnesian cities, a few of which were conquered and annexed, while most of the rest – the most notable exception being Argos – gradually became allies under Spartan hegemony, until a Peloponnesian coalition was an established fact by the late sixth century, and would shortly be turned into a formal league. It was not a league of equals: Sparta had as much voting power as the rest of the allies put together, and she retained the right to initiate proposals. Both chambers of the league – that is, both the Spartans and their allies –

had to agree on large matters such as a declaration of war or peace, but it was often hard for the allies to do more than follow Sparta's lead, especially since Sparta tended to ensure that the allied cities were governed by sympathetic oligarchies.

Sparta had long-standing good relations with the Boiotians and Megarians on the mainland north of the isthmus, and with the island of Aigina, but otherwise her unsuccessful interference in Athenian affairs at the end of the sixth century (see pp. 66–8, 74) marked the end of Spartan growth in mainland Greece: her influence was confined to the Peloponnese and hardly extended further until the Peloponnesian War and the fourth century. Sparta was not on the coast, and had neither the wealth nor the political framework to become a seafaring nation: building, equipping and manning an ancient warship, with some 200 rowers, was incredibly expensive (and they did not trust helots to do the job well) and, as we have seen in the case of Athens, reliance on a fleet tends to shift power down the social scale – something which oligarchic Sparta would never have tolerated.

Leadership in the Persian Wars was thrust upon the Spartans because they had the military expertise other Greek states lacked – they had, in effect, the first standing army, while other armies consisted of amateurs, citizens whose duties included military service – and because they brought with them the other member states of the Peloponnesian League. After that, they were forced to play more of a role in Greek affairs than they might have wanted – and ultimately to confront Athens and her imperialist ambitions, when the future of the Peloponnesian League was threatened.

The Outbreak of the Peloponnesian War

In 446 Athens and Sparta entered into a thirty-year peace, which did nothing to stop each side developing its military potential. The final insults blew up in the 430s, with Corinth, Sparta's greatest ally, usually the target of Athenian manoeuvring.

First, around 438 Athens entered into an alliance with the Akarnanians on the west coast of the mainland. But Corinth considered this coast to be Corinthian colonial territory, so although

Athens was doing nothing literally against the terms of the peace accord, this was a slap in the face for Corinth, and an implicit threat.

Second, there was the Kerkyra affair. Kerkyra (modern Corfu) had been in dispute with its one-time mother city, Corinth, for some years of grim tension and occasional open warfare. Following a defeat in 435 by the island's powerful fleet, Corinth prepared a huge avenging force. In desperation, in 433 Kerkyra called on Athens for help, noting the island's strategic position on the way to southern Italy and Sicily – tempting Athenian ambitions westward – and arguing that war with the Peloponnesian League was already inevitable, so that it would make no difference if Athens alienated Corinth now. In response, the Corinthians issued a warning: Athenian support for Kerkyra would provoke the Peloponnesians beyond the point of no return.

The debate in the Athenian Assembly lasted two days, with the decision going first one way and then the other. Athens had not been particularly expansionist recently, preferring a strategy of preservation and judicious alliances abroad. But faced with the likelihood of war, the Athenians could not afford to let the Corinthian and Kerkyran fleets combine. In the end they voted, cautiously, to enter into a purely defensive alliance with Kerkyra: if the island was attacked they would come to its aid, and they sent a small contingent of ten ships to the island to fulfil this obligation. The Corinthians attacked. The Athenians held back from the engagement for as long as possible, but eventually felt compelled to prevent a massacre of the Kerkyrans. Even so, the Corinthians were successful at sea, and drove the Kerkyrans and Athenians on to land – but withdrew when a further twenty Athenian warships appeared on the horizon.

Third, there was the terrible business of Potidaia, a town on the west coast of Khalkidike, which was a tributary of Athens while retaining strong links with its mother city, Corinth. Athens had recently increased Potidaia's tribute, and then in 432, worried about Corinthian intrigues in the area, she insisted that Potidaia break off relations with Corinth and demolish some of her defences. Potidaia tried to negotiate, but the Athenians sent a sizeable army into the area. This was again a slap in the face for Corinth; once a moderator of Spartan hostility towards Athens, Corinth was now herself consumed by unremitting hostility towards Athens, and threatened to leave the Peloponnesian League if Sparta failed to help. The Spartans promised Potidaia that they would send armed assistance, which arrived in the form of a largely Corinthian army. The two armies clashed, the Athenians won, and the Corinthians were trapped inside the city, along with the inhabitants. The siege lasted until spring 429, with the inhabitants finally reduced by starvation to cannibalism before giving in. The siege cost Athens the enormous sum of 2,000 talents – more than the entire Periklean building programme on the Akropolis. Athens could give no clearer sign of her commitment to war.

Fourth, there was the Megarian Decree. In 432, perhaps in retaliation for the Megarians helping Corinth at Kerkyra, but ostensibly because some Megarians had trespassed on the sacred ground of Eleusis, on the border between Attica and the Megarid, Athens decreed that Megarians were to be excluded from all the harbours of the Athenian Empire, and from the Athenian agora. This insignificant decree – a token economic embargo that could easily be circumvented – became blown out of proportion when the Megarians complained of it to the Spartans and the assembled Peloponnesian League, and the Spartans began to claim, with little plausibility, that it was a breach of the treaty of 446, according to which aggression against each other's allies – the allies as they existed in 446 – was forbidden.

Any of these events could have precipitated the war. There was nowhere else for the energy that had built up over the past fifty years to go. Perikles was walking a fine line between outright confrontation and adherence to the treaty of 446, acting provocatively while waiting for the Spartans to make the first move. However, in 434 the Athenians took the precaution of moving the treasures housed in rural temples in Attica to the safe haven of the Akropolis. By August 432 the Peloponnesian League had voted for war, even though Athens had not broken the actual letter of the terms of the treaty; the Spartans were too afraid of Athenian imperialism to do otherwise, and they also feared the fracture of the Peloponnesian League, since they were being pushed towards war by several of their most influential allies.

Nevertheless, Sparta delayed initiating hostilities, and sent several embassies to Athens, ostensibly to try to avert war, but in fact in an attempt to convince international opinion that they were not the aggressors. First, they invoked the old Kylonian curse (see p. 54), in an attempt to get the Alkmaionid Perikles banished or at least disgraced, and so to destabilize Athens. When this tactic failed, they sent another embassy demanding that the Athenians withdraw from Aigina (a strategic island – the 'eyesore of Peiraieus', as Perikles is said to have described it – conquered by Athens in 457 and recently occupied) and Potidaia, and above all that they repeal the Megarian Decree. Perikles refused, and the Spartans sent a final embassy, insisting that the Athenians relinquish their empire and restore Greek autonomy. The fact that this demand was so utterly unrealistic shows that the Spartans were playing to the crowd.

Fighting finally broke out when the Thebans, anticipating an Athenian invasion of Boiotia (as in the First Peloponnesian War), attacked Plataia. This Boiotian town had long been Athens' ally, had played a glorious part at Marathon, and was a holdout against Theban domination of Boiotia. One night early in March 431 the oligarchic faction in the town let in 300 Theban troops, the advance party of the main army. It all went horribly wrong. The furious Plataians cornered the Thebans in the unfamiliar streets, killed some and captured the rest, while torrential rain delayed the arrival of the main Theban army. By the time they arrived, they could do nothing, since the Plataians bartered the hostages for their withdrawal and then massacred the remaining Thebans and their Plataian conspirators. Wiser minds in Athens saw the value of the hostages in neutralizing the Thebans, but by the time the message reached Plataia, it was too late. The Peloponnesian War began with an act of senseless cruelty, a terrible but true herald of things to come.

Thucydides opens his history of the war with a statement of his belief that it would be the greatest war in Greek history. What follows is a selective account, focusing on the major theatres of the war, but Thucydides was right, because much of the Greek world was convulsed. From Thrace and Macedon to the coast of Asia Minor and the shores of Sicily and southern Italy, Greek cities took the opportunity to settle old scores with their neighbours, protected by an alliance with one or the other of the two superpowers. Moreover, the political rift between Sparta with her support for oligarchy and Athens with her support for democracy was echoed in the strife that tore apart a great many communities. All over the Mediterranean world, Greeks were fighting Greeks; the Olympic spirit of friendly rivalry was shattered.

17

The Arkhidamian War

The Peloponnesian War fell into marked phases, and the first ten years is often called 'the Arkhidamian War', after King Arkhidamos of Sparta, though he was opposed to war in 431 and died in 427. At the start of the war, the Peloponnesians could count on allies from all over the Peloponnese (except for Argos and the Akhaian towns on the north coast, which were neutral), Megara, most of Boiotia, the Phokians and Lokrians on the mainland, and various other mainland states. In the west they had military alliances with Syracuse, which more or less controlled the Greek Sicilians, and with some towns in southern Italy. The Athenians had as allies the 300 states of their Empire, and could also call on Thessalian cavalry units, the Plataians of Boiotia, Kerkyra, Zakynthos and mainland Akarnania. The Spartans were regarded as invincible on land, and the Athenian navy had the same reputation at sea.

Sparta's avowed intention in the war was 'to free Greece' – to put an end to the Athenian Empire, which was portrayed as a form of enslavement of fellow Greeks. But Sparta found itself on the horns of a dilemma. The best way to achieve this goal was to approach the allies directly, and to separate them from Athens by force or diplomacy. But this required a fleet, and Sparta lacked the money and expertise to conduct naval warfare. Even Corinth, with a long-standing navy, was rightly reluctant to challenge Athenian supremacy at sea. At the beginning of the war, Sparta requested a fleet from her Sicilian and Italian allies, but the western Greeks preferred to avoid for as long as possible involvement in the problems of the mainland and the Aegean. Sparta therefore had to adopt a second-best course, dictated by her acknowledged superiority on land.

Ancient Greek warfare invariably involved the devastation of an opponent's farmland, in order to provoke him to give battle – and hoplite battles were usually swift and decisive. The Spartans invaded Attica in most years of the Arkhidamian War; they arrived between the middle and the end of May, when grain crops were ripe enough to either burn or be used for food, and stayed between sixteen and forty days, depending on provisions and the need of the army to be elsewhere: farmers had to return to their lands, and the Spartans could not afford to be away from Lakonia for too long, in case the helots seized the opportunity to revolt. Like any Greek invading army, the Peloponnesians were equipped not just with conventional weapons, but with tools that could be used equally for building a temporary camp, destroying crops, damaging olive trees or clearing roads.

The destruction of the crops and farmhouses was depressing, but it inflicted no long-lasting damage, and was not economically disastrous. As long as Athens had the Long Walls connecting her to Peiraieus, she could import food and other necessities. Siege engines had not yet been developed which could destroy the walls. And Athens, by far the wealthiest state in Greece, had the vast financial resources of the Empire. Apart from a huge capital reserve of 6,000 talents (even after most of the building programme had taken place), at the beginning of the war tribute and reparations brought in 600 talents a year, and a further 400 talents was raised from elsewhere.

Perikles' strategy was to sit and wait – not to wage a war of attrition, but just to wait and to survive. Athens' resources allowed her to do little more than defend herself for about three or four years, and Perikles hoped that the Peloponnesians would give up before Athenian money ran out. He hoped to send the Peloponnesians the message that Athens was invincible. The Peloponnesians lacked the resources, naval and financial, to threaten the Empire, and the city was safe behind its walls. Arkhidamos had conceded to a declaration of war only under extreme pressure from Corinth and other allies; Perikles' best bet was to dishearten the Spartans until they in their turn put pressure on League members to give up. At the same time, he was in no hurry to take any further imperialist action, in the west or anywhere else: he saw that the Empire had reached its limit, and that any further acquisitions during wartime would stretch Athens thin.

The Athenian cavalry emerged for the odd skirmish with the

invaders (especially to protect the farmland close to the city), naval expeditions devastated selected areas of the Peloponnesian coastline and beyond, and the war continued in Khalkidike even after the fall of Potidaia in 429. But none of these actions resulted in important gains or delivered a decisive advantage. Both sides suffered gains and losses. Until 424, the Athenians also invaded the Megarid twice a year, as they had sworn to do in response to the alleged Megarian impiety. Occasionally, there were more significant actions. In 430, for instance, the Athenians stationed a fleet in the Corinthian Gulf at Naupaktos to neutralize the Corinthian fleet, and in 429 they successfully defended it, despite being outnumbered, against a serious Peloponnesian attack.

The strategies of both sides were wrong. The Spartan strategy of regular invasions of Attica did not tempt the Athenians to risk a pitched hoplite battle on land. On the other hand, Perikles had underestimated both the costs of maintaining a navy in war and the stubbornness, or desperation, of the Peloponnesian League. The Spartan tactic did, however, have an unforeseen side effect. Each time the Spartans invaded Attica, everyone who had no other fortress or safe area to hide in took refuge (with all their movable property) within the walls of Athens – not just inside the city itself, but along the narrow corridor of walls leading down to the sea. There was severe overcrowding. In 430 a terrible plague broke out in the city, and over the next four years it wiped out about a third of the Athenian population. There were no hospitals: people died at home or in the street ('like sheep', Thucydides says), and so the plague succeeded admirably where the Spartans could only fail. It broke many Athenians' spirits and, apart from its effect on the general population, it thinned the ranks of fighting men, increasing Athens' financial burden by the necessity of hiring foreign mercenaries. Thucydides has left us a vivid description (2.47–54) of the symptoms – medical and moral – of the plague, but it defies secure identification. Victims ran such a high fever that some threw themselves into cisterns in the hope that the cool water would offer them relief. Most people who contracted the disease died, after a sometimes prolonged illness involving vomiting, diarrhoea, sores and even fits. Thucydides himself contracted the disease, but survived.

Thoroughly dispirited, the Athenian people listened as Perikles' political opponents accused him of cowardice and inactivity. Against his wishes, they sent a mission to Sparta in 430 to sue for peace, but the Spartans' terms – the end of the Athenian Empire – were unrealistic. On top of these troubles, Perikles sent a large force north to try to bring the siege of Potidaia to an end, but succeeded only in infecting the northern army with the plague, carried there by the reinforcements. Egged on by rival politicians, the Athenians charged Perikles with embezzlement (although he was famously incorruptible compared with other politicians) and suspended his generalship. He was found guilty, and fined the enormous sum of 15 talents.

Perikles was reinstated at the beginning of 429, but the elderly statesman died only a few weeks later from the effects of the plague. He had been at the helm of Athenian affairs for many years, and the Athenians would soon learn to miss his experience, wisdom and caution. Above all, he had used his influence to keep Athenian foreign policy and management of the war consistent. From now on the fickleness and inconsistency with which opponents charged the democracy would become more of a factor in Athenian affairs. There were politicians who represented a continuation of Perikles' policies, but his death also gave prominence to his opponents, who had previously been in his shadow. None of these successors had the stature of Perikles. Since they were more nearly equals, the so-called 'fickleness' of the Athenian people depended on which politician's views were found persuasive at any given moment.

Nothing illustrates this better than the most important event of 428, which almost provoked one of the worst atrocities of the war. The oligarchic powers that be in Mytilene, the largest town on Lesbos, were anxious to gain control over the other towns on the island, not all of which would have welcomed it. Knowing that the Athenians would never sanction such a takeover – not for any idealistic anti-oligarchic reasons, but because large units of power are never welcome in an empire – the Mytileneans seceded from Athens. The Athenians first blockaded the island, then besieged the city of Mytilene itself. The Spartans promised help, but delayed and arrived too late – showing how hard it was for them to keep their promise to liberate Greece from the tyranny of the Empire. If they had shown vigour in supporting the rebellion of one of the Athenian allies, others might have taken heart and followed.

In 427 Mytilenean resistance collapsed. Pakhes, the victorious Athenian commander (later to commit dramatic suicide by falling on his sword in the public court where his year of office was being assessed), took possession of the town, sent the ringleaders to Athens, and waited for the Assembly's decision about the town's future – and the Assembly decided to kill all the male citizens of Mytilene, and to enslave the women and children. They felt that they had to stop the rot: if they made an example of Mytilene, perhaps that would prevent further rebellions. After all, their security depended entirely on their Empire. They needed the revenue, and they needed safe passage for grain from the Black Sea through the Aegean.

The Athenian Assembly had voted to execute several thousand people and destroy an entire city. If they had ever occupied the moral high ground, they lost it then. A ship was sent to Mytilene, but the very next day a less harsh mood prevailed in the Assembly. All they could do, however, was send another ship and hope that it would arrive on time. Fortunately, the second ship arrived just as Pakhes was about to carry out the original orders. In the end, 1,000 ringleaders were executed, while the city had to tear down its defences, and accept a heavy fine and a garrison of Athenian soldiers.

Thucydides dramatically cast the debate on the second day in the form of a duel between two speakers, Kleon and the otherwise unknown Diodotos, who had also been the main speakers in the first debate. Kleon was one of the new politicians whose share of the limelight increased after Perikles' death. He was typical of the new breed in two respects. First, although he was as rich as fifth-century Athenian politicians tended to be, it was new money, based on manufacture rather than agriculture, the source of the wealth of the old families; as the comic poets loved to remind their audiences, Kleon's father owned a tanning business. Second, he had become prominent without holding the generalship, but just by his oratorical powers within the Assembly – which is to say that he did not use the traditional channels to power and get elected with the help of influential friends and favours, but he made the poorer people of Athens, who still felt marginalized, his personal clientele.

This became the pattern for politicians in the following century, so much so that the word for 'speaker' (*rhētōr*) became the word for 'politician', generalship became sidelined as a route to power, and politicians tended to be younger, since they did not have to wait until they were thirty (the minimum legal age for holding office) before becoming prominent. Moreover, since they held no official position, they did not have to undergo the assessments to which all magistrates had to submit before and after their term of office. Kleon himself was an exceptional orator, with a voice so strong that he could easily be heard in the open-air meetings of the Assembly and a flamboyant style that was accessible to the ordinary man. He was a democrat who had come to prominence earlier the previous year with the introduction of a heavy war tax on the rich.

Although the people regretted their harsh decision of the previous day, Kleon argued that they should not change their minds. His speech appealed to expediency and attacked any form of moderate imperialism: he wanted to see terror tactics applied to keep the Empire's subjects truly in subjection. But Diodotos argued that it was more in Athens' interest to be seen to be lenient. This is what is really frightening about the debate: Diodotos did not argue on moral grounds that Kleon's proposals were too harsh and cruel; both parties appealed in different ways to Athenian self-interest.

The End of the Arkhidamian War

The following years saw the usual swings and roundabouts of Athenian and Spartan successes and reverses. Athens had signally failed to help Plataia and the town finally fell to the Spartans and Thebans in 427, though the Athenians defeated a Boiotian army in 426; on Kerkyra democrats and oligarchs massacred one another, with the democrats finally proving the more successful and the more bloodthirsty, while Athenian commanders sat by and connived at horrible slaughter; the Athenians achieved some successes in Sicily, in preventing the spread of Syracusan influence and the passage of goods to the Peloponnese from the farms of Sicily; the plague briefly revisited the city; the Spartans carried out their usual invasions of Athenian territory. But there was one critical exception to the generally indecisive state of affairs.

In 425 the enterprising Athenian general Demosthenes successfully fortified the Messenian peninsula of Pylos on the south-west of the Peloponnese, by the bay later called Navarino. This was a clever idea: it could act as a base for disaffected Messenian helots to stir up rebellion, and it was through the helots that the Spartans were most vulnerable. It had the potential to be a war-winning scheme. The Spartans clearly thought so, because they lost no time in attacking the peninsula, with its hastily built fortifications, by land and sea. But the initial Spartan assault on the peninsula was unsuccessful, and then they were routed by an Athenian fleet.

The Spartans had landed 420 men on the island of Sphakteria, just off Pylos. With the defeat and withdrawal of the Peloponnesian fleet, these men were now cut off. The numbers may seem small, but they represented some 10 per cent of the Spartan army, and many of them were proud Spartiates. The Spartan authorities could not endure this loss, and they arranged a truce at Pylos, while they sent delegates to Athens to negotiate an end to the war. They offered to enter into a full alliance with Athens, with each side keeping the territory it currently had. They offered a chance of the old panhellenic ideal of Kimon, in which Athens and Sparta shared the leadership of Greece. Partly out of fear of future Spartan treachery or their inability to rein in their allies, but mainly because their blood was up and they seemed to have the upper hand, the Athenians, led by Kleon, turned down the offer. They wanted to see their enemy humiliated; they wanted sole rule of the Greek world; they preferred the continued killing of fellow Greeks to working at building a lasting peace.

Fighting resumed, but the men on Sphakteria held out longer than expected. There was water on the island, and shade, and when the Spartans offered freedom to any helot willing to run the blockade with provisions for their trapped troops, many jumped at the chance. Back in Athens Kleon, whose refusal of the Spartan peace offer was responsible for the continued fighting, offered to take over command, despite his lack of military experience, and bring things rapidly to an end. He and Demosthenes overran the island, and before long the remaining Spartans surrendered – to everyone's surprise, since Spartans were not supposed to surrender but to die in battle. Two hundred and ninety-two prisoners, among them 120 Spartiates, were taken to Athens. This was the occasion when the Messenians commissioned the statue of Victory at Olympia (see p. 7). The Athenians made a glorious display in the Painted Stoa of captured Spartan shields.

The Athenians were now in a very strong position. They were facing a demoralized and weakened enemy, they held hostages, and they undertook a radical upward revision of the allies' tribute in order to secure their precarious finances. They renewed their peace treaty with Persia, and simultaneously interrupted Spartan delegations to the Great King's satrap in Sardis. They could probably have negotiated peace on very favourable terms, and there was certainly heated discussion of this possibility in Athens and in Sparta. In the meantime, Athens waged a more aggressive war – not the kind of war Perikles had envisaged: they took the island of Kythera, which they could use as a base for interrupting Spartan supplies from Egypt and for raids on the Peloponnese, and nearly risked a hoplite battle with the Spartans outside Megara in 424.

It is a truism that war is hazardous and over-confidence an error. The Athenians devised a bold plan to remove Boiotia from the war, and perhaps to renew hopes of gaining a land empire, by fomenting democratic rebellion in the towns there, and simultaneously launching a large invasion. The secret leaked out and the Boiotians massed an army to meet the Athenian invaders. The battle of Delion in 424 was the first major land battle of the war, and the Athenians were soundly beaten. Apart from light-armed troops, they lost about 1,000 hoplites.

The Spartans followed up this success with an attack on Athenian possessions in the north, under their brilliant general Brasidas, who had made his name as an enterprising and successful commander over the previous few years. The plan was to threaten the Athenian supply of precious metals and timber from Thrace and the grain route from the Black Sea; it was the closest the Spartans could get, lacking a fleet, to an assault on the Empire. The Spartans also used the campaign to defuse tension in their own territory: Brasidas took with him 700 armed Lakonian helots, and at much the same

time the Spartans culled 2,000 helots in Messenia. With a combination of diplomacy and the threat of force, Brasidas succeeded in
persuading several towns in and around Khalkidike to leave the
Athenian alliance, and then laid siege to Amphipolis, the most
important Athenian possession in the region. Before an Athenian
fleet (commanded by the historian Thucydides) could bring help,
Brasidas had offered such favourable terms to the inhabitants of
Amphipolis that they surrendered the city to him without a fight.
Athens never recovered this important outpost. Thucydides' failure
to recover Amphipolis led to his prosecution by Kleon and lifelong
exile. He retired to his family's estates in Thrace, from where he
could survey the war and complete his remarkable history.

Defection from the Athenian Empire in the neighbourhood of
Amphipolis was swift and widespread. The Athenians were demoralized by the succession of recent defeats, and the Spartans seized the
moment to sue once more for peace. Early in 423 the two sides
entered into a one-year truce, to buy time with which to negotiate
a lasting peace. Unfortunately, there were unrelenting hawks on
both sides: on the Spartan side, the Thebans refused to acknowledge
the truce, and Brasidas simply ignored instructions from home and
continued his northern campaigns; on the Athenian side, Kleon kept
stirring things up. Aristophanes, however, used his plays to remind
the Athenians of the benefits of peace. *Peace* (421 BCE) includes the
following wistful lines (571–81):

> Remember how we lived before, my friends,
> In the good old days of peace.
> Remember the dried fruits and the figs,
> The myrtle, the sweet new wine,
> The bed of violets beside the well,
> The olives – how we miss them!
> Here comes the goddess Peace, my friends:
> Implore her to restore these blessings!

Aristophanes is speaking largely for the farmers here; others,
especially the thete oarsmen of the navy and countless artisans,
profited from the war and were presumably happy to see it continue.
In fact, the war caused a huge demographic change in Attica:
whereas the bulk of the population previously lived outside the city,

by the end of the war the proportion had shifted towards the city, as more and more people found urban pursuits.

Skione, a small but strategically placed town in the south of the Pallene peninsula of Khalkidike, was judged to have seceded from the Athenian alliance and surrendered to Brasidas *after* the truce had been signed, and was therefore excluded from the truce, which broadly recognized the status quo in terms of Athenian and Spartan possessions. The Athenian Assembly was furious, and this time there was no Diodotos to oppose Kleon's proposal that all the male citizens of Skione should be put to death.

In 422, once the truce had expired, Kleon took command of northern operations himself. By now Skione was surrounded by a siege wall, so he could ignore it. He retook Torone and several other towns, and then turned his attention to Amphipolis. The two armies met outside the town, and the Athenians were again utterly defeated. They lost 600 men, while the Spartans lost only seven. One of the seven, however, was Brasidas – and among the Athenian dead was Kleon. The Athenians may not have regained Amphipolis, but the two most belligerent men on either side had fallen in a single battle, and now there was nothing to impede a peace treaty.

The treaty that was eventually drawn up in 421 recognized, with minor exceptions, the status quo that had existed before the start of the war. In other words, the Spartans were to abandon Amphipolis and the rest of Khalkidike, leaving Skione to suffer Kleon's posthumous legacy of the execution of all its male citizens. Athens, for her part, was to abandon important gains such as Kythera and Pylos. The peace was to be binding not just on the protagonists, but on all the allies too, and was to last for fifty years. The Arkhidamian War ended in disappointment and frustration for both sides – hardly the right conditions for a lasting peace.

18

The Tipping of the Scales

The Peace of Nikias (named after the chief Athenian negotiator, a prominent dove and panhellenist in the tradition of Kimon) lasted eight years if we wait for the next Spartan invasion of Attica, but considerably less than that if we count the effective resumption of hostilities between the two rival powers.

The peace was a farce from the start. Several of Sparta's most important allies, including the Boiotians and the Megarians, refused to recognize it, the Corinthians did all they could to undermine it, and Sparta's own commander in Khalkidike refused to restore Amphipolis and the other rebellious towns of the region to Athenian hands. Since the Spartan authorities did not punish him, it is clear that their commitment to the peace was fragile. Nevertheless, faced with intransigence from their allies, they entered into a separate treaty between just themselves and the Athenians, one of the most important clauses of which required the Athenians to return the Spartan prisoners from Sphakteria who were still being held in the city.

The willingness of the Athenian doves to carry out their side of the bargain (though they hung on to Pylos) even when the Spartans refused to do their bit brought the entire policy of peace into disrepute in the eyes of the majority in Athens. The Athenian hawks, led by Hyperbolos and Alkibiades, seized the opportunity of the expiry of a thirty-year treaty between Sparta and Argos to demonstrate the inanity of the peace with Sparta, and negotiated an alliance with Sparta's Peloponnesian enemies – the democratic states of Argos, Mantineia and Elis. A last-ditch embassy to Sparta on Nikias' initiative failed to resolve anything, and Athens entered into a 100-year treaty with the dissident Peloponnesian states. The peace was effectively over before it had really started.

Alkibiades was a rare individual. By sheer force of character, by charm and eloquence, he manipulated and influenced everyone and everything around him throughout his colourful life. Flamboyant, passionate, egotistical, opportunist, extremely wealthy and ambitious, he never doubted his destiny and pursued a course of self-interest with rigid determination. He was the essence of the Athenian Empire, admirable and appalling at the same time, and the Athenian people had a love–hate relationship with him, fearing him when he was there and missing him when he was gone. But above all he was an individualist, and therefore at odds with the collectivism of Athenian democracy; he was more concerned with the old heroic values of competition than the quieter virtues of cooperation. And he was a hawk not just for patriotic reasons, but because warfare gave him a chance to shine. His shield was emblazoned with the symbol of his personal and military ambitions – a figure of Eros, the god of passionate love, wielding a thunderbolt.

The year 419 was marked by sabre-rattling from both sides, and a dramatic escalation in tension in the Peloponnese, which broke out into fighting in the following year. The final straw was the threat by one of the Spartans' most important allies, Tegea, that it would save itself by joining the Quadruple Alliance of Athens, Argos, Elis and Mantineia, unless the Spartans did something quickly. Tegea was more or less on the dividing line between the largely pro-Athenian northern Peloponnese and the Spartan-controlled south.

Thucydides once remarked that the Spartans were always slow to go to war, unless they felt some compulsion (*The Peloponnesian War* 1.118). They certainly felt compelled to do so now, since their leadership of the Peloponnese was hanging in the balance. Within a few days King Agis was facing the army of the Quadruple Alliance, including an Athenian contingent, near the town of Mantineia. After some days of dithering on both sides, the Argives came down from the safety of the high ground. There were about 8,000 men on the Argive side and about 9,000 on the Spartan side, but the Argives had the superior position, and the inexperienced Agis, to the fury of his seasoned officers, was rearranging his troops even as the two armies were approaching each other. Nevertheless, and although casualties were heavy on both sides, by the end of the day the Quadruple Alliance had been thoroughly defeated.

The Peace of Nikias was one of the victims of Mantineia, since Spartans and Athenians had clashed in battle; but they tacitly agreed to regard this as an anomaly and carried on as though the peace were intact. The Quadruple Alliance was another casualty of the battle: it fell apart in disarray, with the Argives themselves – under a renewed oligarchy – the first to ally themselves with Sparta. In a single day Sparta held on to the Peloponnese and erased the memory of Sphakteria; more importantly, if they had lost at Mantineia, the Peloponnesian League would have collapsed and the Athenians would have won the war.

Alkibiades was not worried. First, he was looking for a decisive battle on land to destroy Sparta, and this had almost happened without much risk to the Athenians; second, his general policy of resuscitating the war with Sparta by appealing to Athenian pride was gaining ground in Athens, although there was still a strong faction of doves, led by Nikias; and third, the war chest had grown in these years of comparative inactivity. An ostracism in 417 was supposed to remove Alkibiades or Nikias, and so to be a decisive vote in favour of either peace or war, but the two rivals collaborated to make sure that neither of them, but Hyperbolos instead, was sent into exile. The blatant manipulation of the system brought ostracism into disrepute, and it was never used again.

The island of Melos had long irritated the Athenians. It was one of the few places in the Aegean to have resisted joining the Athenian Empire, despite repeated Athenian efforts, both diplomatic and military, and it had supported Sparta in the war. For the Athenian hawks, this was sufficient provocation, and in 416 they launched a large expedition against the island. When called on by the Melian authorities to justify the attack, the Athenians bluntly replied that it had nothing to do with justice or injustice; the reality was that the Athenians had the power to take Melos, and that gave them the right to do so.

The Melians resisted until they were starved into submission. In an action of sickening familiarity, all the men of the island were killed, and the women and children enslaved. The atrocity was compounded because the voters in the Athenian Assembly knew that it was the regular practice of slave traders to leave children and the hard-to-sell elderly by the roadside to die or fend for themselves. But since hubris is bound to be punished, the tragedy of ancient Athens was approaching its climax.

The Sicilian Expedition

In 415 the Athenians launched their most ambitious project yet – a full-scale invasion of Sicily, nominally to protect Athenian allies there against Syracusan expansion, but actually to conquer the island. It is almost incredible that Athens undertook such a massive military strike after sixteen years of a war that had given her plenty of shocks and setbacks. But the hawks had long looked west, and saw the annexation of Sicily as the logical extension of the imperialism which had brought Athens, they claimed, so many benefits. This was the pivotal moment at which Athenian imperialist arrogance led the city into an action which sealed her doom. About two years later the expeditionary force, along with reinforcements that had been sent in the intervening period, was almost wiped out. Athens never fully recovered.

The Athenians might well have won in Sicily, had it not been for incompetence on the part of the commander, Nikias. But he was not supposed to be the overall commander: Alkibiades was, and Alkibiades had considerable flair as a strategist and tactician. Alkibiades was the natural choice to command the expeditionary force, since he had been its champion from the start, arguing that failure to combat Syracusan expansion would be tantamount to abandoning the Empire. Nikias was given joint command, even though he was opposed to the expedition, and had argued, as had Perikles before him, that the preservation of what they had was more important than new acquisitions. As a buffer between these two personal enemies, a third general, Lamakhos, was also appointed.

Having decided to go, the Athenians and their allies prepared a massive armada. A fleet of warships, cargo ships and troop carriers would transport thousands of hoplites and light-armed troops. But in late May or early June, just as the fleet was poised to sail, there was a terrible omen. One night many of the herms in the city were mutilated. Herms were distinctively Athenian milestones or boundary-markers; they were busts of the god Hermes on top of square-cut blocks of stone, each with a prominent erect penis (to ward off evil). On this night their faces were disfigured and their penises were broken off. It may well have been no more than a drunken prank, but it was sacrilege (the equivalent, perhaps, of defacing statues of the Crucifixion), and it struck fear into the hearts of many Athenians. They wanted culprits, undertook a witch-hunt and offered generous rewards for information. In the heat of the moment, Alkibiades and certain of his friends were denounced, not just for the mutilation of the herms, but also for having put on a version of the Eleusinian Mysteries in a private house.

Alkibiades demanded that he be tried for these offences without delay, so that the Sicilian expedition could get under way, but his enemies prevaricated, not wanting the trial to take place while Alkibiades was surrounded by his supporters in the army. The armada set sail towards the end of June. The authorities in Athens soon learnt the names of those responsible for the mutilation of the herms, but in the hysterical atmosphere the whole business of the herms and the profanation of the Mysteries were exaggerated into a conspiracy to overthrow the democracy. Alkibiades had gained enormous popularity as a result of his unique success in the Olympics of the previous year (see p. 11), and Athenians remembered how Kylon had tried to set himself up as tyrant on the strength of an Olympic victory. Besides, Alkibiades was notorious as a man of unbridled lusts – a womanizer and gourmand – and it was commonly felt that such lusts could be satisfied only with tyranny, the power to gain everything for oneself. This feeling was a product of the central Greek moral tenet, 'nothing in excess', and the democracy's insistence on equality.

In Athens there were a number of 'clubs' (*hetaireiai*), which were essentially drinking and dining associations of men of the same age and social standing. They were not generally sources of conspiracy, and many remained purely social groups of like-minded symposiasts, but some, especially those centred on someone with political ambitions like Alkibiades, met to discuss politics and the future of the city. In this way the *hetaireiai* could become political pressure groups, or even seed-beds of revolution. More importantly, even if they were not such pressure groups, they could be suspected of being so: democracy depends on equality, but exclusive clubs undermine equality. In modern Europe, Freemasons are the favourite candidates of conspiracy theorists for the same reason.

So Alkibiades' *hetaireia* fell under suspicion, and a ship was despatched west to bring him back to face trial. In Sicily, after an initial cold reception from the cities of southern Italy and Sicily, the Athenians had at last acquired a base of operations up the east coast from Syracuse, and it was here that the Athenian ship found Alkibiades. He agreed to return home, but as soon as they reached Thourioi he vanished. In Athens, he was found guilty and condemned to death in his absence, but by then he had defected to Sparta. When he heard the news of the verdict, he said, 'I'll show them that I'm alive' (Plutarch, *Alcibiades* 22).

The campaign in Sicily continued for a further two years, but under the half-hearted command of sickly Nikias (Lamakhos died fighting in 414) things went from bad to worse for the Athenians. Any successes were crowned with failures, and the failures gradually counted for more than the successes. Nikias became so famous for his hesitation that already in 414 Aristophanes felt the need for a new pun – 'procrastinikiating' (*Birds* 640). Both sides received reinforcements – the Syracusans from Sparta (with the small size of the expedition reflecting Spartan suspicions about its proposer, the newly installed Alkibiades) and the Athenians in 413 with almost the same numbers as the original expedition. Finally, late in the summer of 413, the Athenians were in a desperate situation: they had just lost over 2,000 men in a single battle, but still had a chance to make a break for freedom and sail home. But there was a total eclipse of the moon, and superstitious Nikias, taking it for a bad omen, refused to retreat for twenty-seven days. The harder-headed Syracusans, Spartans and Corinthians seized the opportunity to inflict a heavy defeat on the Athenian fleet, and then took advantage of their superiority at sea to blockade the Athenians on land. Superstition was now overwhelmed by fear, and the Athenians decided to try to break out. They were again defeated in a vicious battle in the Syracusan harbour.

By now utterly demoralized – after all, were they not supposed to be invincible at sea? – the Athenians refused to take to their remaining ships and chose to try to escape by land. There were

40,000 of them, about half soldiers and the rest camp followers. But the Syracusans had anticipated this move, and placed their men all along the various routes at the places most favourable for ambush. On the sixth day of the retreat half the Athenians – a force led by Demosthenes that had been reduced from 20,000 to 6,000 by constant enemy ambushes – surrendered. On the eighth day the other half, under Nikias, was massacred in disarray: there were only 1,000 survivors. The two Athenian generals were put to death, while their men were kept captive in quarries, and those who did not die of starvation, exposure and their wounds were ransomed or sold into slavery.

Dekeleia and the Ionian War

What with the plague, and now the Sicilian catastrophe, Athenian manpower was reduced to about a third of the numbers at the start of the war. But this was still enough to fight on, though with increasing desperation and reliance on mercenaries. It was already clear by the early spring of 413 that matters in Syracuse were not going the way of the Athenians, and so, with restored confidence, the Spartans prepared to invade Attica and renew the war in Greece. In the previous year the Athenians had joined the Argives in raiding Lakonia itself, and this blatant breach of the peace treaty gave the Spartans their excuse. But this time their invasion had a different purpose: rather than just ravage Athenian territory for a few days, they listened to Alkibiades' advice and decided to occupy a fortress in Attica – to pay the Athenians back for Pylos in their own coin. A sign of the importance of this tactic was that one of the two kings was put in charge of the occupying force.

Dekeleia was the chosen site: it was relatively easy to protect, it was in the heart of good farmland, and it was a looming presence about 20 kilometres from the city. The depressing effect on Athenian morale was increased by material considerations: not only was most Athenian farmland now inaccessible or threatened, but the Spartan presence encouraged slaves from the silver mines in Laureion to run away, depriving Athens of this rich source of income for the remainder of the war. Moreover, the overland route from Euboia was now closed; the island was not only a source of grain but was where most of the Athenian flocks and herds had been kept since the start of the war, and supplies from the island now had to be ferried around Cape Sounion (which was duly fortified). However, Dekeleia alone was not going to win the war for Sparta, any more than the annual Spartan invasions had done in the Arkhidamian War. As long as the Empire was intact, Athens could still import enough through Peiraieus to stumble on.

Since the Spartans now clearly had the upper hand, they were approached in 412 by several Athenian allies who needed their support to defect from the Athenian Empire. These included the important islands of Lesbos, Khios and Euboia. Disturbingly, the delegation from Asia Minor was accompanied by representatives of the two Persian satraps of the region, Tissaphernes and Pharnabazos. The Persians were now prepared to betray their peace treaty with Athens, because Athens had foolishly helped a Persian rebel in Asia Minor a couple of years earlier. In any case, the Persian satraps had a vested interest in seeing Athens lose the war, because as long as the Greek cities in their areas were paying Athens tribute, they were not paying Persia. Urged on by the Great King, they wanted a return to the situation before the Persian Wars, when all the Greek cities of Asia Minor were tributaries of the Persian Empire. The Spartans were prepared to cede the Asia Minor cities in return for Persian funds. Only with such funds could they buy mercenary expertise and build and maintain a fleet. Only with such a fleet could they strike directly at the weakening Athenian Empire.

Alkibiades persuaded the Spartans to focus on Tissaphernes in central Asia Minor rather than Pharnabazos in the Hellespontine region, because Tissaphernes seemed more inclined to bankroll the Spartan enterprise. Alkibiades personally took responsibility for bringing the Khians, with their vital fleet of sixty warships, over to the Spartan cause, and then used the island as a base from which to stir up rebellion in half a dozen coastal towns in Ionia, including Ephesos and Miletos. Tissaphernes was impressed, and promised money. The Athenians had to stop the rot in Ionia. A measure of their anxiety is that they chose this moment to break into a special fund of 1,000 talents, which had been set aside at the beginning of the war for use only in the direst emergency. They sent a fleet of about fifty ships to the Aegean, with Samos as its base. While the Athenians were stationed there, the Samian democrats rose up in rebellion and put an end to the oligarchy which had long ruled the island.

In short order, the Athenians succeeded in securing most of Lesbos and attacking Khios. They next turned their attention to Miletos, but at the impending arrival of a large Spartan and Syracusan force they chose to retreat to Samos. The risk of a battle would have been high, but by failing to take Miletos, the Athenians effectively abandoned Ionia. Things would have gone worse for them had the Spartans acted with more determination, but the Athenians still had the reputation of being superior at sea, and the Spartans took pains to avoid them. Nevertheless, early in 411 the Spartan fleet, based in Miletos, persuaded the island of Rhodes to defect from the Athenians. Even worse, a Spartan army marched north from Ionia to the Hellespont and the town of Abydos came over to their side. The Spartans were now in a position to stir up rebellion in the region and threaten Athenian shipping through the Hellespont. They had at last found a way to strike at Athens' weakness, and from now on the war in the Aegean was more important than any military activities on mainland Greece.

19

Defeat and Civil War

Alkibiades wanted power above all else. He had once been the darling of the democracy, but in 415 his political opponents had manipulated the democratic system to ensure his downfall. By 412 his popularity in Sparta was waning too: his plans for an Aegean takeover demanded more naval daring than the Spartans were prepared to commit, and the Athenians took advantage of their pusillanimity. Moreover, it was widely known that he had had an affair with the wife of King Agis while the king was stationed at Dekeleia, and that she gave birth to his child (whose right to the kingship was later successfully challenged on just these grounds). Alkibiades found it expedient to take refuge with Tissaphernes. There he ingratiated himself by recommending a policy of seeming to favour neither Greek side over the other, but letting them wear each other out, until Persia could reclaim the territories it had lost in 479. Tissaphernes accordingly began to pay the Spartan crews less, and less regularly. He certainly had no desire simply to replace Athenian control of Asia Minor with a Spartan Empire.

Alkibiades was homesick. To his Athenian contacts he began to portray his advice to Tissaphernes as an attempt to undermine Persian support of Sparta. Finally, he came out in the open. He got in touch with the Athenian leaders on Samos, and promised to bring Tissaphernes over to the Athenian side, if they would sponsor his return to Athens. The condition was that the democracy which had expelled him would have to go. In a famous phrase, he described the Athenian constitution, with its notorious preference of equality over efficiency, as 'acknowledged idiocy' (Thucydides, *The Peloponnesian War* 6.89). This was a good moment for Alkibiades to stir up anti-democratic feelings: as a result of the Sicilian disaster, Athens was so poor that it was relying more and more on donations from her wealthy citizens, which were increasingly less voluntary. The rich were losing their capital, and the threat to the Empire threatened their income from foreign holdings. They wanted an end to the war, and control over Athenian resources.

There were essentially two Athenian factions on Samos, and both were prepared to listen to Alkibiades. One was led by Thrasyboulos. Although he was a democrat, he was ready to sacrifice at least some of the institutions of democracy if the result was the survival of Athens, which now depended, he was convinced, on Persian support – and therefore on Alkibiades, since he was best placed to bring in the Persians. In any case, Athens was already a little less democratic than it had been: in 413 a special committee of ten elders, one from each tribe, took over some of the functions of the Council, and in the following year Athenian finances were put in the hands of another specially created committee. Both the Council and the Assembly were losing authority. Thrasyboulos could agree to a moderate, broad-based oligarchy, formed by limiting citizenship to a few thousand men, who would then govern Athens. This would also save much-needed cash, since fewer people would have to be paid by the state for their participation in government.

The other faction on Samos was led by Peisandros. On the face of it, he agreed with Thrasyboulos, but in actual fact he was committed to a narrower oligarchy. At first, both he and Thrasyboulos worked together to persuade the Athenian troops on Samos of the necessity of their proposed actions. There were those who did not trust Alkibiades and argued that he could not fulfil his promises, but the majority was prepared to take the risk. This alternative Athenian Assembly authorized Peisandros to go to Athens and put the same proposal to the Assembly there.

Peisandros' ostensible mission in Athens went well: the Assembly was prepared to make some sacrifices in order to avoid the destruction of the city, even at the cost of allying themselves with the hated barbarians. His covert mission was also successful: he went around the most political of the *hetaireiai* and persuaded them to work for the total overthrow of the democracy and the establishment of a narrow oligarchy. Over the next few weeks Peisandros' agents in Athens created a climate of terror, by means of the judicious assassination of leading democratic politicians and anyone who spoke against their oligarchic proposals.

Peisandros next visited Tissaphernes and Alkibiades in Sardis, both to report on progress and to negotiate the precise terms of Persian support. But negotiations broke down in the face of unreasonable demands from the Great King – Peisandros was prepared, like the Spartans, to sacrifice the coastal towns of Asia Minor, but not to sanction freedom for Persian shipping in the Aegean – and at the same time it became clear that Alkibiades was not as trusted by the Persians as he had made out. Peisandros decided to go ahead with his plans for oligarchy in Athens, but without Alkibiades. However, the failure of this mission to Sardis meant that Thrasyboulos broke from Peisandros: he had been willing to make sacrifices only if Persian help was guaranteed.

Peisandros returned to Athens and within a few weeks he and the more radical oligarchs in Athens had their way. With the city cowed by fear, the Assembly was amenable to a proposal that a board of thirty – the ten elders and twenty others – should be created to take a long, hard look at the constitution. But when this new committee came to make its recommendations to the Assembly a few weeks later, the oligarchs arranged for the Assembly to meet not on the Pnyx as usual, but outside the city walls. This prevented poorer citizens from attending, because they could not afford the armour to protect themselves out in the countryside, which was freely patrolled by Spartan troops from Dekeleia. And then the only recommendation the new committee put to this pseudo-Assembly (clearly having been primed by Peisandros and his colleagues) was that any Athenian citizen could make any proposal he wanted, with impunity, even if – under normal circumstances expressly forbidden by Athenian law – such a proposal was unconstitutional.

Of course, the proposal that was made by Peisandros, and passed, was oligarchic in nature: pay for public service was more or less suspended for the duration of the war, and a new Council of 400 was to be set up with full powers of government. The method of selection of the 400 was also undemocratic: a committee of five, chosen by lot (but from among those present at this pseudo-Assembly), would choose 100 men, who would each co-opt three more. The Assembly was to be limited to 5,000 citizens of hoplite rank and above, and the Council of 400 could convene this Assembly as and when it saw fit. In other words, the 400 were to be the effective rulers of Athens, with the Assembly of 5,000 a sop to more moderate oligarchs, a parody of the democratic Assembly. Moreover, it would be up to a special committee to conduct the census that would lead to the list of the 5,000 – a process which could be prolonged indefinitely to keep the 400 in power. With Thrasyboulos now committed only to democracy, the leader of the moderate oligarchs was a man called Theramenes.

A few days later, surrounded by bodyguards, the oligarchs staged a coup. They burst into the chambers of the official Council, paid off the councillors for the remainder of the year, and instituted the new Council of 400 in their place. One hundred years pre-viously, the last of the tyrants had been expelled from Athens, and democracy had been the Athenian way more or less ever since. But now democratic processes were interrupted. In theory, the 400 would be in power only for a short time, for as long as it took to draft a new constitution for Athens; but it is likely that they had no intention of relinquishing power. They also had no intention of letting people know that the scheme of gaining Persian assistance in the war was dead in the water. After all, their excuse for seizing control was that they and they alone could bring the war to a swift and successful conclusion.

Even though things had not been going well in the Aegean for the Spartans, they had done little or nothing to further their aims in the wider war while Athens had been in the throes of internal strife. They had no need to: they could reasonably expect an oligarchic government in Athens to be prepared to sell Athens to Sparta in return for support for their rule, and indeed the Athenian oligarchs sent a delegation to negotiate terms for peace, thus prov-ing the hollowness of their promise of victory. But the Spartans insisted that they would end the war only if Athens gave up the Empire, and in the face of such intransigence negotiations broke down. A short while later, a Spartan army appeared outside the walls of Athens, presumably to impose their terms, or perhaps in the expectation that at least some of the oligarchs would open the gates to them, but nothing happened, and the Spartans withdrew in disappointment.

In the Hellespont, the Spartans succeeded in persuading several other Athenian allies to secede from the Empire, and the grain route was now in severe danger. The Athenian fleet, with much of the democratic manpower, was still based on the island of Samos. When they heard that the 400 were in power in Athens, there was a strong move to sail to Athens and restore democracy immediately, but that would have meant abandoning the eastern Aegean to the enemy, and Alkibiades, now restored to favour and pretending to be a staunch democrat, rightly curbed such hasty measures. Nevertheless, the army on Samos set itself up as a kind of democratic government-in-exile, and committed itself to the overthrow of the oligarchy in Athens. The combination of the threat from Samos and the Spartan successes in the Hellespont threw the Athenian oligarchs into disarray. None of their plans had succeeded, they had alienated Theramenes and the moderates, and their only hope for remaining in power lay in betraying the city to the Spartans and becoming their puppets.

A Spartan fleet set out, expecting to find either Peiraieus opened by their friends, or the city torn apart by civil strife and therefore easy prey. But the moderates and democrats rose up and seized Peiraieus, and then marched on Athens, not to fight, but to force the 400 to keep their promise of drawing up the list of the favoured 5,000. The Spartan fleet sailed past the mouth of the harbour, but could do nothing more. They turned their attention to their secondary target, Euboia, defeated a scratch Athenian fleet off Eretria, and made it possible for the whole island to rise up in rebellion against Athens. The Athenians were dismayed not just by the loss of this important island, but by the danger they found themselves in. The main Athenian fleet was on Samos: the Spartans could have blockaded Peiraieus and either forced the city to submit, or tempted the Samian fleet to defend Athens at the cost of leaving the eastern Aegean undefended. Fortunately, the Spartans failed to seize the opportunity. Thucydides accused them of lack of nerve, and sarcastically described them as the most helpful enemies Athens could have had (*The Peloponnesian War* 8.96).

It was widely known in Athens that the 400 had intended to betray the city to save their skins. Their last remaining support evaporated, and the Assembly met to transfer power to the 5,000, defined as all those who could afford their own hoplite equipment, as an intermediate step to the restoration of full democracy. The old Council was brought back, and the rule of the 400 was over after only four months. Peisandros and the main oligarchs fled to the Spartans at Dekeleia; others who remained were taken to court at Theramenes' instigation and executed for treason.

The rule of the 5,000 (actually probably nearer 9,000) lasted only a little longer before succumbing to pressure from the oarsmen on Samos. On the restoration of democracy, every male citizen was required to make a solemn promise that he would kill anyone trying to subvert the democracy, or any officer of a non-democratic regime in Athens, or anyone trying to make himself a tyrant, or anyone who collaborated with a would-be tyrant.

War in the Hellespont

One of the first things the intermediate oligarchy of 5,000 did was pardon Alkibiades. But he chose not to come home immediately: 'He had no desire to come back empty-handed, without having achieved anything, and with his restoration accomplished thanks merely to pity and popularity; he wanted to come back in a blaze of glory' (Plutarch, *Alcibiades* 27). At any rate, there was work for him to do. With Euboia went one source of food for Athens; with Byzantion and the Hellespontine towns, and Thasos now in revolt from the Athenian alliance too (it was recovered in 407), the vital grain route from the Black Sea was in deadly peril. Alkibiades set out on a fund-raising expedition in order to finance the Athenian fleet over the next few months.

A series of sea battles in 411 and 410 severely weakened the Spartan fleet, returned much of the Hellespontine area to Athenian control, boosted Athenian morale and secured their route to the Black Sea for the immediate future. Thrasyboulos and Alkibiades were the heroes of the day. Although Alkibiades could not fulfil his promise to bring the Persians over to the Athenian side, the

Athenians forgave him, because of his successes at sea and in raising funds in Asia Minor to pay for the navy.

Once again, the Spartans came to Athens to sue for peace. The terms they offered were that each side should keep the territory it currently controlled, but exchange prisoners and withdraw garrisons from each other's land – that is, the Spartans would abandon Dekeleia, while the Athenians returned Pylos. But with the Spartans controlling so many important islands and cities which had once been Athenian tributaries, the Athenians felt they could not accept these terms. With the benefit of hindsight, of course, the Spartan terms were infinitely preferable to what eventually happened; even in the next century orators looked back on the Athenian rejection of peace at this point as the ultimate folly of a doomed city. But Kleophon, a demagogue in the tradition of Kleon, persuaded the Assembly to reject the offer. Within a year, however, the Spartans had retaken Pylos by force, and so robbed the Athenians of their chief bargaining counter.

Alkibiades badly needed reinforcements in the Hellespont in order to attempt to recover the lost allied towns there. They arrived in the summer of 409, having first waged an inconclusive campaign in Ionia. The following spring, Alkibiades and his fellow generals set to work and in short order, by a combination of diplomacy and military force, they secured several of the rebel Hellespontine towns. But this success was followed by a decisive disaster: the Spartans bypassed the treacherous and self-serving satraps and entered into an agreement with the Persian king himself, Dareios II. The king's younger son, Kyros, was given overall responsibility for the whole Aegean and Hellespontine coastlines, with a mandate to support the Spartans with both men and money. Any last hopes the Athenians might have entertained of reaching an agreement with the Persians vanished.

Alkibiades, however, contrived to make it clear that if anyone could drive a wedge between the Persians and the Spartans, it was he. He made much of his long-standing special relationship with various Persian satraps and dignitaries (this was still a world in which cultural borders could be crossed by aristocratic peers), and this dim hope, along with his acknowledged skills both as a fund-raiser and as a general, made it possible for him to return to Athens in the spring of 407. The Athenian people welcomed him with open arms. They had short memories: he may have achieved some successes in the Aegean and Hellespont, but without a doubt his advice to the Spartans was partly responsible for the terminal condition of Athens. Nevertheless, the Athenians revoked all the outstanding charges against him, had the priests undo the curses they had pronounced after the affair of the Mysteries, and made him commander-in-chief of the Athenian forces with extraordinary powers.

The Surrender of Athens

Alkibiades' sojourn in Athens lasted a little less than six months. His luck was running out.

> Alkibiades seems to be a clear case of someone destroyed by his own reputation. His successes had made his daring and resourcefulness so well known that any failure prompted people to wonder whether he had really tried. They never doubted his ability; if he really tried, they thought, nothing would be impossible for him. So they expected to hear that Khios had fallen too, and the whole of the rest of Ionia, and were therefore irritated when they heard that he had not managed to accomplish everything as quickly or instantaneously as they wanted. They did not stop to consider that he was short of money, and that therefore, as he was fighting people who had a powerful financial backer in the Persian king, he often had to make trips away from the scene of the action, leaving the army to its own devices, to raise money for wages and provisions.   (Plutarch, *Alcibiades* 35)

Plutarch makes some plausible excuses for Alkibiades, but the truth of the matter is that he had simply met his match. A new Spartan commander was active in the Aegean, as bold as Brasidas, and with a healthy contempt for the authorities back home. Lysandros burned with the desire not just to see the Athenians crushed, but to see Sparta elevated to their position in the Mediterranean – with him at the helm of this Spartan Empire. The young

Persian prince Kyros could have found no better shoulders on which to lay responsibility for the war in the Aegean, but Lysandros' independence and tendency to bend the rules earned him the disapproval of more conservative elements back in Sparta. He is reported to have said, 'If there isn't enough lion-skin, one must make patches out of fox-hide', and 'We use dice to cheat boys and oaths to cheat men' (Plutarch, *Lysander* 7 and 8).

By the summer of 407 Lysandros had assembled a fleet of ninety ships at Ephesos. He spent the rest of the year training and preparing his men, avoiding battle with the Athenians, building relationships with the oligarchs of Ionia (whether or not they were currently in government), and flattering his way into Kyros' favour and coffers. Over the next year, Persian money not only paid for his navy, but even enticed non-Athenian oarsmen to defect from the Athenian side. For the first time in the war, the Spartans had as much expertise at sea as the Athenians. It was a critical turning point.

Even though he had fewer ships, Alkibiades was unable to tempt Lysandros to come out and fight. In frustration, he left the bulk of his fleet at Notion, just up the coast from Ephesos, under an inexperienced commander called Antiokhos, and set out in search of adventure, joining Thrasyboulos in the siege of rebel Phokaia. Although Lysandros had resisted being drawn out of the safe harbour of Ephesos as long as Alkibiades was around, when Antiokhos tried the same ruse with a decoy of ten ships, Lysandros pounced. He came out with his entire fleet, and in his first assault succeeded in killing Antiokhos. He chased the remaining nine ships back to Notion, found the Athenian fleet in disarray, and soundly defeated them. It was the end of Athenian attempts to recover Ionia, and more and more towns there went over to the Spartans.

Alkibiades raced back as soon as he heard the news, but it was too late. Desperate for a victory to prop up his reputation at home, he attacked the rebel city of Kyme, but achieved nothing. The Athenians, who had recently endured a Spartan assault from Dekeleia on the very city walls, were not amused, and Alkibiades' enemies took advantage of the grim atmosphere to denounce him. He was removed from his command, and the up-and-coming general

Konon was sent out to Samos to replace him. Alkibiades withdrew to exile in his private fortress on the Khersonese.

By the campaigning season of 406, the Spartan fleet of 170 ships, led this year by Kallikratidas, was more than twice as large as that of the Athenians and sailed freely around the Aegean, undoing Athenian gains on Khios, Lesbos and elsewhere. Finally, Kallikratidas managed to trap Konon in the harbour of Mytilene and blockaded the town by land and sea. The Athenians at home were deeply worried. In a last desperate effort, they melted down sacred statues to raise money to build ships and pay the crews – but the crews were untrained men from every walk of life and stratum of society, even slaves (who were bribed by the offer of freedom), and in having them man the ships, the city was left virtually undefended. Fortunately, the Spartans did not launch a land attack that summer from Dekeleia.

In July this motley fleet of about 100 ships set sail from Athens, under the command of no fewer than eight of the ten generals elected that year. Konon had forty or so ships in Mytilene, but they were trapped. When the Athenian fleet arrived at Samos, they were joined by an allied flotilla. The combined fleet sailed to relieve the blockade at Mytilene. Kallikratidas left fifty ships to enforce the blockade and set out to intercept the Athenian fleet. They clashed close to the Arginousai islands, east of Lesbos. The battle was long and hard, but in the end the Spartans were well and truly beaten, losing seventy-seven ships to the Athenians' twenty-five.

In the emotional seesaw of these closing months of the war, Athenian hopes were again high. Konon was rescued, they had defeated a triumphant Spartan fleet, and they had reason to expect that, having regained control of the sea, they would soon win back their Ionian losses. But they threw it all away. Immediately after the battle, there was fury in Athens that the generals had not stopped to pick up shipwrecked Athenian sailors who were floundering in the water and subsequently drowned. The generals had delegated junior officers to carry out a rescue mission, but it never happened. The generals were summoned home, but two of them, reading between the lines, preferred immediate exile. The other six were arraigned for simultaneous trial.

The trial of the generals became a *cause célèbre*. Emotions ran high, political divisions were close to the surface and reason was replaced by grief and anger. This kind of mass trial was illegal, or at least immoral, since it did not give the defendants time to deliver a speech each. The dubious nature of the procedure was pointed out at the time (and not least by Sokrates, in one of his rare political interventions), and there was much debate and heated argument, but in the end, by a narrow vote, the Assembly went ahead with the mass trial. All six generals were condemned to death and executed. The Athenians had made a public display of their desperation, and everyone knew that such desperation was born out of the secret knowledge that they were losing the war. In fact, the end came quickly.

Now fully driven by the blindness that characterizes so many tragic heroes, the Athenians, at Kleophon's urging, turned down another offer of peace from Sparta. Kleophon argued that the recovery of Ionia and the rebel islands was within their grasp, since the remnants of the Spartan fleet on Khios were hardly seaworthy. This was true, but Kleophon did not allow for the reinstatement of Lysandros, who returned to the Aegean as commander of the Spartan forces in 405. Thanks to his friendship with Kyros, money again became available to pay the Spartan sailors and to fund an emergency ship-building programme. By the summer, he had 150 ships, while the Athenians had 180 stationed at Samos.

Lysandros' men saw some action on the coast of Asia Minor that summer, but his main target was the Hellespont. The Athenians had no choice but to follow him there, to try to neutralize the renewed threat to their grain supply. They beached their ships at Aigospotamoi, but there was not enough food in the neighbourhood to support so many men. In order to gain supplies, the Athenians had to split their forces, with some going to Sestos, about eighteen kilometres down the Hellespont, and others foraging locally.

It so happened that Alkibiades was living nearby, and he still felt sufficient loyalty to the Athenian cause to try to warn the three generals at Aigospotamoi of the weakness of their position, with no proper harbour and no reliable source of provisions. But they rudely sent him packing: 'Others are in command now, not you' (Plutarch, *Alcibiades* 37). This was Alkibiades' last appearance: he was assassinated in 404, apparently by agents of the Persian satrap Pharnabazos.

As the days passed, Athenian discipline grew more and more lax. When Lysandros' attack came, the Athenians were entirely unprepared and he caught most of the ships still drawn up on the shore. All but ten or twelve of the ships were captured or destroyed, and 3,000 men lost their lives while the rest ran away. Grain could no longer get through the Hellespont. It was only a matter of time before Athens was starved into submission. In the city they prepared for a siege and, remembering how they had slaughtered the men of Skione, Melos and elsewhere, they expected the same treatment themselves.

Within a very few weeks, the entire Athenian Empire had collapsed, proving that most of the allies had remained loyal only out of fear or expediency. All over the Aegean, towns and cities opened their gates to Lysandros and his men, hailing him as their saviour and a semi-divine hero. Only Samos loyally held out (and was rewarded by a universal grant of citizenship), but eventually succumbed to siege. After settling affairs in the Aegean, the Spartan fleet sailed for Athens in October 405.

Lysandros blockaded Peiraieus with 150 ships, while both Spartan kings took to the field and the Peloponnesian forces camped just outside the city, within easy view of the walls. Starved of both grain and allies, the Athenians were soon forced to negotiate. There was a division of opinion in Sparta, but in the end Lysandros got his way over the ephors and Spartan allies: Athens was to lose not all her fortifications – the city walls were to survive – but only the Long Walls and the Peiraieus defences; her fleet of warships was limited to twelve; the Empire was formally dissolved; and the pro-Spartan oligarchs exiled after the coup of 411 were to be allowed back. The Athenians accepted these terms. The walls were demolished amid scenes of celebration and the music of pipe-girls. 'People thought that this day marked the beginning of freedom for Greece' (Xenophon, *Hellenica* 2.2.23).

The tragedy had played its course. The city was bankrupt and the countryside had been repeatedly ravaged. Once the queen of the Mediterranean, Athens was now a pawn in a Spartan power struggle: Lysandros desired supreme power in Sparta, and the reason he had argued for less harsh terms for Athens was that he wanted a future ally on the mainland, to add to the many Aegean states who were already loyal to him. Within less than 100 years, Athens had gained a great empire, fought for the best part of fifty years to keep it, but finally lost it. In the end the tables were turned: it was Athens which exchanged autonomy for subjection to a government imposed from outside.

Civil War

To his credit, Lysandros left the Athenians to try to sort out their own constitutional affairs; to their discredit, continued feuding prevented them from doing so. There were essentially three political factions in Athens: the clubs and the returned exiles, who wanted oligarchy and a board of ephors in imitation of Sparta to propose and promulgate their plans; the democrats; and the moderates, who wanted a restoration of the 'ancestral constitution' – essentially the Kleisthenic set-up, with a strong Areiopagos.

Not surprisingly, the three factions failed to reach any kind of compromise, and so the oligarchs sent for Lysandros, who had already imposed narrow oligarchies elsewhere, and arranged for the execution of the most prominent democrat, Kleophon, on a trumped-up charge. Lysandros imposed a junta of thirty, and compromised only to the extent of allowing Theramenes to nominate ten of the thirty, including himself. The thirty were given a brief to restore the ancestral constitution and then govern in accordance with it. Many of the Thirty had been among the Four Hundred of 411, with Sokrates' friend Kritias the most prominent of them.

The Thirty began by bringing to trial and executing a number of democrats on the grounds that they had opposed the peace treaty, but none of these trials or those of more widely unpopular members of the city aroused unrest. People accepted them as the cost of the stability they longed for, and looked forward to the new constitution that would signal an era of peace for Athens and the end of such anarchy. The Thirty apparently wanted to remodel Athens along the lines of the Spartan constitution. They were a body the same size as the Spartan *gerousia*, and they took similar powers: for instance, they gave themselves the power of life or death over anyone resident in Athens who was not a full citizen. They limited full citizenship to 3,000 of 'the best men' (like the *homoioi* in Sparta), while all others – like the *perioikoi* at Sparta – were denied the right to live in the city. Now that Athens had lost its navy, and with it the democratic power of the rowers, the Thirty were trying to return citizens to the land. All this alienated Theramenes, who wanted a citizen body larger than 3,000 and an Assembly with more power than it did in Sparta. Theramenes, after all, had been the chief proponent of the moderate oligarchy of 5,000 in 411.

Democrats either kept quiet or fled. A group of refugees gathered around Thrasyboulos in Thebes. The association of the democrats with Thebes is astonishing, since only a few weeks earlier Thebes had been vociferous in the Peloponnesian League, arguing for the total destruction of Athens. Nevertheless, powerful Thebans already had an eye to the future, and thought that a democratic Athens might make a good ally against the Spartans. In due course, thirty Athenian democrats set out from Thebes, and the number had swelled to seventy by the time they reached Phyle on the southern slopes of Mount Parnes in January 403, where they were reinforced by several hundred mercenaries hired by the wealthy orator Lysias.

The Thirty sent out the whole body of 3,000 citizens against this meagre revolutionary band, but fortune favoured the democrats, and one of the incredible rainstorms that periodically plague the area forced the oligarchs to retire. In a spirit of no compromise, the Thirty outlawed Theramenes and condemned him to death. After drinking the hemlock he flicked out the last drops from his cup (in imitation of the game of *kottabos*) with the words, 'Here's to that fine fellow Kritias!'

With the moderate leader dead, and the most outspoken democrats out of the city, the Thirty set about a reign of terror. First they disarmed everyone except the 3,000, and even sent some Athenians to serve in Lysandros' army. They then began, in the fashion typical of tyrants, to kill their opponents or suspected opponents – about 1,500 men in all – and to confiscate their property for themselves and their followers. It was enough to remind the Athenians that democracy is no less important for what it prevents than for what it provides. Numbers at Phyle swelled, but more gathered in Peiraieus, despite the fact that the port was supposed to be under the control of a board of ten appointed by the Thirty. Others fled to Thebes, Argos and elsewhere. The Thirty secured Eleusis and Salamis, not without bloodshed, and then asked Lysandros for help. He sent a garrison of 700 ex-helots, who occupied the Akropolis. The Thirty alienated even more people by depleting public funds and property, and even robbing the temples, to pay for the Spartan troops.

The garrison tried to cut the line of supplies to Phyle, but Thrasyboulos' men came out against them, attacked their camp and inflicted heavy casualties. This success encouraged more Athenians to join the rebels. Now about 1,000 strong, the democrats left Phyle thinly defended and moved to the hill of Mounykhia in Peiraieus, in order to link up with the democrats there. The oligarchs attacked with superior numbers, but the democrats won, killing Kritias in the process and gaining control of Peiraieus.

The brief and inglorious reign of the Thirty was over. They had failed, at least in military matters, and in Athens the 3,000 deposed them and elected instead a board of ten, one from each tribe. Faced with an even narrower oligarchy, Thrasyboulos' numbers in Peiraieus increased dramatically: men were attracted especially by his offer of citizenship to any who helped him defeat the Ten. Soon he controlled the countryside and was able to lay siege to the city. The oligarchs sent a delegation to Sparta, arguing that Athens would fall under Theban control, and that the democrats were threatening the overthrow of a Spartan-imposed government. Lysandros sent his brother with a fleet to blockade Peiraieus, and came himself with money to hire mercenary troops.

The oligarchs would have preferred to see an army, not just funds, but Lysandros' position in Sparta was not so secure that he could arrange a full-blooded response. Realizing that sooner or later they were going to fail, the Ten showed themselves willing to negotiate, and later in 403 the Spartan king Pausanias brokered a peace between the two sides and withdrew the Spartan garrison. The main terms of the treaty were a political amnesty (for all except the Ten and the highest oligarchic officers, who had to submit to the normal accounting of their office before becoming liable to the amnesty if they passed), the right of oligarchs to leave Athens (many chose to settle in Eleusis, which briefly became an oligarchic redoubt), and compensation for loss of property for the democrats. Work had been in progress for a number of years to write down the complete Athenian law code – what was left of Drakon's and Solon's laws, plus whatever new ones had come into force since Solon's time – and to overhaul the religious calendar, so the fresh start outlined by the treaty went through with no discernible hesitation.

A temporary board of twenty was set up to supervise the city while the restoration of full democracy was put into effect. The returning democrats and the foreigners who had fought alongside them were honoured. Strife was not entirely over, because the oligarchs in Eleusis made one more attempt, in 401, to arm themselves. The democrats responded quickly, though: they besieged Eleusis and killed all the leaders after inviting them to a conference. The oligarchic revolution was finally crushed. The restored democracy considered their overthrow of oligarchy so definitive that they regarded 403 as the start of a new era for Athens, much as the French revolutionaries named 1789 'Year One' of the new epoch.

Athenian democracy had survived its most severe test. The oligarchic revolution certainly arose out of discontent on the part of the wealthy, but it was not a sign of fundamental weakness in the democratic systems or of a deep-seated rift between rich and poor in Athens. No such fault-line laid Athens low, only her own hubris. That tragedy was played out by the end of the Peloponnesian War, and the cruel oligarchy that followed was no more than a cacophonous coda. In the entire 200-year history of Athenian democracy, it was suspended only twice – in 411 and 404 – and both these threats occurred as a result of war, as responses to perceived emergencies. At first, indeed, many saw the Thirty as saviours, bringing peace and a chance to resume normal life and recover the city's fortunes. But they ruled with such cruelty – they were indeed 'ful of cursednesse', as Geoffrey Chaucer put it (*Canterbury Tales* 5.1368) – that within a few years they were universally known as 'the Thirty Tyrants'. Moreover, Sparta's actions in supporting such an appalling

THE HELLENISTIC AND
ROMAN CITY

20

Athens in the Fourth Century

Archaeologists, art historians and casual visitors to the Athenian Akropolis had always noticed a number of holes on the eastern pediment of the Parthenon. The function of some of them was known: in memory of Marathon, Alexander the Great sent back to Athens from his eastern conquests 300 Persian shields which were hung there in a patriotic display. But what was the purpose of the other holes? In 1895 a young American student called Eugene Andrews undertook a remarkable piece of detective work. Perched high above the stony ground on a precarious platform, supported by ropes, he traced the fittings and found that they spelled out an inscription, originally in large bronze lettering, rededicating the temple to the Roman emperor Nero when he visited the city in 61 CE. How did the city reach such a sorry state of subservience that the Athenians would disfigure the Parthenon with a servile text?

Athens emerged from the disasters of the end of the fifth century in tatters, but, astonishingly, with her pride more or less intact. It was, however, a retrospective pride: Athens had abruptly become a city with a past. Abetted by the marked decline in literary evidence about Athens after the conquest of Greece by Philip II of Macedon, this section of the book will cover several hundred years of the city's history: the last years of the Classical period, during which Athens still retained some hope of resurrection; the Macedonian conquest, which ushered in the Hellenistic period, whose chief socio-political feature was that the local politics of the Greek cities became subsumed under the concerns of empires; and finally, the Roman conquest and rule of Greece, which completed this process of the sidelining of Athens, as of other Greek cities. Never again would Greek states make foreign policy for and by themselves: there were always fellow members of confederacies to take into consideration, or external powers and empires to impose policies.

If there is a grand theme unifying Athenian history during this period, it is no longer the city's reaction to the Olympic spirit of Greek cooperation, as it was during the fifth century. The last remnant of that ideal is to be found in Athens' internationalism: because of her glorious past, she had always attracted foreign intellectuals and artists, and this tradition continued with the foundation of schools in the city which established it as the centre of higher education for the Mediterranean world. Instead, what unifies Athenian history from the beginning of the fourth century onwards is the tension between the realities of the present and the receding myth of the past. As long as the city remembered her past, she retained some vitality. But after the Roman annexation of Greece in the second century BCE, she increasingly began to lose her own cultural identity and to become dependent on the largesse of kings, emperors and wealthy individuals, who honoured the city's past by restoring old monuments and building new ones, until Athens looked and was administered more like a Roman provincial town than a Greek citizen-state.

Shifting Alliances and the Renewal of Empire

The Athenians had shown that it was possible for a single citizen-state to rise above all others and to gain great wealth and power. Much fourth-century Greek history is explicable in this context, as various states – especially Athens, Sparta and Thebes – vied with one another in a series of kaleidoscopic alliances to occupy the position Athens had claimed during the previous century. The instability of the fourth century was a direct result of the Peloponnesian War, which had aroused long-standing hostilities between and within states. Oligarchs and democrats clashed and massacred one another; interstate warfare was frequent; political programmes in Athens changed according to the objectives of whichever politician had the ear of the Assembly at the time.

At the end of the Peloponnesian War, Sparta was the leading city of Greece. The Spartans had defeated their rivals and could claim to be the liberators of Greece and protectors of the most cherished Greek values. Never has such a fine claim proved so hollow so fast: they alienated their former allies and tried to replace the Athenian Empire with one of their own. They were supposed to return the Greek cities of Asia Minor to the Persians, in return for Persian backing in the Peloponnesian War, but as soon as Persia was distracted by internal troubles, they set about pushing the Persians out of Asia Minor and subjecting the Greek cities there to their own dominion. So far from granting the former Athenian subject states of Ionia and the Aegean their autonomy, they treated them with even greater harshness. At Lysandros' urging, they imposed pro-Spartan oligarchies or Spartan governors, and tribute, wherever they could, and tried to extend their Empire, or at least their sphere of influence, into northern Greece, Sicily, and even Egypt.

The Persian response to Spartan aggression was to build a fleet (and put in charge the Athenian Konon, who had been living in Cyprus since escaping from Aigospotamoi in 405) and to bribe Greek states to take up arms against Sparta. In 395 a long-standing dispute between the Phokians and the Lokrians escalated into open warfare and then spiralled out of control. The Lokrians called on their Theban allies for help, and the Phokians asked the Spartans to attack Thebes in retaliation. The Athenians, Argives and Corinthians joined the Theban side, with the help of Persian money. The Spartans bungled a two-pronged assault on Boiotia, and Lysandros lost his life fighting there.

Although the anti-Spartan alliance was defeated on land in 394, Konon destroyed the Spartan fleet off Knidos and checked Spartan imperialist ambitions. King Agesilaos of Sparta was forced to focus his military efforts on defence of his homeland rather than on expansion in Asia and, with Persian money brought back by Konon on his return from exile, the Athenians seized the opportunity to rebuild their fortifications, barely ten years after they had been razed to the ground.

With the war in Greece at stalemate and Persia likely to regain her old territories on the Asia Minor coast, Athens' old hostility to Persia led her, encouraged by the hawkish Thrasyboulos and the orator Isokrates, into alliances with Persian rebels and negotiations with former allies in Asia Minor. But the Persians had learnt well how to bring Athens to her knees. They supported a Spartan move to blockade the Hellespont, and Athens again chose submission over starvation. Weakened by constant bickering and warfare, the Greek cities were in no position to resist when in 386 the Spartans and the Persians imposed a peace (usually called the King's Peace), in accordance with which the Asia Minor cities fell under Persian control, for the first time since 479, though Sparta had signed them away in 411. After this, Athenian and Spartan military activity in Asia was severely curtailed.

Throughout this troubled period, there were of course those in Athens who would have preferred peace, but they were in the minority. And the motives of the majority were public knowledge: Athens wanted to regain her Empire. This was the first consequence of the fifth-century myth: an ingrained belief in the city's right to greatness. Despite all the hard lessons of the previous century, despite blatant arrogance and humiliating defeat, the Athenians still needed an Aegean Empire to protect their grain routes and to guarantee a good income (especially after the Persians withdrew their funds), and they thought they could avoid their earlier mistakes. Metics, vital for the Athenian economy, had left in droves after the Peloponnesian War, and needed to be tempted back by renewed prosperity and a Peiraieus which had resumed its former industry.

The terms of the King's Peace explicitly stated that all Greek states (other than those in Asia Minor, which were once more part of the Persian Empire) should be free and autonomous: this was an undisguised attempt to pre-empt Athenian efforts to regain an Empire. The foundations of Empire had already been laid, especially by the military activities of Thrasyboulos in the Hellespont and the northern Aegean in 389 and 388, which gained Athens many allies and lost Thrasyboulos his life. Despite Spartan and Persian opposition, Athenian orators were constantly harping on about Athens' manifest destiny and past glories. In about 390, for instance, Lysias wrote (*Funeral Speech* 2.55–57):

> It took an enormous amount of hard work, it took conspicuous efforts and glorious dangers, but our predecessors liberated Greece. They made their own land supreme, ruled the sea for seventy years, saved their allies from feuding and ensured that

rather than the many being subservient to the few, everyone should have equality. So far from weakening their allies, they not only made them strong, but also increased their own power until the Great King stopped coveting other people's territory, gave up some of his own and was even afraid of losing the rest. In those days no warships sailed from Asia, no tyrant ruled in Greece, no Greek city was enslaved by barbarians; the courage displayed by our predecessors instilled that much caution and respect in all men. And this is why they and they alone necessarily became the champions and leaders of the Greek cities.

The panhellenic nature of the King's Peace could have led Greeks to recognize fellow Greeks as brothers, but bickering and hostilities continued. In 382, while ostensibly on his way north to help towns in Khalkidike against aggression from the citizens of Olynthos, the Spartan commander Phoibidas occupied the Theban akropolis, in direct contravention of the terms of the Peace. Even the pro-Spartan historian Xenophon found it impossible to condone the action. Three years later, when the Thebans, with Athenian help, drove the Spartans out of their city, Sparta responded by invading Boiotia and occupying Thespiai. Athens was looking for a diplomatic solution, but was pre-empted by an attack from the Spartans at Thespiai on Peiraieus. The attack came to nothing, but Athens learnt a lesson in fourth-century international relations: if you are not with them, you are against them.

Athens took advantage of Sparta's unpopularity to increase her imperialist efforts, by usurping the rhetoric of freedom. In 377, at the urging of Kallistratos, the leading statesman of the day, she issued a manifesto: 'Any state, Greek or non-Greek (as long as it is not subject to Persia), may become an ally of Athens and her allies on conditions of freedom and autonomy, and preserve its chosen form of constitution, while having neither garrison nor governor imposed upon it, and without having to pay any tribute' (*Greek Historical Inscriptions* II, 123).

What is significant here is that states were offered an alliance not just with Athens, but with 'Athens and her allies': in this renewed Empire, founded in the summer of 378, the allies had more administrative power than in the fifth century, and tribute (known under the euphemism 'contributions') was pooled; but Athens took upon herself the right to see that action followed debate. Athens had authority rather than legitimate power, but she used that authority to arrogate a position of pre-eminence within the alliance. This was a position from which she could exploit the allies – if she chose to, if imperialists gained power in the city – in a manner which might not differ much from that of the previous century, especially since her propaganda merchants were busy portraying Athens as a potential panhellenic leader against the barbarian Persians.

During the 370s, while the Thebans took control of a Boiotian federal state refounded on democratic lines, the Athenians were building ships and forging alliances, as a bulwark against both Sparta and Persia. Sparta postured and protested ineffectively. The most important member of the Athenian alliance was Thebes, though her membership was fragile and rarely wholehearted. Matters came to a head in 371, after several months of more or less open hostility between Athens and Thebes. The prospect of the final defeat of Sparta seemed remote, and Athens informed her allies that she was going to negotiate a peace with her old rival. But Thebes withdrew from the conference after a deliberate snub by Athens and Sparta. The Spartans invaded Boiotia and faced the Thebans on the plain of Leuktra.

Under the inspired leadership of the philosopher-general Epameinondas, and with the help of their famous Sacred Band (an elite and highly trained force of 300, in which homosexual pairing was encouraged for the sake of loyalty and cohesion), the Thebans routed and massacred the Spartans. Four hundred Spartiates – 40 per cent of all that remained after the war and a marked decline in citizen population – lost their lives, and Spartan power was irrevocably broken. The following year the Thebans invaded Spartan territory, freed the helots of Messenia (denying the Spartans the best of their agricultural land and their way of life), and unified the scattered communities of Arkadia.

One of the three major players in Greece was off the board once and for all. Just to make sure, Thebes spent much of the 360s breaking up the Spartan alliance (which included Athens, now nervous of the Theban threat). The Persians and Boiotians joined forces in 367 to try by diplomatic means to dissolve the Athenian Empire, and Athens' refusal to listen led to a Boiotian fleet under Epameinondas making its presence felt in 364 in the Hellespont, where several of Athens' allies defected.

The period of Theban ascendancy was brief, however. Epameinondas died in battle in 362, and after this Thebes withdrew from the thankless task of attempting, in the face of Athenian and other opposition, to control areas of Greece wider than her local Boiotia. The Athenians took advantage of the vacuum to rebuild her Empire by more aggressive means. Asia Minor was of course in Persian hands, but Athens gradually acquired or reacquired a number of important allies among the Aegean states, though the process was far from smooth and had vociferous opponents at home. Eventually, though, the new Empire (if it deserves the name) came to have about seventy members.

After Leuktra, there was hardly any excuse for the Athenian confederacy: the Spartans were broken, and the Persians were showing no inclination to intervene directly in mainland Greece, as long as the Greeks stayed away from Persian territory. Only pirates remained as a threat to Aegean shipping – so much so that merchant ships were often accompanied by warships. At first Athens was conscientious in avoiding some of the mistakes of the previous century and in keeping to both the spirit and the letter of the manifesto of 377. But gradually tribute-payments were exacted, and the occasional garrison imposed, by Athenian commanders acting with more arrogance than good sense. Moreover, allied wishes were sometimes overridden by the Athenians, who showed an increasing tendency to use the supposedly common tribute for their own military activities; above all, from 368, they were determined to recover long-lost Amphipolis. It was easy for the allies to see these actions as the thin end of the wedge, and a rebellious trickle became a flood in the winter of 357, when Athens was faced with the kind of concerted rebellion that was unknown in the fifth century. Her most important Aegean allies joined forces with the expansionist Persian satrap Mausolos of Karia (of 'mausoleum' fame) and twice defeated an Athenian fleet sent out against them. Athens had to acknowledge that she was never again going to be an imperial power.

Apathy at home and dissent abroad undermined the Athenian will to power, and in 355 Athens formally recognized the independence of the rebel states. She was left with a pitiful 'Empire' consisting of Euboia, the Kyklades islands around Delos, and a few possessions in northern Greece – 'a few wretched islanders', in the words of the orator Aiskhines (*On the Embassy* 71), 'islander' being a derogatory term in Athens. A paltry 45 talents a year was all the income these states provided for Athenian coffers.

Historical hindsight is a wonderful tool; in this case it makes it absolutely plain that all the turmoil of the first fifty or so years of the fourth century was just a storm in a teacup. The real threat lay elsewhere. The 'barbaric' country of Macedon in the north was growing in power and would shortly subdue all the Greek states.

Athenian Politics in the Early Fourth Century

In many respects, Athenian society was unchanged from the fifth century. The peasant farmers who formed the heart of the Athenian way of life still went about their daily business in the same way (once they had recovered from the effects of the war), as did the traders and plutocrats, at a reduced level; religious practices were more or less the same, the great festivals continued, women and slaves were no better off.

Democracy, however, was under attack. Plato thought it was a synonym for anarchy; Isokrates was capable of presenting himself as a true democrat, but really wanted a restoration of the Areiopagos. The virtues of enlightened kingship were being sung by these writers and other philosophers; ultimately, anti-democratic Aristotle, long a resident of Athens, became the tutor of the prince who would become Alexander the Great. And, for whatever reasons, the democracy was somewhat weakened. Since the reforms of 403, a committee (the *nomothetai*, 'law-givers') vetted all laws passed by the Assembly. The size of the committee ranged from 501 to 1,501, depending on the importance of the laws in question, and in the fourth century members were chosen from among the jurors empanelled for that year. At the same time, all proposals passed by the Assembly alone, without the involvement of the law-givers, were downgraded to 'decrees', and since the laws were now written down on stone and displayed, reference to 'unwritten laws' or mere convention was prohibited. Laws were binding on everyone, and were assumed to last for ever, while decrees applied to particular people or situations.

This was a limitation of the Assembly's powers, but the creation of another annual committee did not represent a move towards professionalism, and the character of Athenian democracy remained essentially the same. The Areiopagos Council, however, regained some of its judicial powers, at the expense of the Heliaia, and was once again allowed to supervise the conduct of elected officials. Nevertheless, in about 400, the capacity of the Pnyx was almost doubled, as a symbol that Athenian democracy was not yet defunct. Democracy was deified and worshipped in the fourth century – as a giver of blessings, along with Peace, Good Luck, Persuasion, Rumour and other newly deified abstractions.

For much of the fifth century, military commanders had political power; in the fourth century, as well as orators such as Demosthenes and Aiskhines, it was those who were responsible for the city's finances, especially the Commissioners of the Festival Fund, the money kept aside to pay ordinary people to attend the theatre. The sums of money they wielded were not huge, but they were the closest the city had to professional government officers, in that they were eligible for repeated re-election, and so could use the office as a springboard to political eminence. One continuity with the late fifth century was that politicians came not just from the old noble families, but from a wider social spectrum. Ability, not birth, was the criterion.

Generals were now soldiers rather than politicians, as both spheres demanded professionalism. Warfare was increasingly expensive: warships were just as costly to maintain as before, and the city's coffers were also drained by an increasing reliance on mercenaries, who were better trained and could campaign longer than citizen soldiers. At the same time the rich became more and more dissatisfied with shouldering the burden of the military liturgy (see

p. 174) until this, and the war tax, became shared by groups of people rather than being the responsibility of a single individual. However, one of the last provisions of Kallistratos, the statesman who was prominent in Athens in the 370s and 360s, was that the richest citizens should advance the state the money it would later raise from taxes, when they would be reimbursed. But overall, the rich were less civic-minded in the fourth century than in the fifth, with the result that there was more conspicuous spending on such things as houses, jewellery and monuments. The state let them get away with it, mindful of the social disruptions of the previous century that had pitted rich against poor. Demosthenes managed to get the trierarchy (the liturgy of maintaining a warship for a year) re-established only in 339, when the Macedonian menace demanded emergency measures.

Euboulos was in charge of the Festival Fund continuously from 355 to 344. He came to power after a period of financial crisis, when income from the Laureion mines was significantly lower and the Athenian response was to put pressure on their few remaining allies to increase their contributions. Euboulos, however, recognized the impossibility of an Athenian Empire, and instead promoted a policy whereby Athens took the lead in seeking peace between all the major Greek states, not least so that they could unite against the threat of Macedon to the north. There was life yet in the old slogan of panhellenism. Once this policy failed, Euboulos internalized the focus of Athenian politics and pushed for sound domestic management. Under Euboulos, Athens recovered somewhat – and became accustomed to a reduced role in foreign affairs.

Lykourgos, from an ancient noble family, was already fifty years old when he came to power in 338 with the special title of Steward of the Financial Administration. He controlled Athenian finances for twelve years. Under his regime the annual revenue of Athens soared to 1,200 talents: he reactivated the mines and, since there was general peace in the Aegean, Peiraieus could once again earn its keep. Business was booming and Lykourgos proved that Athens did not need an empire to achieve prosperity. He restocked the temples with treasures, which had been melted down by the end of the Peloponnesian War, and channelled some of the city's surplus money into an extensive building programme. He built shipsheds in

Peiraieus, improved the Pnyx, rebuilt the Theatre of Dionysos in stone, repaired the defensive walls, established the Panathenaic stadium (the basis of the 1896 stadium) to replace the athletic facilities of the agora, tinkered with the Peisistratid Temple of Olympian Zeus, and repaired the Periklean gymnasium at the Lykeion. In short, he reasserted traditional values and set about reviving the glories of Periklean Athens – and adopting a Periklean defiance towards the threat from Macedon.

Fourth-century Athens continued to be haunted by its past. It was not just that orators went on and on about it, but the Athenians also took steps to keep the previous century alive. For the first time the great plays of Aiskhylos, Sophokles and Euripides were preserved and restaged; Plato, Xenophon and other Sokratics set their dialogues in the late fifth century; historians of Athens' past, such as Philokhoros (*c.* 350–260), flourished. The search for meaning – the desire to make sense of the catastrophe and chaos that had defiled the last thirty years of the fifth century – was aided by a new phenomenon. For the first time the written word began to be trusted more than unwritten tradition or the immediacy of living speech. Hence, in combination with nostalgia, we find the revision and publication of the city's laws. Apart from what this tells us about how widespread literacy was in Athens at the time, writing was the way to heal the rift between past and present: the future could rest on the stability and undeniable accuracy of a concrete document. For what underlay both nostalgia and revision was a desire for precision.

An important social institution which exemplifies this trend was the establishment of the *ephēbeia*, a two-year period of acculturation for young men aged between eighteen and twenty (ephebes), following their formal enrolment into a deme. The *ephēbeia* began around 370, but reached its final form only under Lykourgos. It was mandatory throughout the fourth century, but by the middle of the third century it had become voluntary, and so the numbers of young men following the programme dwindled, from about 500 a year at its peak at the end of the fourth century to fewer than fifty a century later, by when it had become a one-year programme, no longer subsidized by the state, but an elite school for its future leaders.

Religious duties were prominent: the young men had to visit all the major sanctuaries of Attica, Athens and Peiraieus. They also had to serve as a garrison, learn military skills, demonstrate these skills in an athletic display before the people and patrol the land. They were free from all other obligations in this period, and were educated in everything from geography and politics to philosophy. At the end of their training, the young men had to take an oath. They called various gods to witness, and then went on:

> I shall not bring shame upon these sacred weapons nor shall I abandon my comrades-in-arms wherever I stand in the ranks. I shall defend both the sacred and the profane aspects of life. I shall hand on the fatherland not smaller than I received it, but larger and better, so far as it lies in my power, with the assistance of all my fellow citizens. I shall obey the officials who govern wisely and the laws, both those which are already established and those which are wisely established in the future. If anyone attempts to destroy them, I shall not allow it, so far as it lies in my power with the assistance of all my fellow citizens. I shall hold in honour the ancestral sanctuaries.
>
> (*Greek Historical Inscriptions* II, 204)

Ephebic training was the closest Athens got to ensuring a degree of professionalism among her soldiers, but it was more significant as an attempt to perpetuate the traditional values which, it was felt, had made Athens great. If Athens was ever to revive, these values needed to be engraved on stone as laws, and on the hearts and minds of the next generation of soldiers and politicians.

Philip of Macedon and Demosthenes of Athens

The Greeks had long had a relationship with various Macedonian rulers, above all because the land was rich in timber, grain and precious metals. Although the Macedonians spoke a version of the Greek language and their kings claimed Greek lineage, they were generally considered to be barbarians, and given to savagery and hard drinking (a reputation which Philip II and his son Alexander the Great did little to remedy). 'Philip,' said Demosthenes (*Philippic* III.31), 'is not Greek, nor is he kin to Greeks. He is a barbarian – and even so he comes from a land which is beneath contempt. He is a plague from Macedon, where even the slaves we used to buy were worthless.' The Macedonians were non-Greek above all because their basic social unit was not the citizen-state, but the tribe: the Makedones were simply the most powerful tribe in the area that therefore came to be named after them. Moreover, all the tribes of northern Greece were still ruled by constitutional monarchies, which Athenians and southern Greeks considered a case of arrested development.

Philip II came to the Macedonian throne in 359. By 355, through a combination of diplomacy, assassination and military force, he had warded off external threats and united the country under his autocratic rule. He developed the army and altered Greek hoplite tactics until he had a stupendous fighting force at his personal command. He could call on an army of 2,000 cavalry and 30,000 soldiers trained to high professional standards, equipped with superior weaponry (especially lighter shields, and a long, sturdy pike which impeded the approach of the enemy line), accustomed to longer periods of warfare than the short Greek campaigning season, and accompanied by fewer camp-followers to allow for greater speed of movement.

Even apart from their lack of professionalism, many Greek states would have to unite in order to field an army of comparable size. But the Greek cities never shared a common view of Philip. Some saw him as a potential champion of Greece against the Persian threat; others saw him as a menace to Greek citizen-state liberty; others saw him as a potential ally who might improve the standing of their native cities. In short, Philip was perceived just as Athens and Sparta had been in the past. Since the Greek states never united, Philip could pick them off one by one, or league by league.

In 357 Philip annexed the former Athenian colony of Amphipolis; Athens was too busy fighting her rebellious Aegean allies to do much more than protest, and the town was never restored, although Philip cleverly used it as a bargaining counter in negotiations with Athens over the subsequent years. By 352 he had made himself master of Thessaly, and so threatened southern Greece. In Athens a young orator called Demosthenes came to prominence with a series of fiery anti-Macedonian speeches. He urged the Athenians to take up arms to defend Amphipolis and the northern cities against Philip, but to no avail.

The name of Demosthenes, the most famous and accomplished orator of the ancient Greek world, will live for ever for his unremitting hostility towards Macedon. Born in 384, a year before his great Macedonian enemy, for thirty years he insisted, against apathy and vociferous opposition, that Philip intended to bring Athens to her knees, by direct assault or by controlling the grain routes. He argued that Athens should take the lead against him, that the Greeks could win and that it would be disgraceful not to try. He appealed often to Athens' glorious past and called on his fellow citizens not to betray it. This was not oratory for oratory's sake, nor mere jingoism: Demosthenes gave all his talents – and even the occasional unscrupulous or specious argument – to the service of the city he loved. He was the son of a wealthy slave-owner, who died young; the guardians of the estate squandered it, leaving Demosthenes with a lifelong attraction to money which caused his exile in 324 when he was convicted of having accepted a large donation from a renegade paymaster of Alexander's who had absconded with a fortune and sought refuge in Athens.

If Demosthenes was loud in his denunciations of Philip, this was partly passion, but partly also due to the fact that there were those in Athens, such as Phokion and Aiskhines, who counselled diplomacy or even submission, on the grounds that Athens was poor and weak: the days of its fifth-century glory were long over, the silver mines were producing far less, there was hardly any allied tribute, and other Greek states were already in discussion with Philip. What chance did Athens have? The answer was 'None', but we can still applaud the will to defend traditional values and freedom to the death. It was the last gasp of Athenian greatness.

The Macedonian Conquest of Greece

In 348 Philip destroyed the Khalkidian town of Olynthos, against feeble Athenian resistance (not least because Philip had been busy bribing Athenian officials), and the other towns in Khalkidike were incorporated into Macedon. Before long, the prize beckoned of expansion further south into the Greek heartland, and east through the Hellespont, which remained as critical to Athens as ever. Feeling the threat, a number of cities from both the mainland and the islands joined Athens in a defensive coalition. Athens became the centre of resistance to Macedon not just because of her standing in Greece and her long interest in the northern cities of Khalkidike, but because of Demosthenes' persuasiveness. At last his convictions became official Athenian policy. War, financed in part by Persia, was waged against Philip in a ragged fashion, until in 340 Philip tried to take Byzantion, and so to impede Athens' grain supply; at the same time he sent a letter to Athens complaining of Athenian aggression and negotiations with Persia. Demosthenes saw this letter as nothing short of an ultimatum, and convinced the Athenians of his view. All-out war on the Greek mainland was now inevitable.

In 338 Philip marched south to the border of Boiotia, where he demanded free passage through the region so that he could invade Attica. There was panic in Athens, vividly described some years later by Demosthenes (*On the Crown* 169–73):

> Evening had come, when a messenger reached the *prytaneis* with the news that Elateia had been taken. At once, they all interrupted their dinner and got up. Some of them began to clear the stall-holders out of the agora and burnt the wicker screens, while others sent for the generals and summoned the public trumpeter. Chaos ruled the city. At dawn the next day the *prytaneis* summoned the Council to their chamber, while you citizens began making your way to the Assembly. Before the Council had finished its discussions or framed any draft proposals, the entire population was sitting up on the Pnyx. The councillors arrived, and the *prytaneis* announced the news they had received and introduced the messenger himself to deliver his report. Then the town-crier asked: 'Who wishes to speak?' Nobody volunteered. The crier repeated the invitation over and over, but still nobody came forward, although all the generals and all the orators were there ... Then I stepped forward and addressed you.

At Demosthenes' urging, the Athenians sent a delegation to the Boiotians, and persuaded them to refuse Philip and accept an alliance with Athens. Alongside Boiotian troops, Athens faced the Macedonians at Khaironeia in Boiotia. Although the armies were numerically more or less equal, and although the Athenians and Boiotians had a good defensive position, the trained and experienced Macedonian hoplites and cavalry cut the Greeks to shreds. Athens and the rest of southern Greece lay open.

Athens was torn, as it had been all along, between conflicting views, with some arguing that the city was doomed unless they negotiated with Philip, and others (chiefly Demosthenes, Lykourgos and Hypereides) arguing for continued resistance, with Persian help. In terror, the Athenians once again contemplated granting citizenship to metics and freeing slaves, for the defence of the city. The Council was in permanent session, ready for any eventuality, and the rural population was brought inside the city walls, as at the start of the Peloponnesian War. Eventually, Demosthenes' political opponents won the day, and Athens bowed to the inevitable.

Philip proved extraordinarily generous: much of what remained of the Athenian alliance was dissolved, but Athens itself was not further punished. Philip's son Alexander, who had been prominent at Khaironeia in command of the cavalry, personally escorted the ashes of the Athenian dead into the city. Demosthenes and his friends continued the verbal assault, but their policies and proposals had been effectively strangled. Philip was granted Athenian citizenship, his supporters gained power in the city and his statue was erected in the agora.

Philip imposed a general confederacy of Greek states, called the League of Corinth, and their first action in 337 was to declare war on Persia. This was good panhellenic propaganda for Philip, and in any case Persia was a serious threat to his expansionist policies. Philip promised to punish Persia for the invasion of Greece some 150 years earlier. But he was assassinated by a disgruntled Macedonian at a wedding party in 336, and Alexander inherited the throne. The rest – this time the cliché is apposite – is history.

21

Hellenistic Athens

After Philip's death, Athens and other cities clamoured for rebellion, but it was no more than wind. Alexander was so powerful that, to Demosthenes' disgust, the Athenians sent a repentant embassy, and the League of Corinth quickly placed command of the war in the East in his hands. Alexander never returned to Greece after 334 and his long campaigns in the East had little immediate effect there. He rarely interfered in Greek affairs, but when he did so he demonstrated a fine touch: in 324, for instance, he ordered every city to take back its political exiles. The edict (issued during the Olympian festival by Alexander's ambassador, Nikanor, the adopted son of the philosopher Aristotle) ensured that each city would remain in turmoil, incapable of uniting either internally or with other cities.

Athenian pride was still fanned by the memory of her fifth-century greatness, but it emerged in rebellious rhetoric rather than action, and the city remained on tense but reasonable terms with the Macedonian authorities. When Thebes, with Persian financial support, rose up in rebellion in 335, it was only because the Athenian army was delayed that the city failed to join the doomed uprising. On Alexander's orders, Thebes was utterly destroyed and her territory was parcelled out among the other Boiotian states.

In the aftermath of the Theban rebellion, Alexander demanded that Athens hand over all those who had preached resistance to Macedon, including Lykourgos and Demosthenes. Athenian diplomats averted the threat, but neither Demosthenes nor Lykourgos remitted his hostility, as a story from a few years later shows. In 324, the Athenians were debating whether or not to award divine honours to Alexander, as the putative son of Zeus. Demosthenes said, 'Let him be the son of Zeus, if he wishes, or even the son of Poseidon' – the implication being that the whole business was artificial and despicable – but Lykourgos topped Demosthenes with his quip: 'What kind of god would he be when worshippers have to purify themselves on *leaving* his sanctuary?' However, expediency ensured that the proposal was passed. As the proposer, Demades, said, 'Better to keep our land than begrudge Alexander heaven.' But the cult was dropped as soon as it was safe to do so, once Alexander had died in 323.

Sparta had refused to join the puppet League of Corinth (or rather, Philip had chosen not to force her to), and revolted in 331, but she and her Peloponnesian allies were crushed and suffered 5,000 casualties. Once again, Athens almost joined the attempt, but pulled back at the last moment. However, there were plenty in Athens who deeply resented their loss of freedom, as well as more specific insults, such as Alexander's intention to throw Athenian settlers off Samos and return the island to its former inhabitants, scattered since 365. In the chaos following Alexander's death, Leosthenes seized the opportunity to stir up rebellion, with the help of the aged orator Hypereides. Athenian anger had been exacerbated by a long-running food crisis: the city could not offer grain merchants enough money to stop them selling elsewhere, and Alexander had been diverting supplies east for his campaigns.

Leosthenes was a hardened military commander, who had grown up among and then in charge of mercenaries serving in the East. Many of these mercenaries had grown to hate Alexander – not least because he had deprived them of work by ordering all the eastern satraps to disband their mercenary forces – and when Leosthenes returned to Athens and was elected general there, he already led an 8,000-strong army. Demosthenes was allowed back from exile and joined the attempt to get Athens to take the lead in a concerted rebellion, against the opposition of Phokion and Demades.

Unsupported by the Peloponnesians or Thebans, the rebels had little chance. At first, however, things went well: troops flocked to the banner of freedom and swelled the army until there were about 25,000 men from over twenty Greek cities; the rebel army took control of Boiotia and bottled up the Macedonians in the Thessalian town of Lamia. The next year, however, Leosthenes was killed and the siege of Lamia was raised by a relieving force. The Athenian fleet was annihilated off Amorgos in the Aegean, and in a final land battle at Krannon in Thessaly the Macedonians defeated the hugely outnumbered Greeks.

Athens again felt deeply threatened, as in 338, but Phokion, well known for his pro-Macedonian position, led the negotiations. The terms were that the Athenians were to hand over the most prominent anti-Macedonians, including Demosthenes and Hypereides, dissolve the democracy in favour of a system of limited franchise, accept a Macedonian garrison in Peiraieus (which would control the city by controlling its essential supplies), not rebuild their lost warships, and pay the Macedonians compensation as well as reimbursing them for the costs of the war. With the help of the newly empowered Areiopagos Council, Demades and the aged Phokion (now in his forty-fifth term as general) became for a while the effective leaders of the city. The Macedonian garrison was the first force to occupy Athenian territory since the Spartans in 403, and it remained there, a symbol of hated occupation, until 229.

Demosthenes and Hypereides fled Athens. With Macedonian agents on his heels, Demosthenes committed suicide by taking poison, which he had concealed in his pen, on the island of Kalauria (modern Poros). Hypereides was less fortunate: he was captured and tortured to death in front of the victorious Macedonian general. The reaction of the mass of the Athenian people to the loss of their citizenship and political power could have been violent, but the Macedonian garrison contained the situation. Thousands of Athenians accepted exile in Thrace, where the Macedonians gave them land; the rest lived on in impotence in Athens. There was a brief backlash of anti-Macedonian feeling in Athens; one of the victims was Aristotle, who had been Alexander's tutor. He found it expedient to flee Athens in 322, and with a reference to Sokrates' trial he said that he did so 'to prevent the Athenians sinning a second time against philosophy'.

Only 9,000 of the former 30,000 citizens could satisfy the new property requirement for citizenship, which was that their estate should be worth at least 2,000 drachmas. Athenian citizenship became the prerogative of a privileged few. This was the end of the world's earliest great democratic experiment; it had lasted a little less than 200 years, from the time of Kleisthenes' reforms. It was also the end of Athenian power: from now on it made little difference whether the nominal ruler of Athens was the assembled people, or an oligarchy, or a single individual, since the destiny of the city was no longer entirely in their hands. Greater powers were always hovering, to dictate the city's future. As a matter of diplomacy, the Macedonian king would write politely to the government with a request that such-and-such might happen, but this was really only a disguised command.

In return for their fealty, cities like Athens received benefactions from the king himself, or from indigenous plutocrats. The old tradition of liturgies continued in this less structured fashion, with the wealthy ensuring that people had enough to eat, subsidizing schools and doctors, financing the construction of temples and other public buildings, and paying for entertainment and amusements. Local politics became increasingly meaningless: there was little point in currying the favour of the Assembly when the Assembly had no real power. But politics, the public life of the city, had previously animated Athens, as it had all Greek citizen-states. So Athens was bound to decline.

The Hellenistic World

Alexander's conquests ineradicably altered the ancient world, and in order to understand many of the events which affected Athens over the next 100 or so years, a more global perspective is needed. The fifty or so years after Alexander's death were scarred by power struggles between several of his generals or their descendants, who set themselves up as rulers of huge tracts of his former Empire. Eventually Antigonos the One-eyed gained power in Asia Minor, Macedon and Greece, while Seleukos took over Syria and the former Persian Empire, and Ptolemy gained Egypt.

Antigonos was a very aggressive ruler, and made largely unsuccessful attempts to seize some or all of his rivals' territory, but the other two joined forces to defeat and kill him in 301. His son Demetrios the Besieger occupied the Macedonian throne until 288, but spent the last few years of his life as a 'guest' of the Seleukids, and it was up to his son, Antigonos Gonatas, to secure the Antigonid kingdom. In other words, it took the best part of fifty years of bloody turmoil before mainland Greece saw any real stability.

The other two kingdoms were more settled, although by the end of the fourth century the Seleukids had lost their eastern lands to the Indian ruler Chandragupta, and later the Parthians (the eastern enemies of the Romans, as the Persians had been for the Greeks) took much of Persia; the rest of the kingdom finally fell to the Romans in the first century BCE. The difficulty of attacking Egypt, surrounded as it was by deserts, ensured its continuing stability and prosperity, until Kleopatra famously chose the wrong side in the Roman civil war and Egypt too was swallowed up by Rome in 30 BCE.

Of the three pillars of Athenian greatness, two were permanently toppled. Athens would never again be a full democracy, and she would never again dominate the sea, although there were periods over the next few centuries when trade picked up. But throughout the Hellenistic period the city flourished as a centre of culture. This was in fact the only true legacy of the fifth century, distinct from the rosy vapours of the myth of past greatness. Athens' prominence as a cultural centre was an extension of the concentration of talent in the city in the fifth century, but it needed an occasional boost. Lykourgos, for instance, gave his patronage and financial support to both Aristotle's Lykeion and Plato's Academy. He also arranged for definitive texts of the plays of the canonical three tragedians to be preserved, disallowing insertions by actors or directors, and revived the city's comic and dithyrambic festivals.

The Hellenistic world was cosmopolitan, and certain of Athens' more parochial ways had to change. Women gradually acquired more freedom, foreign cults entered the religious calendar with more frequency, and the citizenship laws were changed to allow for marriage with foreigners. But through all the changes, Athens was seen not just as a centre of culture, but as the source of culture. The form of Greek used from Spain to India for commercial and diplomatic purposes, called *koinē* ('the common tongue'), was closely akin to the dialect spoken at Athens. Also, tragedy and the symposium – two specifically Athenian cultural artefacts – came to define the hellenized world. A third, Greek rather than just

Athenian, was the gymnasium. An initiative of the early third century helped to spread Athenian culture: in about 280 poets, technicians, musicians and actors based in Athens formed a guild, 'The Craftsmen of Dionysos', who hired themselves out for festivals all over the Hellenistic world – and grew wealthy enough to wield considerable political power in the city.

New tragedies were still written and performed at the Athenian festivals, alongside repeat performances of the accepted fifth-century classics. The same went for comedy too, but here there was a marked evolution of both form and content. Given the city's new powerlessness, there was less point in satirizing contemporary politicians as Aristophanes had done; given that the plays might well be exported to distant lands, parochial references and in-jokes were pointless. But Athens was home to the greatest exponents of New Comedy, especially Menandros of Athens (342–289) and Philemon of Syracuse (360–263). They wrote situation comedies in which Aristophanic fantasy and obscenity were replaced by timeless plots and social archetypes, which appealed to audiences all over the world – and, through their imitations by Roman poets, formed the foundation of what we think of as European comedy.

The fourth century produced amazingly creative sculptors and painters, whose work was characterized by a closer imitation of nature. In sculpture Praxiteles of Athens and Skopas of Paros perfected the languid, sensuous pose, and Praxiteles gave us the first female nude, the Aphrodite of Knidos, for which his model was Phryne, the most famous hetaira in Athens. Lysippos of Sikyon introduced a new canon for the human figure, with longer legs and a smaller head, and positioned so that more than just the front of the body was visible. The full range of emotions could now be expressed on the face or by twisting postures of the body – a satyr turning to look at his tail, a dancer dancing free. Master painters such as Zeuxis of Herakleia on the Black Sea, Parrhasios of Ephesos and Apelles of Kolophon (all of whom lived and worked in Athens at some point in their careers) kept pace with the elegance of innovations in sculpture, and gave their scenes elaborate backgrounds.

Artists in Athens and elsewhere were working with a new aesthetic which tells us a lot about the Hellenistic world. Poetry and the visual arts focused on technique and reflected each other. What was assonance in poetry became the periodic placing of colour and form in painting; poetry in particular was full of such devices, designed to enhance its musicality, playfulness and suggestiveness. Techniques such as filigree, chiaroscuro and gilding were the visual counterparts of the wit and refinement of Hellenistic poetry. The subjects of all media were similar: animals, plants, children, ordinary people, domestic scenes, comic characters, pathetic characters – all portrayed with vigour, a love of detail, a high degree of realism, and psychological insight. Individuals were shown as individuals, rather than as representatives of civic values. The viewer's or reader's emotions were aroused by techniques such as exaggerated realism, often bordering on the grotesque (here we find giants, hunchbacks, dwarfs, cripples) or by pathos or a gentle eroticism.

People still looked back to fifth-century artists for simplicity and greatness of vision, while the Hellenistic world focused on detail – on the expression of individual emotions by the artists, or on scholarship by grammarians. Gradually, however, fewer artists worked with creativity and originality, until in the Roman period mass-production and self-conscious archaism set in. Athens remained a centre of the plastic arts even in the debased period, while Alexandria in Ptolemaic Egypt became the centre of poetry and scholarship (aided by the vast library, whose staff had the aim of collecting every Greek book ever written), and of science, which now became divorced from philosophy and made huge progress. But throughout the Hellenistic and Roman periods Athens' fame was chiefly as an educational centre, the equivalent of a university town, thanks especially to the presence there of the major schools of philosophy and rhetoric.

Rhetoric and Philosophy in Hellenistic Athens

In the fifth century, there were no formal schools of higher education, but a particular speaker might frequent a particular spot (as Sokrates, for instance, could often be found in the shop of Simon the cobbler, near the agora), and people started going there specifically to talk to him, or to listen. In the fourth century, proper schools sprang up. Teachers such as Plato (429–347) and his former pupil Aristotle (384–322) preferred the quieter surroundings of the gymnasia outside the city – the Academy (named after the hero Hekademos) north-west of the city for Plato, and the Lykeion ('Lyceum' in Latin) just to the east for Aristotle. Before long, they bought or built properties adjacent to these gymnasia, and so founded the first recognizable schools of philosophy. The longest-lasting was the Academy, founded by Plato around 375 BCE, which finally closed its doors some time after 529 CE. Oxford and Cambridge have yet to achieve this longevity.

Rhetoric had become an essential tool for politicians from all over the Mediterranean, and Athens also housed schools of rhetoric, of which the first was the school of Isokrates, Plato's contemporary and rival. If Athens retained a cosmopolitan feel in the fourth century, this was due as much as anything to the presence of these two Athenians, who attracted to their schools intellectuals from all over the Greek world, as well as many native Athenians. Plato and Isokrates were the first, but the tradition continued: in Hellenistic Athens teachers were often superstar celebrities. Echoing Perikles' proud boast (see p. 114), Isokrates says (*Festival Speech* 50):

> Where wisdom and rhetoric are concerned, our city has left the rest of mankind so far behind that students here have become teachers everywhere else. Our city has made the name 'Greek' refer no longer to a people but to a cast of thought: people are called 'Greeks' not so much by virtue of their common nature, but because they share our Athenian culture.

Isokrates was born in 436 and lived to be a remarkable ninety-eight years old. He wanted to teach all-round excellence – a kind of practical philosophy – and he targeted the young and rich, with the upper-class assumption that they had the requisite potential. The school flourished. In *Antidosis* (written about 354) he vindicated his teaching. Rhetoric is a skill, not a body of knowledge: an expert orator, like an expert general, marshals and deploys his evidence. Rhetoric gives one useful civic accomplishments, whereas abstract knowledge is useless. Persuasion and the manipulation of the audience's emotions are patently effective in public life. True philosophy, he argued, is rhetoric with a smattering of political education; it trains the mind as gymnastics does the body.

Isokrates might claim that Platonic philosophy was too unworldly to have much value, but the reality was different. As a research institution, Plato's Academy turned out not just an impressive array of scientists, mathematicians and philosophers, but also politicians and military men. Several members of the Academy were invited to redraft the laws of various citizen states. In the long run, however, rhetoric proved more popular than philosophy. In his more extreme moods, Plato despised rhetoric on the grounds that it issued from and perpetuated a system of false values – success and materialism over the true virtue of wisdom. But Isokrates won this battle and rhetoric became an accepted part of the courses offered by even the philosophical schools of Athens, especially by the Peripatetics (the followers of Aristotle) and the Stoics.

In due course of time, philosophy came down from the abstract realms of Platonic metaphysics or Aristotelean intellectualism and polymathy, and learnt also to appeal to a wider audience with promises of self-improvement. All the schools set out to demonstrate how individual human beings should live and provided methods for achieving this goal. The three main branches of philosophy in Hellenistic times were logic (understood as the way or ways of discovering the truth of any matter), physics (the nature of the world and all that is in it) and ethics (how to achieve happiness). Epikouros (341–271), originally from Samos, set up a commune just outside Athens and taught his pupils to withdraw from the world and to live a life of moderation, choosing between competing desires in order to attain freedom from distress – a far cry from the gross hedonism of what has popularly come to be called 'Epicureanism'. The Stoics (named after the Painted Stoa in Athens, where Zeno of Kition in Cyprus (333–262) and Khrysippos from Kilikia (280–206) taught) located human fulfilment in aligning oneself with the rational force which, as Fate, governs the whole universe and every individual life.

The great era of the philosophical schools in Athens continued throughout the third and second centuries. Teaching and being learned began to be seen as professions in their own right; schools – not just the four already mentioned, but Cynics and Sceptics too – disputed points great and small with one another; learning became systematic and spread around the Hellenistic world, and although

Athens remained a centre for all the schools, her dignity in this respect came to be challenged, especially in Roman times, by Alexandria, Antioch and other places. The value placed on education did little to alter elementary schooling, but gradually an intermediate stage evolved, between the elementary schools and attendance at the feet of a philosopher or a teacher of rhetoric, so that in his teens a boy might learn the rudiments of grammar, rhetoric, logic and geometry, to supplement the schooling of his younger years.

But if there was originality within the philosophical schools, the same cannot be said of rhetoric. Quite early in the Hellenistic period, a canonical list was drawn up of the ten Athenian masters of rhetoric (including Lysias, Isokrates, Demosthenes, Aiskhines, Lykourgos and Hypereides) and their speeches were endlessly studied and imitated. Even here, then, Athens' past lingered and affected her present. Pedantic purists refused to use vocabulary or figures of speech which did not have precedents in the works of these masters. Once, the arrogant professor Philagros of Cilicia (late second century CE) in the heat of the moment let slip an 'outlandish' word, and when an opponent sarcastically asked him in which of the classics this word was to be found, he replied that it was to be found in Philagros. Such quick-wittedness was not unusual among the orators, who boasted of their ability to extemporize on any subject. Atticism was worshipped as a virtue in itself, and there were bitter fights, by word and occasionally fist, between its exponents and those of the florid, Asiatic style.

Still, the schools of rhetoric flourished, polished their discipline, and influenced everything from the law and politics to literature, philosophy and education. The high point came in the first and second centuries CE, when Roman emperors endowed chairs in Athens and maintained the schools. It makes some sense to speak by then of a single University of Athens, with a number of teachers whose courses a student could attend. Not only was the salary very generous, but holders of the chair of rhetoric were immune from prosecution and exempt from certain taxes and costs. A sign of the respect given to these teachers is that they were often chosen as Athens' diplomatic representatives abroad. By an unspoken convention, philosophers and teachers were expected to speak their minds, and even the highest dignitaries were expected to tolerate this freedom of speech.

In the first few centuries of the Romans' rule, although their own educational system was adequate, it was still prestigious to study rhetoric and philosophy in Athens, and schools were still being built in the city as late as the sixth century CE. In fact, Horace (Quintus Horatius Flaccus, who studied in Athens) famously said, 'Captive Greece' – by which he meant largely Athens – 'has captured its savage conqueror and introduced culture to rustic Latium' (*Epistles* 2.1.156–7). In many ways, he was right. Athenian sculptors exported their products to Rome, and Roman artists (often Greek artists resident in Rome) imitated Greek originals. It was especially popular for young men from noble Roman families to come to Athens to take part in the *ephēbeia*, as a form of all-round education for body and mind, after the programme was opened up to foreigners in 125 BCE. Athens was the emblem of culture, and learned Romans rapidly became fluent in Attic Greek – though many of them despised the Athenians themselves as not worthy of their great forebears.

Demetrios of Phaleron and Demetrios the Besieger

The violent break-up of Alexander's Empire led to the restoration of a form of democracy in Athens in 318 and the execution of Phokion, but they could not remove Nikanor and his Macedonian garrison from the Mounykhia fortress in Peiraieus, and the following year the Macedonian ruler, Kassandros, forced Athens to give in, and made Demetrios of Phaleron the head of the nominally democratic government. Demetrios, a man of humble origins, now aged about thirty-five, had risen to political prominence a few years earlier. He was a somewhat paradoxical figure: a philosopher (a follower of Aristotle and his successor as head of the Lykeion, Theophrastos of Eresos on Lesbos), a prolific writer on literature, history, philosophy, politics and rhetoric (though only fragments survive), and an able politician who acquired a reputation as a bon vivant.

Demetrios was the 'Supervisor' of Athens for ten years, from 317 to 307. He used not just his famous eloquence, but democratic offices to maintain his power and authority, like a fifth-century statesman. Athens entered a brief period of financial stability, but this was due not so much to any steps Demetrios himself took as to the fact that the state had fewer outgoings: there were no wars, pay for attendance at the Assembly had been dropped, there were only twenty warships to maintain, there was no need for mercenaries since there was the Macedonian garrison, and at the same time the silver mines were productive and Peiraieus was trading.

Demetrios was not entirely a democrat, but he did the best he could for his fellow citizens under difficult circumstances. For instance, he decreased the property qualification for citizenship from 2,000 to 1,000 drachmas. On the other hand, a committee of Guardians of the Laws supervised sessions of the Assembly to ensure that nothing was discussed that was illegal or anti-constitutional (or unfavourable to Demetrios, perhaps). He also abolished some of the ways in which wealthy families had sought self-glorification, such as excessive expenditure on funerals, monuments and women's attire, and made the liturgy of financing choral productions voluntary rather than a legal obligation. The Athenian people responded by erecting statues to him and by not disturbing the peace. But the opponents of Kassandros and Demetrios began to treat with Antigonos the One-eyed in Asia, who had designs on the whole of Alexander's Empire and an enormous army to back him up.

In 314 Antigonos cynically declared that all Greek cities were to be free from garrisons and autonomous. Following this edict, in 307 Demetrios of Phaleron was expelled by Antigonos' son Demetrios the Besieger, who arrived in Athens at the head of an enormous fleet of 250 ships and was hailed as the saviour of the city; Demetrios of Phaleron fled, first to Thebes and then to Egypt, where he helped found the great library at Alexandria and died of a snake-bite.

The transition to the new government was fairly smooth, with few politically inspired executions or exiles. Although the new constitution was called a restored 'democracy', it soon became more or less an oligarchy under the effective rule of Demetrios the Besieger's Athenian sycophants. In the wake of Demetrios of Phaleron's unpopularity (they tore down his statues), a law was passed making it illegal for anyone to open a philosophical school, on pain of death, and giving the state control over the licensing of such schools. The philosophers left Athens in droves, but the following year the law was repealed. Athenian comic poets might gently tease the philosophers, but most people realized that if the city stopped being a cultural centre, it would stop being the centre of anything.

Demetrios kept Athens supplied with grain and timber, and protected the city during his war with Kassandros (307–304). He even undertook some repair work on the Long Walls linking the city to Peiraieus. Some of his more loyal followers began to speak of a new renaissance, a return to the golden ages of Perikles and Lykourgos (who was awarded posthumous honours as a symbol of democracy). But Demetrios took advantage of his popularity – or at least the strength of his sycophants – to override the legal condemnation of one of his followers, to spend state money on his own pleasures, to make the Parthenon his residence when he was in Athens, and to move his concubines with him into the sacred temple. He got away with this outrageous behaviour because the Athenians had deified him and his father:

> On the proposal of Stratokles, the Athenians voted to erect golden statues of Antigonos and Demetrios on a chariot near those of Harmodios and Aristogeiton; to award them both crowns worth 200 talents; to erect an altar and call it 'of the Saviours'; to add two new tribes, Demetrias and Antigonis, to the existing ten; to perform each year for Demetrios and Antigonos contests, a procession and a sacrifice; and to weave their images into Athena's robe.
>
> (Diodoros of Sicily, *Historical Library* 20.46)

It was always possible within Greek religion to worship outstanding men and women after their deaths as heroes, but the cult of living rulers was a more recent borrowing from the East. It is often hard to tell how sincere the Athenians were. A hymn to Demetrios, dating from about 290, included the nearly sacrilegious lines: 'While other gods are far away, or lack ears, or do not exist, or pay no attention to us, we see you present here, not in wood or stone but in reality' (Douris of Samos, Fragment 13). The gods were givers of blessings, powerful beings from elsewhere: so were

Antigonos and Demetrios. So, apparently, were Demetrios' concubines, at least two of whom were honoured as Aphrodite.

The creation of two new tribes involved both constitutional changes (such as the enlargement of the Council from 500 to 600), and further religious honours for Antigonos and Demetrios, since the founders of each of the ten (now twelve) tribes received cult honours. A cult of Demetrios was established at the place in Attica where he had descended from his chariot – parallel to cults in places where Zeus was said to have descended to earth. Demetrios considered himself to be an incarnation of Dionysos, which gave him the licence to party in the Parthenon, and of Demeter, since he provided Athens with grain. As for the weaving of the faces of Antigonos and Demetrios into the design of the robe presented to Athena at the Panathenaia, the consequences were ominous: during the procession a sudden squall broke the ship-cart's mast and ripped the robe. Needless to say, all these cults were repealed after his defeat in 301, at the hands of Kassandros, still his main rival for the Macedonian throne.

After a brief interval during which the Athenians tried to remain neutral between Kassandros and Demetrios, Kassandros installed as the puppet ruler of Athens the Athenian Lakhares, a former democrat who took naturally to tyranny, dissolved the Council and set about stripping Athens of its wealth to pay his troops. 'Lakhares denuded Athena,' said a contemporary comic poet, referring to his removal of the gold plates from Pheidias' statue, and of the Persian shields that Alexander the Great had hung on the Parthenon. But after Kassandros' death Demetrios returned in 295 with a huge army, starved the city into submission (family members fought over who should get to eat a dead mouse), and installed an oligarchy in place of Lakhares, who fled to Boiotia, but could not escape Demetrios' assassin.

In the following years, however, Demetrios' plans for world domination suffered a number of setbacks, culminating in the loss of Macedon, and in 286 the anti-Macedonian alliance backed the rebellious instincts of their sympathizers in Athens. The success of the uprising owed a lot to two individuals. As military commander, Olympiodoros managed to get some of the Macedonian mercenaries to defect from the garrison on Mouseion Hill, and then led the assault on the remainder. Meanwhile, Kallias of Sphettos (the black sheep of a prominent pro-Macedonian family) used his wealth and diplomatic skills to keep the city supplied with both grain and soldiers from Egypt.

Demetrios besieged the city, but quickly agreed to a peace treaty. The Athenian rebellion was part of a concerted plan by his enemies to destroy him, and he was not ready to face them in Attica. Athens regained a measure both of freedom and of democracy. Although Macedonian garrisons remained in Peiraieus and elsewhere in Attica, anti-Macedonian sentiments ran high: a statue of Demosthenes was erected in honour of the great statesman's long fight against the threat of Macedonian rule, and statues of the four kings of the anti-Macedonian alliance were raised in the agora. Without Peiraieus, however, the city was always going to be easy prey; but in 280 Olympiodoros finally succeeded in recapturing the harbour and securing the passage of food and supplies for Athens. The Athenians recovered their confidence enough to send a detachment of 500 horsemen to the north the following year to help turn back an invasion of Greece by marauding Celtic tribesmen.

The true measure of the restoration of Athenian spirits came a dozen years later, when the Athenians, with the encouragement and armed assistance of Ptolemy II, organized a concerted rebellion of Greek states against Macedon (now ruled by Demetrios the Besieger's son, Antigonos Gonatas). Unfortunately, the attempt was premature, and the Peloponnesian states involved in the revolt were largely ineffectual. The Khremonidean War, named after the Athenian statesman who instigated it, was short and bloody, and Athens fell in 263 after a protracted siege.

Gonatas was lenient – he had a soft spot for the city, having studied Stoicism there in his younger days – and the Athenians sycophantically awarded him cultic honours. But the democracy, already severely weakened, was finally destroyed by his giving his puppet governor – the grandson of Demetrios of Phaleron, with the same name – the right to veto any decree or proposal. The city lost the last shreds of its willpower, and never again played any significant part in international politics until the nineteenth century CE. The *ephēbeia* (see pp. 259–60) fell into disuse: Athens had little need now for men with military training. The last men who remembered the days of freedom before the coming of the Macedonians were now dead, and the Athenians numbly accepted Demetrios' presence, along with that of Macedonian garrisons throughout Attica, whose job was to make sure that there was no resumption of disloyalty to the king. Even after Demetrios was replaced in 255 by an oligarchy, every meeting of the Assembly began with prayers for the prosperity of the Macedonian royal family.

The city's decline in status was accurately reflected in its dilapidation. The Long Walls between Athens and Peiraieus collapsed, and were never rebuilt: the city and its harbour were now two separate towns. The volume of trade passing through Peiraieus plummeted, and economically Athens was severely depressed. An aura of genteel decay penetrated even the rosy-tinted spectacles of a contemporary brochure-writer, Herakleides the Critic (*On the Cities in Greece*, Fragment 1.1–5):

> From there you go to Athens. The road is pleasant; it is surrounded by cultivated land and has a gentle appearance. But the city is utterly dry and altogether short of water, and because of its antiquity, is poorly laid out. Most of the houses are shabby, but a few are serviceable. At first sight, visitors would doubt whether this is the renowned city of the Athenians, but before long they would be convinced. The Odeion is the most beautiful in the world. The theatre is remarkable – large and extraordinary. The temple of Athena – the Parthenon, as it is called – is grand and visible from a long way off; it is well worth seeing, perched above the theatre. Sight-seers are amazed by it. The temple of Olympian Zeus is unfinished, but has an incredible design and would be the best temple in the world if it were finished. There are three gymnasia – the Academy, the Lykeion and the Kynosarges – all of which are well supplied with trees and grass. There are all kinds of festivals, and mental diversion and recreation are catered for by a wide variety of philosophers. There are many leisure-time activities and constant spectacles.
>
> Everything that grows from the soil is invaluable and tasty, but there is rather too little of it . . . Spectacles and amusements distract the people's attention from their hunger and make them forget about providing food. But for travellers with their

own provisions there is no city like Athens for pleasure ... In general, where pleasure and the enhancement of life are concerned, Athens surpasses other cities to the same degree that they surpass the countryside. But one must watch out above all for the prostitutes, or one may, without realizing it, be ruined – in a pleasant manner.

22

The Coming of the Romans

For much of the rest of the third century Athens had little political independence, and democracy receded into the background under a series of oligarchic rulers. The city's officers were no longer chosen by lot, but by election, and only the rich played the game of politics. Politicians could be re-elected to key posts year by year, and the Areiopagos gained more and more power at the expense of the Heliaia, the Assembly and the Council. Due both to a declining population and the increasingly cosmopolitan nature of the Hellenistic world, Athenian citizenship laws were relaxed, and an increasing number of foreigners were granted citizenship by naturalization or as a reward for services rendered.

Athens remained officially loyal to her Macedonian rulers until 229, when the city's current leaders, Eurykleides and his brother Mikion, raised 150 talents and bribed Diogenes, the commander of the Macedonian garrisons, to leave Peiraieus, Salamis and Sounion. Diogenes got a posthumous reward too, in that the games instituted in his honour and the grand new gymnasium named after him both outlived him. Athens and Peiraieus were united again – but even this was a sad reflection on Athens' reduced status. The sum involved was fairly substantial, given the poverty of Athens at the time, but the Macedonians would have taken steps to recover Athens if they considered it at all important, and to regarrison it if they considered it a threat.

The Athenians celebrated, however, and under the thirty-year leadership of Eurykleides and Mikion remained prudentially aloof from anti-Macedonian efforts elsewhere in Greece, while strengthening both the defensive walls and ties with Egypt as a buffer against the new, energetic king of Macedon, Antigonos Doson. Even neutrality these days required the support of a world-class leader, and in 224 Athens duly awarded Ptolemy III extraordinary honours:

a thirteenth tribe was created, Ptolemais, with the appropriate cult and priest, and Council numbers were raised to 650. A new athletic festival, the Ptolemaia, was instituted, which in its 100-year history came to rival the other great festivals of Athens. Ptolemy in his turn became the first in a long line of architectural benefactors of Athens by building a gymnasium, the Ptolemaion, on the north side of the Akropolis, which, with its lecture rooms and library, became a favourite haunt of philosophers, as well as a gymnasium for the body.

There were three great wars on Greek soil towards the end of the third century, of which the most significant was the First Macedonian War of 211 to 205. For some years now the Greeks and Macedonians had been aware of 'the cloud in the west' (as one diplomat put it) that was Rome, but this war was the first direct intervention by the Romans against Macedon, as they supported the Aitolian League's attempt to regain its freedom. Having secured most of Italy, Rome was aggressively looking abroad. Athens remained distant, and even supported a delegation to try to stop the war. But power struggles in Alexandria eliminated Egypt's value as an ally, so that when a few years later the Athenians were faced with the threat of renewed hostilities from Philip V of Macedon, they turned for help to an alliance with Rhodes, Pergamon and Rome. The final trigger was an incident in 201. A couple of Akarnanian men entered the sacred precinct of Eleusis during the Mysteries, although they were not initiates. For this act of sacrilege, the Athenians put them to death. The Akarnanians and Macedonians attacked Attica and Athenian shipping, and triggered the Second Macedonian War (200–197).

Athens' suburbs and the countryside were repeatedly ravaged by Philip or his generals in the first year of the war. The city was incapable of defending itself, but was rescued by the Romans and reduced to a minor role in the war. At a conference in Aitolia the Athenians had the opportunity to describe their suffering. As the Roman historian Livy (Titus Livius, *c.* 60 BCE–*c.* 20 CE) reported the Athenians' speech, they regretted the devastation of their land, while accepting that these things happen in war, and focused more on Philip's sacrilege (*History of Rome* 31.30):

> All the tombs and monuments in their territory had been destroyed. The shades of all their dead were exposed, bones

> stripped of their covering of earth. Philip had spread baleful fire
> throughout their ancestral shrines . . . The statues of the gods,
> half burnt and mutilated, lay among the fallen door-posts of
> the temples.

The Athenians were not exaggerating: the archaeological record
shows that the rural sanctuaries of Attica never recovered. There
were literally thousands of these local shrines, and very many of
them were abandoned for ever. Philip's depredations accelerated the
depopulation of the Attic countryside, until great landowners
replaced the old tradition of small farmers; it was only in the fourth
century CE that the rural population picked up again.

    Athenian hatred of Philip was such that they abolished the two
tribes Demetrias and Antigonis, named after former Macedonian
'benefactors', erased all Macedonian names from earlier inscriptions,
tore down all statues to Philip and his ancestors, and formally cursed
him and the whole race of Macedonians. Livy, who was no admirer
of Athens, sarcastically added to his account of these events: 'The
Athenians were making war on Philip with decrees and words –
their only sources of strength' (*History of Rome* 31.44). Their new ally
Attalos I of Pergamon replaced the Macedonians in Athens' good
books: they named a tribe after him, Attalis (so that now they had
twelve tribes again, with Ptolemais the eleventh, and a Council
of 600), with him as the eponymous hero with the appropriate
honours.

    After the defeat of Philip at Kynoskephalai in Thessaly in 197,
the Roman proconsul Titus Quinctius Flamininus cynically or short-
sightedly declared the Greek states free. Athens was sidelined: she
was ignored in the territorial carve-ups following the war, and had
little to do except mediate between Rome and Greek states, and
offer the use of Peiraieus to various Roman fleets. There were many
in the city who feared the growing Roman presence in Greece, but
the pro-Roman oligarchy, the heirs of Eurykleides and Mikion, were
in power more often than not for many years.

    The Second Macedonian War put an end to Macedonian control
of the Greek states. Philip and then his son Perseus concentrated on
the defence and internal security of their reduced kingdom, but
Rome provoked further conflict to make sure that there could never

22. This statue of a seated boxer, from the second century BCE, shows Hellenistic love of realism and detail: notice his cauliflower ears, battered body and thonged hands.

23. A glimpse of Athens in Byzantine times, when small churches abutted ancient ruins and residences.

24. A lithograph of the Tower of the Winds during the period of the Turkish occupation.

25. A view of the Akropolis in 1670, clearly showing how well preserved the temple was before the catastrophic explosion of 1687. The buildings clustered around the temple are the quarters of the Turkish garrison.

26. This vivid drawing of the destruction of the Parthenon by Venetian troops in 1687 shows the size of the explosion and the scale of the destruction. It comes from a book called *Atene Attica*, by Francesco Fanelli, published in 1707, but it copied an original watercolour made on the spot by Giacomo Verneda, an artillery officer in the Venetian army.

27. The first extant photograph of the Parthenon, taken in 1839. It clearly shows not only the mosque, but how utterly ruined the temple was by the explosion of 1687. The original daguerreotype was taken by P. G. Joly de Lotbinière.

28. Christian Hansen's 1836 painting of the Parthenon again shows how utterly ruined the temple was by the explosion of 1687. Hansen's younger brother Theophil was one of the main architects of Athens's neoclassical revival in the nineteenth century.

29. This view, by Louis Dupré, of the Athenian residence of the French consul, Louis Fauvel, early in the nineteenth century, shows some pieces from the huge collection of antiquities he was in the process of collecting, or stealing.

30. A fanciful scene by an unknown artist (copying Ludovico Lipparini) of
Lord Byron pledging allegiance to the Greek cause on the tomb of the heroic warlord
Markos Botsaris. Byron's arrival at Messolonghi in January 1824 brought
hope and funds to the Greeks, who were hard pressed in the
War of Independence.

31. Edward Dodwell's painting (from his 1821 book *Views in Greece*) of the
Athenian market, with the Tzisdaraki mosque in the background.

32. Edward Lear is rather better known today as a versifier, but he painted
some wonderful European scenes, including this one in 1852 of Athens from the west.
The skeletal remains of the Propylaia show how much damage the building had suffered
in the explosion of 1656. Lear has chosen to set his picture in the timeless past,
without showing any houses between the viewer and the Akropolis.

33. This 1863 painting by Giorgio Peritelli of Constitution Square reveals the elegance and charm of nineteenth-century Athens.

34. Starving children in Athens, 1941.

again be a threat from that quarter. In the Third Macedonian War (171–168), Athens' main job was to supply the Roman army with grain, despite having to import it. Most of the Greek cities and leagues had taken the Macedonian side against the Romans, or at least had not actively supported them, and after the successful conclusion of the war the grateful Romans, who were now the only genuine power-brokers in Greece, granted Athens dominion over several Aegean islands, including the wealthy and sacred island of Delos, from which the Athenians expelled the residents and took over the cult and treasury of Apollo. Delos was one of the main centres of Mediterranean trade (especially in slaves), but the Romans insisted that it should be a free port. As a state, then, Athens did not substantially profit from tariffs and taxes, but individual Athenian bankers and merchants grew very rich, and that had a trickle-down effect on the city's economy. And a general increase in Mediterranean trade revived activity in Peiraieus, from which the city could directly benefit. There was money to spare for the repair of public buildings, including the Parthenon, which had been damaged by fire earlier in the century.

For a long while Athens had been fragmented, with areas occupied by foreign and often hostile garrisons. But the long-hoped-for reunification of Attica led to a resurgence of national pride, symbolized by a revival of the cult of Theseus, the founder-hero of Attica. Relations with other Greek states and leagues on the mainland and elsewhere were cordial, and Athens was often called on to arbitrate some dispute or other. Along with peace and prosperity, there was a renaissance of culture: the philosophical schools thrived, and benefactors, especially King Attalos II of Pergamon, began the renewal of the city's crumbling monuments. The magnificent two-storey Stoa of Attalos, built of marble and limestone in the agora, can still be seen in something like its original splendour, since it was rebuilt between 1952 and 1956 thanks to a modern benefaction by the Rockefeller Foundation. Other great stoas built in the second century – the South Stoa and the Middle Stoa – totally changed the appearance of the agora.

Attalos' brother Eumenes II (197–159) also donated a huge stoa on the south side of the Akropolis, to shelter audiences from the Theatre of Dionysos in bad weather; the Seleukid Antiokhos IV tinkered once again with the Peisistratid Temple of Olympian Zeus in 174, and in 60 BCE Ariobarzanes of Kappadokia rebuilt Perikles' Odeion, with the help of Roman architects. All or most of these fabulously wealthy eastern rulers had been educated in Athens, and remembered the city with gratitude. As the years went by, Athens had reason to be grateful that it remained the university town of the Mediterranean world.

Sulla Sacks Athens

As so often in Athens' history, confidence led to aggression and then to repercussions. First, Athens dispossessed the islanders of Delos, and Rome reinstated them; then Athens attempted to annex Oropos (the site of frequent border disputes between Athens and Boiotia) and Rome imposed a heavy financial penalty. By the middle of the 150s, there was considerable tension between Athens and Rome, but Rome still tolerated and even respected its puny but illustrious predecessor. Rome imposed a fine of 500 talents on Athens over the Oropos affair, and in 155 Athens sent a delegation, consisting of the heads of the three main philosophical schools (Academics, Peripatetics and Stoics) to plead for a reduction. The philosophers were successful – the fine was reduced to 100 talents – but they also achieved something more important. While they were in Rome they mesmerized upper-class Romans with their eloquence and learning, and initiated an intellectual revolution. Romans took above all to Stoicism, and it became the fashion for Roman intellectuals and dignitaries to spend some time in Athens at one or more of the schools of rhetoric and philosophy.

Up until the middle of the second century, the Romans had always left Greece after fighting or intervening there. In 148, however, after renewed disturbance in Macedon, the territory became the Roman province of Macedonia, with administrative and military personnel in place; in 146, after the Roman defeat of the Akhaian League and the brutal destruction of Corinth, the governor of Macedonia was also given authority over large areas of southern Greece. Athens was not directly involved in any of this, but even those Greek states which remained nominally free found their power severely limited. The diplomatic Athenian practices of sacrificing to the Roman people and of honouring Rome as the city's benefactor were echoed elsewhere. Athenian trade (chiefly in oil, marble, sculpture, pottery, honey, silver and lead) picked up after the destruction of rival Corinth, and the city provided ships during the Romans' campaign against the Aegean pirates in 102–100. Beneath this calm and cordial veneer, however, discontent raged. In 89 BCE war broke out between Rome and Mithridates VI, the king of Pontos. Within a year Athens had sided with Rome's enemy. It was a fateful decision.

Mithridates was a monarch in the Macedonian mould, capable of assassinating members of his own family to secure his power, and dedicated to an ambitious programme of expansion. His predecessors had long had to deal with Roman interests in the Black Sea region, and Mithridates' ambitions brought him into collision with them. Twice the Romans forced him to return territory he had conquered, but the third time he refused. Roman officials in the area first tried to bribe him and then incited King Nikomedes of Bithynia to attack him. In the course of defeating Nikomedes, Mithridates clashed with Roman troops and then, knowing that war was now inevitable, invaded Phrygia, which was part of the Roman province of Asia. He was welcomed with open arms and rejoicing; oracles foretold the imminent downfall of Rome.

This jubilant and optimistic mood spread to Greece. Athens sent east a delegation, headed by the Peripatetic philosopher Athenion, who returned with Mithridates' promise to replace the unconstitutional regime of the pro-Roman party, and most recently the virtual tyranny of Medeios of Peiraieus, with democracy and autonomy. The Athenians saw Mithridates not just, pragmatically, as a source of grain, but also, ideologically, as the saviour of Greek culture now under threat from the inexorable expansion of the Romans. Given their glorious past, it was their duty, they felt, to support such an effort. Moreover, the Athenians, along with other Greek states, were fed up with the rapacious commercial exploitation of their land by the Romans. Medeios was deposed and Athenion was promptly elected general. Many Athenians left the city in fear, dismayed that the city would bite the hand that had fed it with the gift of Delos and other islands, but the majority supported their new leader.

Mithridates called for a general uprising against the Romans, and there was a terrible massacre of Roman and Italian civilians throughout Asia Minor. Mithridates' general Arkhelaos landed in Greece at the head of a substantial army, having paused on the way only to slaughter the Romans who were occupying Delos, which had refused to follow Athens in rebellion. Arkhelaos replaced Athenion with another philosophically trained Athenian, called Aristion, who made himself the tyrant of Athens and instituted a reign of terror. Aristion and Arkhelaos conquered or won over most of Greece, and Arkhelaos made Peiraieus his headquarts. It was good propaganda for Mithridates to control Athens, the traditional heart of the Greek world, but it made Attica the main site of the war.

Lucius Cornelius Sulla, the mottle-faced future dictator of Rome, arrived in Greece in 87 with 30,000 men, and immediately demonstrated his callous determination by plundering the sanctuaries of Greece, including Delphi, in order to finance his campaign. He pinned Arkhelaos in Peiraieus and Aristion in Athens: with no Long Walls (there had not been enough time to repair them properly), the two towns could not mount a joint defence.

> Sulla was in the grip of a terrible, overwhelming desire to capture Athens, perhaps because he was driven by a kind of rivalry to pit himself against the shadow of the city's past glory, or perhaps because he was angry at the jokes and sarcastic comments with which the tyrant Aristion used to taunt him. . . . Aristion's character was a compound of coarseness and brutality . . . At a time when a medimnos of wheat cost a thousand drachmas in Athens, when people were subsisting on the feverfew which grew on the Akropolis and were boiling up and eating the leather from their shoes and oil-flasks, this man spent all his time partying and gadding about in broad daylight, dancing victory dances and making fun of his enemies.
>
> (Plutarch, *Sulla* 13)

Peiraieus resisted well, because Sulla had no fleet with which to cut off Arkhelaos' supplies, but early in 86 Sulla's men breached Athens' walls and entered the city:

> There was no telling how many people were slaughtered; even now people estimate the numbers by means of how much

ground was covered in blood. Leaving aside those who were killed elsewhere in the city, the blood of the dead in the agora spread throughout the part of Kerameikos that lies on the city side of the Dipylon Gate, and a lot is said to have flooded into the suburb outside the gates as well.   (Plutarch, *Sulla* 14)

Men, women and children, weakened by starvation, were raped and slaughtered. In the first significant vandalism of the city's antiquities, treasures were plundered and carried away to Rome by the shipload, along with nearly all the city's slaves. Sulla later claimed that he gave orders that buildings were not to be demolished, but if this was true it was an order his men widely ignored; many buildings in the agora suffered, and even the Erekhtheion on the Akropolis was damaged by fire. Arkhelaos was eventually driven out of Peiraieus and then it was the port's turn to receive the attention of Sulla's troops. It was totally destroyed, and never fully recovered, because the Athenian economy was too depressed to make it worth spending much money on restoring the port. Athens had learnt the hard way that there was to be no freedom from Rome.

Athens Under Rome

By the following year, Sulla had driven Arkhelaos out of Greece and defeated Mithridates in Asia. The war was over, and one of the chief casualties had been Athens. Although still nominally a free city, not part of a Roman province or a provincial governor's sway, she meekly accepted the reinstatement of the pro-Roman oligarchy, the further weakening of the Assembly, and any other constitutional changes which Rome or her representatives might impose. The city was effectively ruled by three elected officers, the arkhon, the hoplite general and the herald (the president of the Areiopagos), with the help of the Areiopagos Council, which became more and more like the Roman senate. Only a few families, with wealth from banking, landowning or commerce, were involved in politics.

Athens' vassal rank became the status quo in 58 BCE when the Roman province of Macedonia was enlarged to include those few Greek states, Athens among them, which retained a significant degree of self-government and sovereignty. The law, which had been inspired solely by factional fighting within Rome, was repealed three years later, and Athens resumed its status as an independent ally of Rome. The city retained her theoretical autonomy even when southern Greece became the province of Achaea in 27 BCE, but it was a meaningless token of respect. The free cities of Greece were not required to pay taxes to Rome, for instance, but they were often asked for 'contributions', and Roman emperors elevated loyal Athenians to administer the city, or to regulate its financial and political affairs.

Within twenty years in the 40s and 30s, during the appalling Roman civil wars (some of the most significant battles of which were fought on Greek soil), Athens came under the sway of, in turn, Pompey (Cnaeus Pompeius Magnus), Caius Julius Caesar, Marcus Junius Brutus and Caius Cassius Longinus (who were honoured as the new tyrannicides for their assassination of Caesar), Mark Antony (Marcus Antonius) and Octavian (Caius Julius Caesar Octavianus). The city sycophantically honoured each of these incomers, especially because each time it had carefully chosen the losing side: Pompey over Caesar, Brutus and Cassius over Antony, Antony over Octavian. Following the disaster of the Mithridatic War, this was getting to be a bad habit. Sulla said that he spared Athens from total destruction in honour of its glorious past, and after accepting the city's surrender in 48 BCE Caesar echoed the sentiment, but turned it into a pertinent question: 'How often will the glory of your ancestors save you from self-destruction?' (Appian, *Civil War* 2.88). Although he spared the city, he did not hesitate to impose a hefty fine on it for having sided with Pompey – and for having done so not long after he, Caesar, had given the city 50 talents for rebuilding work. The intercession of individual Romans or Athenians restored the city to each successive conqueror's favour, but this could not go on for ever, and the Athenians learnt to bend with the wind. They no longer had either the money or the men to do otherwise.

When Octavian became the Emperor Augustus in 27 BCE, he was granted a monument on the Akropolis, and there was a small temple dedicated to Augustus and Rome just a few metres from the main eastern entrance to the Parthenon. This was typical of what was happening throughout the cities of the eastern Empire, but to its credit Athens resisted Romanization for longer than most. They were slower to grant honours to individual Romans (though those who graduated from the *ephēbeia* automatically became Athenian citizens), they never gave precedence in the Assembly to proposals stemming from Roman authorities, and it was really only under Claudius (41–54) and Nero (54–68) that the cult of the Emperor became a familiar feature of Athenian religion. This reluctance was due largely to nostalgia: the city still wanted to be the equal of the Italian upstart.

But while the process of Romanization could be slowed, it could not be halted or reversed. By the turn of the era Athens, though still sizeable in terms of area and population, was struggling to maintain its cultural identity, and signs of resistance were gradually overwhelmed by the increase in Roman cultural intervention all over the Empire. The historian Cassius Dio reported a miracle that was supposed to have occurred during a visit of the Emperor Augustus to the city in 21 BCE: 'The statue of Athena on the Akropolis, which faced east, turned to the west [towards Rome] and spat blood' (*The History of Rome* 54.7.3). Anti-Roman feelings again flared up in 13 CE, but the disturbance died down of its own accord, and before long all defiance vanished. Even in Hellenistic times Athenians had retained enough pride and sense of a glorious past to show some spirit and courage, but by the time of the Roman emperors the city was a whipped dog.

The Benefactors of Athens

Athens was so poor following its destruction by Sulla that it had to sell the island of Salamis, which had been Athenian territory for centuries and Athenians' place of refuge during the Persian invasion. The Greek cities as a whole were in a parlous state, but Athens suffered as much as any of them in the middle of the first century. The situation was not helped by the exhaustion of the Laureion mines after about 50 BCE. The city was doomed to depend on the tradition, established since the third century, of foreigners giving donations for the building or rebuilding of public edifices. This was a somewhat haphazard process, and many buildings lay more or less in ruins well into the Christian era. The city walls, breached by Sulla, were allowed to crumble and go unrepaired for over 300 years.

The crumbling of old structures, along with the city's need to make amends for having so consistently chosen the wrong side throughout the first century BCE, accelerated the process of Romanization. Not only did architectural styles change (though slowly, because of Roman antiquarianism), but individuals adopted Roman names and manners, and many Romans settled there as traders or exiles, or passed through as students or cultural pilgrims. There was even a special rostrum in the agora, from which visiting Roman dignitaries could address whoever cared to listen. A Roman general on his way east, for instance, could pause from stealing an art treasure or two, and seize the opportunity to present Rome as the heir of the panhellenic fight against barbarian easterners. Gradually, the whole city became permeated by Rome and Romans, until by the end of the first century CE the Theatre of Dionysos was being used for gladiatorial shows and the centre of Athens resembled any other favoured provincial town, with its streets colonnaded in the Roman manner, and orange Roman brickwork replacing Greek marble and limestone.

The Roman financier Titus Pomponius, who settled in Athens not long after the Sullan sack, became such a friend of the city that he was honoured with the nickname 'Atticus'. He lived there for forty years, and was a key figure in reviving the city's fortunes. Not only did he use his fortune to buy grain with which to feed the Athenians in times of trouble, but he acted with great success as the impoverished city's broker whenever it needed to borrow money from Rome, and saved the city from bankruptcy.

In 62 BCE Pompey gave the city, which had scarcely recovered from Sulla's depredations, 50 talents to assist in the restoration of Athens and Peiraieus. To Pompey's irritation, his rival, Julius Caesar, matched the sum ten years later. But the main contribution of Caesar and his adopted son Octavian was the construction of the Roman agora, a little to the east of the old agora. The Roman agora – a large open space surrounded on all sides by colonnades – made the open area of the old agora redundant, and the place that had once been the heart of the city's public life was soon crowded with buildings designed for entertainment and leisure.

By the second century CE, along with other buildings around the edges of the agora, the middle was filled with a huge Odeion, a temple to Ares, and various other smaller buildings and altars. The Odeion was a gift of Marcus Vipsanius Agrippa, the son-in-law, principal general and adjutant of Augustus, who stayed in Athens from 16 to 14 BCE; it seated 1,000 spectators, and was remarkably free of internal supports to aid viewing – until the roof collapsed in the second century CE, and on a reduced scale it became a lecture hall instead. The temple of Ares was actually an old temple from the fifth century BCE, which was moved late in the first century BCE from its original location outside the city to the agora. It was one of several itinerant buildings and monuments, whose relocation was due not just to the fact that the countryside was both increasingly hazardous and increasingly depopulated, but also to the desire of wealthy Romans to honour Athens' past with an antiquarian gesture.

An unknown individual from the first century BCE graced the city with a particularly famous monument. The stunningly beautiful Tower of the Winds still stands in a remarkable state of preservation by the ruins of the Roman agora. The tower is named after the sculpted portraits of the eight winds, one on each face of the tower, and originally it had a weathervane on top to mark the direction of the wind. But it was more than just a primitive wind-gauge: it contained an ingenious water-clock too, and there was a sundial on each of the eight faces, so that passers-by could know the time whatever the weather, and whatever the time of day or night. Another benefactor of the city was Caius Julius Antiokhos Philopappos, the remnants of whose monument (built between 114 and 116 CE) still gleam from the top of Mouseion Hill. Philopappos was the titular King of Kommagene in Asia Minor, a country which had been absorbed into the Roman Empire more than 100 years earlier. He lived in Athens, where he spent some of his wealth putting on festivals and dramas for the people. Herod the Great of Judaea also financed Athenian festivals.

Architecturally speaking, however, the second century CE was the peak of the Romanization of Athens. When Hadrian became emperor in 117 he was heaped with honours by the Athenians, and even venerated as Olympian Zeus on his visit to the city in 124. A thirteenth tribe, Hadrianis, was created in 126, with each tribe now required to supply only forty members for the Council. The previous system was putting too much of a strain on the depleted population. Hadrian, in his turn, oversaw the recodification of the city's laws and the organization of its chaotic finances. With some justification, he saw himself as Athens' new founder, and to mark this he virtually rebuilt the city, which he wanted to make the capital of the eastern part of the Empire. He was a benefactor of many of the provincial cities of the Empire, but he loved Athens more than any other.

He found the older residential areas more or less dilapidated, and decided to build a new quarter, called Hadrianopolis (Roman emperors were not famed for their modesty), just outside the old walls to the east of the city. The centrepiece of the new town was to be the temple of Olympian Zeus, which was finally completed, centuries after its Peisistratid beginnings, in 131 CE, and dedicated with a splendid festival and an address by the arthritic orator Polemon of Karia. The cult statue was modelled on Pheidias' famous original in Olympia. The travel-writer Pausanias found the whole thing too flamboyant and too Roman, especially since there were more statues of Hadrian in the sanctuary than there were of Zeus.

Hadrian also built an aqueduct and a reservoir (which is still in use, in a modernized version), a gymnasium, a fantastic library and archive centre (some of this huge building too is still visible north of the Roman agora: it was so magnificent that later Athenians assumed it was a palace), a pantheon and several other public buildings. In return the Athenians built an 18-metre triumphal arch on the boundary between the ancient city and the new quarter. On one side the legend read, 'This is Athens, once the city of Theseus', and on the other side, 'This is the city of Hadrian, not of Theseus.' The city had been rededicated to the emperor. Hadrian also endowed university chairs to keep Athens as an intellectual centre, and made it the location of annual conferences which were called 'panhellenic', but actually centred more on loyalty to and worship of the emperor. Still, they helped to remind people that Athens was the cultural centre of the world.

After Hadrian emperors had little spare money to spend on rebuilding provincial towns, but wealthy individuals took up the strain. The Library of Titus Flavius Pantainos, which served as a philosophical school as well as a regular library, was built in the early years of the second century next to the Stoa of Attalos in the agora. A huge basilica (commercial and administrative centre) was built in the north-east of the agora; the fountain-houses were restored or replaced. Two or three decades after Hadrian, the greatest private benefactor of the city began his work. Herodes Atticus, born in the village of Marathon, inherited great wealth and made a great deal more as the administrator, for Hadrian, of the province of Asia. His main contributions were the completion in marble of Lykourgos' stadium, the odeion under the south face of the Akropolis (some of the lovely arched windows of which still stand four storeys high), and a temple to Fortune. He was a famous thinker and orator in his day, held a number of administrative posts in Athens, and was the teacher of the philosopher-emperor Marcus Aurelius.

In the third century, however, no major building works were undertaken, and even minor projects were infrequent. The university and the *ephēbeia* barely continued, and the city remained a centre for the manufacture and export of pottery oil-lamps and crude terracotta figurines, but the Roman Empire as a whole was beginning to disintegrate; emperors had other concerns and individuals chose to spend their money on other pursuits. But even in this state of poverty, depopulation and insignificance, Athens had not yet reached its nadir.

ATHENS REDUCED AND REINVENTED

23

Athens Under Byzantion

Sometime in the late Roman or the early Byzantine period, the celebrated gold-and-ivory statue of Athena, sculpted by Pheidias in the heyday of the city's Periklean glory, vanished. Pious Christians could not leave the statue in a building they wanted to turn into a church, and they gave it to the centre of the universe, Constantinople, where it was last noted in the tenth century. There could be no more potent symbol of the city's decline than the loss of this emblem of her Classical greatness.

Moreover, the vagueness of the story reminds us that our sources for the history of Athens in the Common Era are so few that there are decades when Athens is not mentioned in any historical source, and then only in passing. Under such circumstances, the historian has been likened to a man standing outside a walled garden and trying to understand and describe the reality inside with the help of the odd piece of rubbish tossed over the wall. What follows is the result of such meagre pickings.

The Gothic Devastations of Athens

By the second half of the third century, Rome was rent by civil wars and weakened by constant incursions over many of her borders. Even the massive army could not be everywhere at once. It was hardly to be seen when in the 250s Goths, originally from Scythian territory north of the Danube, invaded the Balkans in search of a new homeland. By 258 they had captured Byzantion and were happily employed as pirates in the Black Sea and the Aegean. In 267 the Herulians, one of the Gothic tribes, undertook a more adventurous expedition. They sailed from the Black Sea to Greece, laying waste everything in their path. Soon they reached Athens. As it happens, the Athenians had recently repaired their walls for the first time since the Sullan sack. The co-emperor Valerian (253–60) was concerned about the threat to the provincial towns of the Empire, and wanted them to put up at least a token resistance. But Athens' walls were soon breached and the Herulians swarmed into the city.

Archaeologists have unearthed poignant reminders of the sack, such as a house in whose kitchen lay a mass of smashed kitchen-ware, a handful of bronze coins, and the skeleton of a donkey that had been hastily dragged into the house in a vain attempt to preserve at least this much of the family's possessions. Most of the private houses of the city were burnt or destroyed, and many of the great public buildings in the agora and elsewhere suffered the same fate. The Parthenon was severely damaged by fire. There is an implausible story that the Herulians, poised to burn the libraries of Athens, desisted because they felt that the young men of Athens would be less trouble if they were distracted by their books and studies. But this implies that the Herulians came not just to conquer but to settle, when in fact they were no more than raiders.

The only consolation was that there was not much of a massacre: the inhabitants of the city simply fled to the countryside. Here Publius Herennius Dexippos, annalistic historian and local grandee, hastily formed those who were willing and able into a force of nervous irregulars. Dexippos decided to use guerrilla tactics, and Fragment 28 of his *Scythian History* preserves part of the speech he claims to have given:

> Wars are decided by courage rather than numbers. We have a good-sized force, two thousand in all, and we have this remote spot as a base from which to harm the enemy by attacking him in small groups and ambushing him on his way . . . If they come against us, we shall resist: we have an excellent defensive position here in rough woodland. If they attack us from different directions, they will be repelled by fighting against men who are invisible and use tactics different from those they have met before. Their formation will disintegrate, they will not know where to aim their missiles, they will miss us while continuing to suffer from our attacks. We, however, will be able to shoot accurately from advantageous positions, protected by the trees.

Dexippos went on to explain that the Emperor's fleet was on its way to help them and that he hoped to rouse other Greek cities against the invaders. In the event the first was true, but the second was wishful thinking. But Dexippos and his band of guerrillas did succeed in driving the Herulians out of Attica, and successive emperors gradually finished the task and drove the Goths back across the Danube.

This unlikely military success came too late for the city, however. Athens never recovered. Many of the major buildings were in ruins, and matters were only made worse by the cannibalization of the ruins for material with which a new defensive wall was urgently built. The scale of this wall itself tells a sorry tale: it formed a rough square, from just south of the Akropolis (incorporating the back wall of the Agrippan Odeion) to just north of the Roman agora, but excluding the old agora (which was left ruined for over 100 years) and the Library of Hadrian – or rather, the Library jutted out from the north wall like a grandiose tower. The sides of the square were no more than about 500 metres. The walls were meant only to provide shelter for people and their valuables in an emergency.

Most Athenians now lived and went about their daily business outside these meagre walls. The city's trade in oil-lamps soon revived, even though the Kerameikos, the potters' district, was now undefended. But in other respects the city went into terminal decline. The *ephēbeia* came to an end, and the schools were no longer funded by Rome, but survived on the bequests of grateful students, until the professors came to form the richest segment of society, and because of their relative wealth often wielded administrative power in the reduced city. There were occasional external benefactors, such as the Emperor Constans I (337–50), who gave Athens some grain-growing islands out of respect for Prohairesios of Armenia, one of the most famous (and tallest) rhetorical teachers of his day. But more usually it was the local dignitaries themselves who financed the festivals or paid for maintenance work.

Along with the rest of the diminished population, however, architects and builders survived thanks mainly to the university, which not only attracted enough students to support farmers and artisans, but also built private homes large enough to double as schools, such as the so-called 'House of Proklos', which sheltered

successive generations of heads of the Academy just south of the
Akropolis. Now that the city was a quiet backwater, where the only
ripples were caused by academic arguments, provincial senators
occasionally chose to retire there, and one of them built a huge
villa (known as the 'Palace of the Giants' after the size of its statues)
over the ruins of the Odeion of Agrippa in the old agora, which was
rapidly becoming farmland.

Visitors still came and gawped at the antiquities – Athens was
already a museum – but they were not all impressed. An anonymous
travel writer of the fourth century devoted no more than three
garbled lines to Athens: 'Athens has ancient historical remains and
a remarkable arch where numerous statues commemorate in a
wonderful fashion the wars of ancient times' (*A Description of the
World and Its Peoples* 52). The brevity of this report matched the
destitution of the city. Orators continued to make reference to
the city's splendid past, but one of them was more realistic. Libanios
of Antioch loved Athens: he once said that he would have turned
down sex with a goddess just to smell the smoke of the city; but
when he was offered a professorship there, where he had studied
from 336 to 340, he turned it down because, he felt, it was no longer
a place where an ambitious orator could shine.

Athens had not seen the last of the Goths, however. In 376 they
again crossed the Danube in huge numbers, forced south by the
relentless inroads of the Huns. Rome was hard pressed, and in a
futile treaty of 382 Theodosios I reached a fragile compromise with
them. The treaty left the Balkans vulnerable, however, and the
Goths took advantage. In 395 Alaric and his Visigoths (a huge tribe
formed out of three separate Gothic groups) invaded Greece. The
Roman defences melted away, and Alaric soon appeared outside
the wall of Athens. Then what happened? The historian Zosimus
of the late fifth and early sixth century, who was already convinced
that Athens was under divine protection, tells us, with absolute
certainty, that Alaric was deterred from destroying the city by a
miracle: just as he approached the city, the goddess Athena
appeared, looking just like the ancient statue of Athena Promakhos
sculpted by Pheidias (see p. 108). She patrolled the wall, fully armed,
and seemed capable of repelling any assault. In dismay, Alaric came
to terms with the terrified inhabitants. But is this likely from the

fearsome marauder who went on to destroy Eleusis, Corinth and, in 410, Rome itself? Archaeologists have now unearthed unmistakable evidence that Alaric did sack the city, and did so with just as much vigour as the Herulians 130 years earlier.

From now on the plaintive cries of many visitors to Athens echoed Libanios' assessment of the city. Synesios of Kyrene was a fascinating man, a true reflection of a glorious period of Mediterranean culture when there was enough open-mindedness for pagan and Christian teachers to teach Christians and pagans alike, and the two philosophies mingled in the common search for union with the divine. Two of the great fourth-century Church Fathers, Basil of Caesarea and his contemporary Gregory of Nazianzus, were educated by pagan orators in Athens. So, at much the same time and by the same teachers, was Julian II the Apostate, the celibate emperor of Rome from 360 to 363, who tried in vain to revive pagan learning and to check the rise of Christianity. Synesios was a Christian, but he had been trained as a Neoplatonist, and not only remained fascinated by magic and alchemy, but could not accept central Christian doctrines such as the Resurrection. Naturally, when he was offered a diocese in North Africa, he had profound doubts whether he was the right man for the job. He thought and travelled for six months, and in the course of his travels deliberately took in Athens, as the old centre of pagan culture and the former rival of his beloved Alexandria. He arrived in 410 and after only a few days wrote an elegant but miserable letter home (*Letter* 136):

> Death to the blasted captain who brought me here! Athens no longer has anything sublime except the famous names of places. When a victim has been burnt up in a sacrifice, only the skin remains as a token of the animal that once existed; just so, now that philosophy has departed from here, there is nothing left for the tourist to admire except the Academy, the Lykeion and, of course, the Painted Stoa after which the philosophy of Khrysippos is named – and which is no longer painted anyway, since the proconsul has removed the panels to which Polygnotos of Thasos committed his art. . . . Athens once was home to the wise; now its bee-keepers alone bring it honour.

Christianity Comes to Athens

Synesios' gloom was not entirely justified, because the philosophers did return to Athens and resume their teaching activities, and their students returned, so that there was enough wealth in the city for considerable rebuilding in the early fifth century. But Athens' days as a centre of culture were numbered; the city was a pagan hold-out in a world that was rapidly being overrun by a new faith.

In the course of his world-changing mission, St Paul reached Athens early in 50 CE. As a visiting dignitary, he was invited to address the Areiopagos Council and, cleverly adapting his message to local conditions, he told them that he had come to reveal to them the Unknown God whose altar he had already seen in the city. The sermon he preached did not go down well: the Council was unimpressed and said, in the words of the King James version, 'We will hear thee again of this matter,' which in modern terms is 'Don't call us; we'll call you.' But Paul won a few local converts: 'Howbeit certain men clave unto him, and believed; among the which was Dionysios the Areiopagite, and a woman named Damaris, and others with them' (Acts 17:34).

Nevertheless, Christianity flourished elsewhere in the eastern provinces, if not at first in Athens or the west. By 235 it had eradicated a number of more extreme or eccentric doctrines as heresies and was a force to be reckoned with throughout the Empire. Drawing on the categories and methods of Greek philosophical debate, Christian thinkers were transforming their faith from a passionate branch of Jewish mysticism into an urbane and hellenized religion. They needed to attract not only the poorer members of society, but educated men and women.

At the battle of the Milvian Bridge near Rome in 312 the belligerent Emperor Constantine (307–37) made himself sole ruler of the Empire. In a dream a couple of years earlier his guardian deity Apollo had appeared to him as the sun, accompanied by the goddess Victory, and had indicated that he would reign for thirty years. This was not a normal pagan vision, however: above the sun appeared the Christian cross, and the message that the cross would be his means of victory. At the Milvian Bridge, he therefore sent his men into battle with the sign of the cross on their shields, and although he was heavily outnumbered, he defeated his rival. After this, the superstitious Emperor fostered the new religion throughout the Empire, especially with a massive programme of church building.

By 325 the Athenian Church was substantial enough to be represented at the Council of Nikaia (modern Iznik), where Constantine's delegates decided what would and what would not count as Christian orthodoxy. But the membership of the Athenian church was largely working-class, and it had signally failed to attract many notables. Certain poorer areas of the town were rapidly becoming Christian ghettoes, and the Christians were increasingly antagonistic in the face of polytheistic tolerance of the worshippers of any god. The tenacity of paganism in Athens was due entirely to the presence of the schools, especially Neoplatonism, which offered a viable alternative to Christianity as a way of life and of union with God. The Neoplatonists were big fish in the small pond of Athens; they were an administrative as well as a philosophical presence. And so the early Christian habit of meeting in converts' houses continued in Athens longer than elsewhere; there were no churches, no public places for Christian worship in Athens before the fifth century.

On 4 November 328, the day chosen by his astrologers, Constantine consecrated with extraordinary fanfare the city of Constantinople on the site of ancient Byzantion. Rome remained the sole capital of the Empire, but it was vital for Constantine and his successors to have an imperial headquarters in the east. It was nicknamed 'New Rome', the twin of Rome in an undivided state, and it was almost entirely a Christian city, though Constantine plundered pagan Athens and other cities and sacred sites of the Empire for works of art with which to embellish it. In recompense, he gave Athens yearly grants of grain, and revived the old imperial tradition of funding the professors of the university.

In 364 the new emperor Valentinian I raised his brother Valens to imperial rank, and formally divided the Roman Empire into two halves: he kept Rome and the west, while his brother was awarded Constantinople and the east. From then on there were two Empires, and the star of the eastern half rose as the western half fell and was more or less extinguished by Alaric and his Visigoths. The Roman Empire in the east outlived the one in the west by twelve dynasties, eighty-four emperors and about 1,000 years.

Constantine's benefactions to Athens were no more than a gesture. The shift of the centre of power to Constantinople doomed the southern part of the Greek peninsula to the margins of civilization. Even the great Roman roads, with their ornate milestones, began to suffer from neglect. Athens was further marginalized by steps taken by various Christian emperors to reduce or eliminate pagan religion and culture throughout the Empire. In 435 Theodosios II, who had ascended to the eastern imperial throne in 402 at the tender age of nine months, issued a proclamation that all pagan temples throughout the Empire were to be exorcized and destroyed. Fortunately for tourists and students of architecture, the edict allowed local officials some discretion and was widely disregarded from the outset; then, as the years rolled by, many of the major Athenian temples survived through being converted to churches or, in the case of Hadrian's temple of Olympian Zeus, by being just too big for casual demolition.

Ironically, the wife of Theodosios II was an Athenian-born woman, Aelia Eudokia, whose pagan birth-name was Athenais; she was the daughter of a famous Athenian scholar called Leontios. Although it was an arranged marriage and she converted to Christianity only on the eve of her wedding on 7 June 421, she built one of the earliest churches in Athens, perhaps the earliest, in the precinct of the Library of Hadrian, as part of a programme of redeveloping the city after the Gothic depredations. But she was also an advocate of traditional Athenian learning. She took scholars with her from Athens to Constantinople, and it was largely due to her influence that her husband founded the University of Constantinople, which became a major source of the perpetuation of Greek culture. She herself combined Classical and Christian learning by writing poetic versions of biblical stories, Classical in form and Christian in content. She was a passionate woman, and there were rumours of adultery; in combination with a long-running feud between her and the Emperor's powerful sister Pulcheria, this resulted in her banishment to Palestine in 441, where she died in 460.

If Eudokia represents that strand of Athenian life in the fifth century which was prepared to find some kind of accommodation between what were rapidly becoming conflicting ways of life, another famous resident definitely did not sit on the fence. The Neoplatonic philosopher Proklos of Lykia (412–85) arrived in Athens around 430 and spent the rest of his life there (except for a short period in the late 460s, when further Gothic raids were making life in Athens uncomfortable); from 437 he was head of the Neoplatonic school. Not only did he worship openly in the temples whose destruction Theodosios had ordained, and perform sacrifices there when Theodosios had also (in 438) prohibited such sacrifices throughout the Empire, but he also wrote a sixteen-point refutation of Christianity. Not surprisingly, since it was the Christian monastic copyists whose labours preserved most Greek and Latin literature, this treatise has not survived down to present times.

There is a legend about Proklos, preserved by his pupil and hagiographer Marinos of Samaria, which encapsulates the cusp on which Athens stood at the time (*Life of Proclus* 30):

> How dear he was also to the philosophic goddess is adequately established just by his choice of the philosophic life . . . but the goddess herself also made it perfectly plain when her statue, which had been seated for so long in the Parthenon, was removed in an attempt to move the unmovable. The philosopher dreamt that a beautiful woman came to him and told him to make his house ready as quickly as he could. 'For,' she said, 'the Lady of Athens wants to take up residence with you.'

The Neoplatonists resisted Christianity and felt they were the ones who perpetuated a true path of wisdom, but they were fighting a losing battle. Paganism and heresy were being stamped out all over the Empire. In 527, shortly after his accession to the imperial throne of Constantinople, Justinian I banned any community of the Empire from supporting pagan teaching or teachers. The Academy of Athens, however, fell through a loophole in this law, since it was self-supporting. Two years later, therefore, Justinian issued an edict requiring the final closure of the Academy. He singled Athens out in this way not just because of the loophole: the city had been a centre of pagan culture for so long that it was a mighty symbol, and it was still the centre of Neoplatonic teaching, which with its emphasis on magic was more directly a rival to the new faith. There was an aura of glamour about the professors too, which a good Christian could not tolerate.

There is an apocryphal story that the seven professors of Athens left a couple of years later for the Middle East, where they had heard of a land ruled by a true Platonic philosopher-king. In the event they were disappointed, and they returned. Perhaps they even resumed teaching at some level, even though they were now a persecuted minority. At any rate, Justinian's edict does not seem to have been rigorously or rapidly carried out: thirty years later there was still Academic property for the authorities to confiscate. Nevertheless, 529 is a potent date in the history of Athens: the last of the three pillars of the city's Classical greatness came tumbling down.

The schools were left to crumble, or were transformed into places for Christian study and worship. The same happened to several of the temples in the course of the sixth and seventh centuries. The Parthenon was converted into a church dedicated to the Virgin Mary; this involved no great structural changes, apart from the blocking of the eastern entrance by a new apse and the conversion of the rear room to a narthex, though many of the sculptures were defaced or destroyed. The Hephaisteion was used so rarely, eventually only once a year on the feast day of its patron saint, that the local name for him was Idle St George. The temple of Artemis of the Wild was converted to a church of the Blessed Virgin of the Rock, the Erekhtheion and the Propylaia also became churches. Constantine's victory was complete.

Byzantine Athens

Each time Athens was destroyed by successive Gothic invasions, she rose again in a diminished measure. By the late sixth century, however, even the eastern Roman Empire was under threat from invading Persians and, before long, the irresistible rise of Islam, and Byzantine emperors had little interest in preserving the impoverished and dilapidated towns and villages of the Balkans. When the pagan Slavs invaded Greece in 582, they met no opposition whatsoever: they had arranged for the Persians to distract the Emperor's attention to the east, and the land was theirs for the taking.

Athens was utterly destroyed – not occupied, just destroyed – and this time it was at least two centuries before it began to recover. The Slavs drove the Greeks out of the cities and into the countryside, or even further afield to the islands and elsewhere. Only squatters occupied the ruins of once-grand buildings in the agora, and weeds grew in the pavements of the Parthenon and Propylaia. The theatres and gymnasia collapsed and were plundered for building materials; water supplies and bath-houses dried up; ghosts haunted the sacred places of the Classical past. The invisibility of Athens for the next 200 years is just an aspect of the Dark Age into which Europe as a whole had been plunged by huge invasions and cultural rifts. The Greeks, along with many other peoples, turned in on themselves.

Athens slumbered peacefully, with her noble past remaining only in the form of ancient ruins and a little-altered language, but there was no longer any memory or sense of continuity. When the Emperor Constans II spent the winter of 662–3 in Athens during his campaign against the Slavs, he did so for logistical reasons, not because the city was important. When we hear that Theodore of Tarsus, who as Archbishop of Canterbury from 669 to 690 did more than anyone else to unify British Christians, was educated in Athens, we have to wonder whether he did more than enjoy some learned conversations with the local bishop. Despite the proximity of pagan Slavs, eighth-century inscriptions on a column of the Parthenon show that Christian worship and even the replacement of bishops continued with little interruption.

By the end of the seventh century, the Balkans, along with much of the rest of the Byzantine Empire, had been organized into *themata*. A 'theme' was an administrative unit whose primary purpose was to simplify the collection of the imperial taxes and recruitment of military personnel or labourers; Byzantine bureaucracy was so exact that each theme's governor had lists of all the families in his district and what their special skills were, and could compel them to leave and work in the capital if necessary. Athens was one of the leading towns of the Byzantine theme of Hellas

(Thessaly, Boiotia and Attica). In 732 Emperor Leo III took over from Rome the enormous diocese of East Illyricum (the Balkans, Greece, the Aegean islands, Crete, southern Italy and Sicily), and so for the first time in ecclesiastical terms Athens fell under the jurisdiction of Constantinople. The Pope protested, but the seizure was part of the growing schism between the Eastern and Western Churches, and in any case made sense, since the vast majority of the inhabitants of East Illyricum were Greek-speakers.

The focus of life in Attica was not the city (now little more than the Akropolis) but the surrounding countryside. Rural villages were organized as collectives. Villagers farmed the land in strip cultivation, and every farmer contributed to the total taxes to be paid to central government. Individual farmers owned strips (on which their tax contribution was assessed) or rented land from their neighbours. All shared in communal grazing land, and in facilities such as water-mills, ovens, and wine and olive presses. Over the years, this system allowed successful farmers to grow wealthy at the expense of others, and typically they would move from the countryside to Athens, leaving overseers in charge of their now considerable estates, buy property in the city (the remains of a number of substantial Byzantine mansions have been found), and get involved in provincial government – not least because such positions often entailed exemption from Byzantine taxes. The rich, as usual, could get richer. An area of the city was cleared so that the rich could play *tzykanion*, a form of polo.

For all its insignificance, eighth-century Athens did produce someone who was, by any standards, a remarkable woman. Eirene of Athens was the first woman ever to hold the throne of the Byzantine Empire. Eudokia, as we have seen, had married an emperor, but Eirene was actually the ruler: imported into Constantinople in 769 to marry the imperial heir, in 780, after her husband Leo IV's sudden death, when she was only about twenty-five years old, she successfully challenged the male-oriented norm and proclaimed herself regent and co-emperor until her nine-year-old son came of age. She turned out to be a consummate Byzantine ruler.

She fought off challenges to her rule from both outside and within the Empire, and revealed a deft touch in politics and diplomacy and a ruthless streak in dealing with her enemies. She clearly loved power and recognized that she was good at wielding it; in fact, her son had to incite rebellion in the army to force Eirene to retire and to get himself proclaimed sole Emperor, Constantine VI, even as late as 790. Within two years, however, her period of disgrace was over and she had worked herself back into a position of power in her son's court. By 797 she was ready to strike: her son had no male heir and had lost popularity throughout the Empire. She had him blinded and deposed, replaced governors throughout the Empire whose loyalty was suspect, and ruled as sole Empress (or even Emperor: she deliberately adopted the masculine form for diplomatic purposes) until 802, when her enemies finally managed to get her banished. She died in 803 on the island of Lesbos.

Visits by Byzantine emperors to lowly Athens were rare: apart from that of Constans II in 662–3, only Basil II the Bulgar-slayer came in 1019; he celebrated his defeat of the Bulgars, who had long posed a major threat, with a triumph, offered a mass of thanksgiving in the former Parthenon, and converted some of his booty into gifts for the cathedral, including a golden dove which hung from the roof over the altar and silver panels for the doors. Eirene never returned to her native city, but she did not neglect it. Her army pacified the Slavs in all but a few remote areas of Greece and compelled them to recognize the authority of Constantinople. She promoted deserving members of her family, and raised Athens to metropolitan status, so that it had the same rank as Thessaloniki and Corinth, which ensured the city's continued prominence, if not prosperity. She is also credited with the building or restoration of a number of churches in Athens (though her main building activity was naturally in Constantinople itself), but in the religious sphere by far her most important contribution was that, chiefly by means of the Seventh Ecumenical Council in 787, she restored icons to the churches of the Empire, after recent Iconoclast emperors (including her own father-in-law and, though less fervently, her husband) had removed and destroyed them. For this she is still revered as a saint in the Greek Church.

Athens remained for many decades a quiet provincial town, though plagued by piracy, which was particularly fierce in the eighth and ninth centuries. There was little organized opposition, and pirates often threatened Athens. In 826 and again in 896 they devastated the island of Aigina, within easy sight of Athens. There was in Athens a small colony of Muslims, with their own mosque, from about 900 to 1100, but whether they came as captives or as raiders will never be known. Otherwise the population of Byzantine Athens was largely Greek, with a few Slavs, Albanians and Jews, numbering in total perhaps 7,500.

At the start of the eleventh century the city began to recover some prosperity as a centre for the manufacture of soap, textiles and garments, especially expensive ecclesiastical clothes coloured with the purple dye derived from the murex shellfish. A number of fine churches and monasteries were built, along with new defences. The recovery was in part due to the presence of new arrivals from Italy, hungry for trade, and in part to the fact that the Slavs were now finally pacified, Christianized and integrated into the old population. New confidence – and a newly fortified Akropolis – led the city to revolt against Constantinople around 1040, but the revolt was suppressed by mercenaries under Harald Haardraade (who would die in 1066 in England at Stamford Bridge). In 1147, the fleet of the expansionist Norman king Roger of Sicily, a thorn in the side of Constantinople, found Athens worth plundering (though his primary targets were Thebes and Corinth), and he even removed a number of the town's silk workers. Before long the town returned to the indifferent and impoverished state which had been its lot for so long.

This was the condition of Athens when the scholar Michael of Chonae in Phrygia became one of its most illustrious residents. He was appointed archbishop there in 1182 at the age of forty-four, and left in 1204, abandoning even his books on the arrival of the crusaders with their Catholic faith. Coming from a highly educated and cultured family, he arrived steeped in Classical Greek literature and filled with impressions of the city's past culture and splendours, and was sorely disappointed. In his bleaker moments, he regarded being sent to Athens as akin to exile, and described the city as 'a God-forsaken hole in a far corner of the Empire' and its citizens as 'an uncivilized horde'. These complaints, commonplace among sophisticated Constantinopolitans sent to the provinces, were exacerbated by Michael's awareness of how much the city had lost, though, firm in his faith, he did not regret the passing of pagan religion.

Others at the time also fantasized about Athens' past. The city's reputation as a centre of learning endured to such an extent that the fictitious and scandalous Life of Pope Joan had her educated there even in the thirteenth century. The unreliable English chronicler Matthew Paris (c. 1200–59) says that Greek philosophers came to England early in the thirteenth century from Athens and were expelled by King John because he was afraid that his subjects might deviate from the Christian path, and that John of Basingstoke, the Archdeacon of Leicester, studied in Athens under a brilliant young girl called Constantina, the daughter of the Athenian archbishop. But Paris and his peers lacked the confrontation with reality that brought Michael of Chonae to his senses.

The first sermon Michael delivered in Athens was full of learned references to Athens' past and to ancient Greek literature. The sermon was over-long and far too erudite; the congregation floundered, and Michael later admitted that he might as well have been speaking in a foreign language. Their ignorance and lack of breeding, and their barbaric version of Greek, confounded him. Only the magnificent buildings of the Akropolis, where he had the Propylaia as his residence and the Parthenon as his cathedral, survived intact 'beyond the destruction of time' (wishful thinking!). Everything else was ruined, oppressed between the hammer of the sun and the anvil of an iron soil. Many of the churchmen were more concerned with lining their pockets than saving the souls of their parishioners, who were also oppressed by piracy and the depredations of a swarm of Byzantine bureaucrats, 'thicker than the plague of frogs with which God afflicted Egypt'.

But Michael loved the present inhabitants and did his best to remind them of their past, as a means of restoring their pride; more pragmatically, he campaigned for money, tax-relief, the development of industries in the city, and the curbing of piracy, as well as restoring buildings, including the Parthenon, at his own expense. The campaigns were largely unsuccessful, and towards the end of his life (he died in 1220 on the island of Kea) he wrote a poignant description of the city in a letter to a friend:

> You cannot look upon Athens without weeping. It is not just that she has lost her ancient glory: that was taken from her long ago. But now she has lost the very form, appearance and

24

Athens Under the Franks

In 1205 Athens came under the control of crusading French noblemen, who had massacred the inhabitants of Thessaloniki in 1185
and those of Constantinople in 1204, and were now dividing what
was left of the Byzantine Empire among themselves. The arrival of
Boniface of Montferrat was actually fortuitous, since he frightened
off a worse threat. The collapse of central authority in Constantinople had led to the rise of local warlords, and one of them, Leon
Sgouros (the Curly-head), originally from Nauplion in the Peloponnese, had already burnt the lower town of Athens (so thoroughly
that at least one suburb, over the ancient agora, did not recover
until the eighteenth century) and was besieging the Akropolis. He
hurried north to meet Boniface, but in the event put up no resistance
and retreated back to his stronghold in Corinth. When Boniface
reached Athens, Michael of Chonae, who in this time of anarchy
had taken over the city's secular affairs as well, simply handed the
Akropolis to him, preferring surrender and the plundering of the
Parthenon to needless slaughter and destruction.

Boniface gave Athens to Othon de la Roche, a member of his
entourage from a previously fairly insignificant Burgundian family.
Othon appreciated his sudden elevation and stayed aloof from a rash
attempt by other Frankish nobles a few years later to shake off their
allegiance to the new masters of Constantinople; Athens was duly
rewarded by a visit to the city in 1207 by the newly installed Emperor
Henry of Flanders, who had quickly crushed the rebellion. Just as
Basil II had heard a mass of thanksgiving on his triumphal visit to
the city nearly 200 years previously, so did Henry, but this time it
was a Latin mass celebrated by the French Archbishop Bérard.

Five years later, in gratitude for his help in overcoming Sgouros,
Geoffroy de Villehardouin, the powerful prince of the Peloponnese,
rewarded Othon with the fiefs of Argos and Nauplion in addition to

his extensive territories in Attica, Boiotia, the Megarid, Phokis and Lokris. Of Othon's two capitals, Thebes was the bustling centre of commerce, especially in silk, while Athens was a peaceful backwater, possessed of dignity rather than political or economic importance. Othon ruled his lands as Lord of Athens, a virtual monarch; under him were a number of barons (including members of his own family who had promptly sailed for Greece), then French knights, and so on down the feudal hierarchy to Italian and Jewish merchants (and even a few wealthy Greeks), and finally peasant serfs. Othon was homesick, however, and he returned to France with his immediate family in 1225, leaving the fiefdoms of Athens to his nephew Guy.

The years of peace came to an end in the 1250s. The new ruler of the Peloponnese, Guillaume de Villehardouin, provoked the mainland Latin rulers into a coalition against him, which came to a head at a battle near Megara in 1258. The battle was somewhat incongruous in a Greek setting: armoured knights on horseback charged at one another across a plain, shields emblazoned, pennants flying from helmets and lances lowered. The Peloponnesians won the day, and Guillaume demanded that Guy de la Roche be tried for the crime of insurrection against his feudal superior. The case eventually came before the King of France himself, who could not have cared less, and awarded Guy – the only one who bothered to make the journey to Paris – the title of Duke of Athens, the highest station in the medieval hierarchy after the royal family.

By the time Guy died in 1263, Michael Palaiologos had recovered Constantinople and was clearly intending to restore the old Byzantine Empire in Greece as far as he could. This was the delicate situation Guy passed to his son Jean. Twenty-five years later the conflict between Catholics and Greeks had reached stalemate, and the de la Roche family, represented now by Guy II, had managed to retain all its territory. Guy II inherited Thessaly as well, so that his possessions now encompassed much of northern and central Greece, and his power was felt in the northern Peloponnese and on the island of Euboia too. Flushed with pride, he made an unprovoked assault on Thessaloniki in 1303, with the intention of detaching the city from the Byzantine Empire. The attack was defused, however, by a personal appeal from the French wife of the Emperor, who was living in Thessaloniki, and the huge army returned home and disbanded.

In 1308 the relatively calm fortunes of the Dukes of Athens were abruptly shattered, just as they had reached their peak. On the death of Guy II from cancer, the new Duke, Guy's cousin Gautier de Brienne, faced an invasion of the Catalan Company, a band of highly skilled and highly dangerous Spanish mercenaries. Originally hired by Constantinople to combat the raids of the Turks, they had turned against their paymasters in a series of bloody reprisals for the assassination of their brilliant commander, the renegade Templar Roger de Flor. Having done all they could to disrupt the eastern part of the Empire, and in fact to facilitate matters for the Turks, they turned west and devastated Thrace, their numbers swelled by Turkish soldiers. For three years the catalogue of atrocities in Thrace and Macedonia grew. Then they turned south.

Gautier tried to keep them in check by hiring them for his own ends, to retain his now precarious hold on Thessaly. The Catalans overran Thessaly – and then Gautier made his big mistake. He offered 500 of them permanent employment, and dismissed the rest with the curt suggestion that they should withdraw from the Thessalian districts they now occupied. The enraged Catalans refused and marched to meet him. Early on 15 March 1311 the Catalan force of 7,000 (which included the 500 in Gautier's employ, whom he sensibly released, fearing treachery, to fight alongside their countrymen) defeated his 14,500 troops at a battle close to the Kephissos river; Gautier's 700 heavy knights became bogged down in the marshes, where they were easily slaughtered or captured for later ransom. Gautier was among the first to lose his life. The French rule of Athens had lasted a little over 100 years.

The Catalan Domination of Athens

The Catalans' Turkish allies returned home, but the Catalans themselves stayed, and those who had not brought their families with them took Frankish widows for themselves. They chose one of their prisoners, Roger Deslaur, to organize things for them until in

1312 King Frederick II of Sicily sent them his five-year-old second son, Manfred, as Duke of Athens, with a vicar-general until he should come of age. The Catalans were more than marauding brigands: they were astute enough to appreciate that, if they were to be allowed to survive and settle in war-torn Greece, they would need a strong overlord. Manfred died in 1317, after falling from his horse, and his younger brother became the first in a chain of non-resident dukes, who left the Catalans more or less to their own devices, with the guidance of a vicar-general appointed by the King of Aragon and Sicily.

The Catalans drew up their own constitution and laws, and in the five main towns – Athens, Thebes, Livadia, Siderokastron and Neopatras (modern Ypati) – they established self-governing and self-regulating municipalities, with councils elected for a maximum term of three years, so that (as in ancient Athens) no individual could achieve too much prominence. Each municipality was ruled by a *veguer* (vicar) and a captain, who were responsible for judicial matters and were supported by a council consisting of a judge, an assessor and a notary. Defence was the responsibility of a castellan. Thebes was the capital of their southern territories and Neopatras of the north. Athens was decorative, but the least important of the five municipalities; it was considered an unhealthy location, its chief produce (olive oil) was cheap, its wine was poor and resinous, and the Venetian near-monopoly on trade hindered the development of Peiraieus, or Porte Leone, as it was known at the time.

The protection of the Aragonese–Sicilian kings enabled the Catalans to survive repeated excommunications by a series of popes (which served only to drive quite a few of them into the arms of the Orthodox Church). The grounds given for these interdicts were usually that the Catalans associated with godless Turks, but the fact that the Avignon popes were French and the Catalans had ousted a French family had more to do with it. For a while, the Catalans thrived and increased their territory. Under the ambitious Don Alfonso Fadrique of Aragon, vicar-general from 1317 to 1330, Catalan sway came, largely through piracy, to encompass parts of Euboia, Aigina and southern Thessaly, but he then gave up Euboia in order to keep the Venetians off his back and ceded Nauplion and Argos as a sop to the Peloponnesian Franks, though they were in any case proving reluctant to restore any surviving members of the de la Roche family to their estate.

In addition to excommunication, several popes sought more certain means of damnation for the Catalans. Over the years they tried to interest various parties in expelling them and restoring the French former rulers, but nobody felt inclined to take up the offer. The final major effort from the Avignon papacy came in 1331 when Gautier II, the son of Gautier de Brienne, returned at the head of a papally blessed army to regain his rightful lands. He failed because the Venetians, the main Frankish power in southern Greece, not only refused to support his enterprise, but even renewed their alliance with the Catalans. Gautier besieged various fortresses, but the Catalans sat tight until he ran out of money and returned west.

This was, however, the apex of the Catalan rule of Athens, as niggling warfare, military or diplomatic, with the papacy and their neighbours began to take its toll. Moreover, they had become farmers rather than hardened pirates, and their neighbours smelled weakness and the chance of piecemeal takeover. Some surviving descendants of the de la Roche family made a feeble attempt on Athens in 1370, but without the support of any of the powers in Greece they were easily repulsed. The real threat to Catalan security lay elsewhere.

In 1358 the distinguished Florentine banker and courtier Niccolo Acciaiuoli had been granted, in addition to the substantial Greek territories he already owned in the Peloponnese, the town of Corinth and its unassailable citadel. Niccolo died in 1365, but other members of his family prospered in Greece. In 1374 his cousin's son Nerio Acciaiuoli seized Megara from the Catalans. Five years later, while the Catalan nobles were distracted by internal feuding, the belligerent Navarrese Company captured Thebes. It was a nice irony that the former mercenaries were injured by the latest professional fighters to seek employment in the Greek wars.

A parliament, hastily convened in Athens, now the capital of the south, appealed to Peter IV of Aragon for help against the Navarrese and the traitors who had helped them take Thebes. The king was glad to help, he said, since he considered the Akropolis 'the richest jewel on earth, such that all the kings of Christendom could not create another like it' – hackneyed phrases when applied to Athens, especially by one who had never been there, but significant as the first aesthetic appreciation of the Akropolis after about 1,000 years of Western European silence.

The reinforcements, when they came, were enough only to safeguard the remaining territories, not recoup their losses. Acciaiuoli had already been given Thebes by the Navarrese, and in 1385 he invaded and overran the remaining Catalan possessions almost without a fight. The Catalans, once the terror of Greece, melted away, their numbers thinned by the plague that swept Greece in 1381–2 and their mettle softened by easy living. Only the Akropolis held out, while the king in Aragon dithered. At last, ravaged by famine and the plague, the Catalans surrendered, and on 2 May 1388 Nerio entered the citadel. The anomalous rule of Athens by the piratical Spaniards was over.

The Acciaiuolis in Athens

Nerio's conquest of Athens was only precariously recognized by the Venetians (who embargoed Athenian figs and Corinthian currants) and the Navarrese (who tricked Nerio and imprisoned him for a year). When Nerio was released late in 1390, he was reduced to desperate bargaining with potential allies, and to stripping the Parthenon of Basil II's silver panels, its precious vessels and jewel-encrusted robes to pay his ransom. In Athens itself, however, he strengthened his position by allowing the native Greek population more rights: Greek became once again the official language of the state, and an Orthodox archbishop was allowed to return to his diocese (though not to the Parthenon), after a lapse of 180 years.

Meanwhile, the Turks had taken Neopatras from Nerio and were looming on his northern borders, but their sights were set on Constantinople, and in Greece they contented themselves for a number of years with raids and punitive expeditions against the Peloponnese that largely bypassed Boiotia and Attica. Nerio died on 25 September 1394, after a long illness. He left Boiotia to his son Antonio, the offspring of his affair with an Athenian woman called Maria Rendis, and parcelled out other territories to other Latin heirs (though he lost Corinth to an opportunistic takeover), but whimsically bequeathed the city of Athens to the Cathedral of the Virgin – that is, to the Parthenon. He wanted all the revenue of the city to be put towards the refurbishment of the beautiful monument after he had been forced to despoil it to raise money. This was utterly impractical: St Mary, for all her potency, could not defend Athens, but in his will Nerio had also placed the city under the protection of Venice.

The Greeks resented the fact that Athens, a city with a great past as a centre of pagan and Orthodox culture, now belonged to a Catholic cathedral. The Orthodox archbishop invited the Turks, who were then allied to Constantinople, to drive the hated Latins out of the land. The Turks besieged the Akropolis, but Nerio's Venetian lieutenant, Matteo de Montona, summoned his compatriots from Euboia, to fulfil their part in Nerio's will. The Turks withdrew and from 1395 to 1402 the Venetians were in charge of the city, but Nerio's bastard son Antonio was still dreaming in Thebes of reuniting the two most important parts of his father's former territory.

In 1401 Antonio invaded Attica and besieged the Akropolis, with its fortifications newly repaired by the Venetians. The Venetians sent an army of 6,000 to sack Thebes, but Antonio's force of 300 ambushed them in a defile and massacred them. Early in 1403 the Venetians on the Akropolis capitulated and Antonio reclaimed Athens. By 1405, as a result of skilful negotiating, Antonio had persuaded the Venetians to pardon him and recognize him as the Duke of Athens. The Turks were no longer an immediate threat: they had suffered devastating losses in the east at the hands of the Mongols and were regrouping. By 1435, however, when Antonio died of a stroke after thirty years of relative peace, they were again the power-brokers in Greece and it was only with Turkish approval that the family held on to Athens, while the major powers swirled around them. Finally, in 1456, three years after the fall of Constantinople, the Turks took over. The last Acciaiuoli duke, Franco, abandoned the Akropolis and was allowed by the Turks to retire to Thebes. Late in the summer of 1460 the Turks strangled him.

Athens Under the Franks

In all this time, there was little intermingling between the French (or the Catalans or the Florentines) and the local Athenians in terms of marriage, culture, language or religion: for the first time for several centuries Orthodox Christianity became the faith of the underclass. Like expatriates everywhere, the French were proud of the ways in which they maintained their native culture without becoming tainted by Greek customs; they preferred jousting, hawking and troubadours to peasant festivals, retsina and Homer.

The population of Athens fluctuated throughout the 200 years of Western European rule, but never exceeded about 11,000. The city was attacked no fewer than eight times in this period, and on each occasion was depleted through death and fear. Each time, however, it was restocked by Albanians, returning Greeks, and the dependants of successive masters of the city. Native Athenians were, with rare exceptions, serfs, in feudal bondage to their European masters, not allowed even to own property. One of the exceptions was Dimitrios Rendis (after whom a district of Athens – once a village near the city – is still named), the father of Nerio Acciaiuoli's mistress, whose intelligence was recognized by the Catalans: he became the chancellor of Athens and a valued adviser to the Catalan government, and was allowed to own property and Greek serfs. Others were preferred in other ways, especially as clerks or merchants, but by and large the noble Athenian families lay dormant or oppressed throughout the thirteenth and fourteenth centuries, waiting until they could rise again.

The control of Greece by Frankish powers brought a trickle of European tourists, and of course Athens was high on their list of places to visit. Not everyone bothered to disembark, however, and so the accounts they took back home were often fanciful – and the imaginative interpretations of famous sites by the local tour guides did not help. But the first Western tourist to visit Athens did so by accident. Niccolo da Martoni was ambushed by pirates in February 1395 and ended up on the east coast of Attica. From there, now thoroughly circumspect, he travelled through the night to Athens, to avoid being spotted by brigands. His first glimpses of the ruins at dawn awoke in him a desire to see and know more, and reminded him of snippets of Classical education from his school days, and he engaged a guide to show him around. It would be an understatement to say that he was impressed.

Ciriaco de' Pizzicolli (Cyriacus of Ancona), a passionate antiquarian and restless traveller, visited in 1436 and 1444 and has left us the first surviving sketch of the Parthenon. This sketch is enormously important and enormously controversial: it is the earliest sketch of the sculptures of the temple, but it is hasty and rough, drawn in a single morning from ground level and containing a misleading version of the pedimental sculptures. But he loved Athens. Close to the start of his diary, he wrote breathlessly of 'the huge walls, which have everywhere collapsed because of their great age, and both inside and outside in the countryside incredible marble structures and houses, and sacred shrines and all kinds of statues, outstanding for the wonderful skill of their makers, and vast pillars, but everything everywhere convulsed with great ruins'. Athens still has the same effect on first-time visitors.

Ciriaco busied himself copying inscriptions – no easy job in the days before sites were cleared of weeds and shrubbery, snakes and goats – poking his nose in everywhere, and ignoring the fanciful tales of the guides in favour of his own interpretations (which were not generally much better). The Philopappos monument was still almost complete; by the time of an anonymous Venetian visitor in about 1470, some of it had collapsed. He left us an ecstatic description of the Parthenon – but as an ardent Classicist, nothing at all about life in the lower city, for the Greeks, Albanians and poorer Europeans. This is generally true of visitors to Athens: they counted columns, copied inscriptions and measured temples, but ignored the hustle and bustle around them. It was yet another manifestation of the purist focus on Classical Athens.

25

Ottoman Athens and Elgin's Marbles

With hindsight, it is easy to see the squabbles and power struggles of the Latin potentates in Greece as ostrich-like manoeuvres: they must have realized, had they stopped to think about it for a second, that the Turks were waiting to gobble them up. In 1453, with the fall of the pitiful remnants of the Byzantine Empire, Greece became part of what would become known as 'European Turkey', along with what we now call Serbia, Bulgaria, Romania and so on. There were a few holdouts, but hardly any lasted more than a few years, like the Akropolis, which fell in 1456. The Venetians waged a long and futile war against the Turks from 1463 to 1479 (in the course of which Athens was briefly occupied by the Venetians in 1466), and shorter wars in the sixteenth century, but the balance of power in the eastern Mediterranean remained largely as it had been. The Turks were permanently at war elsewhere, however, and so the Greek peninsula again became largely a quiet backwater.

Once again Athens dropped off the map – literally. There was so little news of it that in 1575 the German classical scholar Martin Kraus, poised to write about the city, had first to write to Constantinopolitan contacts to find out whether it still existed. Athens was remote: it was held by a people assumed to be godless, surrounded by waters rumoured to be infested by pirates (though the Turks were rather good at keeping them down) and land rumoured to be crawling with disease, wolves and brigands. Some maps failed to mark the city, or it was known in letters or maps only in corrupt forms such as 'Satine', 'Sethynes' and 'Cetines'. Once again, for the historian details are often hard to come by and only the surrounding frame is clear.

Ottoman Rule

By the time of its collapse, the Ottoman Empire had deservedly gained a reputation for corruption and cruelty, but this was certainly not the case at the beginning of its rule of the Balkans, nor was it equally the case in all parts of the Empire. Where Athens was concerned, the Turks were aware of the value of their new possession: the Sultan himself, Mehmet II, visited the city for four days in the autumn of 1458, and was overwhelmed by its beauty. He ordered that the Akropolis was to be especially well looked after, expelled the Catholic archbishop, and granted Athenians freedom of worship and, to a degree, self-government under a voivode (governor), a cadi (judge), and a disdar (garrison commander). Athens' privileged position was formalized in 1645, when the city became an appanage of the Chief of the Black Eunuchs, a minor court dignitary, and so less likely to meet the arbitrary cruelty of corrupt administrators. It was rumoured that Athens earned this privilege thanks to the persuasive powers of an Athenian woman who became the sultan's slave and mistress. Apart from the Turkish magistrates most daily business for the Greeks was run by a council of twelve Greek arkhons (mainly from the same few families), one of whose more important jobs was the collection of taxes for the voivode.

The imperial tax system was peculiarly liable to corruption: the voivode paid for his post in advance, and then recouped his expenditure by keeping for himself what remained out of the taxes he collected after he had paid his subordinates. This system meant that the central Ottoman government did not have all the trouble of collecting taxes from around the vast Empire. But not only might a voivode impose high taxes, he could also collect grain and oil in lieu, and then sell these commodities back to his subjects, especially if they were Greeks, for a high price. As if this were not enough, Athenians occasionally had to suffer a higher than usual level of taxation from a rapacious archbishop as well. But, where their voivodes were concerned, the Athenians had the right of appeal to Constantinople if they felt they were being particularly oppressed, and to their credit most voivodes and representatives of the Ottoman government behaved fairly. The penalties for crimes of corruption could be extreme.

For a number of reasons Ottoman rule was not unwelcome in all quarters. Materially, there was hope of advancement, and indeed many Greeks made their fortunes in Asia Minor under the Turks. Muslims regarded trade as an unbecoming occupation for a real man, and Greeks (as well as Jews and Armenians) rushed to fill the gap. As non-Muslims, they were liable to severe taxes, especially on imports and exports (from Athens, chiefly silk, cotton, wax and nuts), but they still prospered. By 1800 Greek merchants had a near-monopoly of maritime trade in the Mediterranean, and matters only improved for them after the last years of the eighteenth century, when Russian vessels gained the right to ply Turkish waters and allowed a number of Greek ships to fly the Russian flag.

In addition to Greek traders, by the eighteenth century a number of Greek families were solidly established in the highest ranks of the Ottoman Civil Service, and in fact came more or less to control the administration of the Empire, either as civil servants in Constantinople or as governors of districts of the Empire. The Phanariotes, as they were known (after the Phanar quarter of Constantinople, where they lived), were the new nobility of Greece, and with their mansion houses and Western European contacts were as alien to their peasant compatriots back home as the most bejewelled and beturbaned Turk. Paradoxically, Greeks constituted both the wealthiest and the poorest members of the Orthodox community of the Turkish Empire.

The backwardness of Athens, and of Greece in general, was a function not just of the poverty and oppression of its inhabitants. The divide between East and West was as solid as the Berlin Wall, and Greece was more or less entirely cut off from all the major intellectual and social movements of Western Europe, from the Renaissance to the Enlightenment. Even in the 1790s there were Greek priests who denounced the views of Copernicus (1473–1543) and insisted that the sun revolved around the earth. If an idea came from the West, it was treated with suspicion or derision – even if it was algebra, atomic theory, optics and acoustics, all of which were condemned by the Greek patriarch in 1819. Athenian ignorance, lamented by Michael of Chonae in the twelfth century, lingered long: there were very few schools in the city until the end of the eighteenth century. Teachers were as rare as doctors or other professionals.

Spiritually, the Turks allowed their subjects freedom of worship. Not only were Christians 'people of the book' (recipients of a revelation acceptable to Islam), but the Turks had practical reasons for their tolerance: successful rebellion would be impossible without the help of the Catholic West, and the Turks wanted to keep the two parts of Christendom divided. Not that the Greeks needed much help in this regard: there was still widespread hatred and suspicion of Catholics in Greece, not just because of the years of occupation, but for the sack of Constantinople in 1204. Successive popes did not help by demanding submission and mass conversion to Catholicism as the price of military assistance against the Turks. So, as far as the Greeks were concerned, at least Ottoman rule would allow them to keep their faith, and therefore the core of their Greekness. In return the Greek Orthodox patriarchs in Constantinople agreed to guarantee the loyalty and quiescence of their followers.

Some Greeks converted to Islam to gain a more secure position in the Empire, or to retain their estates, which otherwise were commonly given to Turkish soldiers as rewards for service and farmed by Greek peasants as sharecroppers or tenants. Two-thirds of the entire tax revenue of the Empire was paid by the Balkans. For this reason alone, the Balkans never underwent mass conversion: Muslims paid less tax than Christians, and the Empire needed the income. Conversion was threatened more often than it was enacted, but led to at least one famous Athenian martyr. In the 1770s young Mikhalis Bakanas, later to become St Michael the Less, accepted death on a trumped-up charge rather than conversion. Another popular Athenian saint is St Philothei, a wealthy woman from the prominent Venizelos family (the district of Athens named after her was once the farmland where she lived), who was famous during her lifetime for her charity towards the poor and who was murdered in 1559 by Turkish hooligans.

At the peasant level, members of either faith borrowed folk rites from one another. Some attended both mosque and church, and saw little difference. Some Christians adopted the Muslim practice of having more than one wife, or of temporary marriage. Church

leaders pontificated about dogma, but peasants were not concerned
with such niceties. At times of drought, which were disturbingly
frequent, Muslims and Christians prayed together for rain – and
even brought in the pagan Africans, former slaves of the Turks, who
lived in some of the caves which pit the Akropolis.

There were rules which kept Greeks second-class citizens: they
were subject to severe punishments and they were not allowed to
carry weapons or be educated or wear green or ride horses or build
houses taller than any Turk's or ring their church bells. No Greek's
word could stand against a Turk's in a law court. Greek women
had to live in seclusion as much as Turkish women. Then there was
the institution of child tribute: at irregular intervals the best and
brightest boys – approximately one in every five – had to be handed
over to the Turkish authorities, and were brought up as Muslims,
destined to join the Civil Service or the army. Oddly, though, this
tribute aroused little protest, and many peasant families regarded it
as a way for their sons to improve their lot. The same goes also for
the removal of girls to become odalisques in a harem. In any case,
these practices did not outlast the seventeenth century.

Throughout the period of Ottoman rule Athens remained
obscure, no more than a large, run-down village; it was the forty-
third largest community in the European territories held by the
Ottomans and you could walk around the wall built towards the
end of the eighteenth century in forty-five minutes. Thessaloniki in
the north was the centre of Ottoman Greece. Athens was split into
two parts: the Akropolis housed the Turkish garrison and their
families, in about 200 dwellings, while Greeks and poorer Turks
(and Albanians and Italians, and a very few Jews) clustered around
the base of the hill to the north and north-east (in the district now
known as the Plaka) in small red-tiled houses. Greeks were not
allowed to set foot on the Akropolis. The ancient agora and the
temple of Olympian Zeus were outside the city, grazing grounds
for sheep, donkeys and camels; storks nested on the tops of ancient
pillars. Manufacturing, which had occasionally given Athens some
degree of prosperity in the previous few hundred years, was reduced
to cottage industry. Athens exported nuts and fruits, and a little
silk, and that was about all. The poverty of the native Athenians
and Albanians was remarked by many visitors. For weeks on end

Peiraieus saw no ships, just fishing-vessels; Europeans traded only with some of the larger islands and with the Peloponnese. Visitors to Athens were often asked for news of the wider world, even of Constantinople.

The latest incarnation of the Parthenon was as a mosque – the Mosque of the Conqueror – while the Erekhtheion became a harem. John Cam Hobhouse, Lord Byron's companion on his first visit to Athens in 1809, recorded seeing Turkish ladies peering down from the Akropolis to the lower town – perhaps wishing they were not so cut off. In all the years that the Turks were in Greece, the two cultures never became more than superficially assimilated. But apart from the fortified village on the Akropolis, Greeks and Turks mingled on a daily basis: the soldiers on the Akropolis had little to do and often came down to the lower town, and other Turks made Athens their permanent home.

In the middle of the seventeenth century there were about 2,000 houses in Plaka, of which about 500 were Turkish. Monuments in Plaka still attest to their presence there: a mosque built soon after the Turkish occupation of Athens in the 1450s; a theological school founded in 1721 by a pious Turk. They also took over older buildings: in the eighteenth century, for instance, a community of Mevlevi dervishes used the Tower of the Winds as their meeting-house. They performed their whirling dance, a kind of moving meditation, every Friday after the noon prayer, and it became a favourite spectacle of tourists in the early nineteenth century.

Bernard Randolph, an English merchant who visited in the 1670s, removed his gaze from the antiquities, and his thoughts from the commonplace contrast between long-lost splendour and contemporary degradation, long enough to have left us some impressions of daily life in Athens at the time:

> The Olive-trees stand so thick to the West of the City that they seem to be a Wood, reaching Six Miles in Length and Two in Breadth ... There are several small Villages, where are very pleasant Gardens, which afford all sorts of Fruit and Saleting [*sic*], having walks round them covered in Vines ... The Vine-yards are planted most betwixt the City, and the Sea. The City is now not above Three Miles about ... The Houses are better

built here than in any part of the Morea [the Peloponnese], most having little Courts, with high Walls in which are Arches with Marble Pillars; few Houses above Two Story high: they are also patcht up with the Ruines of old Palaces, and in most Walls are abundance of old Inscriptions ... The Greeks live much better here than in any other part of Turky ... being a small Common-wealth amongst themselves. They choose eight Magistrates, who adjust all differences, and appear in all Publick Matters ... The City is not walled about, but has Gates at the Streets end, which every Night are shut, to keep out Privateers, who often Land and do much mischief.

Tyranny in Athens and the Destruction of the Parthenon

How did corruption and brutality begin? The Turkish Empire had reached its widest extent by the middle of the seventeenth century, and after that it was whittled away on all sides. The entire Turkish system depended crucially on continuing expansion, so that there was more territory with which its loyal subjects and soldiers could be rewarded. Panic began to set in, and panic among those who wield power is often accompanied by arbitrary cruelty. Another reason was the gradual decline in the population of Greece. By 1676 there were no more than 7,500 inhabitants of Athens, according to Jacques Spon, the French physician, antiquarian and amateur archaeologist whose account of the antiquities of Greece and Asia Minor was the standard work for many decades; and many rural villages had been abandoned as Turks came to own grain-yielding properties, leaving native Athenians only less-profitable produce. So it became harder for the Turkish authorities to raise the taxes demanded of them – and more taxes were required to support an increasing military effort in the face of threats on all sides of the Empire. The circle was particularly vicious for the underdogs.

The gradual collapse of firm central government was matched by the gradual return of piratical slave-traders. Not only did the coastlines become hazardous, but dispossessed or impoverished peasants began to take to the hills and mountains and form bands of klefts (brigands), who preyed indiscriminately on Turks, unwary

European travellers and their fellow Greeks. Klefts were necessarily tough, from living out of doors, and they often kept to a fierce regime of physical fitness as well, with games like tossing the boulder. Ottoman tax collectors were a favoured target. Most of the klefts were utterly unscrupulous, but their attacks on Turks lent them a romantic, Robin Hood image which few deserved. Still, many tales and songs celebrated the deeds of colourful klefts with long, flowing hair tied up under a turban, amazing moustaches, colourful traditional clothes, and pistols and daggers poking out of every fold of their clothing.

The Venetians had never given up their struggle against the Turks in the eastern Mediterranean and the climax of their efforts came in the recovery of the Peloponnese by Francesco Morosini between 1684 and 1715, after a final failed attempt by the Turks to expand into central Europe had left them vulnerable. As soon as he had gained a secure bridgehead in the Peloponnese, Morosini turned his attention to the mainland, and to Athens in particular. The native Athenians welcomed the relieving force (though they buried their valuables, as a precaution) and the Turks took refuge on the Akropolis. They demolished the temple of Athena Nike to shore up the defences with its stones and create space for artillery pieces, and stored their gunpowder, women and children in the Parthenon, on the assumption that the Venetians would never bombard such a cultural treasure.

On 26 September 1687, having been alerted to the whereabouts of the gunpowder by a deserter, the Venetians penetrated the roof of the temple with cannon fire from the nearby Mouseion Hill. Only eleven years earlier a British visitor, George Wheler, had prophetically seen the vulnerability of the Akropolis to bombardment from there. The explosion that followed was so powerful that even the besiegers were showered with fragments of masonry. The temple itself was irreparably damaged by the explosion and the subsequent fire, and 300 people lost their lives. The roof was blown off, the north and south sides of the Parthenon and the walls of the cella were destroyed, and much of the Turkish village on the Akropolis burnt to the ground. The Turks surrendered. Without its central pillars or inner walls, the Parthenon looked like an utter ruin – or rather, two ruins, with just some bits of the western and eastern parts standing. Morosini later added to the destruction by attempting to steal some of the sculptures of the western pediment. In the course of their removal they crashed to the ground and broke to pieces. He and his men had to be content with stealing more accessible pieces.

One of Morosini's officers, Cristoforo Ivanovich, left the following dry account:

> The continuous shelling inflicted considerable damage on the besieged within the narrow enclosing wall of the fortress. His Excellency, informed that the Turks' ammunition, along with the most important women and children, were in the Temple of Minerva ... ordered Count Mutoni to direct his fire there ... There followed a terrible explosion ... In this way the Temple of Minerva, which so many centuries and so many wars had not been able to destroy, was ruined.

The 'Excellency' referred to by Ivanovich was not Morosini himself, who arrived in Athens a few days later, but the Swedish Count Königsmark. By some ironic coincidence, while at university he had written a thesis on 'The Misfortunes of Athens'. The only ray of light in the bleak tale is that a few years previously a Flemish artist in the entourage of the Marquis Olier de Nointel, who visited Athens in November 1674 on his way back from a diplomatic mission in Constantinople, had made some priceless sketches of the sculptures, which more than any other single source allow us to reconstruct them. Perhaps they even compensate for the fact that de Nointel visited Athens only in order to pick up as many antiquities as he could for transport back to France.

The explosion that destroyed the Parthenon is famous, but some thirty years earlier there had been a less well-known explosion on the Akropolis, with a curious tale attached to it. For the Turks the Propylaia was a multi-functional building: it housed the Turkish commander of the Akropolis, but also served as an arsenal and a gunpowder store. On 26 October 1656 lightning struck; there was a terrific explosion, which killed a number of Turks, including the disdar's family, and so severely damaged the Propylaia that for a long while it could no longer function as the entrance to the Akropolis.

The Greek spin on the story is as follows. There is a small church south-west of the Akropolis dedicated, oddly, to St Dimitrios the Bombardier. On 26 October, which is the feast day of St Dimitrios, the congregation was assembled in the church and, the Greeks say, the commander of the Turkish garrison had his big cannon, the Bombardier, primed and ready to fire at the church, out of hatred for all Christians. Just as he was about to fire, the bolt of lightning struck, killing the disdar and his men, and destroying the cannon. The church was saved.

Morosini occupied the Akropolis, but decided that in the long term it was indefensible and left the city on 4 April 1688. The whole exercise had been pointless; the Parthenon had been destroyed for nothing. Athenian refugees left with him: the town was nearly empty, and even the Turks did not bother to reoccupy it. In 1691 they offered an amnesty and three years free of taxes to any refugees who wanted to return and repopulate the place, and they strengthened the fortifications and rebuilt the mosque inside the ruins of the Parthenon: this is the mosque that can still be seen in the earliest photograph of the Akropolis, taken in 1839. Many people did return, but the lower town became very run down and remained that way for years, with collapsed houses and streets clogged with rubble, until the sultan funded a programme of rebuilding and restoration. Matters were not helped in 1715 by the Turkish army, which devastated the town and the countryside while marching to the Peloponnese to fight the Venetians.

Athens' status within the Empire changed for the worse in 1760, when along with other places in Greece it became part of the sultan's own lands. The sultan needed as much money as he could raise, so that instead of a single voivode paying for the right to govern the city, the right to collect taxes for the rest of one's life was auctioned off to the highest bidder. Naturally, the winner needed to recoup his sometimes enormous outlay, and so he imposed ferocious taxes.

By far the worst such governor of Athens was Hadji Ali Haseki (1775–85, 1790–95). Under Haseki hundreds of Greeks, women and men, were thrown into prison, sometimes to die there, and the city suffered under extortionate taxes. A typical despot, he lived in a fine mansion and confiscated rich estates for himself, while the people lived in oppression and poverty. In the 1770s Attica was twice overrun by Albanian troops, who were on the rampage in the Peloponnese after quelling rebellion there for the Turks, until in 1778 Haseki built a new defensive wall around Athens. For building material he ransacked churches and ancient monuments, and after the wall was completed he presented the Athenians, who had formed his labour force, with a bill for its construction. The wall not only kept invaders and pirates out, but made it easier for Haseki to control the passage of taxable goods. It incorporated the triumphal arch of Hadrian, which became the main entry to the city from the east. It is still standing, and is called simply the 'Athens Gate'.

Haseki was recalled to Constantinople in 1785, as a result of complaints from both the Greek and Turkish inhabitants of Athens, but he bribed his way back in 1790 and set about such a reign of terror that before long half the population had fled or was in prison. Eventually the abbot of the Petrakis monastery went to Constantinople to complain and ask for Haseki's removal. But Haseki himself was in Constantinople at the time, and arranged for the abbot's coffee to be poisoned. Fortunately, the abbot took only a sip or two of the coffee, and survived, though 'his beard fell out and his teeth were damaged', according to Panayis Skouzis, a freedom fighter who grew up in Athens during the regime of Haseki. This time the sultan banished the disgraced governor to the island of Kos, where he was executed in 1798. His head was publicly displayed in Constantinople as a warning against future tyrants. People flocked back to Athens and the city soon recovered, until by the beginning of the nineteenth century the population was around 10,000.

Lord Elgin and his Marbles

Traditionally, the Grand Tour on which so many British and European young noblemen embarked in the eighteenth and nineteenth centuries took in (depending on geopolitical circumstances) France, Germany, Switzerland, Italy and the Low Countries. There had always been a trickle of more adventurous visitors to Greece, however, and from the late seventeenth century the fashion of collecting statuary with which to ornament aristocratic estates threatened to add to the trickle as soon as travel to Greece became more practicable, or became desirable because of the wartime closure of France and Italy. One of the main problems as far as Athens was concerned was Turkish paranoia. They did not like people snooping around, especially on the Akropolis where they had their military installations and their modest womenfolk. More people were refused permission to make the ascent than were reluctantly given it.

Otherwise, however, the Turks were warm and friendly towards strangers, and there were quite a few Western visitors in the last quarter of the seventeenth century, by which time there were even a few Europeans living in Athens, as representatives of their countries or as monks establishing a mission. The city was not a complete wreck: there were people prepared to supply what they knew European visitors would require in the way of comfort. At the time of Byron's visit in 1809–10, the voivode was Suleiman Aga, whom Byron described as 'a bon vivant, and as sociable a being as ever sat cross-legged at a tray or table'. The Capuchin monks and various guesthouses offered good lodgings, fellow travellers from Western Europe could provide cultured conversation, and there were no awkward consequences of flirting with a young Athenian woman, because one would soon be on one's way home. Byron even honoured his Lolita, the youngest daughter of his landlady, with a poem, 'The Maid of Athens'.

In additon to tourists, Athens was visited by students of Classical art and architecture. At this time Plaka was not filled with souvenir shops, as it is now. What was a young man to do if he wanted to supplement his sketches or his crude watercolours with a piece of concrete history? By Turkish law, all the antiquities belonged ultimately to the sultan, but a succession of local voivodes were not averse to receiving a bribe (a telescope, or coffee and sugar, would do as well as cash) to allow Westerners to remove the odd inscription or statuette.

Many visitors, before and after Elgin, walked off with little bits of the Parthenon in their packing-cases and boasted of it afterwards in their memoirs. Soon it became a full-blown trade: Turks and Greeks broke bits off the remains and ruins and sold them to tourists. In 1749, for instance, there were still twelve statues on the west pediment of the Parthenon; by 1800 there were only four. Many fragments are now irretrievably lost, but for years bits of the Parthenon turned up all over Europe. A part of the frieze was rescued from a garden in Essex in 1902; no one knows how it got there.

The ancient tradition of the wholesale plunder of antiquities had been revived early in the seventeenth century by collectors such as Thomas Howard, Earl of Arundel, and his contemporary, the Duke of Buckingham, and was encouraged in the following century by the rise of the first great national and imperialistic museums. But though Athens received its fair share of travellers, it remained relatively unscathed by the craze for antiquities until the arrival of a pair of Frenchmen.

Count Choiseul-Gouffier was appointed the French ambassador in Constantinople around 1785. He had already visited Athens in 1780 with a friend, Louis Fauvel, who was a painter and an amateur archaeologist, and now he secured Fauvel an appointment as his representative in Athens. He gained official permission for him to draw and take plaster casts of the antiquities, but privately told him to collect as many of them as he could. These are his actual words: 'Carry off whatever you can. Neglect no opportunity to pillage in Athens and Attica anything that can be pillaged. Spare neither the dead nor the living.' Fauvel was only too ready to obey: he shipped treasures back to France (including, from the Parthenon, a metope and a slab from the frieze) and built up an enormous private collection in his own house in Athens.

Fauvel was well on the way to cornering the market in Athenian antiquities, when the French fell from favour with Napoleon's invasion of Egypt in 1798, and it was the turn of the British. When Thomas Bruce, the syphilitic seventh Earl of Elgin, found himself in 1799 the British ambassador in Constantinople, he imitated the French campaign exactly. His main agent in Athens was a fine Italian painter called Giovanni Battista Lusieri. Elgin's high-minded intention was that the paintings, drawings and plaster casts made by Lusieri and the other artists he engaged would be sent back to Britain for the edification of his countrymen. It was felt that art had reached a dead end and that inimitable models would revitalize a new generation.

Elgin's men had the usual difficulty getting on to the Akropolis, until Elgin extracted a permit from the authorities in Constantinople. This firman instructed the authorities in Athens to allow Elgin's men unimpeded access to the Akropolis, and to let them make drawings and copies of whatever they wanted, to undertake a little amateur archaeology – and 'to take away some pieces of stone with old inscriptions, and figures'. Elgin and his circle were in ecstasy: they were all short of money, none of them intended to return from the East poorer than they started, and they saw this as a way of enriching themselves, as well as preserving the antiquities.

Philip Hunt, Elgin's chaplain, carried the permit in triumph to Athens and hired Greek labourers to collect fragments. Sprinkling threats and bribes wherever he went, he eventually gained permission to remove many pieces from the Akropolis and elsewhere, including the best of the remaining metopes from the Parthenon. He wanted even to dismantle the Porch of the Karyatids from the Erekhtheion and ship it home, but no vessel could be spared for the task and he had to be content with just one maiden, for which he thoughtfully substituted a bare brick pillar. Over the next fifteen or so years, travellers inscribed the brickwork with learned and humorous graffiti defaming Elgin.

The wholesale rape offended nearly everyone; even Lusieri admitted that he had been 'a little barbarous', and the disdar at one point was so upset by the smashing of one of the metopes that he temporarily withdrew his permission. But disappointingly few Greeks raised their voices until later, when the 'theft' of the marbles had become a nationalist issue. Europeans were by far the most vociferous; Edward Dodwell and Lord Byron returned again and again to decrying the 'sacrilege'. But Byron spoiled his campaign by making it personal: the insults ranged from reminding Elgin and the general public that his wife had had an affair to gratuitous mentions of the lord's backward son and syphilitic disfigurement (he had lost much of his nose, leading to merry comparisons between his condition and that of his ancient statues). And his stand against those who ravaged the Parthenon did not prevent him from having an affair with Lusieri's fifteen-year-old brother-in-law and travelling to Malta in 1811 on a ship carrying a cargo of the marbles back to Britain.

Note the date: 1811. Although the most intense work took place for eighteen months during 1801 and 1802, when the best of all the remaining pieces throughout Athens were bought or removed, and although Elgin himself returned to Britain in 1803, Lusieri stayed on, with occasional interruptions, until his death in 1821, dividing his time between quarrelling with Fauvel, extracting more pieces from Athens and elsewhere, and painting (though nearly all his paintings of Athenian antiquities were lost at sea). Over 100 packing-cases of antiquities were shipped back to Britain (one big load was wrecked and had to be salvaged), even apart from the larger sculptures. The scale of the rape is quite astonishing.

Despite the strength of international protest – and one or two unheard voices which suggested that the marbles should be returned to Athens, or might be one day – a parliamentary committee in London exonerated Elgin, on the grounds that he was actually preserving the antiquities against further depredations by the Turks. Strapped for cash, Elgin eventually sold the collection to the British government in 1816 for £35,000 – a fortune, but about half his total expenses and the price he had first asked for. By then, however, thanks to the influence of Byron and other enemies, Elgin's name was mud, and only the undoubted artistic and historical merits of the marbles saved him from a worse outcome. Elgin's financial difficulties did have one result for which we should all be grateful: although he had originally intended to 'restore' the time-worn sculptures, he could not afford to pay for the work. As soon as the marbles went on display in the British Museum in 1817, they began to attract enormous crowds.

It is undoubtedly true that few Turks were interested in the antiquities as such; they were perfectly capable of grinding them up for lime. And, with hindsight, it is perfectly true that had the marbles remained in place on the Parthenon they would have been badly weathered by pollution. Not that they would have remained in place: if Elgin had not taken them, someone else would. One could also argue that the wholesale plunder carried out by Elgin was preferable to the piecemeal pilfering of most of his predecessors, since at least the pieces would remain as a collection.

Nevertheless, the marbles should be returned to Athens. The Greek authorities are capable of looking after them, and the new

Akropolis museum has a room optimistically ready to house them. It is a travesty that there are complementary fragments of the Parthenon sculptures in London and Athens (to say nothing of other Western European museums) crying out for reunification. But it is too late now: the British Museum will never give them back – that would be the thin end of a very thick wedge – and, apart from the notorious and embarrassing occasion in the 1930s when over a considerable period of time they used an abrasive cleaning agent to scrape off what they thought was encrusted dirt, but was actually a combination of ancient primer and natural patina, they have not done a bad job. Perhaps the museum may consider loaning them to Athens on some basis, or even establishing an annexe in Athens. Otherwise, all one can do is regret, and echo the poet Ioannis Ritsos's plaintive cry: 'These stones cannot make do with less sky.'

26

Byron and the War of Independence

Elgin's legacy was not entirely negative. The marbles proved to be the last nail in the coffin of the long-held belief in the superiority of Roman artwork. Elgin's marbles were headline news in Britain, and they added fuel to the smouldering fires of European hellenism. Ancient Greece in general, and Athens in particular, were seen in certain academic quarters, originally in Germany, as having occupied an unapproachable pinnacle of perfection in aesthetic, moral, political and intellectual terms. Athens became the presiding deity of Western humanism. Athenian sculpture and vase-painting were the best the world has ever seen, Athenian architecture the purest of the pure; Athenian democracy was the only true democracy there has ever been, the culmination of the general Greek will to freedom; Athenian society was the perfect blend of liberty and authority. Karl Wilhelm von Humboldt (1767–1835), the educational reformer of Germany, wrote:

> Knowledge of the Greeks is not just pleasant, useful or necessary to us: on the contrary, in the Greeks alone we find the ideal of that which we should like to be and to do. Every part of history enriches us with its human wisdom and human experience, but from the Greeks we take something more than earthly – something godlike.

The ancient Greeks were our ideal future, but it was also they, rather than the more alien Egyptians or Mesopotamians, who gave us our remote ancestry.

The Romantic idealization of Greece quickly spread to Britain. In 1821, in the Preface to his poem *Hellas*, Percy Bysshe Shelley said: 'We are all Greeks ... The human form and the human mind attained to a perfection in Greece which has impressed its images on those faultless productions whose very fragments are the despair

of modern art, and has propagated impulses which can never cease
... to enable and delight mankind until the extinction of the
race.' By 'Greece', Shelley, like most of his contemporaries, meant
'Athens':

> Athens arose: a city such as vision
>> Builds from the purple crags and silver towers
> Of battlemented cloud, as in derision
>> Of kingliest masonry: the ocean-floors
> Pave it; the evening sky pavilions it;
>> Its portals are inhabited
>> By thunder-zoned winds, each head
> Within its cloudy wings with sun-fire garlanded, –
>> A divine work!

> (Shelley, *Ode to Liberty* (1819))

To his credit, Shelley was at least planning to visit Greece at the
time of his death in 1822, and apologized for his 'newspaper
erudition', but most did no more than worship from afar.

The contrast between myth and reality could not have been
greater, since Athens was an impoverished village, with many of its
houses unoccupied, and the rubble of ancient ruins either buried
and forgotten, or almost indistinguishable from the rubble of collapsed houses. But, as we have seen, the myth of Athens had existed
long enough to become deeply rooted. Perikles and the dramatists
initiated it, fourth-century orators perpetuated it, and from Roman
times onwards it was the mark of a cultured gentleman to venerate
fifth-century Athens, while despising or being wary of its current
inhabitants.

The Romantic image of Greece was also perpetuated by numerous artists. There were those who came with antiquarian interests
and drew likenesses of the ruins which were as accurate as their
skills allowed, but there were plenty of others who catered to the
image of Greece in which colourful klefts, shepherds and statuesque
women posed or sat idly among fallen, mossy columns, with rugged
hills in the background and a general air of melancholy for lost
glory. The buyers of such pictures back in Europe thought they
knew Athens: it was the city they had read about in Thucydides
and Plato and Pausanias. They did not want this image disturbed.

William Hazlitt, reviewing an exhibition of the Scottish painter
Hugh William Williams in 1822, praised the artist for 'restoring to
us our old ... true illusion', rather than the 'dry, flat and barren'
landscape of Attica in reality.

There were others whose reflections on past Athenian perfection
gave rise to political concerns for the present. Here is a short passage
from François, Vicomte de Chateaubriand (1768–1848), who visited
Greece in 1806 and afterwards wrote his *Travels in Greece, Palestine,
Egypt and Barbary*:

> From our position we might, in the times of Athens's prosperity,
> have seen her ships setting out from Peiraieus to engage the
> enemy, or to journey to the festival of Delos; we might have
> heard the grief of Oidipous, Philoktetes and Hekabe burst-
> ing from the Theatre of Dionysos; we might have heard the
> clapping of the citizens and the speeches of Demosthenes. But
> alas! From the walls which so long ago echoed to the voices of
> a free people, no sound met our ears apart from a few cries,
> issuing from an enslaved populace.

Over the last half of the eighteenth century, increasing numbers
of travellers returning from Greece included in their memoirs a
call for Greece to be freed from Turkish rule. The philhellenes –
the word means 'admirers of the Greeks' – who began to lobby
for Greek freedom were struck by the contrast between the ideal
of ancient Greek freedom and the servitude of modern Greeks, who
were usually assumed to be direct descendants of Perikles and
company. Philhellenes generally moved at a distance from reality:
they were concerned only with the myth of Athens, and were
capable of ignoring anything which tended to tarnish the glamour.

George Gordon, Lord Byron, was different. When he reached
Athens on Christmas Day 1809, at the age of twenty-one, it was not
his first port of call. He had already travelled through northern
Greece and the Peloponnese, often under conditions of hardship
and danger, and had familiarized himself with the Greek world. He
found what many travellers have found – that the Greeks are a kind
and generous people. He loved Greece ('If I am a poet, the air of
Greece has made me one') and Greeks, whereas most European
visitors were snobbish and rude. He called his fellow travellers,

those with antiquarian interests alone, 'emasculated fogies', and he learnt modern Greek, rather than despising it as a debased version of the ancient language. He especially loved Athens. He could sit in the window of his lodgings in the Capuchin monastery and see 'Hymettos before me, the Acropolis behind, the Temple of Jove to my right, the Stadium in front, the town to the left, eh, Sir, there's a situation, there's your picturesque!'

Byron wanted the Greeks to be free because they were an oppressed people, not just because they were supposed to be the descendants of a supposed freedom-loving people, and some of his most powerful poetry was dedicated to the cause of Greek freedom:

> Fair Greece! sad relic of departed worth!
> Immortal, though no more! though fallen, great!
> Who now shall lead the scatter'd children forth,
> And long accustom'd bondage uncreate?
> Not such thy sons who whilome did await,
> The hopeless warriors of a willing doom,
> In bleak Thermopylae's sepulchral strait –
> Oh! who that gallant spirit shall resume,
> Leap from Eurotas's banks, and call thee from the tomb?
>
> (*Childe Harold's Pilgrimage* II.73.693–701)

> The mountains look on Marathon,
> And Marathon looks on the sea;
> And musing there an hour alone,
> I dreamed that Greece might still be free.
> For standing on the Persian's grave
> I could not deem myself a slave.
>
> (*Don Juan* III.86)

There was nothing here that had not been said before, but Byron was the right man in the right place at the right time. He rode the crest of the wave of the romanticization of Greece and met the rising tide of Greek nationalism, but more importantly he could write with sufficient vigour, enthusiasm and humour to reach a mass audience. Philhellenism became a craze among fashionable ladies and gentlemen; committees were formed to lobby governments and fund resistance (although all too often all they funded were fact-finding missions to Greece). European involvement in Greece was heavily influenced by the Byronic vision of Greece as a 'sad relic', and of noble, almost 'primitive savage' Greeks in need of saving from tyranny, poverty and other evils by the enlightened but sensitive European male.

The Prelude to Revolution

History has shown time and again that education is a critical political factor. All the great movements and paradigm shifts of the European West had passed Athens by, and as long as the Greeks were isolated from the West, there were few voices raised in protest at Turkish rule. In fact, many Greeks were comfortable with their lot (or, as peasants, equally uncomfortable, whoever was in power), and the Church had reached a profitable accommodation, at least partly because of its ingrained hatred of Western Europe. Even most of those who did entertain the idea of Greek freedom dreamt of it some time in the distant future, when Greeks would have grown so powerful in the declining Turkish Empire that they could simply take it over and reinstate the old Byzantine Empire. But in the course of the eighteenth century Constantinopolitan Phanariotes and rich Greek merchants paid for the establishment of schools, the printing of books and the education of Greeks in the West, where they came across the kind of revolutionary ideas which had such momentous consequences in France and developed the concept of Greek nationhood.

There had been calls to revolution before. Above all, in 1770, during the Russo-Turkish war of 1768–74, the Russians encouraged rebellion in the Peloponnese. Unfortunately, however, they followed encouragement with too few soldiers and the uprising was quickly crushed. There had also been isolated voices, crying in the wilderness and seeking martyrdom. Greece offered, above all, Rigas Pheraios (also known as Rigas Velestinlis), who wrote and published pamphlets calling for a revived Greek state on French republican lines and, for a more popular audience, the anthemic *War Song*, which contained the sentiment: 'Better one hour of life as a free man than forty years of slavery and imprisonment.' Pheraios was strangled by the Ottoman authorities in Belgrade in 1798. With his dying words he expressly set himself up as a martyr: 'This is how brave men die. I have sown, and soon the hour will come when my nation will gather the ripe fruit.'

The final factor was the formation of the innocuous-sounding Friendly Society, which became active underground from 1814. Inspired by the martyrdom of Pheraios, the spirit of the French Revolution, the resistance of the Souliotes to Ali Pasha (the ruler of Albania and Epeiros), and the taste of freedom enjoyed by the Ionian Islands under British protection from 1815, the Society, formed in Odessa by three expatriate Greeks, grew – though painfully slowly at first – until by 1821 it had about 1,000 members, especially among the diaspora merchants. Entry into the Society was gained in stages through elaborate rituals, influenced by freemasonry. The sole purpose of the Society was to gain freedom for Greece by means of an armed uprising.

The Friendly Society had an uphill task. Many of the wealthy Phanariotes and ship-owners joined the Church in a thoroughly ambivalent attitude towards Turkish rule, chiefly because they enjoyed so many privileges. Many Westernized Greeks looked to peaceful means, such as education and the pressure of the European powers, to bring about a gradual change in Greece and European Turkey in general. Fortunately for the Society, however, one of the most influential of these Greek intellectuals, disillusioned by British concessions to Ali Pasha, had moved closer to the idea of revolution. The young Corfiot aristocrat, Count John Capo d'Istria (1776–1831) – he later hellenized his name to Ioannis Kapodistrias – met secretly with Theodoros Kolokotronis (1770–1843) and Markos Botsaris (died 1823), two kleft leaders who had taken refuge from Ali Pasha. The brigands and the westernized aristocrat found a common bond in their devotion to the cause of Greek freedom, and they swore an oath that they would do all they could to liberate their homeland from the Turks.

The Friendly Society ignored the ambivalent attitude towards violence of the Phanariotes and the Church, and gained a degree of popular support by promising their peasant countrymen lower taxes, the recovery of their lost lands, and greater stability. There is a nice story from Athens to illustrate street-level resistance to the Turks.

Knowing that war was imminent, the Turks converted the little Athenian church of the Divine Power into a munitions factory. The Greek in charge of turning out cartridges for the Turkish soldiers did indeed make cartridges for the Turks during the day. But at night he made them for the Greeks, and they were smuggled out each morning by an old washerwoman, who hid them under the dirty laundry and took them to the village of Menidi, the centre of revolutionary activity in Attica.

The insurgents were not going to get far without the help of the Western powers. By the end of the eighteenth century, the British and French were concerned to protect their commercial interests in the Middle East and beyond, and the Russians, ever anxious for a warm-water port, had gained the right to act as the protectors of Christians throughout Turkish Europe. Once it was clear that the Turkish Empire was in terminal decline, with revolutions and semi-independent principalities springing up all over the place, the Eastern Question arose: how to ensure stability in the region throughout the process of drastic change, and what to do with it after the Turks had gone. At first, however, no European government countenanced the idea of violent revolution as the way forward.

Greeks had to accept, and exploit, the European construction of their future, in order to marshal for their struggle against the Turks the vital European resources that became free after the end of the Napoleonic wars. Educated Greeks such as Adamantios Koraïs even translated European notions about Greece back into Greek for Europeans to 'discover' as authentically Greek. The lever they used was the Romantic idealization of ancient Greece current among European philhellenes, who responded by increasing pressure on their governments to intervene in Greece. And so the Elgin Marbles and the myth of Athenian perfection had one last contribution to make. As the Greek intellectual Iakovakis Neroulis remarked in 1838, the Greeks owed their freedom to their ancient ruins.

The War of Independence

In March 1821 the Turks were preoccupied with Ali Pasha and had tied up large numbers of their troops from the Peloponnese and northern Greece in an attempt to curb their ambitious vassal. With the Turkish army distracted, and with widespread discontent in Greece as a result of several years of near famine, the Friendly Society seized their moment. An uprising in the northern Balkan territories, led by Alexandros Ypsilantis, the overall leader of the Society, came to a disastrous and unpromising end. Although it was widely expected that the Russians would support any attempt at revolution by Orthodox Christians against infidel Turks, they were actually reluctant to disturb the status quo. It was up to the Peloponnesians, many of whom had existed for a long time on the margins of Turkish rule, to take things further.

On 25 March 1821, now Greece's national day, Giorgios Germanos, Archbishop of Patras and leader of the Friendly Society in Greece, blessed the Greek flag at the Ayia Lavra monastery near Kalavrita before hundreds of Greek irregular soldiers, including Theodoros Kolokotronis. For the first time the battle-cry of 'Freedom or Death' was heard in public. This is the foundation myth of the Greek War of Independence. In actual fact neither of the two protagonists was anywhere near the monastery on the day in question, and there had been sporadic uprisings in the Peloponnese for a week or so before this date, the first probably in the Mani, the rugged middle peninsula of the southern Peloponnese.

Be that as it may, it is certain that over the next few months, in wave after wave of largely uncoordinated uprisings by kleft leaders with their private armies, 15,000 of the 40,000 Turks in the Peloponnese were massacred. The Turks gave as good as they got; there were reprisals not only in the Peloponnese but wherever in the Empire they could find easy targets. The Greek Orthodox patriarch in Constantinople, Grigorios V, was brutally killed. The revolutionaries seized on this murder as propaganda, but since the fifteenth century it had been part of the formal arrangements that the patriarchs were guarantors of the loyalty of their subjects.

By the end of 1821, thanks chiefly to the efforts of Kolokotronis, the Peloponnese was in Greek hands. In January 1822 the Greeks formed a farcical, but defiantly optimistic, provisional government – farcical because it had no power, no money and no country to rule, and was the first of several over the following few years – and as president of the non-existent state they elected Alexandros Mavrokordatos (1791–1865), a prominent Phanariote who had been a friend of Shelley in Italy. The Greeks were trying to show the West that they were going about things in the right, orderly way; but after the French Revolution the European governments were hostile to anything that smacked of republicanism and they remained officially uninterested in the war in Greece until philhellenic pressure grew too strong.

Inspired by events on the Peloponnese, rebellion broke out all over the mainland and on some of the islands. On 26 April 1821 Athens came under attack. The Turks gathered their possessions and families and took refuge on the Akropolis. The Greek soldiers who put them under siege were briefly driven out of the city by a Turkish army in August, which brought much-needed supplies for the beleaguered Turks, but as soon as they left the Greeks resumed the siege. The damage to the ruins was immense, as the Turks moved marble blocks around to act as temporary fortifications, and to make bullets from the lead with which ancient Athenians had joined column drums and other pieces of masonry. The Greeks, it is said, after a while began to send ready-made bullets up to their enemies on the Akropolis to stop them accelerating the ruin of the ancient buildings.

The Turkish garrison lasted on the Akropolis until June 1822, when on one long, hot summer day many of the defeated Turks – men, women and children – who had been promised safe passage, were massacred. Similar massacres and counter-massacres disfigured this atrocious war; the goal of both sides was ethnic cleansing. Meanwhile, on the Peloponnese, feuding between different Greek factions was fast threatening their gains. Disagreement among the Greek insurgents was so fierce that before long there was virtual civil war between two or three factions, and provincial councils, often under the thumb of a local warlord, had taken the place of any form of central government. Mavrokordatos resigned his presidency in disgust. Samuel Howe, an American philhellene and doctor who served with distinction throughout the war, said that the true patriots, rather than those whose goals were glory and booty, were few and shone 'like diamonds among filth'.

Westernized diaspora liberals, backed by the philhellenes, wanted to see Greece rise as a model republic; the klefts wanted a share of power and land in return for their military assistance; the Peloponnesian landowners wanted to retain their feudal estates and the privileges they had enjoyed for so long under Ottoman rule; the island shipowners wanted their slice of the cake too, in return for providing the ships which were used in the war. All of them wanted to get their hands on some of the money that began to flow from Europe. These disagreements, the availability of more Turkish troops after the murder of Ali Pasha, and the arrival in the Peloponnese early in 1825 of the formidable Egyptian troops of Ibrahim Pasha, to whom the sultan subcontracted the task of crushing the insurrection, led to serious setbacks in both military and diplomatic terms. Hundreds of philhellenes had come to fight in the first fifteen months of the war; now they began to return home in disillusionment.

Meanwhile, in Athens successive revolutionary leaders (including the legendary Odysseus Androutsos) came, proved themselves to be inept and despotic bandits, and were murdered by their fellows or died fighting. By 1823 marshy and malaria-ridden Messolonghi was one of the few places in Greek hands north of the Gulf of Corinth, and so it became one of the main destinations for philhellenes arriving in Greece from Western Europe and America. When Byron returned to Greece in January 1824, that is where he went. He landed, dressed absurdly in a pompous military uniform of his own design, to huge acclaim from the weary Greeks, who claimed to see him as a saviour, but also thought he had brought funds with him from England. Byron was no longer content to be a passive figurehead, and he was prepared to dismiss his premonitions of an early death.

Three and a half months later he died pathetically of a fever, but his involvement in the war did more than anything to arouse Western opinion against the Turks and made him a rallying point not only for more philhellenes but for the feuding Greek leaders. Byron did nothing to court the messianic status he gained and was surprisingly modest about becoming a larger-than-life figure. But he had made his political views widely known and, as an A-list celebrity, he was perfect fodder for the gossip columns of the day, so that what he did and said was widely reported. And so he came, willy-nilly, to make Greek independence one of the popular causes of the day. Where popular favour goes, politicians follow, and although the ministers of the British government were almost to a man unsympathetic to Greece and regarded Byron as a disreputable outcast, they were compelled to toe the philhellene line.

By 1826, the Peloponnese had been lost along with thousands of Greek lives, the klefts had returned to their caves in the mountains and Athens was one of the very few places still in Greek hands. In July a Turkish army approached the city. The lower town held out for a while, but fell in August and was badly sacked. It was now the turn of the remaining Greek soldiers and civilians to be besieged on the Akropolis. Athens became the scene of repeated battles, as the Turks attacked the Akropolis, and were themselves attacked by several relieving forces, which rarely achieved their objectives. Finally, in May 1827, there were 10,000 troops stationed in Peiraieus, ready to drive the Turks out of Athens, but the British and Greek commanders did not trust one another, the irregular troops lacked discipline and turned to looting and killing, and the whole enterprise fell apart. When battle was eventually joined, twenty-two of the twenty-six philhellenes in the army died, along with 1,500 Greeks, in the worst military disaster of the war. The Akropolis surrendered on 5 June.

The Turks again occupied the Akropolis, which overlooked a deserted town, battered by fighting and by several years of neglect. The loss of the Akropolis demoralized the freedom fighters: the war was lost and Kolokotronis struggled to keep the last embers of hope glowing. Only Nauplion and a few islands remained in Greek hands, while Ibrahim Pasha was preparing a vast army for the final assault. It seemed that only a miracle would allow the Greeks now to win the war.

The miracle happened. Fearful of further massacres (and wanting to protect their own trading interests), the Western superpowers drew up the Treaty of London, according to which Greece would become a quasi-independent tributary of Turkey, and sent a small, combined fleet to try to arrange an armistice between the warring sides as a first step towards gaining acceptance of the terms of the treaty. Since the Greeks had effectively lost the war, they were keen to accept the treaty, while the Turks naturally rejected it and carried on ravaging the Peloponnese. Under these conditions Admiral Sir Edward Codrington and his French and Russian colleagues had been instructed to do the impossible – to cut Ibrahim's supply route from Egypt, but to do so without any military action, except in the direst emergency.

By October negotiations had been going on fruitlessly for some weeks. The formidable Egyptian fleet of warships and troop-carriers was stationed at Navarino. The much smaller European fleet anchored right inside the harbour, no more than a few hundred metres from the Egyptians, to try to force the issue one way or another. Tempers were becoming frayed and both sides were preparing for battle when the Egyptians made the mistake of firing on an open boat filled with English sailors which was trying to deal with a threatening Egyptian fireship. Four hours later, when the smoke cleared, the Egyptian fleet had been annihilated, without the loss of a single European vessel. There were some 650 European casualties (mostly wounded) compared with 6,000 Egyptian dead and 4,000 wounded. It was the last naval battle in history between fleets consisting entirely of sailing ships, and at a stroke it gave Greece freedom.

The European nations assumed the right to dictate the immediate future of Greece. Russia, Britain and France became the Protecting Powers, to ensure that the Turks left Greece alone. In 1828 Turkish and Egyptian troops evacuated the Peloponnese, though there was still fighting further north, on the mainland. The Greeks drew up a constitution as a republic, and the experienced but autocratic Kapodistrias came to take up the office of the first president of Greece, to try to heal the rifts that threatened civil war and to set the war-torn and impoverished new country on the road towards stability and prosperity.

In Athens, meanwhile, the Turkish garrison hung on, waiting to be paid off by the new Greek government, which was having difficulty raising even this small amount of cash. But everyone knew that the Turkish presence on the Akropolis was a pretence:

the commander himself used to live in more comfortable lodgings in the lower town and walk up to the Akropolis every day to continue the 'siege'. On 31 March 1833 the Turks abandoned the Akropolis, and for the first time for hundreds of years the hill stopped being a military fortress. But a pyramid formed from the skulls of some of the Greeks and Turks who had died on the Akropolis during the War of Independence remained there, next to a heap of bones, until the 1840s.

The War of Independence, the first successful post-colonial revolution in Europe, was not a straightforward affair of glory and heroism against an oppressor. The conventions of European warfare were signally lacking; the war often descended to savagery. The Greeks had different and often irreconcilable motivations, and cancelled out their successes by mutual hostility and scheming that was as bitter as that between Greeks and Turks. Then the presence of the philhellenes muddied the waters, since they too had different motivations, ranging from idealism to thievery, via sheer eccentricity. In the end it was Greek stubbornness, born of their love of freedom, that kept the war going in the face of certain defeat, and the intervention of the European superpowers that brought it to an end. This intervention was aroused by Byron and the philhellenes against the background of European admiration for Classical Athenian perfection. The myth of Athens gained the Greeks their independence.

EPILOGUE

27

The 2004 Olympics

Greece was in the news while I was writing this book, and not just for the prospective Olympics. A bizarre case was going through the courts in Kalamata, in the southern Peloponnese. Twelve British and two Dutch plane-spotters were arrested near Kalamata in November 2001 when they were taking photographs of military planes at an air show. Before leaving for their holiday, the practitioners of this hobby had been warned that the Greeks are highly sensitive about their military installations and equipment, and after arriving they had already been warned off two other prohibited sites; nevertheless, at the air show they went ahead and started taking photographs. The Greeks, ever wary because of continuing tension with Turkey (in theory their NATO ally), which often erupts into near-war, arrested the plane-spotters and charged them with the serious crime of espionage.

The case trickled on. In April 2002 eight of the spotters were found guilty of espionage, and the rest of aiding and abetting it, but the verdict was overturned in November, a year after their initial arrest. I am not here concerned with the ins and outs of the case, but with the way it was reported in the Western press. It is true that the Greeks found it hard to imagine that there was such as thing as plane-spotting for fun – but then it is equally true that it is an odd and eccentric hobby. By and large, the Western press was not concerned with issues like this, but with pouring scorn on the Greeks for their inability to comprehend the innocence of the spotters. The reporters were less interested in whether or not the tourists had broken any Greek law than in finding implicit and explicit ways to arouse derision and contempt in their readers for the poor, backward Greeks.

Greece is no stranger to patronizing attitudes from the West. For Byron Greece was a symbol of perfection, in need of rescue and rehabilitation by the West, since the inhabitants were finding it hard to do it for themselves. The Byronic attitude lingered in fiction and rhetoric long after the War of Independence was over, but in the past seventy or so years it has been overtaken by another, made famous by works of fiction such as John Fowles's *The Magus* or the 1989 film *Shirley Valentine*, or by non-fiction writers such as Henry Miller, Lawrence Durrell and Peter Levi. Here we find Greece portrayed as a place where a Westerner in the throes of an existential crisis might come to discover himself or herself, a place for personal freedom. But it is supposed to have this property precisely because it is primitive, different from the sophisticated and complex West.

It must be admitted, however, that until recently Greece has done little to encourage more egalitarian perceptions by the West. Its political life has often been chaotic and corrupt, and the rocks of feuding upon which the War of Independence nearly foundered have been prominent in more recent struggles too. At the same time, Greece has constantly looked to the West for legitimacy: when it became a full member of the EC in 1981, following some years of associate membership, this was expressly seen as the partial fulfilment of the country's long-term aim for what Konstantinos Karamanlis (1907–98), one of the towering figures of recent political life, called an 'organic Greek presence in the West'. This is the background against which the 2004 Olympics become hugely important. As I warned in the introduction, it is not my intention in this chapter to give anything remotely resembling a history of modern Greece or even Athens. I want only to set the 2004 Olympics in a particular context, by focusing on those aspects of Greece's recent history which have done the most to influence Western perceptions of Athens and Greece.

Scenes from Greek Political Life

Kapodistrias, the first president of the new country, was assassinated in 1831, the victim of a feud with the family of a powerful Peloponnesian warlord. By the time of his death the European powers, despairing of the ability of the Greeks to establish the new country, had dropped the terms of the Treaty of London, and had agreed that Greece was to be a fully independent country under a monarch chosen by them, without Turkish suzerainty. Only someone from outside Greece, it was felt, could rise above Greek squabbles. After some months of chaos Otto, the second son of the fanatically philhellene Prince of Bavaria, was imposed by the Western superpowers, and the republic was replaced by an absolute monarchy.

Othon (to give him his Greek name) was never popular. The absolute monarchy and the effective rule of a small Bavarian coterie was replaced by a constitutional monarchy in 1844; Syntagma (Constitution) Square, the centre of modern Athens, is overlooked by the former royal palace, now the parliament building, and the balcony from which the king read the new quasi-democratic constitution. But even after this bloodless revolution, Othon remained unpopular and he was deposed in 1862. Successive kings descended from the royal house of Denmark – George I, Constantine I, Alexander, George II, Paul and Constantine II – occupied the Greek throne, but their reigns were marked by depositions or near-depositions, abdications or threatened abdications, regencies, periods of exile, and plebiscites to decide whether or not the country really wanted them. George I was assassinated in 1913, and Alexander (who was on the throne as a puppet king only because his father and elder brother had been banished from the country) died of blood poisoning after being bitten by a pet monkey.

During the First World War, in a period known as the Great Schism, the country was divided into two: the southern half was ruled by the king, who inclined towards Germany but wanted to stay out of the war, and the northern half was a republic under Eleftherios Venizelos, who wanted Greece to enter the war against Germany and Turkey. Mud-slinging became rioting and violence, until the anti-German allies blockaded the royalist south into a humiliating submission, from which the monarchy never fully recovered its reputation. Finally, in 1974, by when the monarchy had for a long time been increasingly insignificant and irrelevant, the Greeks voted to get rid of it once and for all, and the country became a full republic.

Governments have not fared much better. Greece has veered

from right to left to the centre, from favouring America to hostility
to America; it was ruled by dictators or military juntas for several
periods of the twentieth century; and governments have succeeded
governments in a bewildering succession of coups and counter-
coups, dynastic politics, riots, revolutions, fresh constitutions, hung
coalition parliaments, scandals, and purges of the Civil Service and
the army. Between 1864 and 1910 there were twenty-one general
elections and seventy distinct administrations (one lasted only a
fortnight), though matters improved hugely in the last quarter of
the nineteenth century after the reformist politician Harilaos Trikoupis forced the king to abandon the practice of appointing his
own prime ministers at whim. Even recently, however, there were
three general elections between June 1989 and April 1990. Karamanlis, twice prime minister and twice president, described being a
politician in Athens as like living in an enormous madhouse. Things
have settled down somewhat in the last decade or so, with PASOK
(the leftist Panhellenic Socialist Movement, formed in 1974) and
New Democracy providing a stable, two-party focus for politics
and politicians.

In the 1920s and 1930s Greece stumbled between monarchy,
dictatorship and republicanism. Following the catastrophic defeat of
the Greek army in Turkey in 1922, King Constantine abdicated in
favour of his son, George II, but the monarchy was so unpopular
that George found it expedient to leave the country the following
year, and in 1924 the monarchy was formally abolished. For several
months, the country was effectively ruled by a revolutionary committee of Venizelist army officers, who were succeeded by the the
dictatorship of the megalomaniacal Theodoros Pangalos (1878–1952).
His rule was marked by pomposity and sabre-rattling against Turkey
and Bulgaria, but little effective action and in 1926 he was over-
thrown in a military coup.

Venizelos was again prime minister from 1928 to 1932 (the only
time between the wars that a government managed to serve out its
term of office) and restored some stability, but he only scraped into
power in 1932, and was defeated in 1933. A period of chaos ensued,
during which Venizelos miraculously escaped an assassination
attempt which left his car riddled with bullets, his bodyguard dead
and his wife wounded. Venizelos was forced into exile in 1935 after

a failed coup, designed to prevent the return of the king; Venizelos's departure and the boycotting of politics by his party allowed the royalists to return to power and restore George II to his throne. The king's solution to continuing turmoil was to acquiesce in the dictatorship of Ioannis Metaxas (1871–1941), who took over in August 1936. What the diminutive dictator lacked in substance he made up in grandiose titles, styling himself 'Father of the Nation', 'First Peasant', and so on.

The army has often taken upon itself the right to interfere in politics, especially in the bloodless coup of 1843 that led to the dissolution of Otto's absolute monarchy, in summoning Venizelos from Crete in 1910, throughout the period between the two world wars, and in the dictatorship of the colonels from 1967 to 1974. Kings too have supported dictatorships or undermined the parliamentary system, as Constantine II did in the mid-1960s by banning elections. Greek political processes have frequently been marred by corruption, vote-rigging, manipulation of the electoral system and outright fraud, and Greek politics remains as dependent on charismatic leaders as it is on policies.

The Great Idea

The driving force behind Greek politics for the first 100 years of the new country's history was the Great Idea, the policy of uniting and incorporating all the main areas of Greece and Turkey where the populations largely spoke Greek. Kapodistrias negotiated a border for Greece which ran from the Gulf of Arta in the west to the Gulf of Volos in the east. This excluded Thessaly, Epeiros, Macedonia, Thrace and the Greek-speaking populations in and around Smyrna and Constantinople in Turkey. Many more Greeks lived outside the borders of the new country than inside. Over the years, as a result of warfare and diplomacy, the new nation gradually expanded: Britain handed over the Ionian Islands as a coronation present to George I in 1864; Thessaly was added in 1881; in 1913, after the Balkan Wars, Greece gained Epeiros, much of Macedonia and Thrace, Crete and most of the Aegean islands; in 1920 and 1923 further tracts of southern Thrace were acquired; and finally, in 1947, the Italians gave up the Dodecanese Islands of the south-eastern Aegean.

There were two main troubles with the Great Idea. First, it encouraged countless politicians to seek popularity by nailing their colours to this mast, while ignoring domestic policy. Greece remained the poorest country in Europe. By 1900 the construction of the Corinth canal and of about 1,000 kilometres of railways (far, far less in proportion to the country's size than the industrialized European nations), and the draining of the marshland of Boiotia, created some of the infrastructure for future growth, but there was little industry, the roads were still terrible, debt repayment amounted to 35 per cent of the national budget and, with the country still heavily reliant on a single crop, currants, imports outweighed exports by 44 per cent. When the price of currants plummeted in 1893, the country was declared bankrupt: it could no longer repay even the interest on its long-standing debts to the Protecting Powers. No sooner would one party raise taxes in order to work towards solving the debt problem than another party would be swept to power on the promise to lower taxes. All available government money went towards the fulfilment of the Great Idea.

Second, the Great Idea was vigorously pursued even when the country was impoverished, in weak negotiating positions, or other-wise incapacitated. In 1897 the Greeks supported the Cretan rebellion against the Turks and only the intervention of the European powers prevented Turkey from invading vulnerable Greece in retaliation. When Venizelos came to power in 1910, he went a long way towards stabilizing the country's economy, but he too was still in the grip of the Great Idea. The dream finally came to grief in 1922.

After the First World War, the European powers awarded Greece huge areas of Turkey around Constantinople and Smyrna, where Greek-speakers were theoretically in the majority. This of course brought the Greeks into conflict with Turkey. At first the war went well, despite the failure of the European powers to provide the support Venizelos had expected, but the new Turkish leader, Mustafa Kemal (soon to be named Kemal Atatürk, the 'father of the Turks'), drew the Greek forces further and further inland, until their lines were stretched too thin and it was hard for supplies to get through. Defeat turned into a rout, and the Greek army was chased back to Smyrna. In a mission that foreshadowed Dunkirk, thousands of civilians and soldiers were rescued by sea – but tens of thousands more were massacred in the conflagration.

Turkey reclaimed the territories, and within a few years a huge 'exchange of minorities' had taken place: 380,000 Muslims left Greece for Turkey, and over a million Orthodox Christians left Turkey for Greece. The good side of the coin was that the incoming Anatolian Greeks imported cultural and practical skills, and industries such as tobacco, which in the future would prove to be the salvation of the country. The Greek economy remained fragile, however, since its main exports were the kinds of luxury or semi-luxury commodities – chiefly currants, tobacco, cotton and oil – which are vulnerable to worldwide slumps. Greece suffered badly, but no worse than many others, after the Great Crash of 1929.

As a result of Smyrna, Britain and France formally renounced their position as Protecting Powers, Venizelos, who had nearly doubled the size and population of Greece after the Balkan Wars, temporarily fell from grace, and though most of the world's Greek-speakers were now contained within the country's borders, the Great Idea was never to be realized in its fullest form: with the removal of most of the Greek population of Turkey, Greece no longer had any claim to Turkish territory. Only Cyprus remained as the chief goal of unificationists and the focus of serious riots, or even international incidents, in 1931 and then almost continuously from 1950 to 1974. The push for unification was finally halted only by a massive Turkish sea and air invasion in July 1974, prompted by the ineptitude of the ruling junta in Greece which resulted in the partition of the island into Greek and Turkish zones, and another 'exchange of minorities'. The island is still the main source of strife between the two countries, though oil in the northern Aegean and the occasional uninhabited islet have also been known to raise the level of tension.

Civil War

The Greeks are still a quarrelsome people, especially when they feel that their honour has been slighted, and vendetta law sat uneasily alongside Western notions of justice for much of the nineteenth century. In the 1850s, for instance, an Athenian man avenged the killing of his son by walking into the house of the killers and murdering every single member of their family, so that the vendetta could not continue with retaliation against his own family. At much the same time a flower-seller in Athens saw a man approach his wife and flirt with her. Not only did passers-by not break up the knife fight that followed, but some of them commended the flower-seller for the accuracy of the thrust with which he stabbed his rival through the heart. There are even more such stories from rural areas.

Several times during the nineteenth and twentieth centuries Greece came close to civil war – never closer than in the Great Schism during the First World War. But it was the Second World War which laid the seeds for true civil war. Between 1940 and 1949 Greece was tortured by constant warfare, in which 600,000 people lost their lives.

In one of the great, forgotten tragedies of the Second World War, about 200,000 Greeks, already suffering under Axis occupation, died of starvation and of hunger-related diseases during the British blockade of the eastern Mediterranean in the first two years of the war. Many of these victims were Athenians, since in the countryside people could find more food, and hoarded what they had rather than sending it to the city. From September 1941 onwards, when the situation became critical, it was a common sight, especially in the slums, to see corpses, often of young children, on the streets, and thousands more were ill and marked by tumours and other effects of malnutrition.

Apart from the occasional German vehicle or patrol, the streets were eerily silent, as no one had the energy to do anything except struggle to keep alive. The poor suffered above all, because the middle classes and others could afford, at least for a while, the exorbitant prices of the black market. Between October 1940, when Greece entered the war, and October 1944, when the Germans left, the price of a loaf of bread went up from 10 drachmas to 34 million drachmas; the cost of cheese multiplied by a factor of nearly two million. For the duration of the war, many people gave up using money and resorted to barter.

The British lifted their blockade of the eastern Mediterranean in the late summer of 1942, and from then on Red Cross deliveries improved matters, but there was still hardship and appalling deprivation, often bordering on starvation and periodically crossing that border. The spirit of the Greeks was never broken, however: they fought back with bullets, demonstrations and strikes, with vivid graffiti and with legendary gestures, as when in May 1941 two young men went up to the Akropolis, past the German guards, and removed the German flag with its hated swastika.

Although the Italians occupied most of the country until they withdrew from the war, the Germans were responsible for two sizeable tracts of land in the north, but most importantly for Athens and Peiraieus. Throughout the occupation, despite the terrible suffering that was visible all around them in Athens, the German occupying forces were taking food for themselves, and it was their financial measures which pushed up inflation. Both Hitler and Mussolini idolized the city as the source of European culture, Mussolini offered no real help, and Hitler even encouraged his subordinates to see the death and suffering of occupied peoples as of minor importance compared with keeping German troops happy and healthy.

The Greek *andartes* – the resistance fighters – were aggressive and occasionally heroic: many of them died in battles with the occupying forces, or after betrayal by informers, and as many as 20,000 civilians died in reprisals – often casual massacres of villagers who happened to live near the site of a resistance attack – during the reign of terror instituted by the Germans after the Italian surrender in September 1943. Many men, women and children were taken to the notorious 'transit camp' at Haidari, near Athens, from where they were led out for mass execution, or deported to one of the concentration camps in Europe, or sent to Germany to work in factories. Over 1,000 villages were looted and burnt to the ground; rape, and the murder even of women and children, were common. Many Greek villagers, and especially orphaned children, eked out a miserable and terrified existence, living more like animals than human beings in the wild or in their ruined homes.

Only 10 per cent of Greece's 80,000 Jews survived the war – the smallest percentage of any country. Most of the survivors came from Athens. Because their first language was Greek (unlike their

Ladino-speaking brothers and sisters in the large community of Thessaloniki), those who did not join the *andarte* bands in the mountains were easily protected and sheltered by sympathetic fellow Athenians. Only about 1,200 obeyed the Germans' order to register as Jews, and they were deported to Auschwitz, where the lucky ones were immediately killed in the gas chambers, and the rest, some 650 men and women, were selected by Dr Josef Mengele, the notorious Angel of Death, for his genetic experiments.

These atrocities and the unbelievable experience of seeing neighbours starve to death radicalized and politicized many Greeks. There were a number of different resistance outfits, with various political allegiances or with none, but gradually the resistance wing of the Greek Communist Party (KKE) became by far the most powerful, even though it was never funded or supported by the British to the extent that some of its rivals were. The Stalinist KKE had long been the bogeymen of modern Greece: they were driven underground in the 1920s by Venizelos and thereby invested with an aura of glamour; Metaxas used fear of communism as a springboard to power in 1936. Their courage as partisans did nothing to tarnish their aura, and at the same time they began to organize themselves into an effective political group. By the middle of 1944, they had eliminated most of their rivals and they controlled much of the countryside, where they even began to set up provisional local governments, while the Germans held the towns and cities.

Although far fewer members of KKE's EAM (the National Liberation Front) or its military arm, ELAS (the Greek People's Liberation Army), were communists than was generally supposed, a significant number were – enough to make prosperous or right-wing Greeks, and the Western powers, Britain in particular, fear a communist takeover of the country after the war. In fact, in Athens and elsewhere, the guerrillas were largely uncoordinated and, even though each group might have a communist adviser, such people varied in influence. Propaganda stories told of rabid Bolshevists preparing to turn beautiful Athens into an oppressive, grey imitation of Moscow, though in fact even most of the paid-up members of the party defied communist doctrine in a number of respects, by remaining committed to a non-exploitative form of capitalism, for instance, and to religion. They wanted to sweep away much of the pre-war state machinery, and to see social reforms and true democracy, but not necessarily a communist state.

But the damage was done, and in 1944 the Germans, with the help of their puppet prime minister Ioannis Rallis, fostered the coalition of disparate Greek groups who were united only by their fear and hatred of communism, and gave them weapons to fight communism in Athens and the countryside. The anti-communists included the former dictator Pangalos and several young men who would later play a role in the military junta of 1967–74. They acted with the same degree of savagery as the Germans or the worst of the ELAS groups, and sowed the seeds for the bloody civil war that was to follow. From February 1944 until liberation in October, there was virtual anarchy in Athens, with frequent round-ups of left-wing suspects by the right-wing Greek authorities, assassinations, hostage-taking, torture, summary executions and street battles.

After the liberation of Greece late in 1944, the British supported exactly the same groups as the Germans. A year earlier, in November 1943, an extraordinary event had taken place in Athens: a British officer had a clandestine meeting with the head of the German Secret Field Police, in order to discuss the possibility of joint action against the perceived Russian threat. The relevant documents have not yet been released, and British authorities have always claimed that this meeting with the enemy was unofficial, but it does harmonize with prime minister Winston Churchill's policies in Greece. Churchill was determined to avoid communism in Greece at all costs, and to see the monarchy restored, and as far as he was concerned anyone who was anti-monarchist was a communist.

Throughout December 1944, in a travesty which was fortunately unique in the war, there were gun battles on the streets of Athens between British troops and street fighters remaining from the resistance. There were as many straightforward freedom fighters, wanting no more than self-determination, as there were genuine communists. Their efforts were futile, however: not only were they up against trained and disciplined troops, who were supported in the air by deadly Spitfires, but Churchill had already reached a secret agreement with Josef Stalin of Russia that Britain and America could have the upper hand in Greece after the war, while Romania could go to Russia. The casual callousness of the negotiations is astounding.

Churchill wrote to Stalin: 'How would it do for you to have ninety per cent predominance in Roumania, for us to have ninety per cent of the say in Greece, and go fifty-fifty about Yugoslavia?' In reply, Stalin ticked the note and passed it back to Churchill.

Churchill's obsession with stamping out communism in Greece left the Greek right wing in firm control of Athens and hence the country as a whole. The new government, which received British and American support, included even some who had collaborated with the Germans, as well as monarchists and Venizelist republicans. Despite their power, the communists were allotted only a few seats in parliament, and the right wing set about manipulating elections and political processes in the most cynical and blatant manner.

The communists, not knowing that they had already been betrayed by Stalin, took to the mountains once again, or regrouped in Yugoslavia and Albania, and fought on. The renewed civil war lasted from 1946 to 1949 and was marked by atrocities at least as appalling as those of the German occupation. In fact, both sides – the right and the left – borrowed terror tactics from the Germans, with round-ups, hostage-taking, and reprisals by special death squads. Thousands upon thousands of people were murdered or imprisoned in concentration camps. The country swarmed with tens of thousands of desperate refugees, who were either trying to escape the horrors of the war or whose villages had been destroyed by Germans or communists.

Neither side could see neutral political ground: if you were not for them, you were against them. Britain was now too bankrupt to support the right-wing authorities, but the Americans more than made up for the loss of British arms and money. On the other hand, Stalin, true to his agreement with Churchill, did not bankroll the Greek communists, although they were constantly waiting for him to do so. The war ended only when Yugoslavia stopped supporting the Greek communists, who were committed to Stalinism, and when the US-backed military defeated them and forced them over the border into Albania. Most of the communists dispersed behind the Iron Curtain, leaving only a legacy of committed governmental suspicion of communism and socialism that plagued Greek politics for the next twenty-five years (to the detriment of much-needed social reforms, which had to wait until the 1980s) and culminated in the colonels' coup in 1967, the implausible excuse for which was the need to pre-empt a communist takeover of the country.

Patronage and Corruption

By the middle of the nineteenth century Greece had the trappings of democracy (though women did not get the vote until the middle of the 1950s), but lacked the infrastructure to implement it. For centuries the Greeks had lived a quasi-feudal existence, in which peasants owed allegiance to wealthy landowners or merchants. The drafting of a more modern constitution by Westernized Greek liberals did nothing to alter the hard fact that Greece continued to survive, as it always had, by a medieval system of patronage. It made a great deal of sense in the Byzantine and Ottoman periods for a poor person to have a patron who could represent him to the powers that be in times of trouble. This system of patronage and nepotism persisted in the nineteenth century, with politicians now as the patrons, demanding votes in return for favours and jobs.

One of the more alarming aspects of the vote-rigging system was the employment by politicians of klefts to intimidate rural peasants into voting the right way. Originally mountain-dwelling brigands preying on Ottoman tax-collectors and everyone else, the klefts had played an important role in the War of Independence as irregular troops. After independence, they were unemployed: new political realities made it hard for them to return to their jobs as the private armies of local warlords, there was insufficient legal employment, and many of them reverted to banditry, or turned to guerrilla warfare in the northern Greek territories still held by Turkey.

The police force and the army were too riddled with corruption and time-serving laziness to come up with any effective answers to a problem that rapidly became endemic. For much of the middle of the nineteenth century, until high levels of emigration to North America solved the unemployment problem, the Greek country-side was not always a safe place to visit. Mark Twain might have made light of his encounter outside Athens in 1867 with people he identified as 'brigands', though they might only have been armed peasants (*The Innocents Abroad*, Chapter 32), but such encounters could be deadly.

Only a few years after Twain's visit, the relative peace of George I's reign was abruptly shattered by an incident with international repercussions. On 11 April 1870 a group of largely English tourists set out from Athens to visit the Marathon battlefield. The English milords – Lord and Lady Muncaster, Frederick Vyner, Edward Herbert and Edward Lloyd, with his wife and daughter – were accompanied by a solitary Italian, Alberto de Boyl, and his manservant. On their way back from Marathon, only a few miles north of Athens (in the village of Kiphissia, now one of the city's more pleasant suburbs), they were captured by a band of over twenty brigands. Tourists had been kidnapped before in Greece, but the incident had always ended satisfactorily, usually with the paying of a ransom. This time, however, it all went horribly wrong, and the incident was the single most important factor in unravelling Western philhellenism and replacing it with its opposite, which still underlies Western European perceptions of Greece.

Lord Muncaster, along with the women and child and de Boyl's servant, were soon released, to present to the Greek government the first of a series of ransom demands that culminated in the insistence on £25,000 and immunity, not just for the kidnappers themselves, but for all brigands everywhere in Greece. The klefts were encouraged in this ridiculous demand by secret contacts with powerful men in Athens, who have never been identified. After a lot of dithering, the Greek authorities, with the reluctant backing of local British and Italian diplomats, sent out a party of soldiers to deal with the situation: the money could easily have been raised by wealthy friends of the captives, but the government could hardly have agreed to any kind of amnesty. The brigands and their prisoners were caught near the village of Dilessi, a little north of the Attic border, on 21 April. The brigands murdered their four prisoners during their largely unsuccessful attempt to escape.

There were many in Britain who regretted the demise of the gunboat diplomacy of an earlier generation in favour of William Gladstone's more enlightened hands-off approach, which allowed others self-determination without being bullied by stronger powers. Even the queen, calling it a 'Greek tragedy', asked for intervention from her government, but Gladstone went no further than diverting a squadron of ships to the area. A farcical enquiry did nothing to quell indignation at Greek inefficiency. The incident was headline news across Europe, and became so notorious that it initiated the gradual end of brigandage: any politician would now be besmirched by contact with such people. The king seized the opportunity to try to weaken the democracy in his favour, the Russians tried to gain more leverage in the country, patriotic Greeks saw it as a chance to whitewash Greece in the eyes of the world by pinning the blame on named or unnamed foreigners, while the guilty parties, the political bosses, went free.

If the nineteenth-century klefts represented one extreme form of corruption, a more insidious form dogged Greece in the twentieth century. The old system of patronage did not die out with the klefts. If you had a job in the Civil Service, which was and still is the major employer in Greece, it was assumed that you might be able to find work for your nephew, or even for your nephew's wife's cousin. Between 1940 and 1970, while the population grew by 19 per cent, the number of civil servants increased by 140 per cent. If there was no real work for these newcomers to do, work would be invented. The result was a proliferation of bureaucracy, which still threatens not just to strangle some offices in Greece, but even to get them into trouble. There have been recent European court cases, since Greece's entry into the European Union, combating the extraordinary powers some offices have to impound goods or tie them up with red tape. Successive governments have promised or attempted reforms, but little seems to get done.

The Akropolis After Independence

The theme of Greek inefficiency spills over from politics and administration to archaeology. A not uncommon view, endlessly deployed in the context of the Elgin Marbles, is that the Athenians cannot even look after their own antiquities – that Britain was right to take them, to save them from the Greeks themselves. But a survey of work on the Parthenon shows that while the argument may have had force earlier, it no longer applies.

The arrival of King Otto and his entourage in Athens in 1834 – he was greeted by an overblown ceremony on the Akropolis – marked the city as the new capital of the monarchy. For a while, a project to turn the Akropolis into the king's palace, incorporating the ancient ruins into a grandiose design, seemed destined to succeed, but common sense prevailed. The Akropolis was, however, ruined by nineteenth-century archaeologists: in their pursuit of the fantasy of fifth-century perfection they eradicated almost all traces of everything from later periods, which were considered 'barbaric', and so they have denied modern visitors any sense of the long history of the hill of Athens. They destroyed the Frankish tower, probably built by the de la Roches; the huge Turkish battlements; the notoriously crumbling houses and shops where the Turkish soldiers had lived; the modifications to the Propylaia which had turned it into a palace; the mosque and its minaret; and even the Byzantine apse in the Parthenon. They eradicated some 1,500 years of Athens' history.

The well-meaning restoration of the Akropolis in the first quarter of the twentieth century by Nikolaos Balanos unfortunately only compounded the problems, by focusing on creating a tourist attraction rather than on historical reality, and especially by using iron and reinforced concrete to join blocks of stone. Before long the iron began to expand, and to crack and stain the marble blocks.

The decay of the monuments on the Akropolis speeded up with the arrival of pollution. Athens' famously dry air became humid, its purity sullied by sulphur and other industrial emissions. Although matters have now vastly improved, Athenian pollution is still firmly lodged in many travellers' minds as a part of their Greek experience and merges with the perception of Greece as inefficient and backward. Its effects on the Parthenon were even more dire. Fragments of masonry fell from time to time, so that the temple had to be roped off for the safety of visitors; some bits of marble could be crumbled in the hand like sugar.

One way and another, then, damage from earthquakes, shelling, fire, ice and Balanos's iron clamps, the corrosive properties of acid rain and various algae and lichens, and the traditions of removing bits of marble for building work elsewhere and bits of sculptures to grace museums and stately homes, had left the Parthenon in a poor state. As recent visitors know, however, the Parthenon is once again being restored. Piece by piece, fragments of marble are being returned to their original positions or replaced. The restoration of the lateral walls in 1841 and Balanos's work were more concerned with creating a viable monument than with issues such as the original location of blocks. But now all this work is being undone, about 70,000 fragments of stone larger than 20 centimetres in size have been catalogued, and wherever possible original pieces are being used in the restoration in their original positions. The aim is to get as close as possible to the astounding level of technical precision of the original builders, whereby blocks were fitted, without mortar, so closely together that even rainwater could not seep in. Some original wooden pins have been discovered during the dismantling process, and they are perfectly preserved, having not been exposed to damp for 2,500 years.

Where damage has been too extensive, new stones are being made from the original marble quarries and, like pieces of an enormous three-dimensional jigsaw puzzle, fitted around the worn edges of original blocks. The important principle of reversibility is being followed throughout. By means of thorough documentation of the whole process, future architects and archaeologists will be able to undo the present restoration, should subsequent discoveries and new techniques make it desirable to do so. Every fragment of stone has its own personal computerized record. Titanium rods are being used instead of Balanos's iron, or the ancients' lead, with a stress factor that will ensure that in the event of a major earthquake the rods will break, not the marble.

This brilliant and painstaking restoration of the Parthenon was initiated in 1985, and will certainly not be finished in time for the 2004 Olympics, as originally planned. If my inexpert eye is any judge, I would guess that another five or six years are needed. But it will be worth the wait. Every piece of original sculpture that remains is being taken to the new climate-controlled museum, and when the reconstruction is complete, exact replicas of all the sculptures, wherever around the world the originals are housed, will once more grace the pediments, friezes and metopes. As much as possible, the reconstruction will also take account of the temple's long history as a church and a mosque.

The astonishingly high level of the work currently being undertaken on the Parthenon delivers an object lesson not just for the Elgin Marbles, which the modern Athenians are obviously perfectly capable of housing, displaying and preserving, but also for the Olympics. It is no longer possible to accuse Greeks of being unsophisticated and behind the times. If they have the will for a project to succeed, it will succeed.

Olympics 2004

In the words of Gianna Angelopoulos, the head of the committee responsible for organizing the Athens 2004 games, 'The Olympics are coming home.' By the time this book is published, the games will be imminent, and many readers will in any case not read it until after the event has come and gone. The organizers are, typically, keeping their cards close to their chest: the official website, for instance, is extremely upbeat and confident, but singularly uninformative. They want to surprise us on the day. Repeated attempts on my part to contact and speak to members of the Greek Olympic Committee have met with frustration, largely out of the fear that I was a journalist wanting to write yet another story on how slow Athenian progress has been towards completion and fulfilment of all the promises on time.

The same crass kind of Western reportage which made a nonsense of the trials of the Kalamata plane-spotters has also spoiled coverage of the preparations for the Olympics. It is true that things did not start well. In April 2000 the President of the International Olympic Committee, Juan Antonio Samaranch, soundly ticked Greece off for its slow start, pointing in particular to the need for 25,000 more hotel rooms, to the failure to complete the road and rail links from the new airport, and to the fact that only 70 per cent of the sports venues were completed. By the end of 2001, however, the IOC reported a 'dramatic' turnaround – but journalists from Western Europe continue to plug the old story of Greek inefficiency.

While the rest of the world scoffed and doubted Athens' ability to host a successful Olympics, the Greek Olympic Committee quietly got on with their business.

One regularly voiced concern has certainly been eliminated: the Greeks (with American and British help, it is said) have closed down the last terrorist group active in Europe as a hangover from the 1970s, the 17 November gang, which successive governments had seemed almost to tolerate, and have pledged 700 million euros for security at the event. Nevertheless, the Western press continues to nag about security and other issues. In April 2003, for instance, it was reported that some of the facilities will not be ready in time for the practice runs and tests required to make sure that everything is up to scratch. This knee-jerk castigation of the Greeks for their inefficiency ignores the fact that not all the Sydney facilities were ready for their tests either.

Part of the problem is that most people fail to appreciate the way things work in Greece. Every square metre of soil potentially contains something of historical interest. Not too long ago, you could turn up fragments of pottery and statuary as you just strolled through the countryside. The Archaeological Service in Greece has enormous power: if your house turns out to be on top of an important site, you can virtually lose rights to your home. In a country whose economy is underpinned by tourism (there are over ten million visitors a year), and where tourists come to see antiquities, not just to enjoy the beaches and the sun, this is understandable in purely economic terms. But the Greeks also care deeply about their past and its preservation.

So every construction for the Olympics, from the gigantic new airport to the stadia and facilities, has to be preceded by intense archaeological exploration and mapping. The level of archaeological interest in the construction of the Athens Metro system in the 1990s may be imagined – and is nicely reflected in permanent displays of archaeological artefacts in two of the central subway stations. In 2001 there was a panic because the discovery of an ancient burial site near Marathon threatened the schedule of the building of the rowing centre; in 2002 the same concerns affected the construction of the Olympic hippodrome, which turned out to be on the site of an ancient temple to Aphrodite and a tomb from the Mycenaean period; the Olympic Village clashed with the site of an aqueduct of the second century CE, part of Hadrian's rebuilding of the city. Compromises were made: the village incorporated the aqueduct into its design, ancient houses were carefully moved 50 metres or so to prevent their being lost for ever, environmental groups have been placated.

Even as recently as February 2003 Gianna Angelopoulos received a rap on the knuckles from the IOC in Lausanne: she was firmly instructed to maintain the sense of urgency and translate all the excellent planning into actual delivery. Transport and accommodation remain complex nightmares for the organizers, and the main stadium's ambitious dome is taking longer than expected to build. Some plans had to be scrapped. The city wanted to plant 30,000 trees to beautify the place, for instance, but the water board told them to abandon the idea. But such things are icing on the cake: the essential work will be finished, the road and rail links will be in place, along with all the facilities, and the Olympics will be a success. As the official website proclaims, 'A new city will be welcoming the world in August 2004.' But how should we measure success?

Atlanta and Sydney are hard acts to follow in terms of razzmatazz. The inspiration to release a flock of doves at the 1896 event has grown into the urge to spend millions of dollars just on superficial entertainment that has nothing to do with sport. My hope is that the 2004 Olympics will see a return, in some measure, to the ancient ideals of austerity, or at least a focus on the sporting events alone, to counterbalance the extravagance of recent events. The settings will be wonderful: cyclists will race around the foot of the Akropolis; the archery contests will be held in the 1896 stadium; everywhere, as usual in and around Athens, there will be a sense of history. The settings and the events alone should provide our entertainment. The Greek sports minister, Evangelos Venizelos, has promised to give the games back their original moral and ideological character. I for one hope he does just that.

One of the suburbs which has been partly taken over by new stadia is called Eirini, which means 'peace'. The IOC has established an International Olympic Truce Foundation. If Venizelos's 'moral and ideological character' includes daring to give prominence to the ancient sacred truce, we should applaud the attempt. It is true that the ancient truce was never meant to stop warfare altogether, but only to protect pilgrims on the way to Olympia and to allow the festival to go ahead without obstruction; but it is also true that as a result of the truce warfare generally subsided, and so de Coubertin's romantic interpretation of the truce may be allowed to stand.

For better or worse, Athens remains a beacon of civilization, and civilization means, among other things, simply being civil to one another. War is the opposite. Besides, sport should be apolitical, a pause between the stresses of daily life and a chance for individuals and nations to meet as equals, with mutual respect. It would be perfect if, with the Olympics coming home to Greece and the whole world watching, a plea could be made for a revival of the ancient truce. For future Olympics, let there be just a few months of ceasefire throughout the world. This may sound pie-in-the-sky idealism, but this is only because it has not been tried before, in the modern world. Who knows? It might work; lives might be saved, and reconciliation rather than fighting might become the way forward. In any case, the proposal could be given teeth by linking it into the threat of exclusion from the games if a ceasefire is not negotiated. For the first time, in 2004 over 200 countries will send competitors to the games. The pressure to take part is enormous; the loss of face for exclusion would be equally great.

If the 2004 Olympics are a success, Athens will have gone a long way towards reconciling the tension between past and future. As we have seen time and again in this book, the city is haunted by its past. One consequence of this today is that it longs to be recognized as a modern city, the equal of other modern metropolises. By solving the complex logistical problems and hosting an international event of this scale, Athens will have earned its right to membership of this fraternity, and may even have created a new past to look back on in future years, rather than being so dependent on the myths of a distant past and on the beneficence of a succession of superpowers, from the Protecting Powers of the nineteenth and early twentieth centuries, to America in the decade after the Second World War and the EU now.

It is not just that the country as a whole will have been modernized as a result of the huge engineering works – road-building, bridge-building, a new airport, a new subway system –

engendered by the prospect of the Olympics. More importantly, Greece will have overcome the deep-rooted problem which under-lies much of the carping that has gone on in foreign presses. This is the common perception of Greece as a *mañana* culture rife with high inflation, corruption and nepotism. But if the 2004 Olympics are a success, Greece will have achieved this on its own, without the kind of outside interference, either well-meaning or hostile, which has dogged her history since the Macedonian conquest of the fourth century BCE. The 2004 Olympics are pivotal: they could be – should be – the start of a whole new era for Athens and the end of modern Greece's 200-year search for legitimacy.

28

Envoi

Greater Athens now houses half of the total Greek population of about eleven million. Its recent growth has been rapid: even the Lykabettos hill was still in the countryside until after the Second World War, and now you would have to say it was in the centre of town. There were two major influxes: in the 1920s and 1930s, after the 'exchange of minorities', when Greeks were driven out of Turkey, and in the 1950s and 1960s, when the peasant economy of the countryside collapsed and people migrated to the towns. There is a third wave today, with the arrival of increasing numbers of Russian and Albanian Greeks (often descendants of former communist guerrillas from the Civil War) and of illegal immigrants.

As you travel around Athens today it is hard to glimpse even its recent past. Most of the nineteenth-century private houses have been torn down to make way for the inexorable expansion of the commercial centre, although many of the wonderful public buildings remain. An early-morning walk in Plaka is essential, to see the charm of its narrow streets before the shops and restaurants open, and before your perspective is distorted by watching out for countless other pedestrians. As for ancient times, the ruins of the Akropolis are still visible from many points, although it is hard to enjoy a stroll around the ruins themselves, as there are invariably too many people on the site, except in winter. As you walk around the centre of town you are sometimes greeted by Classical remains, often below street level, or by a few lofty pillars from the Roman era; and excavations have uncovered much of the agora. But it is hard for the casual visitor to make much sense of these bare footings, and mainly one is faced with the noise and rush of an overgrown modern city.

There is symbolic value in the disappointment many visitors feel in Athens. One of the main points of this book has been to stress that Athens never was what it made itself out to be. It is not now, and it was not then. Yes, the place had more than its fair share of geniuses and wonderful buildings, but there was plenty that was unsound about it, and the myth of Athenian perfection was a creation of orators, starting as early as the fifth century itself. Any modern visitor who feels disappointed is simply suffering from the gap between myth and reality.

But any person or place which has become a myth is subject to a peculiar law – that it is what it has become. We will never know what the historical Jesus was like, or Muhammad, or Sokrates, and the same is true of ancient Athens. In many respects, it no longer matters what the historical reality was like, since as a beacon of civilization it continues to burn brightly. Politicians and thinkers of the eighteenth and nineteenth centuries looked back to the golden age of Athens, and even now the myth of Athens reminds us to aim for ideals, especially in politics.

Athens is always present in the heart and mind of anyone educated in the West who aspires to greatness. It was not just for the Romantics that Athens was an ideal; it was for Perikles and his peers too. Greece has this ability to combine dream and reality, humour and poverty, metaphysics and cunning. The ancient Greeks were not as autonomous as Byron and his peers would have us believe, but they were in love with freedom. The Greeks are united over the centuries by a love of their beautiful land, whether it is as small as ancient Athens or as large as modern Greece. They love the land, the sun, the sea and sky and the white rock, and the light, as clear and intoxicating as the best wine. This love is translated variously into various kinds of action, and some stunningly good poetry (with two recent Nobel prize-winners in Giorgos Seferis (1963) and Odysseus Elytis (1979)), but there are always enough who are prepared to defend infringements of the land's freedom even to death, whether they are klefts in the War of Independence, partisans in the Second World War, or Polytechnic students crushed by the colonels' tanks.

Being a beacon of civilization carries a price. It is not a position that comes of its own accord: like great successes in any sphere at any time, it takes ambition ruthlessly carried out. Is it worth the cost? Do the glories of the Parthenon outweigh the blood and misery of the slaves and subjects whose money and labour were required to build it? This is one of those unanswerable questions, largely because art occupies or should occupy a different universe from the harsh realities of mundane and material life. It is simply not measurable in the same way.

So the moral of this tale is not to be found in any such reflections, but a tragedy is bound to have a moral. With hindsight it is easy to see that if ancient Athens had been a little less arrogant, she might have survived for longer, even granted the law expressed by Herodotos and other ancient thinkers that everything that rises will some day fall. The corollary of this is that the higher something rises, the greater will be its fall. In the modern world, we have many recent or present examples of political arrogance: Robert Mugabe in Zimbabwe, Saddam Hussein in Iraq, and so on. But the highest-riser is the United States of America. America too considers itself a beacon of what passes for civilization in the Western world; time and again over the past thirty years or so America has displayed the arrogance to extend or defend this civilization even by force of arms. Perhaps Athens could continue to be a beacon of civilization in this sense: if America could look back on Athens' story and learn that it is hastening its own fall, it might learn to curtail its use of arms and to become a defender of true culture, not monotonous globalization. The ancient ideal is to respect others, even if their customs are different, rather than trying to impose our values on them.

Maps

A. Central Athens, old and new

B. Attica

C. Central and Southern Greece

D. Greece and the Aegean

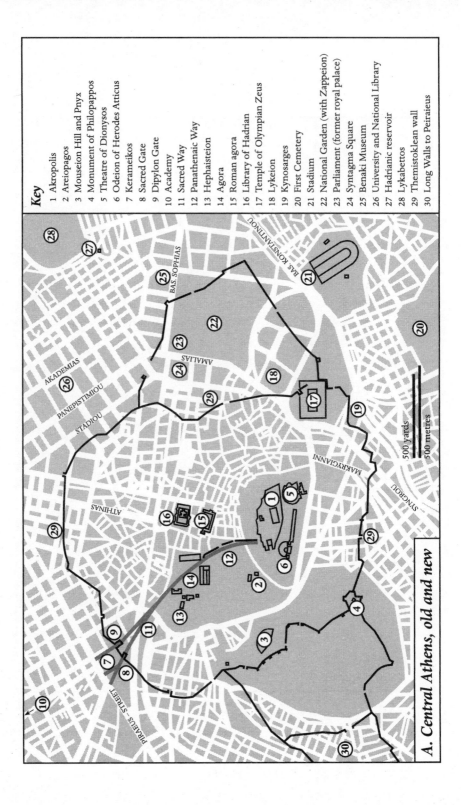

Key

1 Akropolis
2 Areiopagos
3 Mouseion Hill and Pnyx
4 Monument of Philopappos
5 Theatre of Dionysos
6 Odeion of Herodes Atticus
7 Kerameikos
8 Sacred Gate
9 Dipylon Gate
10 Academy
11 Sacred Way
12 Panathenaic Way
13 Hephaisteion
14 Agora
15 Roman agora
16 Library of Hadrian
17 Temple of Olympian Zeus
18 Lykeion
19 Kynosarges
20 First Cemetery
21 Stadium
22 National Garden (with Zappeion)
23 Parliament (former royal palace)
24 Syntagma Square
25 Benaki Museum
26 University and National Library
27 Hadrianic reservoir
28 Lykabettos
29 Themistoklean wall
30 Long Walls to Peiraieus

A. Central Athens, old and new

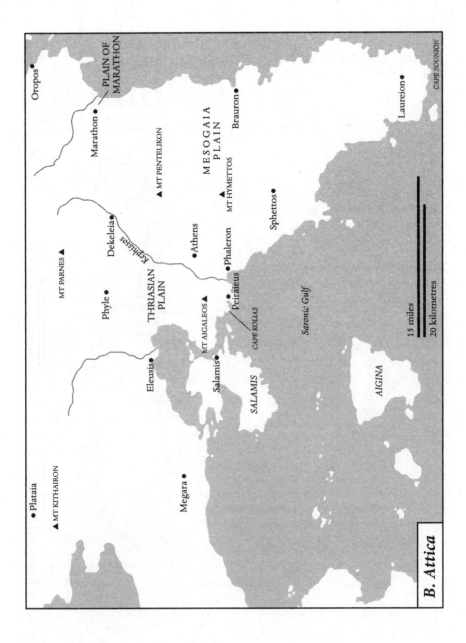

Oropos•

PLAIN OF
MARATHON

Marathon•

▲ MT PENTELIKON

MESOGAIA
PLAIN

Brauron•

▲ MT HYMETTOS

CAPE SOUNION

Laureion•

Dekeleia•

Kephissos

Athens•

Phaleron

Sphettos•

▲ MT PARNES

THRIASIAN
PLAIN

Phyle•

Peiraieus

CAPE KOLIAS

Saronic Gulf

▲ MT AIGALEOS

Eleusis•

Salamis•

SALAMIS

AIGINA

▲ MT KITHAIRON

•Plataia

Megara•

15 miles

20 kilometres

B. Attica

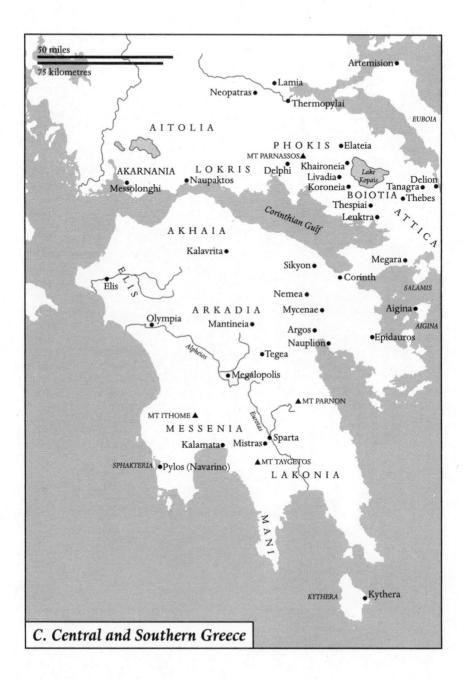

C. Central and Southern Greece

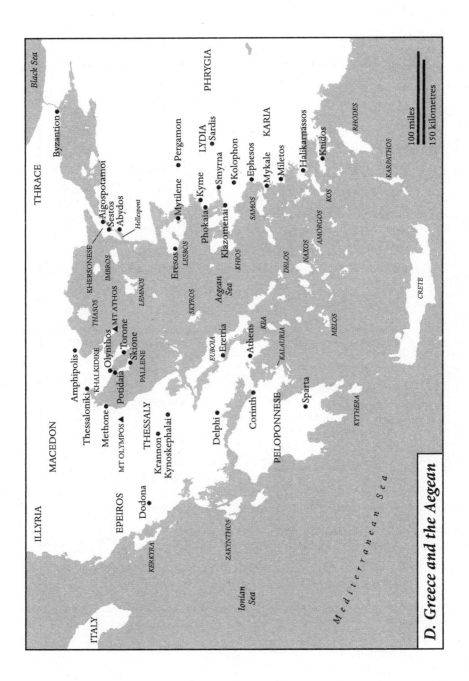

D. Greece and the Aegean

Key Dates

BCE

c. 5000	Athenian Akropolis first inhabited
1500–1200	Mycenaean period
1200–1000	Dorian 'invasion'
1100–800	Dark Age
800–500	Archaic period
800–600	Geometric pottery
776	Traditional starting date of the Olympic Games
c. 750	Homer writes down the *Iliad* and the *Odyssey*, the first extant European literature
635	Attempted tyranny of Kylon in Athens
630–480	Archaic *kouros* statues
630–475	Athenian black-figure vases
621	Drakon's law-code
594	Solon revises Athenian constitution and law-code
566	Reorganization of Panathenaic festival
547–510	Peisistratid tyranny in Athens
530–500	Athenian drama begins to develop out of a long-standing choral tradition
530	Athenian red-figure pottery begins
514	Harmodios and Aristogeiton assassinate Hipparkhos, brother of the tyrant Hippias
508	Kleisthenic reforms
500–340	Classical period
499	Revolt of Ionian cities against Persia
490	First Persian invasion of Greece
487	Democratic reforms reduce the power of the arkhons
480–479	Second Persian invasion of Greece
478	Themistoklean defensive wall built
477	Delian League formed

470–456	Temple of Zeus at Olympia
469	Persian fleet destroyed at Eurymedon
c. 460	Ephialtes sidelines Areiopagos council
454	Athenian fleet destroyed in Egypt; transfer of League funds to Athens
450–429	Perikles ascendant in Athens
447–433	Parthenon built
446	Peace treaty between Athens and Sparta
445	Long Walls connect Athens and Peiraieus
437–432	Propylaia built
431–404	Peloponnesian War
430	Plague strikes Athens
429	Death of Perikles
425	Athenian victory at Pylos
424	Athenian defeat at Delion
421	Peace of Nikias
421–405	Erekhtheion built
415–413	Athenian invasion of Sicily; Alkibiades in exile
411	Oligarchic revolution in Athens; Alkibiades pardoned
406	Deaths of Sophokles and Euripides
404	Defeat of Athens followed by the rule of the Thirty
403	Civil war in Athens; democracy restored
399	Trial and execution of Sokrates
386	The King's Peace, imposed by Sparta and Persia, puts a temporary end to inter-Greek squabbling
378	Formation of Second Athenian League
371	Spartan power broken at Leuktra
338	Macedonian conquest of southern Greece
c. 335	*Ephēbeia* instituted
330–140	Hellenistic period
323	Death of Alexander the Great
322	Lamian War; end of Athenian democracy
317–307	Demetrios of Phaleron rules Athens
286	Athenian rebellion against Macedon
267–263	Khremonidean War
229	Macedonian garrison leaves Athens
197	Roman defeat of Macedonians at Kynoskephalai

146   Roman conquest of Greece
86   Sulla sacks Athens

CE
50   St Paul's mission to Athens
c. 120–35   Hadrian revives Athens
267   Herulian sack of Athens
330   Foundation of Constantinople
364   Division of Roman Empire
393   Theodosios I bans the Olympic Games
396   Alaric sacks Athens
435   Theodosios II outlaws paganism
527   Justinian I outlaws pagan teaching
529   Justinian I closes Academy
c. 582   Slavs sack Athens
732   Athens enters ecclesiastical jurisdiction of Constantinople
1147   Roger of Sicily plunders Athens
1182–1205   Michael of Chonae in Athens
1204   Sack of Constantinople by Crusaders
1205–1311   French control of Athens
1311–88   Catalan control of Athens
1388–1456   Florentine control of Athens
1395–1402   Venetian occupation of Athens
1453   Turkish sack of Constantinople
1456–1821   Turkish rule of Greece
1687   Venetian destruction of Parthenon
1687–8   Venetian occupation of Athens
1775–95   Hadji Ali Haseki rules Athens
1801   Looting of Parthenon by Lord Elgin begins
1809–10   Lord Byron's visit to Athens
1814   Formation of Friendly Society to promote insurrection against the Turks
1821–33   Greek War of Independence
1822   Massacre of Athenian Turks
1827   Turks recapture Akropolis; battle of Navarino
1831   Assassination of Kapodistrias, first president of Greece
1833   Turks evacuate Athens; Greece becomes a monarchy
1834   Athens becomes capital of Greece

1844   Absolute monarchy abolished

1870   The Dilessi incident

1896   First modern, international Olympic Games in Athens

1898–1925   First restoration of Parthenon

1913   Greece gains much territory after Balkan Wars

1914–18   First World War; Great Schism in Greece

1922   Smyrna débâcle

1940–4   Greece occupied by Germans, Italians and Bulgarians

1944–9   Civil War

1967–74   Regime of the colonels

1974   Greece becomes a republic

1985   Second restoration of Parthenon begins

2004   The Olympics return to Athens

Glossary

I have invariably defined technical terms on their first occurrence in the book, but some are repeated, and so it may be useful to have a brief glossary.

agora – a combination of city square, marketplace and administrative centre.

Akropolis – the high point of the city and by Classical times one of the main focuses of Athenian religious life.

Areiopagos – the 'Hill of Ares', a little to the north-west of the Akropolis, which in the Archaic and Classical periods was the meeting-place of an aristocratic council made up of ex-arkhons.

arkhon – literally, 'leader': a term used to describe various high officials of Athenian government at different points of its history. In the Classical period, there were nine annually selected arkhons: the eponymous arkhon (who gave his name to the year), the king arkhon, the polemarch (war-leader), and six *thesmothetai* (originally responsible for law and order).

Assembly – the chief executive organ of democratic Athens, in whose processes every free adult male citizen over the age of twenty could participate.

Council – the main work of the Council was preparing the agenda for the Assembly, presiding over Assembly meetings, and overseeing state finances and officials. It was open to all Athenian citizens over the age of thirty.

deme – something like 'parishes' or 'wards', the demes were the basis of Kleisthenes' reforms. One had to be enrolled in a deme to be an Athenian citizen.

disdar – the garrison commander of a town under Ottoman rule.

drachma – a unit of money within the system where 1 talent = 60 mnas = 6,000 drachmas = 36,000 obols. Greek coinage was not on the whole fiduciary, but was worth its weight: on the Euboïc–Attic scale 1 obol = 722 mg (0.025 oz); 1 drachma = 4.332 g (0.15 oz); 1 mna = 433.2 g (15.16 oz); 1 talent = 25.992 kg (57.31 lb).

ephēbeia – a formal programme of acculturation, initially only for Athenian young men, established in the fourth century BCE.

ephor – in Sparta there were five ephors ('overseers') who, along with the two kings, were the principal authorities.

gerousia – a council of elders, one of the main organs of government in Sparta.

gymnasium – one of the essential features of a Greek town, where men met and socialized or exercised naked (*gumnos* means 'naked'). The three most important gymnasia of Athens were the Academy, the Lykeion (Lyceum) and the Kynosarges.

Heliaia – the Athenian people in their judicial function; a body of 6,000 citizens empanelled each year to serve as jurors in various courts.

helot – the name for an agricultural slave in Sparta.

hetaira – a type of female prostitute in ancient Athens.

hetaireia – a club or association of like-minded men in Classical Athens, formed for social reasons or, sometimes, to take concerted political action.

hoplites – heavily armed foot-soldiers.

liturgy – a public service, either military or relating to a religious festival, which wealthy Athenians were required to carry out.

metic – anyone who was not an Athenian citizen, nor a slave, but who was resident in Athens or Peiraieus for longer than one month. Metics had lesser legal status in Athens, but were required to serve in the army and to pay a residency tax.

ostracism – an invention of Kleisthenes, designed to curb tyranny, whereby each year the Athenian people had the right, if they chose and a minimum of 6,000 votes were cast, to send a prominent public figure into exile for ten years, though with no loss of property rights.

paidagōgos – a male slave who looked after an Athenian boy at home and attended him when he was out and about in public.

palaistra – a wrestling-ground, often found within a gymnasium.

Panathenaia – the central civic festival of the Classical Athenian calendar.

Parthenon – the temple of Athena the Virgin (*parthenos*) commissioned by Perikles and built on the Athenian Akropolis.

perioikoi – free residents of Lakonia who were not slaves, but had no voting rights in Sparta.

Phanariotes – wealthy Greeks from the Phanar quarter of Constantinople who often held important administrative positions in the Ottoman Empire.

phratry – literally a 'brotherhood', the phratries were loose groupings of Athenian citizens with various religious functions, such as naming and welcoming a new-born boy.

Pnyx – the place where the Assembly met, on a low hill to the west of the Akropolis.

prytaneis – the 'presidents' formed the standing committee of the Council who lived continuously, for a tenth of the year, in the Tholos in the agora, so that they were ready to receive any business and to decide whether the full Council should be summoned to prepare the issues for the Assembly.

satrap – rulers of provinces of the Persian Empire, they were semi-independent from the Great King in Sousa and lived like kings themselves, making war on one another, entering into negotiations and deals with others, and occasionally rebelling against the king.

Sophists – 'experts' or 'teachers', the term is used especially of the itinerant teachers of the fifth century BCE who taught a wide range of skills useful to aspiring politicians.

stele – a stone slab used to mark a tomb or inscribed with laws, decrees and other public documents.

stoa – a building consisting chiefly of a long, covered colonnade. The reconstructed Stoa of Attalos in the Athenian agora gives the best impression.

thetes – the lowest of the four property classes in Athens. The highest were those with an estimated annual income of at least 500 *medimnoi* of grain or its equivalent (a *medimnos* was a dry measure of 51.84 litres or 91.24 pints); the next class were the horsemen, with 300–500 *medimnoi*; then there were the hoplites, with 200–300 *medimnoi*; the thetes followed with less than 200 *medimnoi*.

tribe – for the purposes of civic administration, citizens were originally divided between four tribes, but Kleisthenes increased the number to ten. Many boards and committees consisted of ten or multiples of ten, chosen evenly from each tribe.

trireme – a Greek warship, propelled by three banks of oarsmen on each side.

tyrant – a sole ruler who seized power by unconstitutional means, though he was not necessarily a despot.

voivode – the governor of a town under Ottoman rule.

Bibliography

The reader can perhaps guess the enormous amount of scholarly material there is on Athens, and especially on the ancient city. Most of the research for this book has involved the study of such detailed academic books and articles, but anyone with scholarly interests already knows where to find such material (and will be able to recognize my debts), and for the sake of the general reader I have more or less excluded it. What follows, then, is a list of accessible books which I consider reliable and entertaining.

For the study of the ancient world, nothing beats reading the original texts. The translations in the Oxford World's Classics series, and Penguin Classics, are recommended, with the former generally to be preferred to the latter where there are duplicates. In particular, readers of this book will enjoy Herodotos (Oxford), Thucydides (Penguin), Xenophon (Penguin), Aristotle's *The Athenian Constitution* (Penguin) and *Politics* (Oxford), Plato's dialogues (Oxford), Aiskhylos (Oxford), Sophokles (Oxford), Euripides (Oxford), Aristophanes (Penguin) and Plutarch's *Lives* (Oxford).

Kevin Andrews, *Athens Alive* (Athens: Hermes, 1979)

Mary Beard, *The Parthenon* (London: Profile Books, 2002)

Charalambos Bouras *et al.* (eds), *Athens from the Classical Period to the Present Day* (Athens: Kotinos, 2001)

David Brewer, *The Flame of Freedom: The Greek War of Independence 1821–1833* (London: John Murray, 2001)

Robert Browning (ed.), *The Greek World, Classical, Byzantine and Modern* (London: Thames and Hudson, 1985)

Louise Bruit Zaidman and Pauline Schmitt Pantel, *Religion in the Ancient Greek City* (Cambridge University Press, 1992; later reprints have enlarged bibliographies)

Terry Buckley, *Aspects of Greek History 750–323 BC* (London: Routledge, 1996)

John Camp, *The Athenian Agora: Excavations in the Heart of Classical Athens* (London: Thames and Hudson, 1986)

Paul Cartledge, *The Cambridge Illustrated History of Ancient Greece* (Cambridge University Press, 1997); *The Greeks* (2nd edn, Oxford University Press, 2002)

Nicolas Cheetham, *Medieval Greece* (New Haven: Yale University Press, 1981)

Richard Clogg, *A Concise History of Greece* (2nd edn, Cambridge University Press, 2002)

James Davidson, *Courtesans and Fishcakes: The Consuming Passions of Classical Athens* (London: Fontana, 1998)

John Davies, *Democracy and Classical Greece* (2nd edn, London: Fontana, 1993)

Pat Easterling and John Muir (eds), *Greek Religion and Society* (Cambridge University Press, 1985)

Walter Ellis, *Alcibiades* (London: Routledge, 1989)

John Ferguson and Kitty Chisholm (eds), *Political and Social Life in the Great Age of Athens* (London: Ward Lock, 1978)

John Freely, *Strolling Through Athens* (London: Penguin, 1991)

Yvon Garlan, *Slavery in Ancient Greece* (Ithaca, NY: Cornell University Press, 1988)

Christian Habicht, *Athens from Alexander to Antony* (Cambridge, Mass. Harvard University Press, 1997)

Mogens Hansen, *The Athenian Democracy in the Age of Demosthenes* (2nd edn, London: Bristol Classical Press, 1999)

Robert Hopper, *The Acropolis* (London: Weidenfeld and Nicolson, 1971)

Simon Hornblower, *The Greek World 479–323 BC* (3rd edn, London: Routledge, 2002)

Simon Hornblower and Antony Spawforth (eds), *The Oxford Classical Dictionary* (3rd edn, Oxford University Press, 2000)

Joint Association of Classical Teachers, *The World of Athens: An Introduction to Classical Athenian Culture* (Cambridge University Press, 1984)

Roger Just, *Women in Athenian Law and Life* (London: Routledge, 1989)

Donald Kagan, *The Outbreak of the Peloponnesian War* (Ithaca: Cornell University Press, 1969); *The Archidamian War* (Ithaca: Cornell University Press, 1974); *The Peace of Nicias and the Sicilian Expedition* (Ithaca: Cornell University Press, 1981); *The Fall of the Athenian Empire* (Ithaca: Cornell University Press, 1987)

W. K. Lacey, *The Family in Classical Greece* (London: Thames and Hudson, 1968)

Robert Lenardon, *The Saga of Themistocles* (London: Thames and Hudson, 1978)

Alan Lloyd, *Marathon: The Story of Civilizations on Collision Course* (London: Souvenir Press, 1975)

John MacAloon, *This Great Symbol: Pierre de Coubertin and the Origins of the Modern Olympic Games* (University of Chicago Press, 1981)

Douglas MacDowell, *The Law in Classical Athens* (London: Thames and Hudson, 1978)

Molly Mackenzie, *Turkish Athens* (Reading: Ithaca Press, 1992)

Thomas Martin, *Ancient Greece from Prehistoric to Hellenistic Times* (New Haven: Yale University Press, 1996)

Mark Mazower, *Inside Hitler's Greece: The Experience of Occupation, 1941–44* (New Haven: Yale University Press, 1993)

Malcolm McGregor, *The Athenians and Their Empire* (Vancouver: University of British Columbia Press, 1987)

Christian Meier, *Athens: A Portrait of the City in Its Golden Age* (London: John Murray, 1999)

Jon Mikalson, *Athenian Popular Religion* (Chapel Hill, NC: University of North Carolina Press, 1983)

Claude Mossé, *The Ancient World at Work* (London: Chatto & Windus, 1969); *Athens in Decline, 404–86 BC* (London: Routledge & Kegan Paul, 1973)

Oswyn Murray, *Early Greece* (2nd edn, London: Fontana, 1993)

Robin Osborne, *Archaic and Classical Greek Art* (Oxford University Press, 1998); (ed.), *Classical Greece* (Oxford University Press, 2000)

Anthony Podlecki, *Perikles and His Circle* (London: Routledge, 1998)

Jerome Pollitt, *Art and Experience in Classical Greece* (Cambridge University Press, 1972)

J. W. Roberts, *City of Sokrates* (2nd edn, London: Routledge, 1998)

William St Clair, *Lord Elgin and the Marbles: The Controversial History of the Parthenon Sculptures* (3rd edn, Oxford University Press, 1998)

Raphael Sealey, *Demosthenes and His Time: A Study in Defeat* (Oxford University Press, 1993)

Gregory Stanton, *Athenian Politics c.800–500 BC: A Sourcebook* (London: Routledge, 1990)

Judith Swaddling, *The Ancient Olympic Games* (2nd edn, London: British Museum Press, 1999)

Oliver Taplin (ed.), *Literature in the Greek World* (Oxford University Press, 2000)

John Thorley, *Athenian Democracy* (London: Routledge, 1996)

Thomas Webster, *Athenian Culture and Society* (London: Batsford, 1973)

C. M. Woodhouse, *Modern Greece: A Short History* (5th edn, London: Faber & Faber, 1991)

Richard Wycherley, *How the Greeks Built Cities: The Relationship of Architecture and Town Planning to Everyday Life in Ancient Greece* (2nd edn, New York: Norton, 1962)

Index

A bold letter (**A, B, C, D**) after a place name refers to one of the four maps on pp. 382–5. Otherwise, all numbers are page numbers.

Picture Credits

Acropolis Museum, Athens – 16. Antikenmuseum Basel – 18. Benaki Museum, Athens, © 2004 – 23, 24, 29, 30, 31, 34. BPK – 21. British Museum, London – 2, 4, 11, 13, 14. Château Comtal, Boulogne sur Mer – 17. Gennadius Libary, American School of Classical Studies, Athens – 26. Kunstakademiets Bibliotek, Copenhagen – 28. Kunsthistorisches Museum, Vienna – 7. Museo Nazionale Romano (Terme di Diocleziano) Rome © 2003, Photo Scala, Florence: courtesy of the Ministero Beni e Att. Culturali – 22. Museo Ostiense – 3. Museum of the City of Athens – 32. National Archaeological Museum, Athens – 8, 9, 10, 12, 15. Ny Carlsberg Glyptothek, Copenhagen – 5. Parker Library, Corpus Christi College, Cambridge – 20. Private collection – 33. Staatliche Antikensammlungen, Munich – 19. Topham Picturepoint – 25. Vatican, Gregorian Museum of the Etruscan Art, © 1990, Photo Scala, Florence – 1. Vatican Museum, Rome – 6.